T

MANCH

A History of the Regular, Militia, Special Reserve, Territorial, and New Army Battalions since their formation; with a record of the Officers now serving, and the Honours and Casualties of the War of 1914-16.

Compiled by

Captain G. L. Campbell, R.F.A.,

T.F. Reserve of Officers.

The Naval & Military Press Ltd

Published by
The Naval & Military Press Ltd
Unit 10 Ridgewood Industrial Park,
Uckfield, East Sussex,
TN22 5QE England
Tel: +44 (0) 1825 749494
Fax: +44 (0) 1825 765701
www.naval-military-press.com
www.military-genealogy.com
www.militarymaproom.com

Contents

Preface

My reason for compiling these records is that they may be a reply to a remark made to me in November, 1914, by a very high official of Manchester. He said:—

> "I never heard of the Manchester Regiment.
> "It must be proud of its name."

The Regiment *is* proud of its name, and Manchester cannot help but be proud of its Regiment.

I want to thank all those Officers of the Regiment who have so kindly helped me to gather the details together. I could never have done the work without their assistance.

G.L.C.

Aldershot,
April 1st, 1916.

The Manchester Regiment

Depot Headquarters—Ashton-under-Lyne.
Uniform—Scarlet. Facings—White.
Badge—The Manchester City Coat of Arms, superscribed "Concilio et Labore."
Collar Badge—The Sphinx, superscribed "Egypt."
Buttons—The Sphinx in a Garter, surmounted by Crown.

THE REGIMENT

Francis Townley, a member of a Lancashire family, raised a "Manchester Regiment" in Manchester in 1745, in favour of the Pretender Charles Stuart. The Regiment was left as a Garrison in Carlisle by the Pretender on his retreat to Scotland, but soon afterwards it surrendered to the Duke of Cumberland.

There was also a Regiment known as the "Royal Manchester Volunteers," numbered into the line as the 72nd, which was raised in Manchester in 1777, but after taking part in the famous Defence of Gibraltar, was disbanded in 1783.

The Manchester Regiment, as it stands to-day, is one of the three "Civic" Regiments, and was formed on the 1st of July, 1881, from two regiments which had been linked together since 1874—the 63rd (West Suffolk) and the 96th (raised in Manchester in 1824) with the two Militia Battalions formed from the 6th Royal Lancashire Militia. Two additional regular Battalions were added in 1900, but these were disbanded in 1907, and the old Militia Battalions took up their old numbers. There are now six Territorial Battalions, all of which have raised two new Battalions during the present War.

There are in addition twelve Service Battalions, one Second Reserve Battalion, three Local Reserve Battalions, and one Garrison Battalion, made up of Officers, N.C.O.'s, and men who have enlisted for the period of the War only.

There are in all 39 Battalions of the Manchester Regiment, with a total establishment of about 45,000 Officers, N.C.O.'s and men.

The majority of the recruits for the Service Battalions of the Manchester Regiment have come from the City of Manchester, and at least 20,000 have been raised there since the commencement of the War. Captain D. Walkley (late Qr.-Mr. 3 (Reg.) Bn. Manch. R.) is the chief Recruiting Officer, and has as his chief assistants Captain A. Hearsey (Res. of Off.) and Lieut D. H. Bartram.

THE COLOURS

The Battle Honours borne on the Regimental Colours of the 1st, 2nd, 3rd, and 4th Battalions are:—

The Sphinx, superscribed "EGYPT." "EGMONT-OP-ZEE," "MARTINIQUE," "GUADALOUPE," "PENINSULA," "ALMA," "INKERMAN," "SEVASTOPOL," "NEW ZEALAND," "AFGHANISTAN, 1879-80," "EGYPT, 1882," "SOUTH AFRICA, 1899-1902," "DEFENCE OF LADYSMITH."

Those borne on the Colours of the 5th, 6th, 7th, 8th, and 9th Battalions:—

"SOUTH AFRICA, 1900-1902,"
And on the 10th Battalion,
"SOUTH AFRICA, 1901-1902."

1ST BATTALION (63rd Foot).—The Colours carried through the Crimean War are in the possession of the Battalion. New Colours were presented in 1872, and they are still in use.

2ND BATTALION (96th Foot).—The Colours carried by the 96th Foot, which was raised in 1779 and disbanded in 1783, were given to the present 2nd Battalion, and are still kept by them. The new 96th, raised in 1824, received Colours in 1825, and these were carried until 1861, when Maj.-Gen. H. Shirley, C.B., presented new Colours to the Battalion at the Curragh. These were carried until 1886, and were brought home from India by Lt.-Col. W. O. Barnard, with the Colours presented in 1825, and deposited in the Manchester Cathedral. In 1886 Lord Roberts presented new Colours, and these were deposited in the Parish Church, Ashton-under-Lyne, in 1911, on the presentation of Colours to the Battalion by King George at Phœnix Park, Dublin.

3RD BATTALION (Regular).—Raised in March, 1900, and disbanded on 31st March, 1907. Colours were presented on the 24th May, 1902, by Lord Roberts at Aldershot, and are now hung in the Manchester Town Hall.

4TH BATTALION (Regular).—Raised on 1st March, 1900, and disbanded on 28th February, 1907. Colours were presented by the Duke of Connaught, at Cork, on 31st July, 1903, and are now hung in the Manchester Cathedral.

6TH ROYAL LANCASHIRE MILITIA.—The Colours of this Regiment, in use until 1881, are kept at the Barracks, Ashton-under-Lyne.

3RD & 4TH BATTALION (Militia, afterwards Special Reserve). Colours were presented in 1881 and 1883, on these Battalions being formed from the 6th Royal Lancashire Militia.

5TH, 6TH, 7TH, 8TH, 9TH, & 10TH BATTALIONS.—The Colours of these Battalions were presented by King Edward VII. at Worsley Park, near Manchester, in June, 1908.

No Colours have been presented to the new Service Battalion of the Regiment.

It is interesting to note that the present Colours of the 1st, 2nd, 3rd, and 4th Battalions are now in the Officers' Mess at the Barracks, Ashton-under-Lyne. The 3rd and 4th Battalion Colours were left there when the Battalions proceeded to the East Coast at the commencement of the War. On the 16th March, 1915, the Colours of the 1st and 2nd Battalions were deposited in the Officers' Mess with all the honours the Depot could furnish. The 1st and 2nd Battalion King's Colours were carried by Capt. J. H. Holme, Manchester Regiment, who had also carried in 1883 the Queen's olours of the old 3rd Militia Battalion. The Regimental Colours were both carried by Lieut. G. M. Glover, 2nd Bn., Manchester Regt.

THE DEPOT,
Ashton-under-Lyne

In May, 1874, the 63rd (West Suffolk) and the 96th Regiments of Foot became linked together, and formed part of the 16th Brigade of Infantry, the Depôt, or Headquarters, being at the Barracks, Ashton-under-Lyne.

On July 1st, 1881, when the Territorial titles took the place of the old numbers, the Barracks at Ashton-under-Lyne became the Depôt of the Manchester Regiment, and in 1882 the 3rd and 4th Militia Battalions moved there from Salford. There are now twenty-four Battalions of the Manchester Regiment attached to the Depôt—two Regular, two Special Reserve, and 20 Service, Second and Local Reserve. It is here where practically every Recruit of the Manchester Regiment (except those for the Territorial Force Battalions) spends his first few days as a soldier, and is fitted with his uniform, etc.

The officers are:—

Lt.-Col. H. L. JAMES, C.B. (Commanding Depot); Temp. Major J. H. HOLME (Adjutant); Capt. F. J. HEYWOOD (Spec. Res. of Off.); and Hon. Major and Qr.-Mr. G. GARRETT (Quartermaster).

1st BATTALION (63rd Foot)

In 1758 the 63rd was formed from the 2nd Battalion of the 8th (Wolfe's) Foot. The 8th came into existence in 1685, being raised by Lord Ferrars of Chartley. It served in the Irish Campaign of William III., and was in Flanders in 1696-7, and again in 1701, taking part in the siege of 1702. The Regiment shared in the glories of Oudenarde, Ramillies, and Malplaquet. After the Rebellion of 1715 it was called "The King's." It fought at Dettingen and at Fontenoy, and was present later at Falkirk and Culloden.

In 1758 the 63rd formed part of an expedition which sailed to capture Martinique and Guadiloupe. In the spring of 1775 it was landed in Boston, North America, and was engaged in the battles at Bunker's Hill, Long Island, Forts Lee and Washington, Rhode Island, Brandywine, Fort Clinton, Charlestown, Camden, etc. In 1794-5 we find the 63rd back in Flanders, in 1796-8 in the West Indies, and in 1799 in Flanders again, where, under the Duke of York they took part in the battle of Egmont-op-Zee. On October 6th of the same year an unsuccessful attack was made on the French position near Alkmaar, when the 63rd lost over 200 men. In 1800 the Regiment landed at Ellaya De Dominos. The 2nd Battalion of the 63rd served in the Walcheren Expedition, and at the bombardment of Flushing, being disbanded in 1814. The 1st Battalion assisted in the capture of Martinique in 1809, and the following year was engaged at the capture of Guadoloupe. It was again (and for the third time) concerned in the taking of the Island in 1815. In 1826 the Regiment was engaged in Sir William Clinton's Expedition to Portugal, where it remained until 1828. After many years of peace, the 63rd saw service in the Crimean War in 1854. The Regiment was in the rear guard under General Torrens at Alma, and took part in the action late in the day. The 63rd were slightly engaged at Balaclava, but made a very gallant charge at Inkerman. The Regiment, after seeing the fall of Sebastopol, was one of the last to leave the Crimea, having lost in the War, killed or died from wounds and invalided, 48 officers and 999 N.C.O.'s and men. The next campaign of the 63rd was in Afghanistan in 1880-1, and on the return to India marched from Quetta to Dera Ghazi Khaiv, about 400 miles, by the Bozdar route, which lay through a difficult and roadless country.

On July 1st, 1881, the 63rd Foot became the 1st Battalion Manchester Regiment, and as such took part in the Egyptian Campaign of 1882, and was at Ismailia during the battle of Tel-el-Kebir. Afterwards, as a garrison to Alexandria, it was joined by the 2nd Battalion.

The 1st Battalion was in Natal when the War broke out in South Africa in October, 1899. The Battalion took part, with distinction, under Sir Ian Hamilton as Brigadier, in the battle of Elandslaate. After Elandslaagte came Lombard's Kop and Nicholson's Nek, and then Cæsar's Camp, the "key of Ladysmith." Here over four months of fighting, privation, and heroic endurance were spent. After a month's rest the Battalions started on two years' steadv hard work. The first portion included action at Graskop, Amersfort, Van Wyk's, Vlei, and Belfast. Then came marching, convoy duty, and outpost work, enlivened by continual skirmishes. The Battalion also took part in many of Lord Kitchener's "drives."

At the commencement of the present War the 1st Battalion was in India. They came over with the Indian Expeditionary Force, and after being fitted out with winter clothing in the South of France, arrived in the firing line on October 18th, 1914. The first action was at Picantin, on October 23rd. About December 18th the Battalion losses of 8 officers and 100 men were partly made up by the arrival of a draft from England. At Givenchy, on the 20th and 21st of the same month, the Battalion fought for over 30 hours, and succeeded in regaining trenches that had been lost, and holding them against a very considerably stronger force of the enemy. In this action the Battalion losses were 5 officers and over 300 men. The Commander of the Division referred to the Battalion as the "gallant

Manchesters," and the Commander of the Indian Army Corps, in addressing them, said :—

"I want to thank you for your very fine bit of work "in the last fight. You are a very gallant Battalion. "You were holding the most important point on the "right of the British line, and by your gallant conduct "in holding on to it you rendered greater service than "you probably realised. I want to tell Colonel "Strickland in front of you what I think of him. "He is a first-class soldier, and you are a brave lot "of men."

The next big action was at Neuve Chapelle on March 11th and 12th, when the enemy's entrenched position was stormed by our troops. Again the losses were heavy. On April 26th the Battalion took part in the second battle of Ypres, where a considerable number of officers and men were lost, including the Commanding Officer, Lt.-Col. Hitchins.

Up to May 23rd, during seven months' fighting, the Battalion received 38 officers and 1,449 other ranks as reinforcements. During June and July, the Battalion was at La Gorgue. In August it was at Rue de Bris, and at Neuve Chapelle for September, October, and November. From the end of May to the beginning of December the Battalion was continuously employed in trench warfare without engaging in any big actions. On December 9th, 1915, the Battalion embarked at Marseilles and sailed for Mesopotamia.

2nd BATTALION (96th Foot)

The first 96th Foot was raised in 1760 for service under Clive in Southern India, and was disbanded in 1763. When the American War of Independence was at its height, in 1779, another 96th was raised, and this was disbanded in 1783. At the time of the French Revoluntionary War in 1793, a third 96th Regiment was raised, and served in the West Indies, but was broken up four years later at Halifax, Nova Scotia.

In 1803, on the formation of Light Infantry Regiments, the men of the two Battalions of the 52nd Foot who were considered unfit for Light Infantry work were formed into one regiment, and numbered into the line as the 96th. This Regiment took part in the capture of Guadaloupe in 1810, and was disbanded about 1814. In 1816 the 97th

(Queen's German) Regiment became the 96th (or Queen's Own). The 97th came into existence in 1798 as the Minorca Regiment, which was a Regiment of Foreigners raised by Sir John Stuart in Minorca. Though officially known as "A Regiment of Foot in the Island of Minorca," it was more commonly called "Stuart's Regiment," and as such took part in the battle of Alexandria on the 21st March, 1801. The Minorca Regiment was brought into line as the 97th in 1804. It is from the Minorca Regiment and the subsequent 97th that the present 2nd Battalion derives the honours, "Egypt" and "Peninsula."

Early in 1808 the 97th, forming part of the British Army under Lieut.-General Sir A. Wellesley, afterwards known as the Duke of Wellington, proceeded to the Peninsula, and took part in the battles of Vimiera and Talavera. After three years' fighting the Regiment went to Ireland, and was disbanded at Limerick in 1818.

In 1824 the present Battalion was raised by Major-General J. Fuller, at Manchester, mainly from Volunteers from the 94th and 95th Regiments. It was at first quartered at Salford Barracks, Manchester, and afterwards proceeded to Halifax, Nova Scotia. In 1835 the Regiment returned to England, and in 1839 for six months had its headquarters at Bolton-le-Moors, with two Companies at Liverpool, three at Wigan, and three at Haydock.

In 1841 the Regiment went to Australia, and in 1849 to India. When the Crimean War broke out in 1854 the Regiment was ordered to England, and during the next twenty years was stationed in Gibraltar, New Brunswick, South Africa, and India, arriving at Salford Barracks again in 1878. In 1881, owing to the Boer War, the Regiment moved to Malta, and in 1882, as the Second Battalion of the Manchester Regiment, took part in the Egyptian War. Afterwards the Battalion moved to India, and was presented with new Colours by Lord Roberts, near Delhi, in 1886. In 1891, 300 men of the Battalion took part in the Miranzai Expedition. After nearly 18 years' service abroad, the Battalion returned to England in 1898, when four Companies and the Headquarters were stationed at Hulme Barracks, Manchester, and the remaining four Companies at Lichfield.

The Battalion left for South Africa in March, 1900, and participated in the relief of Wepener, the action at Bibbulphsburg, the Caledon Valley surrender, and in the conquest of the Orange Free State generally. It underwent many hardships, more especially from want of clothing and food, and remained at the front until the close of the war. In 1904 the Battalion proceeded to the Channel Islands, and was at the Curragh, Ireland, at the commencement of the present War.

As part of the British Expeditionary Force, in the 14th Brigade, 5th Division of the II. Army Corps, the Battalion arrived in France on August 16th, 1914, and was immediately moved forward to the Belgian frontier. They took part in the fight at Mons on the 23rd, in the rearguard action at Dour on the 24th, Bavay on the 25th, and on the 26th lost 14 officers and over 300 men at Le Cateau. The Battalion was broken up a number of times during the retreat, but Lt.-Col. James, the Commanding Officer, was always able to gather the Companies together again. Then came the advance, and the fighting across the Marne towards the Aisne, when three officers and 105 men were killed and wounded. After some days near Soissons the Battalion left for the North-West of France, and took part in the actions round La Bassée, at Richeburg, Lorgies, La Quinque Rue, and Festubert.

The Battalion served in the trenches opposite Messines from November, 1914, to March, 1915, when it moved to Kemmel, and thence in April to Ypres, where it was kept 91 days in the trenches East of the Yser Canal on the South side of the salient. Here it lost many officers and 685 men killed and wounded only.

At the end of July the Battalion moved back for its first rest of a longer period than six days, three only of which it had had previously since the commencement of the war.

In August the Battalion joined as part of the Fifth Division, the newly-formed 11th Corps, and served in the trenches at Maricourt in the Amiens district. In January, 1916, the 14th Brigade was split up, and the Battalion, with the Brigade Staff, joined the 32nd Division and served in the trenches in front of Albert.

The following officers have commanded the Battalion while in France:—

Lt.-Col. H. L. James, C.B., 16th August to 29th September, 1914, and 16th November, 1914, to 8th January, 1915.

Major W. K. Evans, D.S.O., 29th September, 1914, to 16th November, 1914.

Lt.-Col. R. S. Weston, C.M.G., 8th January, 1915, to 13th November, 1915.

Lt.-Col. N. Luxmore, 13th November, 1915.

3rd and 4th BATTALIONS

The 3rd (Reserve) and 4th (Extra Reserve) Battalions of the Manchester Regiment were formed from what was, until 1880, the 6th Royal Lancashire Militia. During the period 1900 to 1907, when there were four Regular Battalions, the Militia Battalions were numbered 5th and 6th. With the renumbering in 1908 the Battalions got back their old numbers of 3rd and 4th, and became "Special Reserve" instead of "Militia."

Both the Militia Battalions were embodied during the South African War, and on many other occasions since the formation of the old Militia Regiments, have these Militia Units provided big numbers of men as drafts to the Regular Battalions. In peace time they act as a training ground for the Regular recruits. The 3rd and 4th Battalions were both embodied at the commencement of the present War at Ashton-under-Lyne, and left in a few days to take up their coast defence duties on the River Humber. One might almost say that the 3rd Battalion was at the front, as nearly the whole of their original officers and men have gone forward to the 1st and 2nd Battalions as reinforcements. Officers, N.C.O.'s and men have also been sent as drafts to the 6th, 10th, 11th, 12th, and 13th Battalions. Since the commencement of the War the 3rd Battalion has sent out 94 officers and 5,715 other ranks, and the 4th Battalion 47 officers and 2,039 other ranks. The 3rd and 4th Battalions are made up of Special and Line Reservists, re-enlisted old soldiers, the wounded and sick men from the Battalions at the front fit for service again, and men enlisted for the period of the war.

Among the present officers are the following:—

3rd Battalion—

Lt.-Col. H. K. ORAM (Commanding).
Major C. M. THORNYCROFT, D.S.O. (Adjutant).
Hon. Lieut. W. L. CONNERY (Quartermaster).

4th Battalion—

Lt.-Col. J. H. M. JEBB, D.S.O. (Commanding).
Capt. N. W. HUMPHRYS (Adjutant).
Hon. Major H. W. PRICE (Quartermaster).

TERRITORIAL BATTALIONS
(5th to 10th inclusive)

The Battalions all sent officers and men to South Africa during the War of 1899-1902 to serve with the Regular Battalions. For this service the Battalions now have "South Africa," with the years they were represented there, on their Colours.

At the commencement of the present war the Territorial Battalions were embodied, and at about the middle of September, 1914, were sent to Egypt to relieve the Regular Garrison there. The whole of the winter was spent in Egypt, the Battalion proceeding to Gallipoli during the first week of May, 1915. With the exception of one rest of about ten days at Imbros Island, after the attack on the Turkish trenches in June, the Battalions remained in Gallipoli until the general evacuation early in January, 1916. These Battalions form part of the 42nd Division commanded by Maj.-Gen. W. Douglas, C.B., D.S.O., which was known before the war as the East Lancashire Territorial Division.

In September, 1914, the 66th, or 2nd East Lancashire Division, was raised, each original battalion finding a second line. These battalions are now training near Crowborough, Sussex. Later a third line was recruited which is now training near Codford St. Mary's, Wilts.

Each original Territorial Battalion, with its second and third lines, has an establishment of nearly 4,000 officers, N.C.O.'s and men.

General Sir Ian S. M. Hamilton, G.C.B., D.S.O., who was in command of the troops in Gallipoli, describes the advance of the Manchester Brigade (5th, 6th, 7th, and 8th) on June 4th, 1916, as magnificent.

In his despatch describing the fighting of June 4th to 6th, the General says, "The question was now whether this rolling up of the newly captured line from the right would continue until the whole of our gains were wiped out. It looked very like it, for now the enfilade fire of the Turks began to fall upon the Manchester Brigade of the 42nd Division, which was firmly consolidating the furthest distant line of trenches it had so brilliantly won.

"After 1-30 p.m. it became increasingly difficult for this gallant brigade to hold its ground. Heavy casualties occurred; the Brigadier and many other officers were wounded or killed. Yet it continued to hold out with the greatest tenacity and grit.

"Such was the spirit displayed by this Brigade that there was great difficulty in persuading the men to fall back. Had their flanks been covered, nothing would have made them loosen their grip.

"Although we had been forced to abandon so much of the ground gained in the first rush, the net result of the day's operations was considerable: namely, an advance of 200 to 400 yards along the whole of our centre, a front of nearly three miles."

The 9th and 10th Battalions formed part of the 29th Division, which was on the left of the 42nd Division. The Commander-in-Chief, in dealing with the 29th Division's work, praises it in the highest manner possible

5th (Territorial) Battalion

Originally the 4th Administrative Battalion of the Lancashire Rifle Volunteers, formed about 1859, altered later to the 4th Battalion Lancashire Rifle Volunteers, and became, in 1881, the 1st Volunteer Battalion, Manchester Regiment. Present title from 1st April, 1908. The Headquartes are at Wigan, with detachments at Leigh, Patricroft, and Atherton.

After being embodied during the first days of the War, the Battalion was moved to Littleborough, and left England for Egypt during the first week of September, 1914. On May 3rd, 1915, the Battalion left Egypt, and arrived three days later at Cape Helles. At 5 p.m. the Battalion started disembarking, and was taken ashore on trawlers under shell fire from Asia. The night was spent on the beach. The Turks prevented much sleep as this night they counter-attacked the French very vigorously, the gun and rifle fire being practically continuous throughout the night. Next morning, after an early breakfast, the Battalion moved off the sea shore to the top of the cliffs, where they spent the day as Corps reserve, moving up late in the afternoon into dug-outs, and being put into divisional reserve. Next day saw the final advance of the 6th-8th May fighting, the Battalion lending a hand in carrying ammunition up to the guns. About six o'clock at night the Battalion moved out to go into trenches for the first time. Although not actually in the firing line the casualties were numerous chiefly owing to stray bullets and snipers left behind by the Turks.

On Sunday, the 16th, the Battalion moved into the front fire trenches. One week was thus passed in the fire trenches, when the Battalion was taken out for a three days' rest. It was a rest in name only, as the dug-outs were shelled continually by day. The Battalion moved forward 300 yards, 100 yards at a time, digging themselves in. These three advances took our line to within an average distance of 200 yards from the Turks' trenches. The Battalion had had practically no rest for four consecutive days and nights, work on the trenches continuing night and day. On June 1st they were told to expect a Turkish attack, which never came.

June 3rd was occupied in taking up positions ready for the attack next day. At nine o'clock on the morning of June 4th the big bombardment started, and was most intense until 12 mid-day, when the guns lifted on to the Turks' rear trenches and the infantry attacked. The 5th Manchesters were over the parapet, had crossed the Turks' bared wire and taken the first Turk trench in five minutes, which was a very fine perfomance, and not equalled by any other regiment. The losses were small considering the strength of the enemy's position, and this may be put down to the fine charge which demoralised the Turks. Ten minutes after the first Turk trench was taken the two remaining Companies of the Battalion got out of their trenches, pushed on over the first Turk trench, took two more trenches, and then started digging themselves in. The front line had a hot time of it ,as the Turks shelled it very heavily, and later, when the French, Naval, and 7th Manchesters retired the 5th were subject to very heavy enfilade fire, and although suffering heavy casualties stuck to their position until ordered to retire at night, and after the Turks had started cutting off their retreat.

The retirement to the first captured Turkish trench took place at dusk, and was accomplished without the loss of a single man, though several men too badly wounded to move had to be left behind, all those who possibly could being brought back. Shortly after the retirement took place the Turks attacked the Battalion, but were easily driven off.

About sixty prisoners were taken by the Fifth, including several Turkish officers. The Manchester Brigade had held practically the centre of the British line, the Fifth being on the right centre of the Manchester Brigade.

The night of June 4th was quiet. At daybreak of the 6th the Turks attacked our line, but were driven off with loss. On June 9th the Battalion was relieved in the trenches, and went out into reserve. On June 12th the Battalion was taken off the Peninsula and sent to Imbros Island to rest. During its stay at Imbros, the 5th, with the 6th, 7th, and 8th Battalions (the Manchester Brigade), were inspected by General Sir Ian Hamilton, and thanked for the services they had done. On the 21st the Battalion was back on the Peninsula, and by the evening of the 22nd occupied its old trenches. From now onwards the Battalion had a quiet time, never actually taking part in any of the big actions during June and July which occurred on its flanks, never having to do more than support these attacks with rifle fire.

June and July was thus spent, the Battalion taking its turn in the trenches and doing fatigues. August came, and with it the terrible days of the 6th-10th, when the Battalion was knocked about pretty badly due to the big holding attack which was made on the Helles end of the Peninsula while the landing was taking place at Suvla. The part assigned to the Fifth was to take two rows of Turkish trenches after a bombardment by artillery. The Turks had also decided to attack but a day or two later, and had brought up for this purpose the Adrianople Army Corps, the pick of the Turkish Army. When the charge was ordered the men moved forward in a solid line. Few men ever reached the trenches to be taken owing to the Turkish machine guns and enfilade rifle fire. The trenches, too, were packed with Turks two and three deep, making it absolutely impossible for even the finest troops in the world to capture them. The remains of the Battalion trekked back as best it could into their own trenches again. Next morning the remains of the Battalion, helped by another, not of the Manchester Brigade, were ordered to try and take the trenches once again. When the order came to charge the Fifth again leapt over the parapet, but not being supported by this other Battalion, never got far beyond their own parapet, those who were alive scrambling back into the trenches they had vacated only a few minutes before.

Finally, three days later, the Battalion was relieved, and went into the rest camp. It had not been there three days when orders were received to go and relieve the 29th Division. Until the evacuation of Galipoli the Division has held the line which the 29th Division had won.

The Battalion left for Egypt about 7th January, 1916.

The following are the present officers with the dates of their appointments :—

Hon. Colonel—Eckersley, N. off. (Hon. Lt.-Col. ret. Spec. Res.) (Hon. Capt. in Army). 22 Nov. 13.

Lt.-Colonels—

France, W. S., V.D., hon. c. 23 Dec. 05.

Timmis, G. D. (Lt.-Col. ret. Spec. Res.) (Hon. Capt. in Army 6 Feb. 02). *29 July 15.

Majors—

Fletcher, E. 23 June 12.

Darlington, H. C. (t) (Hon. Lt. in Army 24 June 01) (In Command) (*Lt.-Col. 12 Sept. 14). 16 Sept. 13.

Bryan, L. E. G., V.D. (Hon. lt. col.)* 19 Dec. 14. 23 Dec. 05.

Hunter, T., V.D. (Hon. Maj. ret. T.F.). *28 May 15.

Captains—

Cronshaw, A. E. (Hon. Lt. in Army 26 July 02) (*Maj. 31 Aug. 14) 7 Jan. 03. Brown, N. S. (*Lt.-Col. 6 Nov. 14). 13 June 03. Fletcher, C. 23 Dec. 05. Simpson, A. W. W. 10 Jan. 06. Walker, J. S. A. (H) (Empld. under Ministry of Munitions 16 Nov. 15). 16 Sept. 13. (2)Ratcliffe-Ellis A. (*Maj. 21 Dec. 14). *6 Oct. 14. Cherry, J. W. 11 Sept. 14.

Lieutenants—

Wall, J. (*Capt. 17 May 15). 23 June 10. (3)Fletcher, R. L. (*Capt. 26 May 15). 29 June 11. Woods, W. T. (*Capt. 31 Aug. 14). ·10 Aug. 13. (3)Johnson, W. G. E. (*Capt. 4 June 15). 3 Nov. 13. Ainscough, C. (*Capt. 30 June 15). 31 Aug. 14. Johnson, A. E. 31 Aug. 14. (1)Bryham, M. (*Capt. 1 Mar. 15). *29 Dec. 14. (3)Ridge, W. H. (*Maj. 15 June 15). *5 June 1915. 7 Nov. 14.

2nd-Lieutenants—

(1)Allen, G. E. 27 Mar. 14. Bryham, A. L. (*Capt. 31 Aug. 14). 26 Aug. 14. (3)Hewlett, A. (*Capt. 31 Aug. 14). 26 Aug. 14. (2)Lund, G. S. 26 Aug. 14. Burrows, E. J. (*Capt. 23 Sept. 15). 2 Sept. 14. Brown, C. P. 2 Sept. 14. (3)Burrows, M. K. (*Lt. 24 Sept. 15). 12 Sept. 14. Holden, E. N. (*Lt. 24 Sept. 15). 12 Sept. 14. Slaughter, A. 12 Sept. 14. Gordon, F. C. 12 Sept. 14. (2)Rawcliffe, D. M. (*Capt. 18 Nov. 14). 13 Sept. 14. (2)Flinn, R. E. (*Lt. 18 Nov. 14). 30 Sept. 14. (3)Smith, E. H. H. (*Capt. 30 Aug. 15). 30 Sept. 14. (2)Ellis, R. R. (*Lt. 19 Nov. 14). 30 Sept. 14. (2)Clayton, P. C. (*Lt. 18 Nov. 14). 30 Sept. 14. Fisher, E. L. (*Capt 6 Jan. 15). 30 Sept. 14. (2)Prethean, C. (*Lt. 1 Mar. 15). 30 Sept. 14. (1)Stott, T. M. (*Lt. 18 Nov. 14). 30 Sept. 14. (2)Winterbottom, D. D. (*Capt. 1 Mar. 15). 30 Sept. 14. (2)Walmesley-Cotham, T. (*Capt. 20 Jan. 15). 5 Oct. 14. (1)Johnson, H. N. 14 Oct. 14. (3)Field, H. H. (*Lt. 1 Aug. 15). 19 Nov. 14. (2)Fox, J. S. (*Lt. 1 June 15). 1 Dec. 14. (1)Dickey, R. G. A. 1 Dec. 14. (1)Aitkenhead, F. (*Lt. 1 Aug. 15). 15 Dec. 14. (2)Entwisle,

F. W. (*Lt. 1 July 15). 2 Jan. 15. 14 Nov. 14. (2)Ellis, S. R. (*Lt. 1 July 15). 8 Jan. 15. (2)Bryan, J. L. 20 Jan. 15. (2)Davis, L. E. 23 Jan. 15. (3)Widdows, F. M. 24 Jan. 15. (2)Knight, A. R. (*Lt. 1 July 15). Adjt. 15 Feb. 15. (1)Parker, A. S. (*Lt. 24 Sept. 15). 22 Feb. 15. (1)Dickey, J. P. Y. 23 Feb. 15. (2)Griffith, R. B. 1 Mar. 15. (1)Hornabrook, A. W. 4 Mar. 15. (2)Griffith, W. H. E. N. 8 Mar. 15. (2)Smith, H. D. 27 Mar. 15. (2)Blair, R. H. 28 Mar. 15. (1)Goward, E. E. 13 Apr. 15. (2)Batten, P. W. 17 Apr. 15. (2)Charlesworth, J. 24 Apr. 15. (2)McGeorge, T. L. 28 Apr. 15. (1)Pearce, G. O. 29 Apr. 15. (2)Coupe, F. W. 15 May 15. (2)Lamb, E. R. 15 May 15. (1)Makinson, A. L. 26 May 15. (3)Jones, L. T. 1 July1 5. (3)Greenup, G. 1 July 15. (1)Prince, A. E. 1 July 15. (3)Besso, M. 4 July 15. (3)Halliwell, T. 5 July 15. (3)Molyneux, C A. 6 July 15. (3)Hickson, W. O. 7 July 15. (3)Jones, H. (*Lt 10 July 15). 10 July 15. (2)Ellis, H. R. 13 July 15. (2)Brown, G. B. 29 July 15. (2)France, R. A. 1 Aug. 15. Martin, H. Y. 10 Aug. 15. Stewart, T. B. 10 Aug. 15. (3)Wood, J. B. 16 Aug. 15. Hunt, D. K. S. 16 Aug. 15. Kerfoot, E. 17 Aug. 15. Ward, F. J. 22 Aug. 15. (3)Ashworth, R. (*Lt. 27 Aug. 15) Adjt. 27 Aug. 15. Jacobs, R. 30 Aug. 15. (3)Darby, N. L. 31 Aug. 15. (3)Lightbuwn, J. E. 9 Sept. 15. (3)Draper, B. F. 9 Sept. 15. (3)Bergl, L. St. C. 9 Sept. 15. Stevens, D. E. 17 Sept. 15. Bryan, R. T. 1 Oct. 15. Massey, P. E. 2 Oct. 15. Goddbehere, P. 2 Oct. 15. Fletcher, F. L. 8 Oct. 15. Plommer, M. 8 Oct. 15. (3)Ridge, C. S. (*Lt. 19 Oct. 15). 19 Oct. 15. Dickson, S. 28 Oct. 15. Maxted, C. 1 Nov. 15. Travers, H. 1 Nov. 15. Gollop, F. R. 22 Nov. 15. Glover, P. A. 22 Nov. 15. Atkin, H. D. 2 Dec. 15. Stafford, C. A. S. 2 Dec. 15. Urie, W. A. E. 2 Dec. 15. Robertson, W. M. M. 2 Dec. 15. Hawkins, B. L. 2 Dec. 15. Bateman, J. W. 2 Dec. 15. Turpin, A. E. 7 Dec. 15. *24 July 15. Spratling, R. W. 3 Dec. 15. Deighton, R. H. 7 Dec. 15. Soulsby, E. D. 11 Dec. 15. Shaw, G. W. 11 Dec. 15. Coates, C. O. 11 Dec. 15. Britton, H. W. 11 Dec. 15. Jackman, R. J. 11 Dec. 15. Oliver, H. W. 11 Dec. 15. Ogden, W. E. 11 Dec. 15. Downer, F. 11 Dec. 15. Westfield, F. J. 13 Dec. 15. Gregg, R. A. 19 Dec. 15. Fox, J. 19 Dec. 15. Walthew, L. 21 Dec. 15. Finley, J. J. 21 Dec. 15. Phillips, D. H. 21 Dec. 15. Mills, B. H. 21 Dec. 15. Henson, E. D. 21 Dec. 15. Levey, R. P. 21 Dec. 15. Butterworth, N. 31 Dec. 15. Field, N. 31 Dec. 15.

Adjutants—

Sanders, J. M. B., Capt. Leins R. 1 Jan. 13. (2)Knight, A. R., 2nd Lt. (*Lt.) 18 June 15. (3)Ashworth, R., 2nd Lt. (*Lt.) 27 Aug. 15.

Quarter-Masters—

(2)Greenwood, A., hon. lt. 15 Aug. 14. (1)Lock, A., hon. lt. 9 Sept. 14. (3)Wilson, S., hon. lt. 23 Sept. 15.

Medical Officers—

STOTT, Capt. F. W. A., M.B., R.A.M.C. (T.F.) (attd.) 16 July 15. 16 Jan. 15. (2)MARTIN, Capt. W. Y., M.B., R.A.M.C. (T.F.) (attd.) 4 Nov. 15.

Chaplain—

JOHNSON, Rev. P. Y., Chapl. 4th Class (T.F.) (attd.) 29 May 15.

* Denotes Temporary Rank.

OFFICERS OF THE 5TH (TERRITORIAL) BATTALION KILLED, DIED OF WOUNDS RECEIVED IN ACTION, OR DIED

Capt. F. S. BROWN—May 27, 1915.

Captain Frederick S. Brown was a partner in the firm of Messrs. Reynolds and Gibson, cotton merchants, of Liverpool and Manchester. Captain Brown was the son of Mr. James Brown, of Messrs. Eckersley, Limited, cotton manufacturers, Wigan. He was promoted Captain on 16th September, 1906.

Capt. H. M. ROGERS—May 24, 1915.

Captain Henry Milward Rogers, died of wounds received in action. He was 36 years of age, married, and the only son of the late William Rogers, mining engineer, of Coppul, Wigan. Captain Rogers was a member of a Wigan mining engineering firm, and had considerable interests in collieries in Lancashire and South Wales. He was promoted Captain on 17th June, 1915.

Capt. A. C. LEACH—June 12, 1915.

Captain A. C. Leach was the son of Mr. A. H. Leach, of Southport. He was a well-known mining engineer, being a member of the firm of Messrs. Mayhew, Leach, and Mayhew, mining engineers, of Wigan. He was promoted Captain on March 26th, 1913.

Capt. F. A. JAMES—August 18th, 1915.

Captain Francis Arthur James, who died of wounds received in action, was the son of the Rev. C. H. James, Vicar of Haigh, near Wigan. Captain James was 29 years of age. For the five years preceding the war Captain James occupied the position of Vice Principal of the Colvin Talnydar's School at Lucknow, India. Captain James was promoted captain after receiving the wounds to which he succumbed.

Lieut. G. S. JAMES—June 12, 1915.

Lieutenant G. Sydney James was a younger brother of Captain James, and the son of the Rev. C. H. James, Vicar of Haigh, near Wigan. Lieutenant James was a mining engineer in the service of the Wigan Coal and Iron Company, Limited. He was promoted lieutenant on September 16th, 1913.

2nd Lieut. A. C. BROOK—June 13, 1915.

Lieutenant A. C. Brook was the son of Mr. Arthur Brook, of the Treasury, and he was associated with his uncle, Mr. T. J. Hirst, of Meltham Hall, and Mr. C. Lewis Brook, of Harewood Lodge, in the management of the business of Jonas Brook and Brothers, Limited, sewing cotton manufacturers, Meltham Mills, near Huddersfield. Lieut. Brook was 31 years of age. He was promoted lieutenant on September 12th, 1914.

2nd Lieut. T. C. WALKER—June 12, 1915.

Second-Lieutenant Thomas Cartmell Walker was the youngest son of Mr. T. A. Walker, of the Pagefield Ironworks, Wigan. Lieutenant T. C. Walker, who was twenty years of age, was on the point of proceeding to Cambridge when the war broke out. He joined the 5th Battalion on October 13th, 1914.

MISSING.

Capt. D. D. WINTERBOTTOM, from Aug. 7, 1915.
Lieut. C. AINSCOUGH, from May 19, 1915.
2nd Lieut. L. E. DAVIS, from Aug. 7, 1915.
2nd Lieut. F. L. MCGEORGE, from Aug. 7, 1915.

WOUNDED.

Major A. E. CRONSHAW.
Capt. A. L. BRYHAM. 9 Aug. 15.
Capt. H. H. CUNNINGHAM. 18 May 15.
Capt. A. HEWLETT.
Capt. J. M. B. SANDERS.
Capt. W. J. WOODS.
Lieut. P. C. CLAYTON. 6 Aug. 15.
Lieut. B. L. FLETCHER. 12 June 15.
Lieut. P. C. FLETCHER. 26 May 15.
Lieut. A. E. JOHNSON. 12 June 15.
Lieut. W. G. E. JOHNSON.
Lieut. A. S. PARKER.
2nd Lieut. G. E. ALLEN. 9 Aug. 15.
2nd Lieut. C. P. BROWN.
2nd Lieut. E. J. BURROWS. 12 June 15 and 9 Aug. 15.
2nd Lieut. M. K. BURROWS, 12 June 15.
2nd Lieut. R. G. A. DICKEY. 6 Aug. 15.
2nd Lieut. F. C. GORDON. 12 June 15.
2nd Lieut. H. N. JOHNSON. 13 June 15.
2nd Lieut. H. J. PORTER. 6 Aug. 15
Hon. Lieut. and Qr.-Mr. TAYLOR.

N.C.O.'S AND MEN OF THE 5TH (TERRITORIAL) BATTALION KILLED OR DIED OF WOUNDS RECEIVED IN ACTION.

Date List Published.	
3 7 15.	1997 Cpl. J. Lowe.
	332 Cpl. W. Millington.
	1557 L/Cpl. W. Davenport (d.w.)
	2404 Pte. H. Hessey (d.w.)
5 7 15.	1298 Pte. A. Jones (d.w.)
6 7 15.	1126 Pte. J. Aldred.
	1978 Pte. R Causey.
	1720 Pte. R. Collinge.
	1414 Pte. J. Ferguson.
	2361 Pte. J. Fox.
	1375 Pte. J. Gregory.
	2368 Pte. N. Lewis.
	2028 J. McGann.
	1304 Pte. A. E. Regan.
	1526 G. Shepherd.
	34 G. W. Smith.
	2366 Pte. E. C. H. Slater.
	2256 Pte. C. H. Taylor.
	2229 Cpl. C. Foster.
	2032 Sergt. W. Fowler.
	2374 Pte. T. Halliwell.
	103 Pte. J. Hersnip.
	1265 Pte. W. Holland.
	1659 Pte. J. Holmes.
	180 Sergt. J. Horrocks.
	1194 Pte. T. Kelly.
	1794 Pte. J. T. Lindsay.
	1979 Pte. J. Mahon.
	6111 Pte. S. Mortimer.
	1859 Pte. W. Myers.
	256 Sergt. J. Pickles.
	1944 Pte. J. S. Smith.
	999 Pte. R. Smith.
	213 Sergt. S. Whittle.
	2175 Pte. E. Wilson.
	1562 Pte. W. Winstanley.
	1802 Pte. W. Wood.
	2363 Pte. R. Woodhall.
	2084 Pte. A. Young.
20 7 15.	1650 Pte. A. H. Birchall.
	1584 Pte. J. Bolton.
	2136 Pte. J. W. Brennand.
	2086 Sergt. J. Bridge.
	1677 Dr. W. Brindle.
	2056 Pte. F. Birke.
7 7 15.	1493 Pte. T. Barrow (d.w.)
	1474 Pte. H. Thomas (d.w.)
9 7 15.	2116 Pte. J. Dean (d.w.)
	1309 Pte. W. Duddle (d.w.)
	1555 Pte. G. Jones (d.w.)
	2117 Pte. A. Rothwell (d.w.)
	2342 Pte. T. Sweeney (d.w.)
12 7 15.	1844 Pte. S. Lawton.
	2371 Pte. W. Talbot
17 7 15.	2264 Pte. J. Austin.
	2008 Pte. G. Bainbridge.
	211 Pte. A. Banks.
	922 Sergt. W. Bruinson.
	218 Sergt. A. Mc. N. Boyle
	1951 Pte. P. Brown.
	1929 Pte. W. Campsall.
	2359 Pte. C. Devereaux.
	1563 Pte. T. Downing.
24 7 15.	1888 Pte. J. Longson.
6 8 15.	2231 Pte. C. Cragg (d.w.)
17 8 15.	1745 Pte. W. Barlow.
	1508 Pte. C. Clements.
	2819 Pte. C. Garside.
	2360 Pte. H. A. Hilton.
	261 Sergt. A. Sanderson.
	1956 Pte. A. Graham (d.w.)
	2278 Pte. H. Smith (d.w.)
21 8 15.	2197 Pte. J. Moardman (d.w.)
	1406 Pte. J. Brown (d.)
24 8 15.	1228 Pte. G. Halliwell (d.w.)
25 8 15.	1830 Pte. A. Johns.
	2681 Pte. G. Moores.
	1656 Pte. J. Bolton (d.w.)
	2640 Pte. H. Jephson (d.w.)
	1444 Pte. W. Jarvis.
	1458 Pte. O. Ditchfield (d.)
	1688 Pte. H. Mason (d.)
	2484 Pte. J. W. Burke.
	1581 Pte. W. Dandy.
	2628 Pte. A. Jones.
	2521 Pte. L. Parry.
	2243 Pte. S. Pinckrance.
	2910 Pte. J. Gregson.
18 9 15.	1537 Pte. J. Dainteth.
	1146 Pte. J. Martland.

Date List Published.	
	1924 Pte. A. Callaghan.
	2053 Pte. J. Daniels.
	1309 Pte. R. Eckersley.
	1374 Pte. R. Hesford.
	2293 Pte. W. B. Jones.
	1542 Pte. S. Kay.
	1763 L/Cpl. J. Lacey.
	1967 Pte. J. McCoombes.
	2092 Pte. T. Middlehurst.
	947 Pte. W. Moss.
	1750 Pte. J. Rathbone.
	2223 L/Cpl. F. Rowlandson.
	2093 Cpl. H. Rudd.
	1812 Pte. W. Smith.
	1366 L/Cpl.J. Telford.
	1501 L/Cpl. J. G. Telford.
	1751 Pte. A. Webb.
	1807 Pte. J. Wilkinson.
23 7 15.	1971 Pte. E. Bentham.
24 7 15.	2048 Pte. T. Carney.
	2072 Pte. P. Harrison.
	2155 Pte. J. Houghton.
1 9 15.	1811 Pte. J. W. Rhodes (d w.)
2 9 15.	1415 Sgt. E. Horsfield (d.)
8 9 15.	1291 Pte. G. Bowden.
10 9 15.	1291 Cpl. C Acton.
	1167 Cpl. J. Banks.
	1449 Pte. R. Boardman.
	1921 Pte. G. Carr.
	2542 L/Cpl. A. Cheetham.
	1769 Pte J. Dowd.
	2788 Pte. J. T. Fox
	2097 Pte. H. Harrison.
	2372 Pte. C. Heaton.
	2341 Pte. J. Heaton.
	1249 Sgt. J Howard.
	1491 Pte. C. P. Johnson.
	2860 Ptei. H. Keefe.
	2818 Pte. E. Pollard.
	3004 Pte. R. J. Priestley

Date List Published.	
22 9 15.	3181 Pte. Ashroft.
27 9 15.	1896 Pte. R. Downham.
	2121 Pte. F. J. Walker.
29 9 15.	2952 Pte. J. Rooks.
27 10 15.	987 L/Cpl. F. Clay.
	2619 Pte. S. R. Hall.
	2290 Pte. R. Jones.
1 11 15.	991 Pte. R. Taylor (d.)
23 11 15.	1638 Pte. Calderbank (d.)
3 12 15.	1825 Pte. J. Duddy (d.w.)
10 12 15.	1911 Pte. T. Horrocks.
	2791 Pte. T. Roden.
	2045 Pte. J. Winnard.
27 12 15.	1958 Pte. J. France (d.w.)
29 12 15.	1004 Co.-Q.M.-Sergt. J. M. Tickle.
17 1 16.	3558 Pte. J. Cosgrove (d.)
24 1 16.	2435 Pte. B. Duckworth (d.w.)
29 1 16.	1290 Pte. R. H. Summers.
31 1 16.	1933 Pte. T. Dean.
4 2 16.	1360 Pte. R. Houghton (m.k.)
	2673 Cpl. G. Bickley (d.w.)
	1282 Pte. F. Unsworth.
	3082 Pte. J. Wilkinson.
	1329 Sgt. J. Williams.
	1875 Pte. Worthington.
10 9 15	2533 Pte. T. Carey (d.w.)
	2276 Cpl. F. Baron (m) (b.k.)
	1772 Pte. E. Loughlin (m) (b.k.)
	2013 Pte. C. Southern (m) (b.k.)
	2017 Pte. E. Southern (m) (b.k.)
	2023 Cpl. S. Stockton (m) (b.k.)
	126 Sgt. J. Topping (m) (b.k.)
11 9 15.	1523 Pte. E. Chadwick (d.w.)
	639 Pte. E. Houghton (d.w.)
	2066 Pte. W. McDonald (d.w.
	2740 Pte. E. Rawlinson (d.w.)
	1266 Pte. G. Smith (d.w.)
	2785 Pte. T. Tither (d.w.)
	360 Sgt. R. Baxendale (d.w.)

6th (Territorial) Battalion

Originally the 7th Administrative Battalion of the Lancashire Rifle Volunteers, altered later to the 7th Battalion Lancashire Rifle Volunteers, and became on 1st April, 1880, the 2nd Volunteer Battalion, Manchester Regt. Present title from 1st April, 1908. The Headquarters are in Stretford Road, Hulme, Manchester.

The Battalion was mobilised on August 4th, 1914, on the outbreak of War, and moved to Littleborough, where is was encamped until September 10th, when it embarked for Egypt with the rest of the East Lancashire Division.

The Battalion was in Egypt, first at Alexandria and afterwards at Cairo.

On May 3rd, 1915, the Battalion left Egypt for the Dardanelles, and arrived three days later at Cape Helles, where it disembarked that evening in lighters, and was marched up to the top of the cliff above "W" Beach. The Battalion came under shell fire when landing. Next day it proceeded with the 5th and 7th Battalions into dug-outs about a mile further inland. There, on the 8th May, the Battalion witnessed a very heavy bombardment and attack, the men being utilised in carrying ammunition to the guns. That night the Battalion moved up into reserve trenches, half occupying trenches already made; the remainder had to advance about 500 yards on the Krithi round and dig themselves in. Some men were lost in the night, and there were quite a number of casualties in these trenches from dropping bullets. On the 16th the Battalion moved into the front line, and occupied trenches on the right of the Brigade. The night was very wet, and the trenches were full of water when morning came. The Battalion remained in these trenches, except for two days' rest, until the 10th June, and during the period there much work was done improving the trenches,and on the left a long trench was cut to the right to connect up and consolidate the line. This trench helped very much in keeping enemy sharpshooters from slipping through. The line was then complete. The Battalion also advanced forward about 200 yards, and dug a firing trench with its three communication trenches in the night about May 30th. This was a fine piece of work, and carried out splendidly by the Battalion. The digging was done in the open. The work was continued from May 30th to June 3rd, digging and improving the new lines. June 3rd was all in preparation for the attack on the 4th June.

On the 4th June, at 9 o'clock prompt, a big bombardment started, and was carried on until mid-day, when the guns lengthened their range on the rear trenches of the enemy, and the attack was started by the Infantry. The 6th Manchester Battalion was over the parapet in one rush, three companies charging the Turkish trenches, the nearest being some 200 yards away. In 20 minutes the men were in possession of the three Turkish trenches. The losses in this charge were very heavy. At 12-15 the second line moved, one company of the 6th Manchesters going to the second objective to the left of the 8th Battalion. They advanced 400 yards in front of the trenches taken by the first-line, and dug themselves in. This was a very fine bit of work, but, unfortunately, the right of the line having to fall back, eventually the men had to retire from this position at night. It was brilliantly held during the day, and considerable losses were inflicted on the Turks, who attacked in force. Subsequently the Battalion held their ground, although heavily attacked by the Turks. About 200 prisoners, including several officers, were taken by the 6th. The Manchester Brigade held this line until relieved on the 9th June, when they went into reserve.

On the 12th June the Battalion was sent to Imbros to rest. There the Manchester Brigade was inspected by General Sir Ian Hamilton, and thanked for their services. On the 21st they returned to Cape Helles, and on the 22nd were sent to the front-line trenches. During the remainder of June and July, except for one small attack on the left of the line, it had a quiet time, although there was considerable activity in bombing on both sides.

In August once more the Battalion was in for strenuous days. On the 6th August, the 5th Manchester Battalion had a very stiff fight, and on the 7th the 6th Battalion were ordered to charge the Turkish trenches. After a very severe bombardment by the guns three lines were launched, at successive intervals of a quarter of an hour, but the Turkish artillery, machine gun and rifle fire was so intense that, although the men were going with great dash, they were unable to reach the trenches, and a few returned. During this period the Turks continuously bombarded with their guns, and the Battalion had a good many casualties in the trenches.

On the 13th August the Battalion was relieved and went into rest again. Three days afterwards it took over the trenches west of the line, to relieve the 29th Division, and remained on this sector until it was finally withdrawn from Gallipolo. During this period the Battalion's trenches were once or twice mined by the enemy, and suffered considerable casualties; also bombing on both sides was very active.

The Battalion left for Egypt about the 7th January, 1916.

The following are the present Officers of the Battalion :—

Lt.-Colonels—

(1)Heywood, G. G. P. 1 Sept. 11.

(2)Davies-Colley, T. H. (Hon. Maj. ret. T.F.) *28 Sept. 14.

Majors—

(1)Pilkington, C. R., C.M.G. (Hon. Lt. in Army 19 Aug. 01) (*Lt.-Col. 1 June 15) 24 July 08.

(1)Worthington, C. S. 25 Feb. 14.

(3)Lowe, H. D. *9 Sept. 14. 1 Sept. 11.

Captains—

(2)Frank, N. G. (*Maj. 1 June 15). 22 Oct. 06. Bennett, J. R. 15 Oct. 13. (2)Pilkington, E. F. (*Maj. 1 July 15) 12 Feb. 14. (1)Davies, O. St. L. (*Maj. 1 June 15). *5 Aug. 14. 9 Jan. 04. (1)Bolton, D. C. 26 Aug. 14. (3)Brierley, H. C. *1 Oct. 14. (2)Blayney, J. J. *24 Oct. 14. Helm, J. H. *24 Oct. 14. (3)Melvill, M. G. D. *24 Oct. 14. (2)Whitworth, J. H. *31 Oct. 14. (1)Blatherwick, T. 1 May 15. (1)Aldous, F. C. 21 May 15. (1)Blatherwick, F. 4 June 15. (1)Heywood, A. G. P. 7 Oct. 15.

Lieutenants—

(1)Thomson, A .D. 26 Aug. 14. (1)Hammick, H. A. (*Capt. 4 June 15). 26 Aug. 14. McDougall, S. *24 Oct. 14. (2)Brooks, A. B. *24 Oct. 14. (3)Collier, S. F. (*Capt. 27 Aug. 15) Adjt. *31 Oct. 14. Lingard, J. R. *31 Oct. 14. (2)Hoare, B. S. (*Capt. 1 Aug. 15). *31 Oct. 14. (1)Molesworth, W. N. (*Capt. 4 June 15). 21 May 15. (2)Maxwell, K. G. (*Capt. 14 Sept. 14). 21 May 15. (1)Hellawell, H. S. (*Capt. 4 June 15). 21 May 15. (1)Heywood, H. C. L. 21 May 15. (1)Sellars, E. L. 4 June 15. (2)Hargreaves, C. A. 25 Aug. 15.

2nd-Lieutenants—

Bedford, R. H. 26 Aug. 1.4 (3)Houghton, J. R. (*Lt. 27 Aug. 15). 2 6Aug. 14. Kershaw, G. V. (*Lt. 18 June 15). 31 Oct. 14. Bridgford, S. L. 31 Oct. 14. Rainbow, J. 31 Oct. 14. (2)Anderton, C. A. (*Lt. 1 Aug. 15). 31 Oct. 14. (2)Bridgford, R. R. (*Lt. 1 Aug. 15). 31 Oct. 14. (1)Collier, S. (*Lt. 4 June 15). 31 Oct. 14. (2)Tattersall, J. B. 31 Oct. 14. (2)Fox, C. H. (*Capt. 1 Aug 15). 31 Oct. 14. (2)Fox, G. W., Adjt. *(Capt. 11 Oct. 15). 1 Feb. 15. (2)Tattersall, F. G. 8 Feb. 15. (3)Bloomer, H. S. (*Lt. 27 Aug. 15). 18 Feb. 15. Whitehead, J. S. 18 Feb. 15. (1)Rowsell, H. W. 18 Feb. 15. (1)Cadman, W. H. 8 Mar. 15. (3)Oliver, A. D. (*Lt. 27 Aug. 15). 10 Mar. 15. (3)Steele, E. (*Lt. 27 Aug. 15). 10 Mar. 15. Whiteside, D. 8 Apr. 15. (2)Holmes, A. B. (*Lt. 11 Oct. 15). 9 Apr. 15. 4 Mar. 15. (1)Kershaw, G. G. (*Capt. 4July 15). 25 Apr. 15. (1)Barber, L. H. 21 May 15. Burett, C. 6 June 15. (3)Chadwick, J. H. (*Lt. 10 Nov. 15). 14 June 15. (3)Sutcliffe, N. W. (*Lt. 10 Nov. 15). 25 June 15. (2)Hunter, D. F. (*Lt. 2 Nov. 15). 25 June 15.

(2)Vass, W. A. E. (*Lt. 2 Nov. 15). 25 June 15. (2)Oughtred, E. N. (*Lt. 2 Nove. 15). 25 June 15. (2)Platt, E. L. (*Lt. 2 Nov .15). 25 June, 15. (2)Stockdale, F. (*Lt. 2 Nov. 15). 25 June, 15. Hay, F. McK. 27 June 15. (2)Tweedale, G. (*Lt. 10 Nov. 15). 31 July 15. (3)Gibson, R. E. 9 Aug. 15. (3)Greenleaves, H. L. 10 Aug. 15. Worthington, T. R. 12 Aug. 15. Crossley, F. 12 Aug. 15. Bennet, J. 12 Aug. 15. Braithwaite, W. 12 Aug. 15. Bowers-Taylor, A. 12 Aug. 15. (3)Allen, C. R. (Capt. 10 Nov. 15). 15 Aug. 15. Hartshorn, E .P. 24 Aug. 15. (3)Morison, A. J. 28 Aug. 15. (2)Bloomer, W. C. K. 2 Sept. 15. (3)Whittaker, L. A. 2 Oct. 15. (3)Hollins, E. TH. 2 Oct. 15. (3)Vipond, H. 2 Oct. 15. (3)Booth, C. V. 2 Oct. 15. (3)Chew, H. 2 Oct. 15. (3)Benton, F. C. 2 Oct. 15. (3)Leighton, H. 2 Oct. 15. (3)Mawson, R. H. 2 Oct. 15. (3)Wigelsworth, C. E. 2 Oct. 15. Rhoades, E. A. 14 Oct. 15. (3)Walton, R. W. 14 Oct. 15. (3)Back, L. E. 14 Oct. 15. Cronopulo, D. W. 18 Oct. 15. Maitland, E. F. 22 Oct. 15. Horsfield, J. F. 27 Oct. 15. (3)Horrocks, A. J. 28 Oct. 15. Wood, D. G. 1 Nov. 15. (3)Heydon, A. 5 Nov. 15. (2)Kirk, R. 6 Nov. 15. Wilson, L. A. 16 Dec. 15. Bate, H. R. 16 Dec. 15. Allison, W. F. 21 Dec. 15. Hargreaves, T. A. 21 Dec. 15. Hinchcliffe, G. 21 Dec. 15. Bateman, R. A. 21 Dec. 15. Powell, J. R. 21 Dec. 15. Jackson, H. 21 Dec. 15. Knott, E. 1 Dec. 15. Keys, S. 25 Dec. 15. Barrow, R. H. 31 Dec. 15.

Adjutants—

(1)Holberton, P. V., Capt. Manch. R. (Maj. in Army). 4 Nov. 11. (3)Collier, S. F., Lt. (*Capt.) 16 June 15. (2)Fox, G. W., 2nd Lt. (*Capt.). 1 Oct. 15.

Quarter-Masters—

Vass, W., hon .m. (Empld. Recg. Duties). 25 July 05. Wynne, W., hon. lt. 5 Aug. 14. (2)Arkinstall, W. W., hon. lt. 10 Feb. 15. (3)Corrie, J. T., hon. lt. 17 Sept. 15.

Medical Officers—

(1)Norris, Capt. A. H., R.A.M.C. (T.F.) (attd.) 21 Dec. 12. 22 June 09. (2)Fitzgerald, Capt. W.E., M.B. R.A.M.C. (T.F.) (attd.) 6 Apr. 15. 6 Oct. 14.

Chaplain—

Challenor, Rev. J. W., TD, Chapl. 1st Class (T.F.) (attd.). 24 Oct. 11. 24 Oct. 91.

* Denotes Temporary Rank.

OFFICERS OF THE 6TH (TERRITORIAL) BATTALION KILLED, DIED OF WOUNDS RECEIVED IN ACTION, OR DIED.

Capt. W. N. Bazley—23 May, 1915.

Captain W. N. Bazley died from wounds received in action. He joined the Mounted Infantry Company of the old 2nd Volunteer Battalion Manchester Regiment.

now the 6th Territorials, over 20 years ago. At the outbreak of the South African War he entered the 77th Imperial Yeomanry as a non-commissioned officer, and became an honorary lieutenant in the Army while on active service. His promotion to the rank of captain came on September 1st, 1911. Captain Bazley was connected with the yarn trade of Manchester. He was 42 years of age.

Capt. H. T. CAWLEY—23 Sept., 1915.

Captain H. T. Cawley was the son of Sir Frederick Cawley, M.P., and was himself M.P. for the Heywood Division of Lancashire. He was killed while defending a crater which had been made by a Turkish mine in front of our trenches. Capt. Cawley was promoted captain on 1st June, 1913.

Capt. R. G. EDGER—4 June, 1915.

Captain Robert Gerald Edgar was the only son of Mr. R. A. Edgar, solicitor, Manchester. He was born 10th May, 1885, and educated at Rugby and Oriel College, Oxford. He was admitted a solicitor, and became a member of the firm of Boote, Edgar, Grace, and Rylands in April, 1911. Whilst at Alexandria he assisted in the preparation of the prosecution, before a court-martial, of a German spy, who was found guilty and sentenced to penal servitude for life. He was for some time commandant of the prisoners camp at Alexandria. He was promoted captain on August 26th, 1914.

Capt. S. F. JACKSON—4th June, 1915.

Captain Stanley Foster Jackson, who was 27 years of age, was a stockbroker carrying on business in Manchester, and was a son of the late Mr. Foster Jackson, of Old Trafford. He was an enthusiastic sportsman, and has often turned out for the Lancashire Rugby team. He was promoted captain on July 20th 1912.

Capt. J. HOLT—4 June, 1915.

Captain J. Holt was the elder son of Alderman Edward Holt, of Woodthorpe, Prestwich, and Windermere, an ex-Lord Mayor of Manchester, and was 33 years of age. He was educated at Rugby and Christ Church, Oxford. He was promoted to captain on December 20th, 1911.

Capt. A. D. HUNTER—7 Aug., 1915.

Captain A. D. Hunter was promoted to captain on October 24th, 1914.

Capt. E. KESSLER—4 June, 1915.

Captain Edgar Kessler was the eldest surviving son of Mr. P. W. and Mrs. Kessler, of Fernlea, Falloweld, Manchester. He was promoted captain on August 26th, 1914. Captain Kessler was interested in the well-known shipping firm of Kessler and Co., of Dale Street, Manchester.

Capt. H. B. PILKINGTON—4 June, 1915.

Captain Hugh Brocklehurst Pilkington was the second son of Mr. and Mrs. Charles Pilkington, of the Headlands, Prestwich. He was educated at Winchester and Trinity College, Cambridge, and was 28 years of age. He was a director of the Clifton and Kersley, the Outwood, and the Pilkington Colliery Companies. When at Winchester and Cambridge he was a member of the Rifle Volunteer Corps, and in 1909 he joined the 6th Battalion of the Manchester Regiment. He was promoted captain on February 24th, 1914.

Capt. A. D. THOMPSON—7 Aug., 1915.

Captain A. D. Thompson was promoted to lieutenant on August 26th, 1914, and to captain while in Gallipoli with the 6th Battalion.

Capt. W. H. WAINE—7 Aug., 1915.

Capt. W. H .Waine was appointed a temp. captain in the 14th (Reserve) Battalion Manchester Regiment on February 8th, 1915. He left Lichfield, where his Battalion had been training, to join the Med. Exped. Force on May 13th, 1915, and was attached to the 6th Battalion when killed in action.

Capt. A. J. WALKER—7 Aug, 1915.

Captain A. J. Walker was the younger son of Mr. J. C. Walker, of Henley-on-Thames. Captain Walker was probably the youngest officer of his rank in the British Army, having been promoted captain before he was 19 years of age. He was educated at Wellingborough School, and was a fine athlete, gaining his colours in the cricket and football elevens.

Lieut. A. C. BROOKE TAYLOR—4 June, 1915.

Lieutenant A. Cuthbert Brooke Taylor was the second son of Colonel and Mrs. Brooke Taylor, of Bakewell, Derbyshire, and only transferred from the 6th Battalion Sherwood Foresters, in which he had served for several years, to the 6th Manchesters in the spring of 1914. He was educated at Cheltenham College and Manchester University, where he took the engineering course, and subsequently became A.M.I.C.E. On transferring to the 6th Manchesters in 1914 he was appointed musketry instructor to the Battalion. Lieutenant Brooke Taylor was in his 28th year.

Lieut. A. N. MILNE—7 Aug., 1915.

Lieut. A. N. Milne joined the 6th Battalion as a Second Lieutenant on April 25th, 1915. He enlisted in the Battalion on mobilisation.

Lieut. E. W. PEARSON—7 Aug., 1915.

Lieut. W. E. REISS—8 Aug., 1915.

Lieut. W. E. Reiss was serving in the 6th Battalion before the war. He was promoted lieutenant on July 20th, 1912.

Lieut. E. F. THORBURN—4 June, 1915.

Lieut. Edward Francis Thorburn was the youngest and only surviving son of Lieut.-Colonel William Thorburn, M.D., F.R.C.S. Lieut. Thorburn was educated at Marlborough, and was a member of the Officers' Training Corps there. He obtained a commission in the second line of the 6th Manchesters, and went to Southport for training, where he specialised in signalling duties. Early this year he accompanied the drafts that were being sent out to Egypt. He was 21 years of age. He was promoted lieutenant on 31st October, 1914.

Lieut. E. T. YOUNG—4 June, 1915.

Lieutenant Edmund Turner Young was the eldest son of the late Colonel T. P. Young and Mrs. Young, of Stand Hall, Whitefield, Lancashire, and of Marple, Cheshire. Lieut. Young, who was 31 years of age, was promoted lieutenant on August 26th, 1914.

2nd Lieut. R. C. BROOKS—4 June, 1915.

Second-Lieutenant Rowland Causer Brooks was the second son of Mr. Buckley Brooks and Mrs. Brooks, of the Manor House, Hale Barns, Cheshire. He joined the 6th Battalion Manchesters after the Battalion had gone to Egypt. He did his training with the Second Reserve at Southport, and early this year went to join the Battalion at Khartoum. Second Lieutenant Brooks was interested in the management of Holts Derby Brewery, Manchester.

2nd Lieut. R. N. COMPTON-SMITH—29 May, 1915.

Second-Lieutenant R. N. Compton-Smith joined the 6th Battalion on September 5th, 1914.

2nd Lieut. A. J. J. DONALD—4 June, 1915.

Second Lieutenant Alan James Ingram Donald was the eldest son of Dr. and Mrs. Archibald Donald, of Manchester. He was 21 years of age. He received his education at Winchester, and proceeded to New College, Oxford, where he was a member of the Officers' Training Corps. Lieutenant Donald applied for a commission the day after the declaration of war, and went in September with his Battalion to Egypt.

2nd Lieut. R. KILLICK—19 May, 1915.

Second-Lieutenant R. Killick had served in the Indian Volunteers as a lieutenant when he was gazetted to the 6th Battalion on August 29th, 1914.

2nd Lieut. T. R. MILLS—4 June, 1915.

Second-Lieutenant T. R. Mills was the only son of Mr. and Mrs. T. H. Mills, of White Bank House, Brinnington, Stockport. Second-Lieutenant Mills was 28 years of age, and was educated at Harrow and Trinity College, Cambridge. He was gazetted to the Battalion on August 5th, 1914.

MISSING.

Lieut. S. McDougall, from 7 Aug., 1915.
2nd Lieut. J. Rainbow, from 7 Aug., 1915.

WOUNDED.

Major C. R. Pilkington—4 June, 1915.
Major C. S. Worthington—4 June, 1915.
Capt. O. St. L. Davies—27 May, 1915.
Capt. J. H. Helm—29 July, 1915.
Lieut. F. C. Aldous—19 May, 1915.
Lieut. T. Blatherwick—4 June, 1915.
Lieut. Carey (Attached).
Lieut. H. A. Hammick—14 June, 15.
Lieut. G. V. Kershaw—7 Aug., 1915.
Lieut. J. R. Lingard—21 Aug., 1915.
Lieut. J. A. Rule (Attached)—7 Aug., 1915.
2nd Lieut. W. Braithwaite.
2nd Lieut. W. H. Cadman—10 June, 1915.
2nd Lieut. S. Collier—24 May, 1915.
2nd Lieut. C. A. Hargreaves.
2nd Lieut. E. P. Hartshorn—16 Sept. 1915.
2nd Lieut. H. S. Hellawell—14 June, 1915.
2nd Lieut. H. C. L. Heywood—12 May, 1915.
2nd Lieut. W. N. Molesworth.

N.C.O.'S AND MEN OF THE 6TH (TERRITORIAL) BATTALION KILLED OR DIED OF WOUNDS RECEIVED IN ACTION.

Date List Published.	No.	Name
15 6 15.	1741	Pte. Huipar.
21 6 15.	1871	Cpl. C. W. Miller.
3 7 15.	1998	Pte. J. D. Denham (d.w.)
	976	L/Cpl. H. M. Plant (d.w.)
	2145	Pte.
	2253	Pte. J. H. Bebbington.
	1810	Pte. C. H. Cooper.
	2446	Pte. W. W. Daws.
	2389	Pte. D. G. Lancaster.
	2336	Pte. T. Penny.
5 7 15.	1525	Pte. A. F. Cummock (d.w.)
	1932	Pte. W. Wilkinson.
6 7 15.	1903	F. E. Allen.
	682	Cpl. H. P. Clinch.
	2378	Pte. H. Coope.
	1509	Pte. S. H. Cumpsty.
	2359	Pte. J. J. Dunkerley.
	1619	Pte. J. F. Elton.
	2247	Pte. S. H. Forbes.
	1374	Pte. A. H. Fry.
	1959	Pte. F. Graham.
	2434	Pte. G. Griffiths.
	1805	Pte. H. Griffiths.
	2219	Pte. F. Halliday.
	1688	Pte. A. Haughton.
	1618	Pte. H. Haynes.
	1676	Pte. W. Hays.
	2176	Pte. G. A. Holden.
	2166	Pte. Z. Holme.
	2410	Pte. W. T. Horrocks.
	1441	Pte. L. Huff.
	1838	L/Cpl. J. Jones.

Date List Published.	
	985 Pte. T. H. Hayward.
	1729 Pte. S. Kershaw.
	2164 Pte. N. V. Lloyd.
	2089 Pte. C. H. Neaves.
	1479 Cpl. C. A. G. Rutter.
	2366 Pte. E. C. H. Slater.
	2256 Pte. C. H. Taylor.
8 7 15.	1413 Pte. A. Hobday (d.w.)
	1678 Pte. E. A. Heap (d.w.)
	1971 Pte. C. S. Wardley (d.w.)
9 7 15.	2198 Pte. N. Bickerton (d.w.)
	1866 Pte. W. H. Booth (d.w.)
	2118 Pte. L. Evans (d.w.)
	1953 Pte. W. Evans (d.w.)
	2460 Pte. H. W. Higgins (d.w.)
	1818 Pte. G. A. Hill (d.w.)
9 7 15	2031 Pte. J. Hough (d.w.)
	2386 Pte. H. Kay (d.w.)
	1755 Pte. J. Kerwin (d.w.)
	1667 Pte. G. A. Roberts (d.w.)
17 7 15.	2370 Pte. E. Bateson.
	1309 Pte. W. Bleeckley.
	2083 L/Sergt. L. D. Boyd.
	1620 Pte. I. A. Brittain.
	1450 Pte. T. F. Chilton.
	1578 Pte. C. B. Clayton.
	1480 Pte. S. C. Clayton.
	92 Sergt. J. Clegg.
	1753 Pte. A. Cluff.
	2340 Pte. A. Collinge.
	2486 Pte. J .D. Cooney.
	2451 Pte. J. Dawson.
	2319 Pte. M. Duggin.
	57 C.-Q.M.-Sergt. J. W. Wilson.
	2243 Pte. E. Wood.
	1539 Cpl. S. Woodhead.
20 7 15.	1731 Pte. W. R. Barker (d.w.)
	261 Sergt. A. Fleming (d.w.)
	2309 Pte. H. A. Sames (d.w.)
24 7 15.	1184 L/Sergt. E. J. Cory.
	2087 Pte. C. A. Cross.
	2081 Pte. J. C. Foley.
	2142 L/Cpl. S. Heydon.
	1316 Cpl. H. Mould.
	218 Sergt. J. Orme.
	9448 Pte. J. Pollitt (d.w.)
	565 Pte. H. H. Taylor (d.w.)
	2174 Pte. J. Gilbert (d.w.)
6 8 15.	2286 Pte. A. C. Yates.
17 8 15.	1717 Sergt. C. J. Boyes Varley.

Date List Published.	
	1967 Pte. L. Lilley.
17 7 15.	1996 Pte. H. N. Laimbeer.
	1878 Pte. J. A. Lee.
	190 L/Cpl. W. Leigh.
	2277 Pte. T. F. Marsden.
	2312 Pte. C. L. Mellor.
	1654 Pte. W. Mercer.
	2097 Pte. F. T. Mills.
	421 Cpl. P. Newlove.
	2484 Pte. R. Nightingale.
	778 Sergt. E. Norton.
	1869 Pte. P. Parker.
	2161 Pte. H. Penn.
	840 L/Cpl. J. B. Pickup.
	1806 Pte. S. B. Pilling.
	2212 Pte. T. C Porter.
	2401 Pte. T. R. Rennick.
	2453 Sergt. G. A. Richards.
	1466 Pte. C. R. Rimes.
	1391 Pte. W. T. Robinson.
	758 L/Cpl. J. K. Senior.
	1818 Pte. J. F. Sickson.
	176 Sergt. E. Sorton.
	142 Pte. W. Taylforth.
	2162 Pte. T. H. Taylor.
	2175 Pte. R. Torkington.
	2306 Pte. N. S. F. Tozer.
	1670 Pte. S. Trueman.
	1709 Pte. C. Uttley.
	1901 Pte. A. J. Walters.
	1591 Pte. C. Walton.
17 7 15.	2062 Pte. E. Williams.
	1035 Pte. O. Wilson.
3 11 15.	1558 Pte. A. Burgess.
	2637 Pte. A. E. Heeley.
4 11 15.	1870 Pte. S. G. Stables (d.w.)
8 11 15.	2764 L/Cpl. S. C. Berry (d.)
	1857 Pte. H. Williams.
15 11 15.	1953 Pte. W. Evans (d.w.)
16 11 15.	1792 Pte. R. Gunn (d.)
23 11 15.	2399 Pte. H. Hornbrook.
	2059 Pte. J. Matthews.
8 12 15.	2350 Pte. R. Anderson (d.)
6 12 15.	3391 Pte. F. Nightingale.
8 12 15.	2286 Pte. W. Ashton.
	2221 Pte. C. Buckley.
	1613 Pte. F. Crewe.
	2210 Pte. E. M. Grimshaw.
	1911 Pte. W. Leighton.
11 12 15.	2241 Pte. T. Hockill (m.k.)

Date List Published.		
21. 8 15.	1977	Pte. E. O. Bleackley (d.w.)
	1876	Pte. N. D. Howarth.
	459	Pte. S. Nicholas.
	2303	Cpl. A. G. Richards.
	2060	Pte. R. H. Cooper.
	2098	Pte. H. C. Darlington.
	2804	Pte. R. Stear.
	2342	A. S. Anderson (d.)
	2471	P. Tabb (d.)
	2710	Pte. W. F. Hahn.
	2897	Pte. W. Taylor (d.)
18 9 15.	1638	Pte. T. P. Bromhead.
	2285	Pte. V. R. Clarke.
24 9 15.	1538	Pte. E. Partt.
	2095	Pte. T. Taylor.
2 10 15.	2509	Cpl. A. E. Wright.
5 10 15.	1915	Pte. F. N. Williams.
8 10 15.	2540	Pte. R. W. Turner.
11 10 15.	1176	Pte A. S. Ballingall (d.)
	1665	Pte. G. E. Broome.
	3090	Pte. L. P. Whitehead.
22 10 15.	2154	Pte. W. H. Bourne.
	2852	Pte. F. Dearden.
	2915	Pte. D. Ferguson.
26 8 15.	2033	Sgt. L. Bennett.
8 9 15.	1271	Cpl. C. W. Miller.
	1738	Pte. A. M. Doig (d.w.)
	2252	Pte. J. Kelsay (d.w.)
	2407	Pte. J. H. Tyldesley (d.w.)
9 9 15.	1927	Pte. C. H. Barlow.
	1742	Pte. J. Blacklock.
	252	Sgt. H. Cloy.
	2039	Pte. J. H. Cottrill.
	2762	Pte. W. Gonde.
	2801	Pte. F. Gralfsky.

Date List Published.		
16 12 15.	2358	Pte. F. H. Moss.
29 12 15.	2000	Pte. J. S. Horne.
"	2327	Pte. W. Reid.
5 1 16.	2363	Pte. O. Marsden.
15 1 16.	1491	Pte. P. K. Ballantyne (m.k.)
	1565	Pte. A. Finningley (m.k.)
	2458	Pte. E. E. Garrard (m.k.)
	2380	Pte. L. A. Johnson (m.k.)
	1147	L/Cpl. W. Roberts (m.k.)
	2685	Pte. S. Rogers (m.k.)
	1801	Cpl. A. H. Smith (m.k.)
	1929	Pte. G. Walton (m.k.)
18 1 16.	2471	Pte. P. Tabb.
29 1 16.	2397	Pte. R. Corbishley.
	1544	Pte. R. B. Hand.
31 1 16.	2369	Pte. H. G. Austin.
	2126	L/Cpl. W. L. Cundall.
	2287	Pte. A. Daber.
	2325	Pte. T. H. Garner.
	2109	Pte. F. Pollick.
	1897	Pte. W. M. Rankin.
	1949	Pte. W. E. Ward.
	1680	Pte. G. Whittaker.
	2463	Pte. C. P. Wild.
	2829	Pte. D. Gray
	2714	Pte. H. Heath.
	3018	Pte. F. Llewellyn.
	2797	Pte. H. V. Loughland.
	2270	Pte. H. G. Metcalfe.
	1169	Pte. F. Murphy.
	3296	Pte. R. Ollerenshaw.
	1704	Pte. P. E. Taylor.
	1643	L/Cpl. F. Thompson.
	1631	Pte. E. Tomlin.
	1473	Pte. H. A. Leach (d.w.)

7th (Territorial) Battalion

Originally the 33rd Battalion Lancashire Rifle Volunteers, altered later to the 16th Battalion, and became in 1881 the 4th Volunteer Battalion, Manchester Regiment. Present title since 1st April, 1908. The Headquarters are in Burlington Street, Manchester. The Battalion was embodied during the first few days of the War and sailed for Egypt on September 10th, 1914. It remained there until May 2nd, 1915, when the Battalion was moved to Galipoli, landing on the 7th.

The Battalion's first experience of the fire trenches was on May 11th, 1915, when it relieved the Wellington Battalion, New Zealand Brigade. It received its baptism of fire on the night of May 12th, 1915. For two hours the whole of the guns on both sides, and the guns of the British and French Fleets bombarded the opposing lines of trenches. During an interval in this bombardment, a party of 100 officers and men who had gone out with rations, machine-guns, and also with the object of digging a communication trench, was caught in the open and suffered badly from shell fire, both from our own "Unders" and the enemy's "Overs." Some of the party were fortunate enough to scramble back to the face of the cliff they had just ascended, and so get cover. The others, however, had to lie flat in the open for about an hour. It was here that the Battalion first had any of its members killed, three men being killed, nine wounded, and one officer and one N.C.O. missing. Fortunately, the officer turned up the following day. His companion, however, was never seen again.

The Battalion's first charge against the enemy was made on May 13th, 1915, by "B" Company, who went forward, and along with the 89th Punjabis, gained about 50 yards of ground. The Battalion was relieved after about a week in the first line trenches, by the Royal Fusiliers, and went into Reserve.

The Battalion was sent up to the trenches again on the 25th May, and on the evening of the 26th relieved the 5th Battalion Manchester Regiment. On the night of May 28th "B" and "D" Companies were ordered to go out 150 yards and dig a new trench, thus bringing our lines up to the Naval Division, which was on our right. "A" and "C" Companies were told off to dig the communicaton trenches between the new lines and the old. The digging in was completed despite a galling fire at close range, though the price paid in officers and men was necessarily heavy, the casualties includng Captain Rylands and 2nd-Lieutenant Brown killed. Lieutenant Whatley did great work during the first night's digging. The 5th Battalion Manchester Regiment took over the new line of trenches on May 31st.

The big attack on June 4th was participated in by the whole Battalion, "A" and "C" Companies being in the first line, and "B" and "D" Companies in the second line. They charged as far as the third Turkish trench, but had to retire to the second, as number three proved to be a "dummy trench," and it was in this retirement that the Battalion suffered so heavily. At the close of the day there were only five officers and about 250 N.C.O.'s and men left out of the whole Battalion. The killed included Major J. H. Staveacre, who was in command (Col. Gresham having been invalided), Lieutenants Freemantle, Thewlis, Dudley, and Ward. The command of the Battalion then devolved upon Captain and Adjutant P. H. Creagh. The remnant of the Battalion was relieved and sent to the Island of Imbros for a much-needed rest, their first in over a month's fighting, during which the casualties had reached no less a figure than 650.

Returning to Gallipoli after a week's rest, the Battalion took part in the big demonstration of August 6th and 7th. On the night of August 6th "B" and "D" Companies were ordered to reinforce some men of the Worcesters, who were believed to be holding part of a Turkish trench 300 yards to the left front. These Companies got to within 50 yards of this trench, but had to retire after losing about 60 men. The enemv opened a very rapid fire upon them, and their numbers did not admit of any further attempt being made.

On August 7th "B" and "C" Companies made an attack on the ground between the East and West Krithia Nullahs, but had to retire, this being an almost impossible place to attack from that point. They were caught by machine-gun fire in the bottle neck of the Nullah just before it branched out East and West.

Nothing of note happened after this date until the Battalion was suddenly called from the rest camp to relieve the 29th Division, who were being sent to Suvla Bay.

September 15th was an unlucky day for "C" Cmopany, who lost 32 men killed and one wounded in an enemy mine explosion. On December 4th, the Turks exploded another mine in almost the exact spot, and this time "B" Company lost one killed and four wounded.

On the evacuation of the Peninsula, the Battalion proceeded to Alexandria, and from thence to Cairo and Tel-el-Kebir.

The following are the present officers of the Battalion, with the dates of their appointments:—

Hon. Colonel—

WINGATE, Gen Sir F. R., G.C.B., G.C.V.O., K.C.M.G., D.S.O. 16 Dec. 14.

Lt.-Colonels—

(1)Gresham, H. E., T.D. 14 May 15.

(2)Pollitt, J. B., V.D. (Lt.-Col. & Hon. Col. ret. T.F.). *28 Sept. 14. 2 Jan. 2.

Majors—

(1)Hertz, G. B. 4 Jan. 11.

(1)Whishaw, E. R. *30 Sept. 14. (Maj. Army 1 Jan. 09).

Davies, H. G. (Q.). 1 Oct. 14.

Hawkins, H. (Hon. Lt.-Col. T.F.). *23 July 15. 20 Nov. 14.

Captains—

(1)Fawcus, A. E. F. (*Maj. 4 June 15). 1 Mar. 07. (1)Brown, J. N. 1 Mar. 07. bt. maj. 3 June 15. (1)Norbury, C. 14 June10. (1)Smedley, H. 5 Oct. 12. (1)Higham, C. E. 4 Dec. 13. (1)Nelson, D. *5 Aug. 14. 7 Jan. 11. (1)Ward Jones, A. T. 2 Sept. 14. Hardiker, J. O. (*Lt.-Col. 17 Aug. 15). *4 Sept. 14. Eaton, H. R. (H.) (Asst. Dist. Offr. S. Prov., Nigeria, 12 Jan. 14). 25 Sept. 14. (1)Williamson, C. H. 26 Sept. 14. (1)Norbury, B. 26 Sept. 14. Creagh, J. R. (*Maj. 4 July 15). *1 Oct. 14.

Lieutenants—

(1)Townson, E. (*Capt. 29 May 15). 22 June 13. (1)Tinker, A. H. (*Capt. 4 June 15). 4 Dec. 13. (1)Chadwick, G. (*Capt. 24 Aug. 15). 2 Sept. 14. (2)Irwin, W. L. *1 Oct. 14. Nasmith, G. W. (*Capt. 1 Dec. 14). *1 Oct., 14. Eaton, T. R. (*Capt. 1 Dec. 14). *31 Oct. 14. (3)Ingham, B. *31 Oct., 14. Nidd, H. H. *26 Nov. 4. Davies, H. B. F. (*Capt. 1 Dec. 14). *26 Nov .14.

2nd Lieutenants—

(1)Lockwood, G. S. (*Lt. 2 Sept. 14) H 18 June 13. (1)Hamilton, G. C. H. (*Lt. 2 Sept. 14). 30 Dec. 13. (1)Thorpe, J. H. (*Lt. 2 Sept. 14). 1 Jan. 14. Creery, W. F. (*Capt. 4 July 15). 9 May 14. (1)Ross-Bain, G. 4 Aug. 14. (1)Norbury, D. (*Lt. 4 June 15). 4 Aug. 14. (1)Hayes, F., late Capt. (*Capt. 29 May 15). 5 Aug. 14. (3)Heathcote-Hacker, V. St. C. (*Capt. 1 Dec. 14). 20 Aug. 14. (2)Nation, W. A. C. (*Capt. 1 Oct. 15). 2 Sept. 14. (2)Bentham, R. (*Lt. 1 Dec. 14). 2 Sept. 14. (1)Palmer, F. C. (*Lt. 4 June 15). 2 Sept. 14. (3)Grant, R. W. G. 2 Sept. 14. (2)Norris, G. W. 2 Sept. 14. (2)Rowbotham, J. E., Adjt. (*Maj. 1 Sept. 15). 14 Sept. 14. Whitley, N. H. (*Lt. 4 June 15). 17 Sept. 14. Tinto, W. A. (*Lt. 1 Dec. 4). 1 Oct. 14. (1)Collier, H. 1 Oct. 14. (2)Braithwaite, R. H. (*Capt. 1 Oct. 15). 22 Oct. 14. Hawkins, G. H. A. (*Lt. 1 Dec. 14). f.c. 26 Nov. 14. (1)Sivewright, W. J .(*Lt. 29 June 15). 26 Nov. 14. (2)Hurlbatt, E. S. (*Maj. 9 Nov. 15). 1 Dec. 14. (1)Marshall, J. (*Lt. 4 July 15). 24 Dec. 14. (1)Norbury, M. 24 Dec. 14. Bennett, N. B. (Brig. M.-G. Odr.) (*Capt. 1 Oct. 15) 24 Dec. 14. (2)Schofield, J. A. (*Capt. 1 Oct. 15). 9 Feb. 15. (3)Adamson, W. (*Capt. 1 May 15), Adjt. 1 Dec. 14. (1)Ward,

G. H. 22 Feb. 15. (1)BURN, F. G. (*Lt. 1 July 15). 9 Mar. 15. WILD, H. E. 11 Mar. 15. SUTHERLAND, J. W. 11 Mar. 15. GRANGER, T. E. 11 Mar. 15. GRANGER, H. M. 11 Mar. 15. SMITH, T. H. 11 Mar. 15. BATEMAN, M. 11 Mar. 15. MORTEN, J. C. 11 Mar. 15. (2)ALLAN, G. A. (*Capt. 1 Oct. 15. 21 Mar. 15. (2)BOLTON, R. L. (*Lt. 1 July 15). 21 Mar. 15. BRYAN, C. J. 27 Mar. 15. KAY, H. N. 27 Mar. 15. DOUGLAS, C. B. 27 Mar .15. (1)WOOD, C. S. 27 Mar. 15. HARRIS, L. G. 13 Apr. 15. BELL, R. 13 Apr. 15. BAKER, R. J. R. 13 Apr. 15. (2)POTT, F. M. 16 Apr. 15. (2)HEATHCOTE-HACKER, R. N. G. 20 Apr. 15. MCCROSSAN, C. G. 21 May 15. (2)BROWN, J. 29 May 15. (2)SCHOLFIELD, F. B. 3 June 15. HOBDEY, A. C. 4 July 15. (2)BISHOP, H. O. 4 July 14. (2)BRITTAIN, T. E. 20 Aug. 15. (2)WOODALL, C. H. 2 Aug. 15. (2)SMITHIES, A. 20 Aug. 15. (2)MORRIS, D. 20 Aug. 15. (2)BOON, A. 20 Aug. 15. WILSON, S. J. 30 Aug. 15. HOPWOOD, N. 8 Sept. 15. (2)EDGE, N. 10 Sept. 15. (2)HAMMOND, G. G. 10 Sept. 15. COOPER, C. M. 12 Sept. 15. BROMLEY, J. T. 12 Sept. 15. WOOD, T. W. 13 Sept. 15. MARSLAND, N. (*Lt. 17 Sept. 15). 17 Sept. 15. (2)ALDRED, A. G. 17 Spt. 15. BROADHURST, R. P. 24 Sept. 15. JESSOP G. 28 Sept. 15. 7 Apr. 15. PELL-ILDERTON, P. 30 Sept. 15. FRANKLIN, G. W. F. 2 Oct. 15. BARRATT, W. H. 2 Oct. 15. STIEBEL, J. S. 2 Oct. 15. TAYLOR, L. 7 Oct. 15. DUNCAN, J. 14 Oct. 15. GRESTY, W. 8 Nov. 15. ROBINSON, H. J. 8 Nov. 15. TANNER, H. P. 8 Nov. 15. MORRIS, E. T. 12 Nov. 15. VOLLMER, H. P. 20 Nov. 15. ROBINSON, P. 20 Nov. 15. LEAKE, E. G. 28 Nov. 15. HODGE, A. 7 Dec. 15. PHILLIPOWSKY, I. R. 7 Dec. 15. PRIESTLY, H. 7 Dec. 15. FORD, S. C. 7 Dec. 15. RUDD, P. 14 Dec. 15. ROBSON, J. W. 16 Dec. 15. JOYE, L. H. J. 19 Dec. 15. NORBURY, G. 2 Dec. 15. BARKER, A. T. 21 Dec. 15. HOLLAND, H. 21 Dec. 15. GROSART, W. D. 2 Dec. 15. TAAFE, C. R. O'R. 21 Dec. 15. BRETON, H. M. 21 Dec. 15. SMITH, J. W. 21 Dec. 15. WOOD, H. A. 21 Dec. 15. EARWAKER, R. N. D'O. 21 Dec. 15. LINGARD, W. 21 Dec. 15. STRATTON, R. D. 21 Dec. 15. LECOMBE, P. H. 25 Dec. 15. HAYES, J. M. 31 Dec. 15.

Adjutants—

(1)CREAGH, P. H., D.S.O., Capt. Leic. R. 12 June 11. (2)ROWBOTHAM, J. E., 2nd Lt. (*Maj.) 1 Dec. 14. (3)ADAMSON, W., 2nd Lt. (*Capt.) 1 May 15.

Quarter-Masters—

(1)SCOTT, J., hon. m. 10 Dec. 04. (2)DERBYSHIRE, J., hon. lt. 24 Oct. 14. (3)GITTINS, T., hon. lt. 11 June 15.

Medical Officers—

FARROW, Capt. J. F., R.A.M.C. (T.F.) (attd.) 6 Mar. 14. 6 Sept. 10. (2)CREAGH, Capt. P. N., R.A.M.C. (T.F.) (attd.). 15 Apr 15 15 Oct. 14.

* Denotes Temporary Rank.

OFFICERS OF THE 7TH (TERRITORIAL) BATTALION KILLED, DIED OF WOUNDS RECEIVED IN ACTION, OR DIED.

Major J. H. STAVEACRE—4 June, 1915.

Major J. H. Staveacre commenced his military career in the ranks of the 4th Volunteer Battalion Manchester Regiment. At the outbreak of the South African War he transferred to the Earl of Chester's Yeomanry, and served during the campaign as a sergeant. In May, 1905, he took a commission in his old regiment, the 4th Volunteer Battalion Manchester Regiment, which, on the formation of the Territorial Force, became the 7th Battalion Manchester Regiment. He was promoted captain in March, 1906, and major in August, 1912. Major Staveacre was in command of the 1/7th Battalion Manchester Regiment in Gallipoli when he met his death, and had the distinction of being mentioned in Sir Ian Hamilton's despatches. He was 43 years of age, and a partner in the firm of Leinster Bros. and Staveacre, London, Manchester, and Londonderry, shirt manufacturers.

Capt. T. W. SAVATARD—29 May, 1915.

Captain T. W. Savatard had been a member of the 7th Battalion Manchester Regiment since 1909, and was promoted captain in 1912. He was the son of the Rev. Louis Savatard, Vicar of Holy Trinity Church, Darwen, and was 37 years of age. Captain Savatard was an inspector at the head offices of the Manchester and County Bank.

Capt. R. V. RYLANDS—29 May, 1915.

Captain Rylands was the son of Mr. R. W. Rylands, of Manchester. He matriculated when 16, and entered the University to study law. Captain Rylands was a member of the firm of Boote, Edgar, Grace, and Rylands, solicitors, of Manchester. He was a lieutenant of the 7th Manchester Regiment (Territorials) when war broke out, and was promoted to a captaincy on September 27th, 1914, on proceeding to Egypt. He was 23 years of age.

Lieut. A. H. BACON—6 Aug., 1915.

Second-Lieutenant Alan Harvey Bacon was the second son of Capt. W. C. Bacon, of Withington. Lieutenant Bacon was educated at South Manchester School and Rossall, at which latter he was for four years a cadet in the School Corps. By profession he was an engineer. He was 27 years of age. He was promoted lieutenant on December 1st, 1914.

Lieut. G. W. FREEMANTLE—4 June, 1915.

Lieut. Freemantle received his commission as lieutenant

on June 22nd, 1913. He was employed at the Manchester Corporation Sewage Works at Davyhulme as chemical analyst. He received his education at Manchester University, and he joined the Officers' Training Corps there.

Lieut. H. D. THEWLIS—4 June, 1915.

Lieut. Harold D. Thewlis was the only son of Mr. J. H. Thewlis, of Victoria Park, Manchester. Lieutenant Thewlis, whose father was formerly Lord Mayor of the city, was 24 years of age. He was an old Manchester Grammar School boy, and he took the B.Sc. degree at the University of Manchester. He was at the Cheshire Agricultural College at Holmes Chapel when war broke out. He was a member of the O.T.C. at the University, and received a commission in the 7th Battalion Manchester Regiment (Territorial Force) in 1912. Lieut. Thewlis was promoted to lieutenant on September 2nd, 1914, when he accompanied the Battalion to Khartoum.

2nd Lieut. T. F. BROWN—29 May, 1915.

Second-Lieutenant T. F. Brown was gazetted 2nd September, 1914, and proceeded with the Battalion to the Sudan. He was 20 years of age, and an Irishman. Lieutenant Brown was killed during an advance made by the Battalion on 28th May, 1915.

2nd Lieut. L. DUDLEY—4 June, 1915.

Second-Lieutenant C. Leonard Dudley was educated at Uppingham, and on leaving school entered the office of the late Sir William Pollitt, then manager of the Great Central Railway. He resigned when war broke out in South Africa to join the 21st Company of the Cheshire Imperial Yeomanry, and saw service for 18 months against the Boers, receiving the South African medal with four clasps. Before the South African War, Second-Lieutenant Dudley had been a member of the old Mounted Infantry Company of the 4th Manchesters. After his return he went to British Columbia and was associated for four years with the Canadian Pacific Railway. Immediately on the outbreak of the present war he joined his old regiment, now the 7th Manchesters, went to Khartoum in September, and acted as Censor for a time at Halfa, until he was recalled to join his regiment for the Dardanelles.

2nd Lieut. H. M. GRANGER—29 May, 1915.

2nd-Lieut. H. M. Granger joined the 1/7th Battalion Manchester Regiment as a private just prior to the Battalion leaving for Egypt in September, 1914. He was given his commission in March, 1915, and died of wounds received in action on 29th May, 1915, in the Dardanelles. Lieutenant Granger was 20 years of age, and was educated at Denstone College, Staffs. He took a keen interest in sport, taking a prominent part in Rugby football, cricket, golf, and boxing. His brother, Second-Lieut. E. Granger, who also holds a commission in the 1/7th Battalion Manchester Regiment, is a prisoner of war in Constantinople.

2nd Lieut. F. LOMAS—4 June, 1915.

MISSING.

2nd Lieut. G. H. WARD, from 4 June, 1915.

Second-Lieut. G. H. Ward was gazetted to the 7th Battalion Manchester Regiment, on 22nd February, 1915, and joined the Battalion at Cairo in April, 1915, a few days before it sailed for the Dardanelles. He was missing after the big action of 4th June, 1915. Lieut. Ward had been for some years in the Educational Department of the Egyptian Government.

WOUNDED.

Capt. G. CHADWICK—4 June, 1915.
Capt. H. B. F. DAVIES—7 Aug., 1915.
Capt. C. E. HIGHAM—4 June, 1915.
Capt. D. NELSON—13 May, 1915.
Capt. H. SMEDLEY—29 May and 17 Sept., 1915.
Capt. A. H. TINKER—13 May, 1915.
Capt. C. H. WILLIAMSON—4 June, 1915.
Lieut. G. C. H. HAMILTON—4 June, 1915.
Lieut. G. S. LOCKWOOD—29 May, 1915.
Lieut. N. NORBURY—4 June, 1915.
Lieut. F. C. PALMER—4 June, 1915.
Lieut. W. J. SIVEWRIGHT—7 Aug., 1915.
Lieut. N. H. P. WHITLEY—4 June, 1915.
2nd Lieut. M. BATEMAN—4 June, 1915.
2nd Lieut. H. C. FRANKLIN.
2nd Lieut. F. HAYES—7 July, 1915.
2nd Lieut. J. C. MORTEN—4 June, 1915.
2nd Lieut. T. H. SMITH—4 June, 1915.
2nd Lieut. J. W. SUTHERLAND—4 June, 1915.

PRISONER OF WAR.

2nd Lieut. T. E. GRANGER (Wounded)—4 June, 1915.

N.C.O.'S AND MEN OF THE 7TH (TERRITORIAL) BATTALION KILLED OR DIED OF WOUNDS RECEIVED IN ACTION.

Date List Published.	
14 6 15.	1738 Pte. T. Barton (d.w.)
3 7 15.	1712 Pte. A. Burgess.
	1655 Pte. W. Hunt (d.w.)
	1179 Pte. H. Lowry (d.w.)
	429 Pte. W. A. Nuttall (d.w.)
	2347 Pte. R. R. Wolstencroft (d.w)
6 7 15.	2313 Pte. H. Jennings.
	2368 Pte. C. Super.
7 7 15.	2002 Pte. P. Millington (d.w.)
	1761 Pte. T. Henshall (d.w.)
	2269 Pte. J. Moran (d.w.)
	176 Cpl. P. Percival (d.w.)
	1937 Pte. P. Sowden (d.w.)
	20 Co.-Sgt.-Mjr. F. Hundy (d.w)
9 7 15.	1000 L/Cpl. E. Bromley.
	2011 Pte. W. Collins.
	2333 Pte. C. Davies.
	2164 Pte. T. Hobbs.
	1278 Pte. R. H. Passand.
	5454 Pte. A. R. Phillips.
	1671 Pte. W. Rawson.
	1675 Drm. R. S. Smith.
	1846 Pte. S. Taylor.
	714 L/Cpl. G. Winterbottom.
	1939 Pte. A. Wood.
9 7 15.	2266 Pte. C. Carpenter (d.w.)
	2381 Pte. J. Chantler (d.w.)
	1821 Pte. J. F. Parsonage (d.w.)
	1788 Pte. J. Ward (d.w.)
15 7 15.	2436 Pte. T. Byrne (d.w.)
17 7 15.	2121 Pte. J. Wrigley (d.w.)
19 7 15	2009 Pte. A. Bree.
	1617 Pte. G. S. Brooks.
	1301 Pte. J. E. Dodds.
	1144 L/Cpl. R. Dooler.
	2450 Pte. J. Harling.
	1259 Pte. P. Heath.
	1748 Pte. R. Lamb.
	1898 Pte. W. Lees.
	2374 Pte. H. B. Lowerson.
	2160 Pte. J. Lyons.
	1874 L/Cpl. A. Morris.
	2322 Pte. A. Wharmaugh.
	203 Pte. J. T. Jackson (d.w.)
20 7 15.	2433 Pte A. Milligan (d.w.)

Date List Published.	
5 7 15.	2178 Pte. A. Boaler (d.w.)
	2014 Pte. R. R. Heseltine (d.w.)
	1639 L/Cpl. A. McLesa (d.w.)
	1698 Pte. E. Morris (d.w.)
	2316 Pte. A. Powell (d.w.)
	1367 Pte. M. Walsh (d.w.)
	980 Pte. W. Bleasdale.
	164 C.-Sgt.-Mjr. S. R. Cookson.
	1212 Pte. J. Cox.
	2098 Pte. T. B. Dawson.
	2247 Pte. W. H. Dingle.
	2130 Pte. B. Fisher.
	2362 Pte. J. A. Graham.
	2397 Pte. H. Granger.
	1196 Pte. G. Hodgkins.
	1358 Pte. W. Horrax
	1935 Pte. F. Keeble.
	1674 Dr. H. Kelly.
	1331 L/Cpl. A. Kenyon.
	2408 Pte. J. Milligan.
	2455 Pte. S. Newbould.
	1485 Pte. A. Partington.
	1283 Pte. G. Robertson.
25 8 15.	1689 Pte W. H. Russell.
	2032 Pte. J. E. Shepherd.
	1657 Pte. W. H. Smith.
	1659 L/Cpl. W. H. Smith.
	2057 Pte. S. Walker.
	521 Sergt. H. Webster.
	1725 Pte. R. White.
	1311 L/Cpl. L. Wilson.
	2406 Pte. D. Winter.
	1924 Pte. S. Worrall.
9 15	3014 Pte. S. Barber.
	1402 L/Cpl. B. Cawley.
	3033 Cpl. R. Cunnington.
	1520 Cpl. W. Jepson.
	1807 Pte. H. Leaver.
	1361 Pte. E. McClure.
	2805 L/Cpl. F. H. Rideal.
27 9 15.	2215 Cpl. A. Banks (m.k.)
	896 Pte. G. Bowe (m.k.)
	1431 Pte. F. Cavanagh (m.k.)
	2262 Pte. H. Clare (m.k.)
	2192 Pte. A. W. Cowan (m.k.)

Date List Published.	
24 7 15.	2402 Pte. J. Brown (d.w.)
26 7 15.	1500 Pte. H. McHugh (d.w.)
6 8 15.	1438 Pte. W. F. Pease (d.w.)
17 8 15.	2375 Pte. E. Thomas (d.w.)
	2399 Pte. J. D. Green.
21 8 15.	1313 Pte. F. Penty.
	1397 Pte. C. Hawley.
24 8 15.	3090 Pte. H. Dale (d.w.)
	2586 Pte. H. H. Hammond (d.w.)
25 9 15.	473 Sergt. T. Arnold.
	2403 Pte. E. Balon.
	1347 L/Cpl. T. Barnett.
	1178 Pte. S. Hodson (m.k.)
	2351 Pte. F. Hunt (m.k.)
	1823 Pte. J. Jones (m.k.)
	2036 J. Kelly (m.k.)
	2361 Pte. J. H. Kershaw (m.k.)
	2282 Pte. F. Lomas (m.k.)
	1296 L/Sgt. R. Longshaw (m.k.)
	1647 L/Sgt. D. H. S. McKie (m.k.)
	1945 Pte. E. Maby (m.k.)
	2177 Sergt. G. Marvin (m.k.)
	1882 Pte. J. W. Morris (m.k.)
	1605 Pte. A. Page (m.k.)
	48 L/Cpl. W. Peacock (m.k.)
	2300 Pte. W. Pickles (m.k.)
	2044 L/Cpl W. R. Rawlinson (m.k)
	2355 Pte. F. Royle (m.k.)
	1956 Pte. C. Starkey (m.k.)
	1413 L/Cpl. J. Verity (m.k.)
	1893 Pte. J. Whalen (m.k.)
	1775 Pte. H. Whalley (m.k.)
	1573 Pte. A. Williams (m.k.)
	2458 Pte. M. V. Williams (m.k.)
	1561 Pte. T. Pannell.
	1699 Pte. H. J. Dunstall.
29 9 15.	1570 Pte. J. M. Leigh.
30 9 15.	2067 Pte. C. Ross.
5 10 15.	1165 Pte. E. Adderley (d.w.)
	490 Cpl. A. Anderson (d.w.)
	1740 Pte. W. A. Ayres (d.w.)
	1228 Cpl. J. Berry (d.)
	2438 Pte. A. Billington (d.w.)
	2143 Pte. G. C. Boucler (d.w.)
	2290 Pte. G. Brown (d.w.)
	1179 Pte. T. Burgess (d.w.)
	2255 Pte. C. C. Chadwick (d.w.)
	2125 Pte. C. E. Clarke (d.w.)
	2311 Pte. J. Cleino (d.w.)
	1662 Pte. R. C. Collins (d.w.)
	2315 Pte. J. Draper (d.w.)

Date List Published.	
	1931 Pte. T. A. Davies (m.k.)
	1772 Pte. H. Dillon (m.k.)
27 9 15.	2077 Pte. W. Leyland (m.k.)
	2432 Pte. H. Finch (m.k.)
	2217 Pte. J. Fisher (m.k.)
	2364 Pte. F. Fitchett (m.k.)
	1700 Pte. J. Fitzsimmons (m.k.)
	2302 Pte. F. Gamble (m.k.)
	2176 Pte. J. Gibbon (m.k.)
	2212 Pte. P. Goulden (m.k.)
	1352 Pte. F. Hallam (m.k.)
	2401 Pte. W. Henritt (m.k.)
	891 L/Cpl. F. Peers (d.w.)
	2119 L/Cpl. W. Pope (d.w.)
5 10 15.	2132 Pte. A. E. Raper (d.w.)
	1258 Pte. J. W. Phodes (d.w.)
	2003 Pte. J. Sanderson (d.w.)
	1384 Pte. B. Thornley (d.w.)
	1385 Pte. R. Walker (dw.)
	2270 Pte. S. Webb (d.w.)
21 10 15.	2296 Pte. J. T. Wild (d.w.)
1 11 15.	1277 Pte. W. Chadwick.
2 10 15.	1958 Pte. J. Bancroft.
3 10 15.	3231 Pte. L. Stoddard.
4 10 15.	295 Co.-Sgt.-Mjr. A. W. Leigh.
	1107 Pte. P. Dinsdale.
	3051 Pte. W. F. Oldfield.
8 11 15.	2515 Pte. C. V. Ashton (d.)
	3232 Pte. L. Bracegirdle (d.)
9 11 15.	1416 Pte. T. Lyons.
16 11 15.	1456 Pte. J. Gregory.
	1401 Pte. J. Reid.
23 11 15.	2243 Pte. J. P. Shipley.
26 11 15.	2274 Pte. G. Bowden (d.)
29 11 15.	2257 Pte. W. Brookes.
	2428 Pte. L. Oakes.
	1943 Pte. C. Vardin.
7 12 15.	1479 Pte. A. Connell (d.w.)
8 12 15.	1245 Pte. H. Morris (d.w.)
	1784 Pte R. Nickeas (d.)
3 12 15.	1943 Pte. C. W. Vardin.
7 12 15.	268 Pte. J Eardley.
10 12 15.	1799 Pte. H. Hilditch (d.)
11 12 15.	2758 Pte. W. Hall (d.)
18 12 15.	3080 Pte. T. Shaw.
27 12 15.	2956 L/Cpl. G. Salt (d.w.)
29 12 15.	1282 Pte. J. W. Mauley (k.)
	1941 Pte. W. Bour.
	3461 Pte. H. N. Harrison.
	2681 Pte. T. Pain.
	3018 L/Cpl. R. M. Smith.

Date List Published.	
	1921 Pte. G. Fawdry (d.w.)
	1926 Pte. A. Gillibrand (d.w.)
	1720 L/Cpl. H. Hargreaves (d.w.)
	2378 L/Cpl. E. Harrison (d.w.)
	1627 L/Cpl. W. Hinchcliffe (d.w.)
	238 Sergt. F. Holcroft (d.w.)
	2386 Pte. J. H. Holland (d.w.)
	750 Pte. H. Jones (d.w.)
	1663 Pte. W. Kellett (d.w.)
	1442 Pte. R. McWilliam (d.w.)
	1681 Pte. R. Merriman (d.w.)
26 8 15.	1856 Pte. S. Holmes.
	1841 Pte. G. Keegan.
	1040 Pte. T. Thompson.
	2226 L/Cpl. H. O. T. Wilde.
	1354 Pte. R. Williams.
	2045 Pte. F. Anderton.
	3035 Pte. H. Davies (d.w.)

Date List Published.	
	3091 Pte. G. Watkins.
3 1 16.	3242 Pte. G. T. Hill.
	3197 Pte. C. V. Renshaw.
5 1 16.	3669 Pte. S. Haufman.
	3642 Pte. A. H. Woodward.
	3662 Pte. R. Marshall (d.w.)
24 1 16.	1968 Pte. R. E. Bannon.
29 1 16.	1888 Pte. F. C. Barks.
28 1 16.	1566 Pte. W. Twiss (d.w.)
	1897 Pte. J. Counsell (m.k.)
3 9 15.	2424 Pte. G. Charlton (d.)
9 9 15.	1873 Pte. E. Bridge.
	2409 L/Cpl. H. S. McCarthney.
	1723 Pte. T. Lyth (d.w.)
10 9 15.	756 Pte. H. Butcher (d.w.)
	1858 Pte. G. Jacques (d.w.)
	2554 Sgt. H. Clare (d.)

8th (Ardwick Territorial) Battalion

Originally the 40th Battalion Lancashire Rifle Volunteers, altered later to the 20th Battalion, and became in 1881 the 5th (Ardwick) Volunteer Battalion, Manchester Regiment. Present title since 1st April, 1908. The Headquarters are in Ardwick, Manchester.

The Battalion was embodied during the first week of the War, and after waiting for some time in Manchester were moved to Littleborough. From here the Battalion was moved early in September, 1914, to Egypt, and there completed their training. On November 7th, 1914, the Battalion took part in the annexation of the Island of Cyprus. The Battalion embarked for Gallipoli on May 3rd, 1915, and arrived at Cape Helles three days later, where they were landed. Nothing of importance took place during May, though the Battalion had a fair number of casualties.

The attack on June 4th commenced at 12 o'clock noon. The advance was divided into two lines, the first moving off at 12 o'clock and the second at 12-15. The Battalion went forward with great gallantry, and it was during this first charge that so many officers and men were lost. The second line followed, and captured all before them. At 5-30 p.m. orders were given to retire on to the main Turkish trench. There was a great difficulty in getting the men back, as they were certain that if they were reinforced they could hold on to the advanced position. Major F. I. Bentley (now Lieut.-Colonel) who was in command of the Battalion (Lieut.-Col. Heys having taken over command of the Brigade) was able, about nine o'clock in the evening, to get the majority of the remaining men back to the main Turkish trench. The fighting continued until June 8th. Lt.-Col. Bentley, in describing the fighting of June 4th to 8th, says :—

> "On June 5th, none of the officers (22 in number) of "the 8th Manchesters who went into action were left, "with the exception of Capt. Barlow, who was with the "machine guns, and myself. The casualties, as far as "I can estimate, were nearly 500 killed and wounded. "I cannot adequately describe the devotion and "bravery of the men I had the honour to command. "Every man behaved nobly, and it is really difficult to "single any particular unit, which did better than "another. The medical arrangements, the com-"missariat, and the getting up of ammunition were "perfectly carried out."

About the middle of June the Battalion was taken off the Peninsula, and sent to Imbros Island for ten days' rest. During their stay at Imbross the Battalion, with the rest of the Battalions of the Manchester Brigade, were inspected by General Sir Ian Hamilton, who thanked them for the work they had done.

The Battalion took part in the action of August 7th to 11th, when the Southern force kept the Turkish troops occupied during the landing at Suvla Bay.

In August the Battalion, as part of the 42nd Division, relieved the 29th Division, and until the evacuation of Gallipoli they continued to hold the line originally won by the 29th Division. The Battalion returned to Egypt about January 7th, 1916.

The following are the present Officers, with the dates of their appointments :—

Hon. Colonel—

Barlow, J., M.V.O., V.D. (Hon. Maj. ret. Vols.) (Maj. T. F. Res.) (N.R.A. Sch. of Musk..) 3 Dec. 06. In Command.

Ross, E. H., Leic. R. 22 June, 15.

Lt.-Colonel—

(1)Bentley, F. T., T.D. 4 June 15.

Majors—

(2)Crosland, J. C. H. (*Lt.-Col. 28 Sept. 14). 7 Mar. 14. (1)Stephenson, H. M. 8 Aug. 14.

Captains—

(1)Mandley, H. C. F. 21 Apr. 10. (1)Bluhm, Q. M.. 27 Apr. 12. (1)Lings, H. C. I. of M. 7 Mar. 14. (3)Halstead, H. D. (*Maj. 2 1June 15). *5 Sept. 14.

Lieutenants—

(1)Moore, C. G.(*Capt. 30 May 15) 27 Apr. 12. (1)Robinson, F. (*Capt. 30 May 15). 20 Oct. 12. (1)Marsden, A. G. (*Capt. 5 June 15). 30 May 14. Higham, C. S. S. (*Capt. 14 Oct. 15). *14 Oct. 15.

2nd Lieutenants.

(1)Wallwork, E. (*Lt. 30 May 15). 28 Feb. 13. (1)Clear, A. (*Lt. 18 Nov. 14). 8 June 14. (1)Barlow, A. E. (*Capt. 5 June 15). 4 Aug. 14. Percival, R. L. 5 Aug. 14. (1)Horsfall, E. (*Capt. 15 Aug. 15). 6 Aug. 14. (1)Yeld, R. B. (*Lt. 4 June 15). 7 Aug. 14. (1)Railton, O. C. (*Lt. 5 June 15). 7 Aug. 14. (1)Morley, H. L. C. (*Lt. 4 June 15). 7 Aug. 14. (2)Howarth, F. A. (*Maj. 21 Apr. 15). 12 Aug. 14). (2)King, R. H. (*Lt. 21 Apr. 15). 14 Aug. 14. Agelasto, E. J. 15 Aug. 14. (1)Hepburn, H. W. (*Lt. 4 June 15). 15 Aug. 14. (1)Bluhm, C. (*Lt. 4 June 15). 18 Aug. 14. Ryley, D. A. G. B. (*Lt. 21 Apr. 15). 26 Aug. 14. (2)Cowan, P. C. (*Lt. 1 Aug. 15). 26 Aug. 14. (2)Coombee, H. B. (*Lt. 1 Aug. 15). 3 Sept. 14. (2)Beaumont, T. S. (*Maj 21 Apr. 15). 10 Oct. 14. Elton, H. G. (*Lt. 18 Nov. 14). 10 Oct. 14. (3)Whitworth, H. (*Lt. 18 Nov. 14). 10 Oct. 14. (2)Crews, A. J. (*Capt. 21 Apr. 15). 10 Oct. 14. Higham, C. (*Capt. 21 Apr. 15). 10 Oct. 14. (2)Williams, M. W. A. (*Capt. 21 Apr. 15). 10 Oct. 14. (2)Thody, C. J. (*Lt. 18 Nov. 14). 10 Oct. 14. (3)Hearne, J. E. (*Capt 18 Sept. 15). 10 Oct. 14. Yates, C. P. 10 Oct. 14. (2)File, R. M. (*Lt. 1 Aug. 15). 10 Oct. 14. Mackinson, J. R. (*Lt. 4 June 15) (Adjt. Comd. Depot). 10 Oct. 14. (2)McDougall, G. (*Lt. 21 Apr. 15). Adjt. 10 Oct. 14. (1)Forbes, A. (*Lt. 30 July 15). 10 Oct. 14. Norris, W. 4 Feb. 15. Rushton, A. 4 Feb. 15. (2)Greenwell, G. H. (*Lt. 1 Aug. 15). 4 Feb. 15. (2)Chadwick, F. N. 15 Feb. 15. Hall, B. C. 25 Feb. 15. Eller, C. R. 28 Feb. 15. (2)Bailey, K. V. 1 Mar. 15. Salomon, S. 6 Mar. 15. Kirby, R. V. D. 6 Mar. 15. Deakin, C. K. 25 Mar. 15. (3)Abbott, H. (*Lt. 28 Sept. 15). 12 Apr. 15. Smith, J. B. 16 Apr. 15. (3)Butterworth, H. (*Lt. 28 Sept. 15). 16 Apr. 15. Makinson, H. 16 Apr. 15. (3)Heath, L. M. (*Lt. 30 July 15). 16 Apr. 15. Leach, J. 16 Apr. 15. (2)Haslam, H. 18 Apr. 15. (3)Peach, L. Du G. 19 Apr. 15. (1)Murdoch, F. J. T. 24 Apr. 15. Greenhalgh, H. J. 27 Apr. 15. Teare, H. J. 27 June 15. (3)Whitley, L. G. M. 29 June 15. (3)Orford, H. S. 29 June 15. (3)Balmforth, A. (*Lt. 21 Sept. 15), Adjt. 1 July 15. (3)Symonds, F. H. 1 July 15. (3)Horner, C. C

4 July 15. (3)WOODS, J. R. (*Lt. 22 Sept .15). 4 July 15. MARSHALL, W. D. (*Lt. 30 July 15). 4 July 15. (3)MICHAELIS, E. 6 July 15. (3)GIBBONS, W. 8 July 15. (3)WILLETT, E. (*Lt. 22 Sept. 15). 10 July 15. (2)BARDSLEY, R. C. 21 July 15. (3)HALL, R. A. 9 Aug. 15. (2)REES, F. B. 12 Aug. 15. (3)LOCAN, W. A. (*Lt. 14 Oct. 15). 17 Aug. 15. (3)HOPKINS, O. W. 5 Sept. 15. (2)EVANS, J. G. 7 Sept. 15. (3)BRITTOROUS, F. 20 Sept. 15. (3)FARMER, G. G. 20 Sept. 15. (3)HASLEHAM, G. H. 20 Sept. 15. (3)JACKSON, J. A. 20 Sept. 15. (3)BOWKER, J. S. 26 Sept. 15. (3)ROTHWELL, J. 29 Sept. 15. (3)MICHAELIS, A. V. 2 Oct. 15. FRANKENBERG, S. S. 8 Oct. 15. (3)DARWIN, J. H. B. 11 Oct. 15. (2)HASLAM, C. 12 Oct. 15. (3)FOSTER, F. 13 Oct. 15. MACDONAL, A. L. 20 Nov. 15. CHAPLIN, S. S. 20 Nov. 15. ASHE, E. N. 27 Nov. 15. COLLINS, S. T. 2 Dec. 15. HALLETT, L. 2 Dec. 15. THOROGOOD, E. L. 2 Dec. 15. BRUCE, J. P. 2 Dec. MAWDSLEY, F. A. 2 Dec. 15. METCALFE, H. R. 2 Dec. 15. WIGHTMAN, A. B. 6 Dec. 15. COLLIER, F. 6 Dec. 15. LORENZEN, C. C. 6 Dec. 15. HOAL, E. G. 6 Dec. 15. HOLDAWAY, N. A. 6 Dec. 15. PORTER, R. P. 6 Dec. 15. NEWTON, C. R. 6 Dec. 15. MAYER, J. S. 6 Dec. 15. THORP, S. 6 Dec. 15. COLLIS, E. W. 7 Dec. 15. BRIGGS, E. H. 11 Dec. 15. EVANS, G. H. 16 Dec. 15. REEVE, G. N. B. 16 Dec. 15. HOBROUGH, F. R. 16 Dec. 15. COPE, G. Q. 16 Dec. 15. PETERS, W. H. 17 Dec. 15. WALKER, H. E. 19 Dec. 15. MORAN, J. 19 Dec. 15. ROBINSON, C. F. 19 Dec. 15. EVERETT, H. 23 Dec. 15. PETRIE, W. H. 23 Dec. 15. CARBERRY, A. A. 23 Dec. 15. SENIOR, H. G. 23 Dec. 15. ROYLE, G. A. 23 Dec. 15. LOVE, J B. 30 Dec .15. FRANKLIN, P. G. 30 Dec. 15. LOCAN, L. T. 31 Dec. 15.

Inst. of Musk.—
(1)LINGS, H. C., Capt. 20 Jan. 15.

Adjutants—
(1)COLLINS, C. H. G., Capt. D. of Corn. L.I. 1 Sept. 12. (2)McDOUGALL, G., lt. 21 Apr. 15. (3)BALMFORTH, A., 2nd Lt. (*Lt.) 21 Sept. 15.

Quarter-Masters—
(1)STEWART, W H., hon. lt. 1 May 13. (2)MARTIN, J. S., hon. lt. 10 Oct. 14. (3)TARPEY, W., hon. lt. 4 July 15.

Medical Officers—
(2)WILSON, Capt. G. R., M.B., R.A.M.C. (T.F.) (attd.) 19 Oct. 15. (2)CASE, Capt. H. W., M.B., R.A.M.C. (T.F.) (attd.) 10 June 15. 10 Dec. 14.

(Attached)—
(1)MURPHY, P., 2nd lt. (*Capt.) Manch. R. 18 Aug. 15.

* Denotes Temporary Rank.

OFFICERS OF THE 8TH (TERRITORIAL) BATTALION KILLED, DIED OF WOUNDS RECEIVED IN ACTION, OR DIED.

Lieut.-Col. GEORGE W. HEYS,—4th June, 1915.

Lieut.-Col. George W. Heys joined the 8th Battalion Manchester Regiment in August, 1890, and in 1914 he was gazetted command of the Battalion, succeeding Col. W. E. Lloyd. During the South African War he was selected to command the active service company of Volunteers raised from the 5th (Ardwick) and the 10th (Oldham) Battalions of the Manchester Regiment. On mobilisation on August 4th, 1914, Col. Heys received orders for his Battalion to proceed to Egypt, and he was in command of the troops at the time of the annexation of the Island of Cyprus. On January 20th, 1915, he returned to Egypt, where he resumed command of the whole of the Battalion. On May 1st the Battalion left Cairo and proceeded to Gallipoli, where on June 4th, owing to wounds and subsequent death of Brigadier-General Noel Lee, he was placed in command of the Brigade. It was whilst inspecting a main Turkish trench which had just been captured in the afternoon of this day that Col. Heys was killed. He was 48 years of age. Col. Heys was an hon. captain in the Army 20th November, 1902, and was promoted Lieut-Colonel on 7th March, 1911.

Captain DUDLEY H. STANDRING—28th May, 1915.

Captain Dudley H. Standring died from wounds sustained on May 28th, 1915. He was educated at Conway and spent some time in Canada. He was a director of Messrs. John Standring & Co., Ltd., smallware manufacturers, of Livesey Street Mills, Manchester. He was second in command of "B" Company, and was on several occasions mentioned in despatches. He was in charge of "D" Company at the time of his death. Capt. Standring was promoted captain 5th February, 1913.

Capt. E. G. W. OLDFIELD—5th June, 1915.

Capt. E. G. W. Oldfield was the only son of the late Rev. Edmund Oldfield, Rector of St. Elizabeth's, Reddish. He was 33 years of age. He obtained his captaincy on 8th June, 1906. He rendered service in the South African War as a trooper in the Imperial Yeomanry. It was upon his return to this country that he was given a commission in the Ardwick Battalion. For five years the Company which he commanded—"F" Company—was awarded the Cup for general efficiency. He was a prominent member of the Fine Cotton Spinners and Doublers' Association, and was a conspicuous worker on behalf of the Church Lads' Brigade.

Capt. HERBERT JOHN ROSE—4th June, 1915.

Captain Herbert John Rose was one of the most popular officers in the 8th Battalion Manchester Regiment. In his younger days he took a great interest in the work of the Church Lads' Brigade, and was a prominent Church worker. Before he was given a commission in the 8th Battalion Manchester Regiment he was for some years Colour-Sergeant in "F" Company of the old 2nd Volunteer Battalion Manchester Regiment (now the 6th Battalion Manchester Regiment). He was killed whilst charging a Turkish position. Capt. Rose was promoted captain on 8th June, 1906.

Capt. ARCHIBALD JAMES HEPBURN—29th May, 1915.

Capt. Archibald James Hepburn was the only son of Mr. and Mrs. W. A. Hepburn, late of Crumpsall, and now of Lytham. He was 33 years of age, and was a well-known member of the Manchester Amateur Dramatic Society. He was educated at Sedburgh. For some years he was the manager of the Square Bleaching Works, Ramsbottom. He joined the Territorial Force in 1910, and was promoted Captain on February 5th, 1913. He was killed by a sniper.

Lieut. W. J. DE VERE SCOTT—29th May, 1915.

Lieut. W. J. De Vere Scott, who joined the Battalion in Egypt, was killed during a sand-bag advance which the Battalion made over a distance of two hunderd yards. He was a Lecturer on History at the University, Cairo. Lieut. Scott joined the 8th Battalion on 22nd February, 1915.

Lieut. S. HEYWOOD—4th June, 1915.

Lieut. S. Heywood was a son of Mr. Fred Heywood, of Crumpsall, and was educated at Uppingham. He was one of the most popular officers in the Battalion. He was killed whilst leading his men in the charge on June 4th. A well-known golf player, he assisted North Manchester, and in 1914 was awarded the Houldsworth Cup. He was 25 years of age. Lieut. Heywood was promoted lieutenant on 6th December, 1909.

Lieut. S. HALL—4th June, 1915.

Lieut. S. Hall joined the Ardwick Battalion two years ago. He was the son of a well-known builder and contractor. Before taking up his residence at Blackpool he resided at Withington, near Manchester. He was 30 years of age, and was a prominent figure in Manchester and Blackpool golfing circles. Lieut. Hall was promoted Lieutenant on 3rd May, 1913.

Lieut. J .W. WOMERSLEY—4th June, 1914.

Lieut. John William Womersley was the eldest son of

Mr. Frederick Womersley. He was 31 years of age. Educated at Mill Hill School, he was a partner in the firm of Messrs. Womersley and Tweedale, Chartered Accountants, of Manchester. He had been connected with the 8th Battalion Manchester Regiment for several years, and filled the position as signalling officer, being promoted lieutenant on 25th May, 1914.

Lieut. R. MARSDEN—4th June, 1915.

Lieut. Reginald Marsden was in the service of the Lancashire & Yorkshire Railway Company at Trafford Park and the Ship Canal Depots. He was a son of the late Mr. G. W. Marsden, of Wakefield. He was 23 years of age, and was an all-round sportsman. He married in Cyprus the daughter of the late Archdeacon Spencer. Lieut. Marsden was the scout officer of the Battalion, and was promoted lieutenant on 30th May, 1914. For some years he was a member of the Manchester Y.M.C.A. Rugby and Cricket Clubs.

Lieut. W. H. INGRAM—4th June, 1915.

Lieut. W. H. Ingram was the eldest son of the late Mr. William Henry Ingram, of Cross Street, Manchester. He was educated at Clifton College, and in Sussex. In his younger days he was in the employ of the Fine Cotton Spinners' Association, and was for some time engaged at their mills at Lille. He was a director of the firm of Messrs. Crosses and Winkworth, of Bolton. He rejoined the 8th Battalion Manchester Regiment as a lieutenant at the outbreak of war after a short retirement. He was 31 years of age. Lieut. Ingram was promoted lieutenant on 26th Aug., 1914.

2nd Lieut. P. C. JOHNSON—16th May 1915.

Second-Lieutenant Percy Clarkson Johnson was previously an officer in the old 5th (Ardwick) V.B. Manchester Regiment, and served in the South African War in the old 6th Battalion Manchester Regiment, and was an honorary captain in the Army by reason of that service. He was on a visit to England when war broke out—he resided in Rhodesia—and applied for a commission in the 8th Manchesters. He was in charge of a Maxim gun, and was the first officer of the 8th Battalion to be killed in Gallipoli. Lieut. Johnson was gazetted on 7th August, 1914.

2nd Lieut. E. W. WESTBROOK—8th November, 1915.

Second-Lieutenant E. W. Westbrook, who was 22 years of age, resided at Silver Hill, Hyde. He was a member of a well-known legal family, his father, the late Mr. G. J. Westbrook, having a very considerable practice, being for many years Clerk to the County Justices at Hyde and Dukinfield. His two eldest brothers maintain a partnership in the legal profession at Hyde and Stalybridge.

2nd Lieut. F. HELM—4th June, 1915.

Second-Lieutenant F .Helm, who was 34 years of age, was a son of Mr .and Mrs. John Helm, of Lindfield, Wilmslow, and was in the service of the Calico Printers' Association. He was well-known in amateur theatricals. At the outbreak of war .he enlisted in the Earl of Chester's Yeomanry, and was given a commission in the 8th Manchesters on 15th August, 1914. He was a most popular officer.

2nd Lieut. A. BOWEN—7th August, 1915.

Lieutenant A. Bowen accompanied a draft abroad in July, 1915, and was second-in-command of "A" Company. He was killed in the operations on the 7th August, 1915. Lieut. A. Bowen was gazetted on 18th August, 1914.

2nd Lieut. W. NORRIS—7th August, 1915.

Second-Lieutenant Norris, who was killed in the operations of August 7th, joined the Battalion abroad in July, 1915. He was second-in-command of "B" Company.

MISSING.

Lieut. A. BOWEN, from 7 Aug., 1915.
2nd Lieut. W. NORRIS, from 7 Aug., 1915.

WOUNDED.

Major H .M. STEHENSON—27 May, 1915.
Capt. Q. M. BLUHM—7 June, 1915.
Capt. COLLINS—19 May, 1915.
Capt. H. C. F. MANDSLEY—19 May, 1915.
Capt. H. C. LINGS—7 June, 1915.
Capt. C. G. MOORE—19 May, 1915.
2nd Lieut. C. BLUHM—7 June, 1915.
2nd Lieut. E. HORSFALL—1 June, 1915.
2nd Lieut. J. R. MAKINSON—30 May, 1915.
2nd Lieut. H. L. C. MORLEY—1 June, 1915.
2nd Lieut. F. J. T. MURDOCK—7 June, 1915.
2nd Lieut. O. C. RAILTON—7 June, 1915.
2nd Lieut. M .S. TAYLOR—12 June, 1915.
2nd Lieut E. WALLWORK—7 June, 1915.
2nd Lieut. C. P. YATES—7 Dec., 1915.
Hon. Lieut. and Qr.-Mr. W. H. STEWART—14 July, 1915.

N.C.O.'S AND MEN OF THE 8TH (TERRITORIAL) BATTALION KILLED OR DIED OF WOUNDS RECEIVED IN ACTION.

Date List Published.	No.	Name
3 7 15.	2432	Pte. H. Burrows.
	357	Cpl. A. Day
	1595	Pte. W. Harrop.
	1614	Pte. T. O'Neill.
	1996	Pte. P. W. E. Slattery.
	2127	Pte. E. Wheeler.
	555	L/Cpl. A. Morton (d.w.)
	1082	Pte. W. Overend (d.w.)
	2375	Pte. P. Rowson (d.w.)
	2237	Pte.Pte. W. Towler (d.w.)
	979	Pte. J. E. Welfare (d.w.)
5 7 15.	1890	Pte. J. E. Flynn (d.w.)
	2332	Pte. T. E. Pidley (d.w.)
	1853	Pte. W. Harris (d.w.)
	1239	Sergt. J. Hall (d.w.)
	1918	Pte. T. Leigh (d.w.)
	1770	Pte. J. Lomax (d.w.)
	2076	Pte. W. Powell (d.w.)
	2235	Pte. C. Stott (d.w.)
6 7 15.	1809	Pte. T. Bridgwood.
	1371	Pte. T. Bryen.
	1678	Pte. J. Comerford.
	1756	Pte. C. H. Corleth.
	506	L/Sergt. J. R. Higgins.
	2283	Pte. F. Kight.
	1674	Pte. P. Langley.
	1758	Pte. W. Croon.
	1927	Pte. J. Stobe.
7 7 15.	2446	Pte. J. Farrell (d.w.)
	2486	Pte. J. Halme (d.w.)
7 7 15.	625	Sergt. A. Hand (d.w.)
	2392	Pte. C. E. Robinson (d.w.)
	2454	Pte. S. B. Thomas (d.w.)
6 7 15.	1559	Pte. J. W. Allen.
	1810	Pte. J. H. Ashby.
	1545	Pte. J. Bates.
	1860	L/Cpl. P. A. M. Bruneth.
	1692	Pte. P. Blakey.
	1694	Pte. J. Bray.
	2517	Pte. B. Brown.
	1488	L/Cpl. W. Bryan.
	609	Sergt. A. Cadmore.
	2197	Pte. F. Charlton
	2419	Dr. J. Clarkson.
	1688	Dr. J. W. Cleminson.
	2411	Pte. J. Corcoran.
	1546	Pte. J. Craven.
	1696	Pte. E. Eardley.
	1874	Pte. C. Foster.
	1212	Pte. H. Fullen.
	2447	Pte. D. Garcham.
	2205	Pte. W. Goodman.
	2425	Pte. F. Gregson.
	2457	Pte. J. Gubshon.
	2526	Pte. S. Harrison.
	2058	Pte. A. Hudson.
	2481	Pte. R. Johnson.
	1427	Pte. W. E. Kerridge.
	3170	Sergt. E. Kershaw.
9 7 15.	1485	Pte. W. Kilroy.
	263	Sergt. R. F. Leake.
	1911	Pte. J. Limb.
	2277	Pte. J. McPhee.
	1891	Pte. H. A. Morris.
	2544	Pte. H. J. Mottram.
	126	Pte. A. Newton.
	2443	Pte. J. Pass.
	1922	Pte. J. Fane.
	2275	Pte. E. Pennington.
	2414	Pte. W. R. Reid.
	2032	Pte. J Robinson.
	1556	Pte. T. Shaw.
	2201	Pte. T. Stanway.
	1435	L/Cpl. H. Steeles.
	2458	Pte. R. A. Tate.
	1098	Pte. J Thatcher.
	2055	Pte. A. Tudsbury.
	1778	Pte. P. H. Tyrrell.
	344	L/Cpl. T. Wade.
	2030	Pte. H. P. Warner.
	1863	Dr. A. Winstanley.
	1955	Pte. J. Wood
	1734	Pte. P. Worthington.
12 7 15.	1974	Pte. J. W. Crearorex.
15 7 15.	2437	Pte. T. Shepley (d.w.)
	2218	Pte. J. T. Berry (d.w.)
17 7 15.	1962	Pte. T. W. Sutcliffe (d.w.)
20 7 15.	2161	Pte. C. Beamish (d.w.)
22 7 15.	1983	Pte. J. Taberner.
26 7 15.	2469	Pte. T. Cannon.
	2452	Pte. W. Connor.
	2352	Pte. A. Cook.
	1877	Pte. J. Matthews.
6 8 15.	2229	Pte. W. Almond.
	2119	Pte. H. Barker.
	837	Sergt. F. A. Boden.

Date List Published.	No.	Name
	1110	Pte. L. Edwards.
	585	Pte. W. Davies.
	2357	Pte. A. Downs.
	1795	Pte. A. Fairclough.
	2082	Pte. H. Featherstone.
	1875	Pte. J. E. Flattery.
	1978	Pte. H. Ford.
	1914	Pte. N. Gill.
	2249	Pte. J. Gooch.
	1591	Pte. T. Griffiths.
	2438	Pte. J. Heathcote.
	1636	Pte. R. Hurst.
	1885	Pte. F. Jones.
	1728	Pte. P. McDermott.
	2536	Pte. J. Mann.
	1741	Pte. D. Noble.
	1748	Pte. P. O'Connor.
	2226	Pte. A. E. Price.
	2516	Pte. R. W. Procter.
	1587	L/Cpl. T. Scott.
	1583	Pte. E. Smith.
	1808	Pte. H. Staley.
	2553	Pte. J. Stone.
	1921	Pte. A. H. Tingle.
	1544	Pte. A. Upton.
	2509	Pte. W. Wescombe.
	2224	Pte. R. Williams.
6 8 15.	2347	Pte. C. Wilson.
	2532	Pte. R. Wood.
	50	Sergt. C. Whittaker (d.)
	2541	Pte. T. H. Bardsley.
	1786	Cpl. C. Harling (d.w.)
17 8 15.	2396	Pte. J. Gannon.
	1085	Pte. E. Goacher.
21 8 15.	1936	Pte. H. Breakey.
	2191	Pte. G. Finn.
	1403	Pte. J. H. Rimmer.
24 8 15.	1426	Pte. R. Marsden.
	1609	Pte. C. Patteh.
25 8 15.	2522	Pte E. Illidge.
7 9 15.	2396	Sergt. J. Stone
	3289	Pte. J. Bottomley.
	2303	Pte. J. R. Entwistle.
	2579	Pte. W. Foran.
	306	Co.-Q.M.-Sergt. E. Garside.
26 8 15.	1389	Sgt. F. Jackson (d.w.)
	1783	Pte. E. S. Jones (d.w.)
31 8 15.	367	Co.-Q.M.-Sgt. W. H. Hordsworth.
1 9 15.	2403	Pte. T. Hevison (d.)
2 9 15.	1657	Pte. J. H. Hartley (d.w.)
9 9 15.	7	Cpl. C. Carruthers (d.w.)

Date List Published.	No.	Name
	2378	Pte. W. Burton.
	3420	Pte. W. Johnson.
	199	Co.-Sergt.-Mjr. A. Kelly.
	1517	Pte. J. Lynde.
	2500	Pte. W. C. Nelson.
	2339	Pte. J. Osborne.
	2933	L/Cpl. H. Owen.
	1277	Cpl. H. Ramsden.
	1392	Sergt. R. Spense.
	3188	Pte. C. S. Stening.
	2747	Pte. J. Waugh.
	1441	Pte. J. Worrall.
27 9 15.	2259	L/Cpl. A. Creight.
	2010	Pte. A. Goodfellow.
	1364	L/Cpl. A. Horden.
	2524	Pte. P. K. E. Cartney.
29 9 15.	2676	Pte. C. Kemp
30 9 15.	1434	Pte. F. Thurston.
6 10 15.	1780	Pte. A. Bayliss
	2509	Pte. F. W. Forrester.
	1243	Pte. S. Hamleth.
13 10 15.	3118	Pte. C. F. Reilly.
14 10 15.	2591	L/Cpl A. Ross.
20 10 15.	3051	Pte. J. T. Tew.
21 10 15.	3146	Pte. W. Hindle.
27 10 15.	2069	Pte. L. H. Jones (d.)
1 11 15.	2122	Pte. W. Thompson (d.)
2 11 15.	2933	Pte H. Whitehead.
9 11 15.	2440	Pte. J. Moran.
3 12 15.	1953	Pte. J. Brown (d.w.)
7 12 15.	6	Co.-Q.M.-Sgt. Kealing (d.
8 12 15.	3670	Pte. T. Beddows.
18 12 15.	2808	Pte. C. Harry (d.)
29 12 15.	63	Co.-Sgt.-Mjr. Saton (d.) (P. of W.)
5 1 16.	2199	Pte. S. Bowes.
	2772	Pte. H. Hitchen
	1932	Pte. P. O'Brien.
	2967	Pte. H. K. German.
7 1 16.	2846	Sergt. J. Mitchell.
24 1 16.	1704	Pte. A. Lees.
7 1 16.	2834	Pte. T. Tollitt (d.)
28 1 16.	3369	Pte. J. J. Bedford (d.)
	2932	Pte. S. Roberts (d.)
14 1 16.	2070	Pte. J. W. Terry (d.)
	1765	Pte. H. Couzens (d.w.)
	2331	Pte. A. Davies (d.w.)
	291	Sgt. J. W. Sutton (d.w.)
10 9 15.	1814	Pte. R. Benson (d.w.)
	3187	Pte. T. F. Smethurst (d.
	1615	L/Cpl. W. Walley.

9th (Territorial) Battalion

Originally the 6th Battalion Lancashire Rifle Volunteers, altered later to the 7th Battalion, and became in 1880 the 3rd Volunteer Battalion, Manchester Regiment. Present title since 1st April, 1908. The Headquarters are at Ashton-under-Lyne, where the Battalion was embodied early in August, 1914. After remaining some days at their homes, the men were moved to Littleborough, where the East Lancashire Territorial Division was being gathered together. The Battalion left England early in September for Egypt, where it remained for the winter. On May 5th, 1915, the Battalion sailed from Port Said for Gallipoli, and was landed at Seddul Bahr four days later. The Battalion came under fire the next day, but did not occupy first line trenches for some days. During the last week of May it was attached to the 29th Division.

In the action of June 4th to 8th the Battalion held a third line trench in support of the Manchester Brigade. This was an exceedingly important position, and had to be held at any cost.

While the landing at Suvla Bay was being carried out, the Battalion was one of those occupying that position of the Southern line called the Vineyard. With the object of drawing the enemy away from Suvla Bay a number of fierce attacks were made by the Allies, and it was here that Lieut. W. T. Forshaw gained the V.C.

The following is the official notification issued by the War Office of the King conferring the V.C. upon Lieut. Forshaw :—

Lieutenant William Thomas Forshaw, 1/9th Battalion, the Manchester Regiment (Territorial Force).

For most conspicuous bravery and determination in the Gallipoli Peninsula from 7th to 9th August, 1915.

When holding the north-west corner of the "Vineyard" he was attacked and heavily bombed by Turks, who advanced time after time by three trenches which converged at this point; but he held his own, not only directing his men and encouraging them by exposing himself with the utmost disregard to danger, but personally throwing bombs continuously for 41 hours.

When his detachment was relieved after 24 hours he volunteered to continue the direction of operations.

Three times during the night of 8th-9th August he was again heavily attacked, and once the Turks got over the barricade, but after shooting three with his revolver he led his men forward, and captured it.

When he rejoined his Battalion he was choked and sickened by bomb fumes, badly bruised by a fragment of shrapnel, and could hardly lift his arm from continuous bomb throwing.

It was due to his personal example, magnificent courage, and endurance that this very important corner was held.

The Battalion left Gallipoli during the general evacuation, and is now back in Egypt.

The following are the present Officers of the Battalion, with the dates of their appointments :—

Hon. Colonel—

Wainwright, C. R., T.D. (Lt.-Col. ret. T.F.) 1 Apr. 14.

Lt.-Colonel—

(3)Wade, D. H. 17 July 13.

Majors—

(3)Garside, E. 20 Apr. 12.
Nowell, R. R. (*Lt.-Col. 9 July 15) 4 Nov. 14.
(2)Heywood, C. C. (*.Lt.-Col. 28 May 15). 21 Nov. 14.
Howe, E. H. (Hon. Maj. ret. Vols.) *23 July 15. 18 Mar. 15

Captains—

Lees, *R.*, I of M. 26 Oct. 06. (1)Howorth, T. E. (*Maj. 9 Feb. 15). 20 May 09. (1)Platt, T. A. 20 Apr. 12. (1)Woodhouse, F. 17 July 13. (3)Okell, G. H. 18 Oct. 13. (1)Kershaw, F. W. 4 Nov. 14. (2)Scott, E. H. (*Maj. 23 July 15). *7 Nov. 14. 7 Feb. 06. (3)Thornes, W. G. D. *6 Dec. 14. Richardson, E., s. 9 Feb. 15.

Lieutenants—

(3)Birchenall, A. G. (*Capt. 12 Oct. 14). 13 Nov. 12. (2)Stephenson, D. B. 17 July 13. (1)Makin, F. A. 24 Jan. 14. (1)Handforth, G. W. *Capt. 28 July 15). 24 Jan. 14. (3)Makin, G. *Capt. 19 Oct. 14). 7 June 14. (1)Shaw, H. C. 2 Sept. 14. (1)Wood, R. G. 4 Nov. 14. (1) Forshaw, W. T. 4 Nov. 14.

2nd Lieutenants—

(1)Hyde, T. G. (*Lt. 4 Nov. 14). 27 Apr. 14. (1)Parker, L. A. (*Lt. 4 Nov. 14). 8 May 14. (1)Lillie, W. H. (*Lt. 4 Nov. 14). 2 Sept. 14. (1)Sutton, O. J. (*Capt. 20 Oct. 15). 2 Sept. 14. (1)Shatwell, H. G. (*Lt. 1 July 5). 2 Sept. 14. (1)Wade, J. M. 2 Sept. 14. Marsden, P. S. (*Lt. 16 Aug. 15). 2 Sept. 14. Butterworth, H. E. 2 Sept. 14. (1)Cooke, C. E. 2 Sept. 14. Broadbent, J., T late Maj. 5 Sept. 14. (2)Barratt, W. M. 12 Oct. 14. (2)Sampson, H. V. (*Capt. 24 Nov. 14). Adjt. 12 Oct. 14. (2)Brister, J. F. (*Capt. 24 Nov. 14). 12 Oct. 14. (3)Wilkinson, N. (*Capt. 23 June 5). 12 Oct. 14. (2)Allen, V. M. B. (*Lt. 24 Nov. 14). 12 Oct. 14. (1)Robinson, B. F. (*Capt. 9 Sept. 15). 12 Oct. 14. (2)Leaver,

W. E. (*Capt. 24 Nov. 14). 12 Oct. 14. (2)Knight, H. H. (*Lt. 24 Nov. 14). 12 Oct. 14. (1)Needham, O. S. (*Lt. 9 Aug. 15). 2 Oct. 14. (1)Connery, A. W. F. 12 Oct. 14. (2)Oppenheimer, E. N. (*Capt. 9 Sept. 15). 12 Oct. 14. (2)Ruttenan, S. W. (*Lt. 24 Nov. 14). 12 Oct. 14. (2)Cooke, L. H. (*Lt. 20 Oct. 15). 12 Oct. 14. (2)Greenwood, W .G. 12 Oct. 14. (2)Hill, R. (*Lt. 19 Aug. 15). 6 Nov. 14. (1)Bury, W. N. B. (*Capt. 9 Sept. 15). 7 Nov. 14. (1)Naylor, S. (*Capt. 9 Sept. 15). 7 Nov. 14. (1)Ablitt, W. J. 1 Jan. 15. (1)Fielding, P. P. 20 Jan. 15. (3)Jackson, R. H. (*Lt. 23 June 15). 24 Mar. 15. (1)Hampson, F. C. 27 Mar. 15. (3)Grove, J. P. (*Capt. 23 June 15). 27 Mar. 15. (1)Ainsworth, T. 12 Apr. 15. (2)Barratt, G. H. (*Lt. 20 Oct. 15). 13 Apr. 15. (1)Demely, W. H. 13 Apr. 15. (1)Ingham, H. (*Capt. 20 Sept. 15). 13 Apr. 15. (1)Ainsworth, P. (*Lt. 20 Oct. 15). 17 Apr. 15. (2)Smith, E. N. (*Lt. 20 Oct. 15). 18 Apr. 15. (1)Beard, F. 18 Apr. 15. (2)Brickman, I. P. (*Lt. 20 Oct. 15). 18 Apr. 15. (1)Balmford, E. 5 May 15. (2)Winkworth, L .S. 18 May 15. *7 Apr. 15. (2)Sinclair, W. G. 19 May 15. *9 Apr. 15. (2)Till, G. F. 26 May 15. *22 Apr. 15. (2)Donaldson, R. C. 31 May 15. *29 Apr. 15. (1)Brister, B. H. 10 June 15. (3)Hayward, G. E. (*Lt. 7 Oct. 15). 11 June 15. (1)Dale, R. J. N. 18 June 15. (2)Green, A. 21 June 15. (1)Tommis, J. R. 21 July 15. (3)Watts, F. (*Capt. 28 Oct. 15). 25 July 15. (3)Hill, C. E. 27 July 15. (3)Ward, R. (*Lt. 7 Oct. 15). 9 Aug. 15. (3)Waring, J. F. (*Lt. 7 Oct. 15). 9 Aug. 15. (3)Barnes, B. M. 17 Aug. 15. (3)Garside, F. (*Lt. 7 Oct. 15). 17 Aug. 15. (1)Gray, A. 21 Aug. 15. 10 Apr. 15. (3)Sidebotham, W. F. 21 Aug. 15. (3)Gough, H. S. 21 Aug. 15. (3)Whitehead, C. S. 31 Aug. 15. (3)Harrison, A. J. 1 Sept. 15. (2)Lindley, E. W. 4 Sept. 15. *29 July 15. (3)Kelly, R. 6 Sept. 15. (3)Henthorne, A. 7Sept. 15. (3)Hesketh, H. R. 10 Sept. 15. (2)Gossling, D. F. 10 Sept. 15. (2)Pilling, F. 17 Sept. 15. Rawlins, T. A. (*Capt. 21 Sept. 15). 21 Sept. 15. (2)Jones, A. S. 2 Oct. 15. (3)Mylius, S. 22 Oct. 15. (3)Ellis, H. C. (3)Bennett, H. 8 Nov. 15. (3)Forge, E. R. 8 Nov. 15. (3)Vipond, F. E. 20 Nov. 15. Spargo, H. J. 20 Nov. 15. (2)Shanahan, J. E. 30 Nov. 15. *29 July 15. Langton, R. S. 1 Dec. 15. Hartley, W. S. 2 Dec. 15. Stern, H. S. 2 Dec. 15. Pitt, B. I. 2 Dec. 15. Haydock-Wilson, H. 2 Dec. 15. Spink, L. R. 7 Dec. 15. Wilkinson, J. Y. 17 Dec. 15. MacDonald, G. 17 Dec. 15. Bamforth, V. 21 Dec. 15.

Inst. of Musk.—

(2)Lees, R., Capt. 15 June 13.

Adjutants—

(1)Dearden, J. A. Capt. Manch. R. 12 Mar. 12. (2)Sampson, H. V., 2nd Lt. (*Capt.) 23 June 15.

Quarter-Masters—

(1)Connery, M. H., Qr.-M.r (hon. capt.) ret. pay, hon. m. 22 Apr. 09. (2)Connery, J., Hon. Lt. 17 Jan. 15.

Medical Officers—

Frankish, Maj T., M.B., R.A.M.C. (T.F.) (attd.) 9 Mar. 15. (2)Whitehead, Capt. G., M.B., R.A.M.C. (T.F.) (attd.) 3 May 15. 3 Nov. 14.

Chaplains—

Burrows, Rev. F. H., M.A., Chapl. 4th Class (T.F.) (attd.). 13 May 09. (2)Sanderson, Rev. G. P. M., Chapl. 4th Class T.F.) (attd.). 12 June 15.

* Denotes Temporary Rank.

OFFICERS OF THE 9TH (TERRITORIAL) BATTALION KILLED, DIED OF WOUNDS RECEIVED IN ACTION, OR DIED.

Lt.-Col. F. H. Cunliffe—25 May, 1915.

Lt.-Col. F. H. Cunliffe was in command of 2/9th, and went to Gallipoli to command the 1/9th. He was a Lieut-Col. Retired T.F., and rejoined on Sept. 28th, 1914.

Major W. H. Archbutt—8 Feby., 1915.

Major W. H. Archbutt proceeded to Egypt with the Battalion in September, 1914, where he died.

Major A. Hilton, R.A.M.C.—4 Apr., 1915.

Major A. Hilton was attached to the 9th Battalion from the R.A.M.C. He proceeded to Egypt in September, 1914, and died while acting as Medical Officer to the Battalion.

Capt. F. Hamer—7 June, 1915.

Captain Frank Hamer was 35 years of age, and a son of Mr. William Hamer, an ex-Mayor of Ashton-under-Lyne. He was in business at Ashton as a chartered accountant. In 1904 he was elected to Ashton Town Council in the Liberal interest for Portland Place Ward. He received his commission in the Ashton Battalion in 1904, and was promoted captain on December 7th, 1911.

Capt. H. Sugden—21 June, 1915.

Captain Harold Sugden succumbed to wounds in hospital at Alexandria. He was in business as an auctioneer and valuer. He was 36, and had served for a good many years in the Home Defence Forces. He was promoted captain on July 6th, 1910.

Lieut. J. M. Robson—17 July, 1915.

Second Lieutenant John M. Robson died from enteric in hospital at Alexandria. He was the elder son of Mr.

and Mrs. George Robson, of Ashton-under-Lyne. He was gazetted on the 14th November, 1914.

2nd Lieut. A. H. HUDSON—14 June, 1915.

Second-Lieutenant Allan Harrison Hudson was 20 years of age, and the only son of Mr. Jervis Hudson, of Hyde. In 1913 he was articled with the firm of Messrs. Brown, Briggs, and Symonds, solicitors, Stockport. He volunteered shortly after the war broke out, and was gazetted on the 14th November, 1914. He went to Egypt early in April, and after remaining there seventeen days was sent to the Dardanelles.

2nd Lieut. F. JONES—24 May, 1915.

Second-Lieutenant Fred Jones was serving before the war, and was made sergeant just before mobilisation. On leaving for Egypt he was given a commission on September 30th, 1914. He had been an assistant master in an Ashton Council School.

2nd Lieut. A. E. STRINGER—7 June, 1915.

Second-Lieutenant A. E. Stringer was gazetted to the 9th Manchesters on September 2nd, 1914.

2nd Lieut. P. A. WOODHOUSE—11 Sept., 1915.

Second-Lieut. Percy Aspden Woodhouse enlisted in the 11th Hussars early in the War, and was gazetted a second-lieutenant in the 9th Battalion early in 1915. He died of dysentery, and was buried at sea. Second-Lieut. Woodhouse was the only son of Mr. and Mrs. C. H. Woodhouse, of Blackburn. He was 23 years of age.

MISSING.

2nd Lieut. J. M. WADE—9 July, 1915.

WOUNDED.

Lt.-Col. D. H. WADE—24 May, 1915.
Major R. B. NOWELL—7 Aug., 1915.
Lieut. O. J. SUTTON—7 Aug., 1915.
2nd Lieut. E. BALMFORD—13 July, 1915.
2nd Lieut. A. W. F. CONNERY—5 July, 1915.
2nd Lieut. P. S. MARSDEN—12 June, 1915.
Hon. Major and Qr.-Mr. M. H. CONNERY—22 June, 1915.

N.C.O.'S AND MEN OF THE 9TH (TERRITORIAL) BATTALION KILLED OR DIED OF WOUNDS RECEIVED IN ACTION.

Date List Published.		Date List Published.	
3 7 15.	1866 Pte. T. Bell.		1606 Pte. W. Townley.
	1690 Pte. A. Gee.		1413 Pte. T. Penny (d.w.)

Date List Published.		Date List Published.	
	2216 Pte. A. Hare	6 7 15.	1809 Pte. I. Smith (d.w.)
	1401 Pte. E. Hodgkiss.	7 7 15.	2003 Pte. F. Ballard.
	2151 Pte. W. S. Foden.		1393 Pte. P. Tilbury.
	2192 Pte. J. Jones.		1957 Pte. J. Rowbottom (d.)
	2085 Pte. H. Bailey (d.w.)	25 8 15.	1289 L/Cpl. G. Massey.
	1652 Pte. R. Stott (d.w.)		2082 Pte. F. H. Walker (d.w.)
	1746 Pte. T. Chapman (d.)		745 Pte. A. Booth.
9 7 15.	2175 Pte. F. Farier.		1342 Pte. H. Bradbury.
	786 Pte. J. Coffey (d.w.)		2330 Pte. H. Chadwick.
	1760 Pte. J. H. Cooper (d.w.)		2946 Pte. W. B. Forrister.
	1390 Pte. A. Hague (d.w.)		1568 Pte. A. V. Goddings.
	1524 J. W. Jenneys (d.w.)		2971 Pte. A. G. Harling.
	1872 Pte. H. Ogden (d.w.)		1324 Pte. S. J. Hillan.
	1775 Pte. W. Postle (d.w.)		1189 Pte. H. Newton
	1178 Pte. H. Redfern (d.w.)		1850 Pte. D. Nuttall.
12 7 15.	1855 Pte. J. E. Swain (d.)		2095 Pte. J. J. O'Connor.
	555 Pte. W. Barker (d.w.)		1909 Pte. A. Smith.
15 7 15.	1000 L/Cpl. E. Earnshaw.		1252 Pte. E. Smith.
	1546 Pte. J. Finnighan.		2742 Pte. J. Speddings.
	1859 Pte. E. Heineman.		2625 Pte. J. Walker.
	69 Sergt. H. Illingworth.		2616 Pte. J. Bardsley.
	2238 Pte. J. Love.		1535 Pte. J. H. Connolly (d.)
	2126 Pte. J. Martin.		1863 Pte. W. Adshead (d.w.)
	1415 L/Cpl. W. Halon	24 9 15.	2089 Pte. P. Storns.
15 7 15.	1734 Cpl. H. Matthews.	30 9 15.	2941 Pte. J H. Brown.
	2012 Pte. J. Tetlow.	5 10 15.	1314 Pte. J. W. Andrew.
	1380 Pte. B. Rawlings		1618 Pte. C. Higgins.
	1354 Pte. W. Shuttleworth.		1402 Pte. C. Turner.
	1044 Pte. T. Gorman (d.w.)	6 10 15.	2195 Pte. H. Kenyon.
	1821 Pte. G. W. Hudson (d.w.)	11 10 15.	2356 Pte. F. Smith.
26 7 15.	1152 L/Cpl. J. Blandford.	13 10 15.	2897 Pte. H. Clegg
20 7 15.	1484 Cpl. J. Hughes (d.)	21 10 15.	921 Cpl. H. Bolten (d.w.)
26 7 15.	1488 Pte. R. Burgess.	13 11 15.	2139 L/Sergt. G. Higham (d.w.)
	1128 Sergt. H. Earle.	2 12 15.	2049 Cpl. C. W. Gibson (d.w.)
	1660 Pte. H. Garside.	3 12 15.	1947 Pte. H. Rhodes (d.w.)
	1853 Pte. A. Lewis.		1998 Pte. S. Armitage.
	1851 Pte. W. Mather.	7 12 15.	1787 F. Jones (d.w.)
	1927 Pte. J. Sellars.	11 12 15.	1210 Pte. J. A. Crane (d.)
	2193 Pte. S. Steflox.	26 12 15.	3321 Pte. J. Gallagher.
6 8 15.	2066 Pte. J. Crompton (d.w.)		1641 Pte. E. Green (d.w.)
	1298 Pte. E. Martyn (d.w.)	29 12 15.	3291 Pte. A. Jones.
17 8 15.	2183 Pte. E. Hargreave (d.w.)		3090 Pte. J. Lawton.
	1920 Cpl. W. Mitcheson (d.w.)		2757 Pte. W. Lilley.
	2202 Pte. J. Hague (d.)		3340 Pte. C. Booth.
	1218 L/Cpl. J. Hollingworth (d.)	1 1 16.	3281 Pte. J. Fearnaley (d.w.)
21 8 15.	1922 Pte. E. Kelly.	3 1 16.	2297 Pte. S. Mather (d.)
	1501 Pte. G. Markham.		2282 Pte. J. Finucane (d.)
26 8 15.	1155 L/Cpl. W. Burke (d.)		1423 L/Cpl. A. Burgess (d.w.)
	2207 Pte. B. Thompson (d.)		1271 Sgt. J. Taylor (d.w.)
10 9 15.	31 Sgt. T. Lomas.		449 Dr. F. Wyatt.
	1557 Pte. J. Walker.		

10th (Territorial) Battalion

Originally the 56th Battalion Lancashire Rifle Volunteers, altered later to the 22nd Battalion, and became in 1880 the 6th Volunteer Battalion, Manchester Regiment. Present title since 1st April, 1908. The Headquarters are in Oldham.

The Battalion, after being embodied, left for Egypt on 10th September, 1914. On 5th May, 1915, they sailed for Gallipoli, arriving four days later. The Battalion was in reserve for some days, and afterwards, owing to the heavy casualties sustained by the Hampshire Regiment and the Royal Fusiliers, the 10th Manchesters filled the gaps in the two Battalions.

The first big battle the 10th Manchesters were in was on the 4th to the 6th of June, 1915, when the Battalion fought with the 29th Division (Regulars) on the left of the line below the village of Krithnia. The fighting was of an exceptionally sanguinary character, and officers and men acquitted themselves admirably, gaining the warmest of praise from the men of the 29th Divsiion. They advanced over five lines of Turkish trenches at the point of the bayonet, driving the Turks before them in disorder. The men showed wonderful coolness and courage in a perfect hail of shrapnel and machine gun fire, and in spite of the fact that many of their officers had fallen.

Captain Booth showed exceptional courage in leading several charges, and there were numerous instances of personal bravery amongst N.C.O.'s and men.

Subsequently the Battalion was got together, and it was found the casualties for this battle alone amounted to over 450, a big percentage of these being killed.

The next big engagement was on the 19th-20th of June, when the Battalion was in the second line of trenches and were called upon to repel a sudden attack by the Turks, who came on in overwhelming numbers. After very severe fighting the Turks were driven back with heavy losses.

In the August operations at Cape Helles the Battalion was again engaged, having been reinforced by a draft from the 2nd line. The Battalion was too weak in numbers still to hold any appreciable length of the line, but about about the 7th of August relieved the 6th Lancashire Fusiliers in the fire trench, and fought stubbornly and bravely against the repeated attempts of the enemy to recapture the Vineyard trenches.

From the middle of August to the evacuation of Gallipoli very little information has come through of the Battalion. The Battalion has lost about 200 officers, N.C.O.'s and men killed in action and 20 are missing, 540 having returned to England wounded and sick.

The following are the present officers of the Battalion, with the dates of their appointments :—

Hon. Colonel—

Patterson, W., V.D. (Lt.-Col. ret. T.F.) 19 Dec. 13.

Lt.-Colonels—

(1)Rye, J. B., V.D. 18 Dec. 13. (2)Patterson, W., V.D. (2)Patterson, W., V.D. (Hon. Col.) *27 Sept. 14.

Majors—

(1)Bamford, P. (Hon. Lt. in Army 2 June 01). 12 Oct. 12. (3)Hardman, G. W. (Hon. Lt. in Army 6 July 02). 2 Sept. 14.
(2)Shiers, J. T. (Maj. ret. T.F.) *1 Oct. 14.

Captains—

(1)Wilde, L. C. 30 Apr. 04. (1)Booth, A. C. 13 Feb. 07. (1)Newton, G. R. (H) I. of M. 14 June 07. Newton, J. A. 1 July 11. (1)Stott, G. E. 12 Oct. 12. (1)Griffiths, D. E. G. 9 Aug. 13. Leach, A., Brig. M.G. Offr. 31 Aug. 14. (1)Sutcliffe, H. 31 Aug. 14.

Lieutenants—

(1)Hardman, F. 8 June 12. (1)Wilkinson, L. St. G. (*Capt. 4 July 15). 15 July 13. (1)Pochin, G. D. 9 Aug. 13. (1)Stott, P. 30 Aug. 14. (1)Park, D. 30 Aug. 14. (1)Wilde, R. W. 31 Aug. 14. (3)Lee, A. E. 9 Mar. 14. Stott, J. 8 Apr. 14. (1)Taylor, J. A. C. 6 Aug. 14. (3)Bleakley, J. F. 2 Sept. 14. (2)Maw, A. (*Capt. 10 Jan. 15). 5 Sept. 14. (3)Gillespie, P. (*Lt. 10 Jan. 15). 5 Sept. 14. (1)Butterworth, A. (*Capt. 14 Sept. 15). 12 Sept. 14. (1)Rodgers, G. (*Capt. 28 Nov. 14). 1 Oct. 14. (1)Rowbotham, J. C. S. 1 Oct. 14. (3)Rye, E. 1 Oct. 14. (2)Maw, A. R. (*Lt. 7 Aug. 15). 1 Oct. 14. (2)Boyd, J. (*Lt. 1 Oct. 14). 14 Oct. 14. (1)Mercer, F. (*Lt. 1 Oct. 14). 14 Oct. 14. (1)Hassall, H. (*Lt. 1 Oct. 14). 14 Oct. 14. (2)Wallwork, H. (*Capt. 1 Oct. 14). 14 Oct. 14. (2)Scholefield, F. (*Capt. 24 Aug. 15), Adjt. 14 Oct. 14. (1)Tweedie, F. I. G. (*Lt. 1 Oct. 14). 14 Oct. 14. (3)Gill, C. I. (*Capt. 21 Sept. 15). 14 Oct. 14. (2)Taylor, G. B. (*Lt. 1 Oct. 14). 14 Oct. 14. Taylor, J. (*Capt. 1 Dec. 14). 1 Dec. 14. (1)Wallwork, E. 1 Dec. 14. (2)Wild, H. (*Lt. 7 Aug. 15). 14 Jan .15. (1)Stanford, R. V. 15 Jan. 15. (1)Hampson, H .J. 2 Feb. 15. (1)Sutton, D. H. 7 Feb. 15. (2)Preston, W. (*Lt. 7 Oct. 15). 8 Feb. 15. (1)Kershaw,

J. H. 10 Feb. 15. (1)BEVERIDGE, J. E. 11 Feb. 15. (3)JONES, J. F. (*Capt. 25 Sept. 15). 12 Feb. 15. (1)COOPER, C. H. 12 Feb. 15. (2)STEVENS, H. C. G. (*Lt. 7 Oct. 15). 12 Feb. 15. (2)ABBOTT, H. (*Lt. 7 Oct. 15). 12 Feb .15. (1)BAXTER, G. V. 13 Feb. 15. (1)GARDNER, R. L. 13 Feb. 15. (2)HASLEWOOD, W. A. 15 Feb. 15. (3)HUGHES, B. E. H. 16 Feb. 15. CRAWSHAW, G. W. (*Capt. 24 Aug. 15) (Brig. M.-G. Offr.) 8 Mar. 15. (2)HAYWOOD, T. C. 9 Mar. 15. (2)BLETCHER, T. (*Lt. 7 Oct. 15). 9 Mar. 15. (2)QUARMLY, F. R. 9 Mar. 15. (2)DAVIES, C. R. (*Lt. 7 Oct. 15). 15 Mar. 15. (2)SEWELL, F. R. 16 Mar. 15. (3)CARSON, R. M. (*Capt. 29 Sept. 15). 18 Apr. 15. (1)FAULKNER, T. (*Lt. 6 Aug. 15). 18 Apr. 15. (1)KIRK, J. L. 24 Apr. 15. (2)BOOTH, C. H. 1 May 15. (2)ROOKE, W. H. C. 26 May 15. *5 May 15. (3)BOUSKILL, C. (*Lt. 29 Sept. 15). 7 June 15. (3)WILKINSON, F. R. (*Lt. 29 Sept. 15). 7 June 15. (3)KILNER, H. A. 14 July 15. (3)TWEEDALE, A. 16 July 15. (2)BAIRD, S. 4 Aug. 15. (2)STONES, N. 25 Aug. 15. (3)SCHOFIELD, W. (*Lt. 29 Sept. 15). 31 Aug. 15. (3)HOWARTH, F. 5 Sept. 15. (3)HOLT, S. 5 Sept .15. (3)HIRD, A. 9 Sept. 15. (3)HOWELLS, J. C. 9 Sept. 15. WOODHEAD, J. 10 Sept. 15. (3)WITHAM, A. W. 10 Sept. 15. DUMUGHN, F. L. 10 Sept. 15. (3)HORSFALL, M. 10 Sept. 15. HARRY, G. O. M. 12 Sept. 15. (2)WHITTAKER, E. N. 17 Sept. 15. (2)SUTTON, V. 17 Sept. 15. (2)BAXTER, H. J. 18 Sept. 15. MALLALIEU, J .T. 20 Sept. 15. (2)FRIPP, G. C. 29 Sept. 15. ALLEN, A. F. 20 Nov. 15. FEARNE, S. 2 Dec. 15. SMITH, R. A. 2 Dec. 15. JUPP, J. M. S. 2 Dec. 15. ROBERTS, J. P. 17 Dec. 15. HUDDLESTON, N. C. 17 Dec. 15. PRESTON, J. L. 17 Dec. 15. KERSHAW, G. H. 19 Dec. 15. FOY, C. 19 Dec. 15. JACKSON, T. H. 19 Dec. 15.

Inst. of Musk.—
(2)NEWTON, G. R., Capt. 9 July 09.

Adjutants—
(1)DE PENTHENY-O'KELLY, E. J., Maj. R. W. Fus. 28 Nov. 13.
(2)SCHOLEFIELD, F., 2nd Lt. (*Capt.) 24 June 15.

Quarter-Masters—
(2)OGDEN, T C., Hon. Lt. 23 Sept. 14. (1)WYNNE, A. G., Hon. Lt. 11 June 15. RENNIE, J., Hon. Lt. 18 June 15.

Medical Officers—
(2)FORT, Capt. H. M., M.B., R.A.M.C. (T.F.) 8 June 12.
(1)BAIRD, Capt. L. B., R.A.M.C. (T.F.) (attd.) 1 Apr. 15. 5 Sept. 14. (2)FARQUHAR, Capt. J., M.B., R.A.C.M. (T.F.) (attd.) 22 July 15.

Chaplain—
ORTON, Rev. J. W., V.D., Chapl. 1st Class (T.F.) (attd.) 1 Apr. 08. 6 Dec. 12.

* Denotes Temporary Rank.

OFFICERS OF THE 10TH (TERRITORIAL) BATTALION KILLED, DIED OF WOUNDS RECEIVED IN ACTION, OR DIED.

Capt. J. H. CLEGG—22 June, 1915.

Captain James Hamer Clegg was 27 years of age. He is the only son of Mr. and Mrs. Charles Clegg, of Wilmslow, and the joint managing director of Clegg Brothers, Limited, Mumps Mill, Oldham. When the Regiment left for Egypt Lieutenant Clegg stayed behind for a time to take charge of the men who had not volunteered for foreign service. He also assisted in the formation of two reserve battalions before setting sail for Egypt. He was promoted captain on November 28th, 1914.

Capt. G. W. OWEN—22 June, 1915.

Captain George Webster Owen, when a youth, joined the ranks of the old 2nd Volunteer Battalion Manchester Regiment, attaining the rank of sergeant. He was in the Officers' Training Corps at the University, obtained a commission in April, 1900, and was gazetted captain on August 31st, 1914. Captain Owen was 32 years of age, and in business was a yarn agent in Manchester.

Capt. H. L. J. SPIELMAN—13 Aug., 1915.

Captain Harold Lionel Spielmann was the younger son of Sir Isidore Spielmann, and was educated at Clifton Pembroke College, Cambridge. In September, 1914, he was gazetted to the 10th Battalion. He was promoted captain on November 28th, 1914.

Lieut. J. CLEGG—27 May, 1915.

Lieut. J. Clegg was promoted lieutenant on August 31st, 1914.

Lieut. F. N. G. GRIFFITHS—2 June, 1915.

Lieut. F. N. G. Griffiths was promoted lieutenant on August 31st, 1914.

2nd Lieut. R. G. L. ASHCROFT—6 June, 1915.

Second-Lieutenant Robert Geoffrey Lees Ashcroft was 19 years of age, and the son of the late Mr. James Henry Ascroft, and nephew of the late Mr. Robert Ascroft, a former member for Oldham. He was educated at Charterhouse School, which he left in July, 1914. Shortly after the war was declared on August 25th, 1914, he joined the 1/10th Manchester Battalion, and he went with them to Egypt and later to the Dardanelles.

2nd Lieut. T. KIRK—6 June, 1915.

Second-Lieutenant Tom Kirk was the elder son of Mr. and Mrs. George S. Kirk, of Princes Road, Heaton Moor. Second-Lieut. Kirk rejoined his old regiment, the 6th Manchesters, as a private at the outbreak of war, and went into training at Littleborough, and later proceeded to Egypt. He was recently promoted to a commission in the 10th Manchesters, and with this regiment was despatched to the Dardanelles. He was a very prominent member of the Heaton Mersey Lacrosse Club, and played for Lancashire County. He was also a member of the West Heaton and Northern tennis clubs, and represented his county in this sport.

WOUNDED.

Capt. A. C. BOOTH—18 June, 1915.
Capt. A. LEACH—4 Aug., 15.
Capt. G. R. NEWTON—27 June, 1915.
Capt. G. E. STOTT—6 July, 1915.
Capt. H. SUTCLIFFE—6 June, 1915.
Lieut. P. STOTT—6 June, 1915.
2nd Lieut. A. BUTTERWORTH—6 July, 1915.
2nd Lieut. J. B. EMMOTT—6 June, 1915.
2nd Lieut. J. L. KIRK—10 Aug., 1915.
2nd Lieut. H. R. B. NEVINSON—6 June, 1915.
2nd Lieut. E. WALLWORK—24 May, 1915.

N.C.O.'S AND MEN OF THE 10TH (TERRITORIAL) BATTALION KILLED OR DIED OF WOUNDS RECEIVED IN ACTION.

Date List Published.	
3 7 15.	2136 Pte. R. Lane.
	1994 Pte. A. Ogden.
	1094 Pte. E. Wanener.
	1981 Pte. J. Currie (d.w.)
	1590 Pte. J. Curre (d.w.)
5 7 15.	1019 Pte. P. Cartledge.
	1609 Pte. A. Fozzard.
	905 Pte. E. Fitton.
	2179 Pte. E. R. Smalley.
	1810 Pte. A. Snow.
6 7 15.	1492 Pte. T. Healey (d.w.)
	1898 Pte. W. Howard (d.w.)
	1252 Pte. J. E. Morgan (d.w.)
7 7 15.	821 Pte. D. J. Thomas (d.w.)
9 7 15.	1497 L/Cpl. R. Adams.

Date List Published.	
	1473 Sergt. R. Smith.
	1333 Pte. T. W. Stanton.
	1542 L/Cpl. T. H. Strachan.
	1611 Pte. H. Styles.
	2285 Pte. J. L. Taylor.
	2194 Pte. W. Taylor.
	1530 Pte. R. Urmston.
	2017 Pte. J. Walker.
	1236 Pte. T. Ward.
	1152 Pte. H. Ward.
	1152 Pte. H. Watson
	987 Pte. A. Wood.
9 7 15.	2019 Sergt. J. W. Wood.
	1749 Pte. F. Wyall.
	2278 Pte. J. Bamford (d.w.)

Date List Published.	
	1943 Pte. H. Anderson
	2214 Pte. H. Bailey.
	1666 Pte. S. Bairstow.
	2224 Pte. W. Buckley.
	2305 Pte. T. Cheetham.
	2096 Pte. T. Claber.
	644 Pte. H. Clark.
	1837 Pte. H. Clegg.
	'470 L/Cpl. T. H. Crew.
	1320 Pte. F. Drabble.
	50 Co.-Sqr.-Mjr. F. Dunkerley.
	141 Pte. J. Fitten.
	2108 Pte. P. Fitzjerald.
	2314 Pte. A. Fletcher
	1751 L/Cpl. F. Perbutt.
9 7 15.	1722 Pte. H. C. Gledhill.
	1887 Pte. J. Greaves.
	1258 Pte. F. Greenwood.
	1975 Cpl. F. Hadfield.
	560 Sergt. H. Hinchcliffe.
	1763 Sergt. S. Holden.
	1290 L/Cpl. G. H. Horton.
	1548 Pte. H. Huxley.
	1980 Pte. H. Jackson.
	1663 Pte. J. Kelly.
	213 Sergt. T. Kitson.
	455 L/Cpl. J. H. McPlegor.
	2155 Pte. P. Honks.
	1154 Pte. W. Moss.
	1936 Pte. H. Powwel.
	342 Cpl. J. W. Rose.
	2173 Pte. H. Saint.
	2178 Pte. H. Stinger.
	1481 Pte. S. Smedley.
6 8 15.	1680 Pte. J. Rennie.
	1431 Pte. A. Norman (d.)
21 8 15.	1788 Pte. P. Clegg
	1737 Pte. J. Patchett.
25 8 15.	2134 Pte. J. T. Kirkman (d.w.)
	2873 Pte. F. Sykes.
	1865 Pte. W. H. Rothwell.
	1351 Pte. A. Hitchen.
	1779 Pte. T. Little.
17 9 15.	1624 Pte. M. Crawshaw.
	2954 Pte. F. Moran.
	1526 Sergt. F. Bowden.
	2315 Sergt. T. Gardiner.
	1361 Cpl. J. Greenwood.
	3006 Pte. V Hadfield.
	2807 Pte. J. Hallam.
	39 Sergt W. Hutton.

Date List Published.	
	670 Pte. R. Edwards (d.w.)
	902 Pte. J. Paider (d.w.)
	2063 Pte. J. Ramsden (d.w.)
12 7 15.	382 Dr. T. Black.
	1862 Pte. J. Byne.
	2092 Pte. W. Carter.
	1608 Pte. W. Eastwood.
	1120 Sergt. S. Fallows.
	823 Pte. J. W. Hadfield.
	1866 Pte. F. Holt.
15 7 15.	2270 Pte. J. Needham (d.w.)
	943 L/Cpl. W. Currie (d.w.)
17 7 15.	2052 Pte. J. Clansey.
	829 Cpl. W. Kidd.
	2282 Pte. F. Smith.
	2087 Pte. J. Burgess (d.w.)
	996 Pte. J. C. Burke (d.w.)
	1560 Pte. J. Goldsby (d.w.)
	2169 Pte. S. Robinson (d.)
20 7 15.	1498 Pte. S. Booth (d.w.)
	2204 Pte. W. Wilkinson(d.w.)
	1797 Pte. A. Mellor (d.)
24 7 15.	2227 Pte. J. Charlesworth.
	2232 Pte. G. H. Cook.
	1559 Dr. C Dean.
	2041 Sergt. E. Drinkwater.
	1635 Pte. E. Elson.
	1535 L/Cpl A. Grady
	1567 Pte. G. Neilson.
	2196 Pte. G. Travis.
	1579 Pte. J. Vaudrey
	2264 Pte. J. Lyon.
	2212 Pte. W. Ashton (d.)
26 7 15.	1600 Pte. J. J. Johnson(d.w.)
	1736 Pte. A. Newton.
27 9 15.	1234 Pte. C. Bannister.
	2182 L/Cpl. A. A. Snare.
1 10 15.	2532 Pte. H. Schofield.
5 10 15.	1075 Pte. W. Seville.
5 10 15.	2337 Pte. As. Aspin.
	2472 Pte. J. Holden.
	1540 Pte. F. Lowe.
8 10 15.	2906 Pte. H. Cocker.
27 10 15.	2619 Pte. F. Hoyle.
8 11 15.	2586 Pte. J. Cooper.
	2925 Pte. T. Hague.
15 11 15.	2342 Pte. C. Stafford (d.)
2 10 15.	2306 Pte. P. Ridings.
5 10 15.	1460 Pte. J. Richardson.
23 11 15.	2398 Pte. A. Starkey (d.)
	1917 Pte. T. H. Knott (d.)

Date List Published.		Date List Published.	
	2127 Cpl. G. A. Jones.	30 11 15.	1839 Pte. G. Hague.
	1864 Pte. F. Mellor.		2068 Pte. R. Burgess (d.w.)
	1867 Pte. F. Stott.	29 12 15.	695 Pte. H. Jones.
	2969 L/Cpl. E. Turner.		2217 Pte. E. Bellby.
	1550 Pte. R. Whittaker.	26 12 15.	2613 Cpl. J. Hilton.
	201 Sergt. W. Wyke.	3 1 16.	993 Cpl.S. Francis (d.)
21 9 15.	2789 Pte. W. H. Bellheus.		3020 Pte. T. Littlewood (d.)
22 9 15.	2570 Pte. H. Bradley.	5 1 16.	3118 Pte. H. Kenworthy.
	1692 Pte. J. Bardsley.	7 1 16.	3217 Pte. F. H. Stott (d.w.)
	2222 L/Cpl. F. Broadbent.	24 1 16.	452 Pte. R. Burrows (d.)
	2687 Pte. M. Kelly.		3874 Pte. A. E. Turner (d.)
	3140 Pte. W. Lindsay.	28 1 16.	2505 Pte. H. Morgan (d.)
	1540 Pte. H. J. Lowe.	2 9 15.	1740 Pte. A. Connelly.
10 9 15.	673 Cpl. J. Coleman (d.w.)		

SERVICE, SECOND RESERVE & LOCAL RESERVE BATTALIONS

The 11th, 12th, 13th 16th, 17th, 18th, 19th, 20th, 21st, 22nd, 23rd, and 24th are "Service Battalions." The 14th is a "Second Reserve Battalion," and the 25th, 26th, and 27th are "Local Reserve Battalions."

All the Officers, N.C.O.'s and men of these Battalions, except the officers and N.C.O.'s who have been loaned by the Regular Army for training purposes, are serving for the period of War only. The officers hold temporary rank in the Regular Army.

11th (Service) Battalion

Raised at the Barracks, Ashton-under-Lyne, in August, 1914. Composed of the first men to come forward at the commencement of the War. Is in the First New Army, and has a considerable number of Regular officers. Trained at Grantham and Whitley, under Lt.-Col. B. A. Wright, D.S.O.

The Battalion embarked during the first week of July, 1915, to join the Mediterranean Expeditionary Force. One Company, under Major Bates, in the "Empress of Britain," and the remainder, under the Commanding Officer, in the "Ascania." The Battalion assembled on the Island of Imbros, fourteen miles from the Gallipoli Peninsula. It formed part of the Brigade which made the first landing in Suvla Bay on the night of August 6th, 1915. The disembarkation was successfully made in six feet of water, and under rifle and shell fire, there being several casualties before the men got ashore. After assembling on the beach the Battalion moved north, and, in the dark, rushed the Turkish trenches and the fortified signal post at Kemikli Point, afterwards fighting its way along the high ridges to the North of the Bay in order to cover the left flank of the landing. They were strongly opposed, and were held up by heavy rifle and shell fire after advancing about three miles, but maintained their position until supported, shortly after dark, by two battalions of another Division, when they dug in for the night.

Early on Sunday (8th August) the Battalion, which had suffered heavily, and was badly in need of food, water, etc., was relieved, and taken into reserve. It was in reserve that day and during the operations of the 9th and 10th August, but lost four officers and several men.

The Battalion received letters of congratulation on their behaviour from two Divisional Generals.

During the landing and the subsequent fighting, Lt.-Col. B. A. Wright, D.S.O., was in command of the Battalion with Captain H. Ellershaw as his Adjutant, both of whom were wounded.

Between the 6th of August and the Battalion's departure from the Peninsula in the early winter, eight officers and over 100 other ranks were killed in action or died of wounds, and 10 officers and 330 other ranks wounded. 40 N.C.O.'s and men being missing.

The Battalion left Gallipoli on December 19th, 1915, for Imbros Island, and proceeded to Alexandria a month later.

Among the present officers of the Battalion are :—

Lt.-Col. B. A. WRIGHT, D.S.O. (Commanding).

Capt. H. ELLERSHAW (Adjutant).

Hon. Lieut. C. H. FRAZIER (Quartermaster).

12th (Service) Battalion

Raised at the Barracks, Ashton-under-Lyne, in August, 1914. In the Second New Army. First training at Wool, under Lt.-Col. H. C. E. Westropp (now Brig.-Gen.), and afterwards under Lt.-Col. E. G. Harrison, C.B., D.S.O.

The Battalion joined the British Expeditionary Force in France, leaving England on 14th July, 1915. The first few days were spent at the overseas base in camp, the

Battalion afterwards moving north by road to Ondidou, where they were billetted until early in August, when they were ordered to Hooge, where they have since taken their share of trench work. Lt.-Col. Harrison was wounded while in command of the Battalion, Major Nash taking command in his absence.

Included among the present officers are:—

Lt.-Col. E. G. HARRISON, C.B., D.S.O. (Commanding).
Major E. J. MCFARLANE (Adjutant).
Hon. Lieut. G. RITT (Quartermaster).

13th (Service) Battalion

Raised at the Barracks, Ashton-under-Lyne, in September, 1914. In the 3rd New Army. Commenced training at Eastbourne, 19th September, 1914, and moved to Seaford (Sussex) on 29th September, 1914. The Battalion remained there until 3rd December, when they moved back into Eastbourne into billets. Between 2nd and 19th March, 1915, the Battalion was at Maidstone and Knockholt, moving to Seaford on the latter date. During June, July, and August it was in Aldershot refitting prior to sailing for France on 6th September, where they formed part of the British Expeditionary Force.

The Battalion arrived in the trenches seven days later, and until the 18th was attached to the 148th Brigade at Hebuterne for instruction. Between 22nd September and 21st October the Battalion occupied trenches at Foucaucourt on the Amiens-Peronne road. On 27th October they left Marseilles on the "Saturnia" and disembarked on 6th November at Salonika. For the next month they were training near Salonika, and have since then been engaged in digging trenches for the defence of the town and road making.

The Battalion is now with the Salonika Expeditionary Force. The casualties while in France were very small.

Among the present officers of the Battalion are:—

Lt.-Col. H. J. JONES, C.B., D.S.O., who has been in command since formation.
Capt. F. O. THORNE (Adjutant).
Lieut. F. O. MEDWORTH (Acting Quartermaster).

14th (Second Reserve) Battalion

Raised at the Barracks, Ashton-unde-Lyne, in November, 1914. Has a Wigan and District Pals Company. The

Battalion was in the 4th New Army as a Service Battalion, but has now been made a Reserve Battalion to the 11th, 12th, and 13th Service Battalions. The Battalion is stationed at Lichfield. Over one hundred officers are training with the Battalion.

Up to the end of 1915 over 80 officers and 900 N.C.O.'s and men have proceeded overseas as drafts to Service Battalions.

Among the present officers are:—

Lieut.-Col. T. M. GREER (Commanding).
Capt. J. J. MACC. GREER (Adjutant) .
Hon. Lieut. J. R. JONES (Quartermaster).

15th (Service) Battalion.

The formation of this Battalion was cancelled. A number of 2nd-Lieutenants have been posted to the Battalion, but they are all attached to other units of the Regiment for training or have proceeded overseas.

MANCHESTER CITY BATTALIONS (16th to 23rd inclusive)

The Battalions were raised in Manchester from warehouse and other employees in the City, by the Lord Mayor of Manchester (Sir D. MacCabe), assisted by a committee of gentlemen connected with the big commercial houses in the City. The first four Battalions formed the 111th Brigade, and were under Brig.-Gen. H. C. E. Westropp, who had Major C. L. R. Petrie, D.S.O., as Brigade Major. The remaining four form the 126th Brigade, under Brig.-Gen. F. J. Kempster, D.S.O.

Both Brigades Marched Past Lord Kitchener in Manchester on Sunday, March 21st, 1915, and were very highly praised by him.

The Brigades were afterwards re-numbered, and included in the 37th Division. The 24th (Oldham) Battalion came in in place of the 23rd Bantam Battalion.

16th (Service) Battalion (1st City)

Recruiting commenced on August 31st, 1914, at the Artillery Headquarters, Hyde Road, and the next day the

Lord Mayor attested over 600 men. The companies were arranged here, and the men put through their first recruit drills before moving to Heaton Park into tents. Huts were specially built in Heaton Park, and were occupied until early in April, 1915, when the Battaloin moved to Grantham, the Reserve Companies being left at Heaton Park to form the Battalion Depot. These Reserve Companies became part of the 25th (Reserve) Battalion on 7th September, 1915.

From Grantham the Battalion moved to Larkhill, near Salisbury and from there joined the British Expeditionary Force early in November, 1915. The Battalion has been in action while in France.

The training of the Battalion was under Lt.-Col. J. C. Crawford's direction up to 10th March, 1915, when he was appointed to command the 1st (Regular) Battalion of the Manchester Regiment. Lt.-Col. Crawford was succeeded by Major C. L. R Petrie, D.S.O., who is still in command of the Battalion.

Among the present officers of the Battalion are:—

Capt. E. G. SOTHAM (Adjutant).
Hon. Lieut. J. T. BALL (Quartermaster).

17th (Service) Battalion (2nd City)

Recruiting commenced on September 2nd, 1914, at the Artillery Headquarters, Hyde Road. The men were here posted to the companies, and put through the early stages of their training. After a long wait the Battalion was moved to Heaton Park into tents. Huts were afterwards provided. Heaton Park was left early in April, 1915, when the Battalion was moved to Grantham, the Reserve Companes being left behind to form the Battalion Depot. On September 7th, 1915, these Reserve Companies formed part of the 25th (Reserve) Battalion.

From Grantham the Battalion moved to Larkhill, near Salisbury, and from there joined the British Expeditionary Force early in November, 1915. The Battalion has been in action while in France. The training has been carried out under the direction of Lt.-Col. H. A. Johnson, who is still in command of the Battalion. Among the other officers are:—

Capt. C. L. MACDONALD (Adjutant).
Hon. Lieut. T. A. YARWOOD (Quartermaster).

18th (Service) Battalion (3rd City)

Recruited at the Albert Hall, Manchester, during the early portion of September, 1914. The men were posted to the companies at the City Hall, Deansgate, and afterwards went into quarters, which had been arranged for them, at the White City. The Battalion later moved into huts at Heaton Park. These were occupied until early in April, 1915, when the Battalion was moved to Grantham, the Reserve Companies being left behind to provide the Battalion Depot. On September 7th, 1915, these Reserve Companies were formed, with the Reserves of the 16th and 17th Battalions, into the 25th (Reserve) Battalion.

From Grantham the Battalion moved to Larkhill, near Salisbury, and from there joined the British Expeditionary Force early in November, 1915. The training has been carried out since the Battalion was formed under the direction of Lt.-Col. W. A. Fraser, who is still in command. Among the other officers of the Battalion are:—

Capt. G. E. HOARE (Adjutant).
Hon. Lieut. T. C. PIERCE (Quartermaster).

19th (Service) Battalion (4th City)

Recruited at the Albert Hall, Manchester, during the early portion of September, 1914. The early training under Lt.-Col. G. G. P. Heywood, who died shortly after his appointment, took place at the City Hall, Deansgate, and afterwards at Belle Vue. The Battaion moved into huts at Heaton Park in November, where they remained until early in April, 1915. On the Battalion moving to Grantham, the Reserve Companies were left at Heaton Park to form the Battalion Depot. On September 7th, 1915, these Reserve Companies became part of the 26th (Reserve) Battalion.

From Grantham the Battalion was moved to Lark Hill, near Salisbury, and from there joined the British Expeditionary Force early in November, 1915. Bt.-Col. E. A. Kettlewell followed Lt.-Col. Heywood in command of the Battalion, being succeeded, in June, 1915, by Lt.-Col. Sir H. B. Hill, Bt., who is still in command.

Among the present officers of the Battalion are:—

Capt. J. W. MYERS (Adjutant).
Hon. Lieut. J. O'MALLEY (Quartermaster).

20th (Service) Battalion (5th City)

Recruiting commenced at the Albert Hall on November 16th, 1914, and finished on the next day. The men were sent to Morecambe into billets, where they remained the whole of the winter. Early in April, 1915, the Battalion was moved to Grantham, the Reserve Companies going to Heaton Park, Manchester, to form the Battalion Depot. These Companies formed part of the 26th (Reserve) Battalion on its formation on September 7th, 1915.

The Service Battalion was afterwards moved from Grantham to Lark Hill, near Salisbury, and from there joined the Britsh Expeditionary Force early in November, 1915. The early training of the Battalion was under the direction of Bt.-Col. A. J. Arnold, D.S.O.

The following are among the present officers of the Battalion :—

Lt.-Col. S. MITCHELL (Commanding).
Capt. F. BRYANT (Adjutant).
Hon. Lieut. A. A. CAIN (Quartermaster).

21st (Service) Battalion (6th City)

Recruiting commenced at the Albert Hall on November 17th, and finished on the 21st. The men were sent to Morecambe into billets, where they remained the whole of the winter. Early in April, 1915, the Battalion was moved to Grantham,the Reserve Companies going to Heaton Park, Manchester, to form the Battalion Depot. These Companies formed part of the 26th (Reserve) Battalion on its formation on September 7th, 1915.

The Service Battalion was afterwards moved from Grantham to Lark Hill, near Salisbury, and from there joined the British Expeditionary Force early in November, 1915. The early training of the Battalion was under the direction of Bt.-Col. W. W. Norman, who is still in command.

Among the present officers of the Battalion are :—

Capt. H. J. BROOKS (Adjutant).
Hon. Lieut. R. WATERHOUSE (Quartermaster)

22nd (Service) Battalion (7th City)

Recruiting commenced at the Albert Hall on November 23rd, and finished on the 30th. The men were sent to

Morecambe into billets, where they remained the whole of the winter. Early in April, 1915, the Battalion was moved to Grantham, the Reserve Companies going to Heaton Park, Manchester, to form the Battalion Depot. These Companies formed part of the 27th (Reserve) Battalion on its formation on September 7th, 1915.

The Service Battalion was afterwards moved from Grantham to Lark Hill, near Salisbury, and from there joined the British Expeditionary Force early in November, 1915. The early training of the Battalion was under Lt.-Col. C. de C. Etheridge, D.S.O.

The following are among the present officers of the Battalion :—

Lt.-Col. P. WHETHAM (Commanding).
Capt. J. E. TOWNSEND (Adjutant).
Hon. Lieut. E. L. MAIDEN (Quartermaster).

23rd (Service) Battalion (8th City)

This Battalion is composed entirely of men who are between the heights of 5ft. 0in. and 5ft. 3in. Recruiting commenced on November 26th, 1914, and the Battalion was completed on December 2nd. The men were sent on enlistment to Morecambe, and were quartered in billets all the winter. Early in April, 1915, the Battalion was moved to Grantham, the Reserve Companies going to Heaton Park, Manchester, to form the Battalion Depot. These Reserve Companies formed part of the 27th (Reserve) Battalion on its formation on September 7th, 1915.

The Service Battalion was afterwards moved from Grantham to Lark Hill, near Salisbuy, and from there joined the British Expeditionary Force early in November, 19S15. The early training of the Battalion was carried out under the direction of Lt.-Col. Sir H. B. Hill, Bt.

The following are among the present officers of the Battaion :—

Lt.-Col. R. P. SMITH (in Command).
Capt. St. G. W. MILLER (Adjutant).
Hon. Lieut. L. CUNLIFFE (Quartermaster).

24th (Service) Battalion (Oldham)

Raised by the Mayor of Oldham in October and November, 1914, from men employed in the Odham district. Huts were built at Chatterton, near Oldham, for the

Battalion, and these were occupied during the winter. In April, 1915, the Battalion was moved to Grantham, and from there to Lark Hill, near Salisbury. Early in November, 1915, the Battalion joined the British Expeditionary Force. The early training was carried out under the direction of Lt.-Col. W. T. W. Scott.

The Reserve Companies were moved to Heaton Park in April, 1915, to form the Battalion Depot, and on September 7th formed part of the 27th (Reserve) Battalion.

The following are among the present officers of the Battalion :—

Lt.-Col. J. B. BATTEN (in Command).
Lieut. G. B. DEMPSEY (Adjutant).
Hon. Lieut. A .M. WINDER (Quartermaster).

25th (Local Reserve) Battalion

Formed on September 7th, 1915, at Heaton Park, Manchester, from the Reserve Companies of the 16th, 17th, and 18th (Service) Battalions. The Battalion was afterwards moved to Prees Heath, Shropshire, and on December 31st, 1915, to Southport, where they occupy billets.

The following are among the officers of the Battalion :—

Lt.-Col. F. R. MCCONNELL (in Command).
Capt. A. HARREY (Adjutant).
Hon. Lieut. C. W. BLACKFORD (Quartermaster).

26th (Local Reserve) Battalion

Formed on September 7th, 1915, at Heaton Park, Manchester, from the Reserve Companies of the 19th, 20th, and 21st (Service) Battalions. The Battalion was afterwards moved to Prees Heath, Shropshire, and on December 31st, 1915, to Southport, where they occupy billets.

The following are included in the officers of the Battalion :—

Bt.-Col. B. R. HAWES, C.B. (in Command).
Capt. C. JOYCE (Adjutant).
Hon. Lieut. T. B. HALL (Quartermaster).

27th (Local Reserve) Battalion

Formed on September 7th, 1915, at Heaton Park, Manchester, from the Reserve Companies of the 22nd, 23rd, and

24th (Service) Battalions. The Battalion was afterwards moved to Prees Heath, Shropshire, and on December 31st, 1915, to Southport, where they occupy billets.

The following are included in the officers of the Battalion :—

Lt.-Col. H. LEDWARD (in Command).

Capt. W. PAYNE (Adjutant).

1st GARRISON BATTALION

This Battalion was formed towards the end of 1915, and is composed of officers, N.C.O.'s, and men who are permanently unfit for active service abroad, but are fit for garrison service overseas. The Battalion is stationed at Knowsley Park, Prescot, under the command of Lt.-Col. H. W. K. Bretherton.

1st CADET BATTALION

This Battalion, which was founded in 1888, is now under the command of Captain G. F. Faulkner, Recruiting Officer, Manchester Recruiting Area.

Lieut.-Col. H. Ledward, the Commanding Officer, and all the other officers (except one who is unfit) serving at the commencement of the War are now in the New Armies or the Territorial Force.

A considerable number of N.C.O.'s and men have enlisted in various branches of the Service.

The present officers are :—

Capt. G. F. FALKNER, Cadet Major (in Command).

Lieut. J. HAMER, Cadet Captain.

Cadet 2nd-Lieut. E. HULME.

Cadet 2nd-Lieut. J. A. O'BRIEN.

Cadet 2nd-Lieut. K. BURKE.

Cadet 2nd-Lieut. A. ROGERSON.

Cadet 2nd-Lieut. A. L. ALDRIDGE (Quartermaster).

The Headquarters are in Poplar Street, Ashton Old Road, Manchester.

HONOURS, DECORATIONS MEDALS, Etc.

Awarded to Officers and men of the Manchester Regiment during the present War, for services in the field :—

Awarded Victoria Cross—

Lieut. W. T. Forshaw, 9th Bn. (T.F.)
2nd-Lieut. James Leach.
9016 Sergt. John Hogan, 2nd Bn.
168 Private I. Smith, 1st Bn.

To be Brevet Colonel—

Lt.-Col. E. P. Strickland, C.M.G., D.S.O.

To be Companion of the Order of the Bath—

Lt.-Col. H. L. James.

To be Brevet Lt.-Colonel—

Major W. P. E. Newbigging, D.S.O.

To be Brevet Major—

Capt. P. V. Holberton.
Capt. J. N. Brown, 7th Bn. (T.F.).

To be Companion of the Order of St. Michael & St. George—

Lt.-Col. (temp.) C. R. Pilkington, 6th Bn. (T.F.)
Major R. S. Weston.

To be Companion of the Distinguished Service Order—

Major (temp. Lt.-Col.) C. S. Worthington, 6th Bn. (T.F.)
Major C. M. Thornycroft.
Capt., now Major W. K. Evans.

Awarded Military Cross—

Lieut. V. A. Albrecht.
Lieut. (now Capt) B. G. Atkin (Attd. W. Afr. R.).
2nd-Lieut. M. K. Burrows, 5th Bn. (T.F.)
Lieut., now Capt. (temp.) A. B. Close-Brooks (Spec. Res.).
2nd-Lieut. (temp. Lieut.) S. Coller, 6th Bn. (T.F.).
2nd-Lieut. C. E. Cooke, 9th Bn. (T.F.).
Capt. (temp.) G. T. Ewen (Spec. Res.).
Capt. (temp. Major) A. E. F. Fawcus, 7th Bn. (T.F.).
2nd-Lieut. L. Findlater (Spec. Res.).
Capt., now Major N. B. de L. Forth.
Lieut., now Capt. W. R. Freeman.
Lieut. H. J. Gwyther (Spec. Res.).
Capt. (temp.) H. A. Hammick, 6th Bn. (T.F.).
Lieut., now Capt. J. S. Harper.
2nd-Lieut. (temp. Lieut.) H. Hassall, 10th Bn. (T.F.).
Capt., now Major J. R. Hellis.
Capt. (temp.) G. S. Henderson.
Capt. C. D. Irwin.
Capt. B. V. Mair.

Lieut., now Capt. E. L. Musson (Attd. K. Afr. Rif.).
Lieut., now Capt. (temp.) R. H .R. Parminter.
Capt. J. M. B. Sanders (Adjutant), 1/5th Bn. (T.F.).
Lieut., now Capt. A. J. Scully.
Capt. (temp.) W. N. Shipster.
2nd-Lieut. (temp. apt.) O. J. Sutton, 9th Bn. (T.F.).
2nd-Lieut., now Capt. G. W. Williamson (Spec. Res.).
Lieut. R. G. Wood, 9th Bn. (T.F.).
No. 3154 Reg. Sgt.-Maj. W. Finney.

Promoted 2nd Lieutenant—
Sergt. T. Ruddy.
Act. Co. Sgt.-Major H. M. Paton.
Sgt.-Major P. Murphy.
Act. Sgt.-Major H. Franklin.
Act. Sgt.-Major S. Taylor.

Mentioned in Despatches—

Lt.-Col. H. L. James, C.B.	19 Oct. 14.
Major W. P. E. Newbigging, D.S.O.	19 Oct. 14 and 15 Oct. 15.
Capt. F. H. Dorling	19 Oct. 14.
Capt. F. S. Nisbet (since dead)	do.
Capt. H. Knox	do.
Lieut. J. H. L. Reade (since dead)	do.
Lieut. J. S. Harper	do.
2nd-Lieut. J. Leach, V.C.	22 Dec. 14 & 17 Feb. 15.
Lt.-Col. E. P .Strickland, C.M.G., D.S.O.	17 Feb. 15.
Capt. W. K. Evans, D.S.O.	17 Feb. 15 & 5 Apr. 15.
Lieut. A. J. Scully	17 Feb. 15.
Lieut. E. R. Vanderspar (since dead)	do.
Lieut. (temp.) S. D. Connell (since dead)	do.
2nd-Lieut. G. Dixon	do.
2nd-Lieut. R. T. Miller	do.
2nd-Lieut. G. W. Williamson	do.
Qr.-Mr. and Hon. Lt. W. L. Connery	do.
Lt.-Col. (temp.) B. D. L. G. Anley, D.S.O.	5 Apr. 15.
Lt.-Col. H. W. E. Hitchins (since dead)	do. & 15 Oct. 15.
Major R. S. Weston	5 Apr. 15.
Capt. J. R. Heelis	do.
Capt. W. N. Humphreys	do.
Capt. C. D. Irwin	do.
Capt. B. V. Mair	do.
Capt. A. K. D. Tillard	do.
Lieut. A. Barker	do.
Lieut. W. R. Freeman	do.

Lieut. R. H. R. Parminter do.
Lieut. H. T. Pomfret do.
Capt. C .A. Bolton 20 May 15.
Lt.-Col. H. C. Darlington, 5 Bn. (T.F.) 22 Sept. 15.
Lt.-Col. C. R. Pilkington, 6 Bn. (T.F.) do.
Lt.-Col. W. G. Heys, 8 Bn. (T.F.) (since dead) do.
Major C. S. Worthington, 6 Bn. (T.F.) do.
and 11 Dec. 15.
Major J. H. Staueacre, 7 Bn. (T.F.) do.
Capt. W. T. Woods, 5 Bn. (T.F.) do.
Capt. P. V. Holberton do.
and 11 Dec. 15.
Capt. H. B. Pilkington, 6 Bn. (T.F.) (since dead) do.
Capt. (temp.) H. A. Hammick, 6 Bn. (T.F.) do.
and 11 Dec. 15.
Capt. P. H. Creagh, 7 Bn. (T.F.) do.
Capt. E. G. W. Oldfield, 8 Bn. (T.F.) (since dead) do.
Capt. H. J. Rose, 8 Bn. (T.F.) (since dead) do.
Capt. H. D. Standring, 8 Bn. (T.F.) (since dead) do.
Capt. H. C. Lings, 9 Bn. (T.F.) do.
Lieut. G. S. James, 5 Bn. (T.F.) do.
Lieut. R. G. Wood, 9 Bn. (T.F.) do.
Lieut. (temp.) O. J. Sutton, 9 Bn. (T.F.) do.
2nd-Lieut. M. K. Burrows, 5 Bn. (T.F.) do.
Major C. M. Thornycroft, D.S.O. (Spec. Res.) 15 Oct. 15.
Bt.-Major (temp. Lt.-Col.) E. G. Harrison, C.B., D.S.O. do.
Capt. E. A. Buchan, D.S.O. (since dead) do.
Capt. (temp.) A. B. Close-Brooks (Spec. Res.) do.
Capt. (temp.) G. T. Ewen (Spec. Res.) do.
Capt. H. J. Gwyther (Spec. Res.) do.
Capt. J. R. Gwyther (Spec. Res.) do.
Capt. (temp.) G. S. Henderson do.
Capt. (temp.) W. N. Shipster do.
Lieut. V. A. Albrecht do.
2nd-Lieut. L. Findlater (Spec. Res.) do.
Capt. J. M. B. Sanders, 5 Bn. (T.F.) 11 Dec. 15
Capt. P. H. Creagh, D.S.O., 7 Bn. (T.F.) do.
Capt. (temp. Major) A. E. F. Fawcus, 7 Bn. (T.F.) do.
Lieut. W. T. Forshaw, V.C., 9 Bn. (T.F.) do.
2nd-Lieut. P. C. Clayton, 5 Bn. (T.F.) do.
2nd-Lieut. (temp. Lieut.) S. Collier, Bn. (T.F.) do.
2nd-Lieut. A. N. Milne, 6 Bn. (T.F.) (since dead) do.
2nd-Lieut. E. P. Hartshorn, 6 Bn. (T.F.) do.
2nd-Lieut. (tem. Capt.) O. J. Sutton, 9 Bn. (T.F.) do.

No.	Name	Date
	2nd-Lieut. C. E. Cooke, 9 Bn. (T.F.)	do.
	2nd-Lieut. H. Hassall, 10 Bn. (T.F.)	do.
—	C. S. Maj. Wood, 2 Bn.	19 Oct. 14.
—	C. Qr.-Mr.-Sgt. J. Morris, 2 Bn.	do.
—	Sgt. Winterbottom, 2 Bn.	do.
—	,, M. Richards, 2 Bn.	do.
—	,, Rice, 2 Bn.	do.
	Pte. Hodge, 2 Bn.	do.
4722	C. S. Maj. R. Wilson, 1 Bn.	17 Feb. 15.
9016	Sgt. J. Hogan, V.C., 2 Bn.	do.
779	,, H. Massey	do.
666	,, T. Ruddy	do.
888	,, F. Snow, 2 Bn.	17 Feb 15 & 5 Apr. 15.
899	Cpl. T. Duffy, 1 Bn.	17 Feb. 15.
1175	,, C. W. Matters	do.
1015	L/Cpl. W. Coleshill, 1 Bn.	do.
2263	,, F. Brooks	do.
2016	Pte. A. A. Metcalfe, 1 Bn.	do.
906	,, J. Mitchell, 1 Bn.	do.
6047	,, W. Cleaver	do.
3154	Reg. Sgt.-Maj. W. Finney, 1 Bn.	5 Apr. 15.
5522	Co. Qr.-Mr.-Sgt. R. J. Stanley, 1 Bn. (killed)	do.
3649	Qr.-Mr.-Sgt. J. T. Connery, 2 Bn.	do.
988	Sgt. C. Boardman, 2 Bn.	do.
1367	Act. Sgt. E. Kent, 2 Bn.	do.
8050	Act. Sgt. W. H. Robinson, 2 Bn. (killed)	do.
269	Pte. R. Dakin, 2 Bn.	do.
2443	,, Pte. G. Gillagan, 2 Bn.	do.
213	Sgt. S. W. Whittle, 1/5 Bn. (T.F.) (Killed)	26 Aug. 15.
449	L/Cpl. F. Catterall, 1/5 Bn. (T.F.)	do.
44	Co. Sgt-Maj. F. Hay, 1/6 Bn. (T.F.)	do.
155	Co. Sgt.-Maj. J. Hurdley, 1/6 Bn. (T.F.)	do.
1184	L/Cpl. B. C. Cory, 1/6 Bn. (T.F.)	do.
1045	L/Cpl. A. Senior, 1/6 Bn. (T.F.)	do.
1801	Pte. A. B. Smith, 1/6 Bn. (T.F.)	do.
2046	,, N. T. Wills, 1/6 Bn. (T.F.)	do.
1738	,, A. M. Doig, 1/6 Bn. (T.F.)	do.
1493	,, R. Cutter, 1/6 Bn. (T.F.)	do.
2478	,, R. Nashim, 1/6 Bn. (T.F.)	do.
2049	L/Cpl. H. S. McCartney, 1/7 Bn. (T.F.)	do.
1536	Pte. J. Connolly, 1/7 Bn. (T.F.)	do.
1904	L/Cpl. J. Frank, 1/7 Bn. (T.F.)	do.
3757	Sgt.-Maj. P. Murphy, 1/8 Bn. (T.F.) (Attd. from Manch. R.)	do.

306	Co. Sgt.-Maj. E. Garside, 1/8 Bn. (T.F.) (Killed)	do.
397	Cpl. J. Williams, 1/8 Bn. (T.F.)	do.
2093	Pte. G. Evans, 1/8 Bn. (T.F.)	do.
1155	,, W. Burke, 1/9 Bn. (T.F.)	do.
1904	,, J. E. Taylor, 1/9 Bn. (T.F.)	do.
969	,, T. Weston, 1/9 Bn. (T.F.)	do.
1428	,, G. A. Smith, 1/9 Bn. (T.F.)	do.
6968	C. S. Maj. J. Harrison	15 Oct. 15.
4811	Sgt. (Act. S.M.) C. Yeates	do.
4306	Sgt. C. Ross	do.
1136	L/Cpl. J. H. Worcester	do.
3913	Pte. P. Logan	do.
2659	Pte. R. W. Ward, 1/5 Bn. (T.F.)	11 Dec. 15.
890	Pte. R. Bent, 1/5 Bn. (T.F.)	do.
815	L/Sgt. A. McDonald, 1/6 Bn. (T.F.)	do.
1825	Pte. J. Murphy, 1/6 Bn. (T.F.)	do.
2410	Cpl. F. White, 1/7 Bn. (T.F.)	do.
1590	Sgt. W. McLaughlin, 1/7 Bn. (T.F.)	do.
180	Sgt. S. Bayley, 1/9 Bn. (T.F.)	do.
2103	Cpl. T. Picford, 1/9 Bn. (T.F.)	do.
2148	L/Cpl. S. Pearson, 1/9 Bn. (T.F.)	do.
1294	Pte. F. Chevalier, 1/9 Bn. (T.F.)	do.
1160	Drummer H. Broadhurst, 1/9 Bn. (T.F.)	do.
8008	Sgt. R. E. Povah, 11 (S.) Bn.	do.
3574	Pte. (Act. Cpl.) J. Gregory, 11 (S.) Bn.	do.
7891	L/Cpl. C. McLean, 11 (S.) Bn.	do.
3661	Pte. J. Benson, 11 (S.) Bn.	do.
3009	Pte. F. Coates, 11 (S.) Bn.	do.

Awarded Distinguished Conduct Medal—

2892 Cpl. F. Baddley, 1/10 Bn. (T.F.)
1395 Sgt. J. Bates, 1 Bn.
180 Cpl. S. Bayley, 1/9 Bn. (T.F.).
824 L/Cpl. R. Benson, 1 Bn.
890 Pte. R. Bent, 1/5 Bn. (T.F.)
2244 L/Cpl. G. T. Beuan, 1 Bn.
9143 Pte. A. D. Bloor, 2 Bn.
1015 Act. Sgt. W. Coleshill, 1 Bn.
2363 L/Cpl. F. Crooks, 1 Bn.
1328 Pte. J. Curry, 1 Bn.
1493 Pte G. R. Cutter, 1/6 Bn. (T.F.
1843 Pte. A. Davies, 1/5 Bn. (T.F.)
95 Acting Cpl. J. Deruin, 1 Bn.
8581 Sgt. J. Devonshire, 1 Bn.
8878 Cpl. H. Dixon, 2 Bn.

1738 Pte .A. M. Doig, 1/6 Bn. (T.F.)
899 Cpl. T. Duffy, 1 Bn.
2086 Pte. E. J. Edwards, 1 Bn.
239 L/Cpl. M. Flannery, 1 Bn.
1056 L/Cpl. C. A. Gavins, 1 Bn.
2393 Pte. W. Glenn, 1 Bn.
969 Sgt. H. Grantham, 1/9 Bn. (T.F.)
3574 A/Cpl. J. Gregory, 11 (S.) Bn.
7280 C.S. Maj. H. Harland, 1 Bn.
232 Sgt. F. Harrison, 2 Bn.
2016 Cpl. (now 2nd-Lieut.) E. P. Hartshorn, 1/6 Bn. (T.F.)
2478 Pte. R. Hashim, 1/6 Bn. (T.F.)
44 Co./Sgt. Maj. F. Hay, 1/6 Bn. (T.F.).
7624 C.S. Maj. H. Heywood, 1 Bn.
2179 Pte. T. Higgins, 1 Bn.
2322 Pte. A. Hilton, 1/5 Bn. (T.F.)
155 C.S.M. J. Hindley, 1/6 Bn. (T.F.)
— L/Cpl. (Acting Sgt.) C. F .G. Humphries, 1 Bn.
101 Pte. W. Kelly, 1 Bn.
1787 Cpl. J. Le Cras, 1 Bn.
7657 C.S. Major J. Lemon, 2 Bn.
9005 Co.-Sgt.-Maj .E. Maquire, 1 Bn.
1118 Sgt. J. Martin, 1 Bn.
1405 Cpl. J. McCartney, 1/5 Bn. (T.F.).
— L/Sgt. A. McDonald, 1/6 Bn. (T.F.)
1590 Cpl. C. McLaughlin, 1/8 Bn. (T.F.)
8673 Pte. W. McMullen, 2 Bn.
2016 Pte. A. A. Metcalfe, 1 Bn.
906 Pte. J. Mitchell, 1 Bn.
40 L/Sgt. H. Mort, 1/7 Bn. (T.F.)
— Pte. J. Murphy, 1/6 Bn. (T.F.)
2148 Pte. O'Connor, 1/8 Bn. (T.F.)
6141 Sgt.-Maj. J. Parker, 2 Bn.
2148 L/Cpl. S. Pearson, 1/9 Bn. (T.F.)
2103 L/Cpl. T. Pickford, 1/9 Bn. (T.F.)
1228 Pte. F. Richardson, 1 Bn.
2263 Pte. M. Richardson, 1/7 Bn. (T.F.).
1045 L/Cpl. W. A. Senior, 1/6 Bn. (T.F.)
8737 Pte. J. E. Shalliker, 2 Bn.
1358 L/Cpl. C. J. Silvester, 1/9 Bn. (T.F.)
888 Co.-Sgt.-Maj. F. Snow, 2 Bn.
2109 Pte. W. Stanton, 1/8 Bn. (T.F.).
2023 Pte. S. Stockton, 1/5 Bn. (T.F.)
2078 Pte. A. Summers, 1 Bn.
301 Pte. J. Ward, 2 Bn.

2659 Pte. R. W. Ward, 1/5 Bn. (T.F.)
7424 Sgt. H. Waters, 2 Bn.
2410 Pte. F. White, 1/7 Bn. (T.F.)
1114 L/Cpl. A. Willis.
1073 L/Cpl. T. Willis, 2 Bn.
4722 C.S. Major R. Wilson, 1 Bn.
1745 L/Cpl. C. C. J. Wood, 1 Bn.
936 Cpl. W. Wrixton.

Awarded Croix de Chevalier (France)—
Major (temp. Lt.-Col.) N. Luxmore.
Capt. (temp. Major) A. F. F. Fawcus (T.F.)
Lieut. A. Barker.

Awarded Croix de Guerre—
Lieut. R. G. Wood, 9 Bn. (T.F.)
9005 Co S. Maj. E. Maquire, 1 Bn.
2957 Pte. J. Grimes, 1/5 Bn. (T.F.)
779 Sgt. A. Massey, 2 Bn.

Awarded Medaille Militaire—
C. Qr.-Mr. Sgt. J. Morris.
1130 Sgt. A. McDowell, 1/6 Bn. (T.F.)

Awarded Cross of the Order of St. George of Russia—
899 Cpl. T. Duffy (3rd Class).
4884 Sgt. J. C. Tallantire, 2 Bn. (4th Class).
168 Pte. I. Smith, V.C., 1 Bn. (4th Class).

Awarded Medal of St. George of Russia—
5865 A/Sgt. E. Stockdale, 2 Bn. (1st Class).
824 L/Cpl. R. Benson, 1 Bn. (3rd Class).
1733 L/Cpl. A. Whiteley, 2 Bn. (3rd Class).
1745 Cpl. C. J. Wood, 1 Bn. (4th Class).

CASUALTIES.

The War of 1915-16.

Regular, Special Reserve, and New Army

(The Casualties of the Territorial Battalions are shown separately under each Battalion).

OFFICERS KILLED OR DIED FROM WOUNDS RECEIVED IN ACTION.

Baldwin, Brig.-Gen. (temp.) A. H. 10 Aug. 15.
Bates, Major (temp.) H. C., 11 (S.) Bn. 7-11 Aug. 15.

BEDFORD, 2nd Lieut. C. C., 1 Bn. 13 Mar. 16.
BELL, 2nd Lieut. (temp.) E. V., 11 (S.) Bn. 7-11 Aug. 15
BENTLEY, 2nd Lieut. C. L., 2 Bn. 28-29 Oct. 14.
BROCKLEHURST, 2nd Lieut. (temp.) J. S., 14 (Res.) Bn. attd. 11 (S.) Bn. 1 Nov. 15.
BRODRIBB, Lieut. W. C., 2 Bn. 26 Aug. 14.
CAMPBELL, Lieut. (temp.) H., 11 (S.) Bn. 22 Aug. 15.
CAULFIELD, Lieut. J. C., 2 Bn. 18 Nov. 14.
CHITTENDEN, 2nd Lieut. A. G. B., 2 Bn. 9 Sept. 14.
CONNELL, Lieut. S. D., 1 Bn. 21 Dec. 14.
CREAGH, Capt. L., 1 Bn. 20-21 Dec. 14.
CURTIS, 2nd Lieut. W., 1 Bn. 13 or 14 Mar. 15.
DAVIDSON, Lieut. R. I. M., 1 Bn. 24 Nov. 14.
DAVIES, 2nd Lieut. R. C., 1 Bn. 11 Mar. 16.
DUNLOP, Capt. F. C. S., 1 Bn. 8 Nov. 14.

FARRAR, 2nd Lieut. H. R. 24 Dec. 14.
FISHER, Capt. H., D.S.O., 1 Bn. 16 Dec. 14.
FOWKE, Capt. M., 2 Bn. 26 Aug. 14.
GUDGEON, 2nd Lieut. S., 3 Bn. (Spec. Res.) attd. 2 Bn. 14 May 15.
HALLER, Capt. (temp.) J. H. L., E. Surr. R. attd. 2 Bn.
HEALEY, 2nd Lieut. P., 3 Bn. (Spec. Res.) attd. 1 Bn. L. North Lanc. R. Oct. 15.
HEYWOOD, 2nd Lieut. H., 1 Bn. 25 Sept. 15.
HITCHIN, Lt.-Col. H. W. E., 1 Bn. 26 Apr. 15.
HORRIDGE, 2nd Lieut. R., 2 Bn. 17 Nov. 14.
JOHNSTON, 2nd Lieut. (temp.) R. L., 17 (S.) Bn. 13 Dec. 15.
JONES, 2nd Lieut. (temp.) T. A. E. E., 11 (S.) Bn. 7-11 Aug. 15.
LAITHWAITE, Lieut. (temp.) J., 20 (S.) Bn. 24 Feb. 16.
LEE, Brig.-Gen. (temp.) N. (Hon.Col. 6 Bn.) 22 June 15.
LYNCH, Capt. R. F., 1 Bn. 11 Mar. 16.
MACKAY, 2nd Lieut. C. L., 5 Bn. Worcester R. attd. 2 Bn. 7 June 15.
MARSLAND, Lieut. (temp.) S. H. 11 (S.) Bn. 7-11 Aug. 15.
MARTEN, 2nd Lieut. H. H., 2 Bn. 13 Aug. 15.
MCKIEVER, 2nd Lieut. V. C., 3 Bn. (Spec. Res.) attd. 2 Bn. 18 May 15.
NELSON, 2nd Lieut. (temp.) J. L., 18 (S.) Bn. 10 Mar. 16.
NICHOLSON, 2nd Lieut. —, Cheshire R. attd. 2 Bn. — Nov. 14.
NISBET, Capt. F. S., 2 Bn. 26 Aug. 14.

NORMAN, Lieut. S. S., 1 Bn. 20-21 Dec. 14.
PARKER, Capt. E. D., 2 Bn. 20 Mar. 1915.
PARKER, Lieut. —, R.A.M.C. attd. 11 (S.) Bn. 7-11 Aug. 15.
PIERCE, Capt. W. G. K., 2 Bn. 26-27 Oct. 14.
PYMAN, Capt. J., attd. from 3 Bn. Bord. R. 18 Nov. 14.
READE, Lieut. J. H. L., 2 Bn. 28-29 Oct. 14.
REID, 2nd Lieut. W. M., 23 (S.) Bn. 27 Feb. 16.
ROBERTS, 2nd Lieut. G. B., Indian Army attd. 1 Bn. 11 May 15.
ROBINSON, Lieut. K., M.B., R.A.M.C. attd. 12 (S.) Bn. 27 Sept. 15.
RYMER, Capt. (temp.) J. H., 11 (S.) Bn. 7-11 Aug. 15.
SAPORTAS, Lieut. (temp.) H. A., 2 Bn. 16 July 15.
SILLERY, Major J. J. D., 11 (S.) Bn. 7-11 Aug. 15.
SMITH, Lieut. (temp.) J. H. M., 2 Bn. 9 Sept. 14.
STOKOE, 2nd Lieut. (temp.) J. C., 14 (Res.) Bn. attd. 6 Bn. N. Lanc. R. 11 Dec. 15.
TILLARD, Capt. A. G., 2 Bn. 20 Oct. 14.
TONGE, 2nd Lieut. (temp.) W. R., 17 (S.) Bn. 12 Jan. 16
TRUEMAN, Capt. C. FITZ G. H., 2 Bn. 26 Aug. 14.
VANDERSPAR, Lieut. E. R., 2 Bn. 24 June 15.
WALKER, 2nd Lieut. R. F., 2 Bn. 21 Oct. 14.
WASHINGTON, 2nd Lieut. J. N., attd. R.F.C. 2 Oct. 15.
WICKHAM, Lieut. (local Capt.) T. S., D.S.O., 1 Bn. 25 Aug. 14.
WILKINS, 2nd Lieut. A. R., 3 Bn. (Spec. Res.) attd. 1 Bn. 11 Mar. 16.
WILSON, 2nd Lieut. A. K., 1 Bn. 20 Mar. 15.

ACCIDENTALLY KILLED.

JUKES, Lieut. (temp.) M. E. E., 14 (Res.) Bn. 4 Sept. 15
TOWNSEND, 2nd Lieut. (temp.) A. E., 18 (S.) Bn. 26 Nov. 15.

DIED.

BERTRAM, Major W., 11 (S.) Bn. 18 Feb. 15.
HADFIELD, Lieut. (temp.) J. R., 13 (S.) Bn. 22 Mar. 16.
HEYWOOD, Col. B. C. P., T.D., 19 (S.) Bn. 29 Oct. 14.

OFFICERS MISSING.

BALSHAW, 2nd Lieut. W., 2 Bn. from 26 Aug. 14.
BAXTER, Lieut. (temp.) P. R. E., 1 Bn. from 11 Mar. 16
BURDON, Lieut. J., 1 Bn. from 13 Mar. 16.
EWEN, Capt. (temp.) G. T., 3 Bn. (Spec. Res.) attd. 1 Bn. from 11 Mar. 16.

GLEN, 2nd Lieut. D. A., attd. R.F.C., from 30 Dec. 15.
LANE, 2nd Lieut. E. A. M. 1 Bn. from 11 Mar. 16.
MANSERGH, Capt. W. G., 2 Bn., from 26 Aug. 14.
MORRIS, 2nd Lieut. C. 1 Bn. from 11 Mar. 16.
OWEN, Lieut. A. P., 3 Bn. (Spec. Res.) attd. 1 Bn. from 11 Mar. 16.
ROBINSON, 2nd Lieut. A. H., 1 Bn., from 18 June 15.

OFFICERS WHO ARE "PRISONERS OF WAR."

BROWN, 2nd Lieut. A. W., 3 Bn. and R.F.C., from 11 Nov. 15.
BURROWS, 2nd Lieut. R. F. G., 2 Bn., from 26 Aug. 14.
BUTLER, 2nd Lieut. W. E., 2 Bn., from 26 Aug. 14.
MILLER, Capt. R. T., 3 Bn. (Spec. Res.) attd. 2 Bn., from 26 Aug. 14.
MORLEY, Capt. C., 2nd Bn., from 26 Aug. 14.
WYMER, Capt. G. P., 2 Bn., from 26 Aug. 14.

N.C.O.'S AND MEN OF THE 1ST, 2ND, 3RD, AND 4TH BATTALIONS KILLED OR DIED OF WOUNDS RECEIVED IN ACTION.

Date List Published.		
27 10 14.	2/9227	L/Cpl. T. Comer.
	2/176	Pte. T. Cowley.
	2/126	Pte. J. Howard.
	2754	Pte. A. aines.
	2/9441	Pte. F. Lord.
	2/2528	Pte. A. Mangan.
	2/9873	Sergt. A. G. Rehm.
	2/2324	L/Cpl. J. Rourke.
	2/271	Pte. R. Stubbs.
	2/78	Pte. J. Sturt.
	2/2187	Cpl. E. Walker.
	2/2614	Pte. W. Andrews (d.w.)
	2398	Pte. E. Clayton (d.w.)
17 11 14.	2/9836	Cpl. J .Cockrane (d.w.)
18 11 14.	2/9893	Pte. W. Burns.
	2/9427	Pte. J. Dillon.
	2/2657	Pte. J. Flannery.
	2/7984	Pte. R. Furnival.
	2/410	Pte. H. Hilton.
	2/8545	Pte. G. Leadsom.
	2/63	Pte. R. McKew.
	2/2027	Cpl. W. T. Marsh.
	2/386	L/Cpl. W. Massey.

Date List Published.		
16 12 14.	2/2303	L/Cpl. W. Bradshaw(d.w.)
	9595	Pte. J. Hibbert (d.w.)
	9586	Pte. F. Hirst (d.w.)
19 12 14.	9260	Pte. J. Broomhead.
	8825	Pte. J. Duke.
	2792	Pte. W. Gribbin.
	2692	Pte. W. Nelson.
	689	Pte. F. Hanlon.
	8066	Pte. W. Stanley.
	9213	Pte. W. Shann (d.w.)
	2/2436	Pte. J. Carter (d.w.)
	2/249	Pte. T. Powell (d.w.)
19 12 14.	2/8956	Pte. F. Woodhead (d.w.)
23 12 14.	2/9280	Pte. W. Browne.
	2/9639	Cpl. J. Clarke.
	2/8760	Pte. W. Cook.
	2/2060	Pte. G. Corbett.
	2/9503	Pte. W. Dennison.
	2/9543	L/Cpl. W. Henshaw.
	2/8692	Pte. E. Hutchinson.
	2/9754	Pte. G. Jackson.
	2/9606	Pte. W. Johnstone.
	2/86	Pte. W. Letford.

Date List Published.		
	2/8731	Co.-Sgt.-Mjr. J. Morris (d.w)
18 11 14.	2/226	Cpl. E. Seall.
	2/8670	Pte. T. Walkden.
19 11 14.	2/9332	Pte. J. Wyche.
20 11 14.	2/9498	Pte. T. Johnson.
	2/2115	L/Cpl. A. Kenderick.
	2/2401	Pte. H. Larrard.
	2/2655	Pte. G. Turner.
	2/2546	Pte. J. Waterson.
	2/9594	Sergt. P. Rothwell (d.w.)
21 11 14.	2/8942	Pte. J. Cooke (d.w.)
23 11 14.	2403	Pte. A. W. Andrews (d.w.)
27 11 14.	2/6365	Cpl. J. Murray.
1 12 14.	2/9250	Pte. W. Hilton (d.w.)
	2/8888	Pte. J. Tomlinson (d.w.)
4 12 4.	8035	Pte. T. Jackson (d.)
5 12 14.	2/2595	Pte. G. Brickman (d.w.)
7 12 14.	2/303	Pte. H. Richards (d.w.)
9 12 14.	6689	Cpl. W. Gregory (d.w.)
	2/439	Pte. J. J. O'Brien (d.w.)
	1/9656	Pte. J. Bradbury.
8 1 15.	1/7935	Pte. R. Bradshaw.
	1/1952	Pte. W. Burgess.
	2/5782	Pte. J. Cain.
	8212	Pte. —. Chadderton.
	2/2650	Pte. F. Clark.
	2/7997	Pte. J. Connor.
	2/8869	Pte. C. England.
	2/8718	Pte. W. G. Grinstead.
	2/1213	Cpl. A. Hopson.
	2/9420	Pte. A. Leonard.
	2/2550	Pte. J. Leonard.
	2/9279	Pte. J. McKeowan.
	2/9736	Pte. J. McManns.
	2/8632	Pte. H. Nowell.
	8616	Pte. J. O'Donnell.
	2/8198	Pte. M. O'Mara.
	2/9168	Pte. G. Scott.
	2/2725	Pte. W. Walker.
13 1 15.	2/2202	Pte. C. J. Claxton (d.w.)
18 1 15.	1/234	Cpl. T. Barrett.
	1/9102	Pte. J. Cowan
	1/1353	Pte. A. Holland.
	1/1725	Pte. W. Redford.
	1/2331	Pte. R. Taylor.
	1/897	L/Cpl. A. Walker.
	2/62	L/Cpl. H. Hughes (d.w.)
	1/2099	L/Cpl. H. Windle (d.w.)
19 1 15.	1/1999	L/Cpl. W. Barnard.
	1/1622	L/Cpl. J. Connock.
	2/512	Cpl. P. Faulkner.

Date List Published.		
	2/413	Pte. T. Melia.
	2/375	Pte. J. Moir.
	2/2452	Pte. H. Newton.
	2/2530	Pte. G. Percy.
	2/2507	Pte. F. Preston.
	2/2626	Pte. J. Pritchard.
	2/6507	Sergt. T. Rice.
	2/9161	Pte. H. Saxon.
	2/7960	Pte. J. Woods.
29 12 14.	1/955	Pte. J. Butterworth.
	1/2399	Pte. R. Lawler.
	1/7729	Sergt. R. Shaw.
	1/1797	Pte. G. Parkinson (d.w.)
6 1 15.	1696	Pte. McSweeney.
	1/2256	Pte. J. Ogden.
	2/1037	Pte. C. Rogers.
	1647	Pte. E. Thompson.
	1/1120	Pte. F. Watts.
8 1 15.	1/49	Pte. J. Beresford.
	179	Sergt. J. Borth.
	1/5876	Pte. A. Ride.
	1/1007	Pte. F. Robinson.
	1/2418	Pte. C. J. Shennan.
	1/1834	Pte. M. P. Smith.
	1/2239	Pte. R. Smith.
	1/1450	Pte. T. Spike.
	1/742	Pte. W. Thomas.
	1/2010	Pte. A. Taite.
	1/200	Pte. J. Walker.
	1/1929	Pte. J. Walwork.
	1/2173	Pte. D. Watts.
	1/1873	Pte. E. White.
19 1 15.	1/2114	Pte. J. McDonald.
	1/1587	Pte. C. Ormonde.
	1/9810	Pte. W. Plant.
	1/1729	Pte. T. Sandiford.
5 2 15.	2/1842	Pte. I. L. Jutsum (d.w.)
	4722	Co.-Sgt. R. Wilson (d.w.)
9 2 15.	6880	Pte. J. Bradley.
	8927	Pte. J. Hannon.
	189	L/Cpl. W. Gill.
11 2 15.	1/1794	Pte. J. Edmondson.
	2/7241	Pte. R. Kent.
	2/9258	L/Cpl. E. Kirivan.
	1/1907	Pte. W. Light.
	2/1814	Sergt. J. T. McGarry.
12 2 15.	2/5827	Pte. F. Battie.
	2/9068	Pte. W. Clarke (d.w.)
15 2 15.	1/1801	Pte. S. E. Warwick (d.w.)
	1/1124	Pte. T. Cowshill.
16 2 15.	2/1745	Pte. W. France.

Date List Published.

20 2 15. 1/2181 Pte. G. Hall.
1/2075 Pte. A. G. Hancock.
1/2128 Pte. J. Hegarty.
1/761 L/Cpl. H. Hill.
1/1125 Pte. J. Hopkins.
1/2123 Pte. C. Houlahan.
1/1419 Pte. E. J. Johnson.
1/6097 Pte. T. Judge.
1/1826 Cpl. J. McGivern.
1/1343 Pte. D. Mahoney.
1/7848 Pte. W. Mercer.
1/8981 Pte. E. Mulrooney.
1/1380 Pte. G. W. Newins.
1/959 Pte. J. Nolan.
1/1694 Pte. M. Noon.
1/2235 Pte. A. Peach.
1/823 Pte. W. Perry
1/1021 Pte. J. Power.
1/1667 Pte. J. Ralphs.
1/8748 Pte. J. Randall.
1/1119 Pte. T. Anderson.
1/2341 Pte. E. Arties.
1/1626 L/Cpl. W. H. Atherton.
1/1876 Pte. W. H Beech.
1/1644 Pte. F. Beevor.
1/1486 Pte. J. Beswick.
1/1970 Pte. E. Birch.
1/795 Pte. W. H. Bourgaize.
1/7887 Dr. W. Brandon.
1/2237 Pte. H. Buckley.
1/1144 T. Byron.
1/1805 Pte. T. Cosgrove.
1/1661 Pte. T. Cunane.
1/998 Cpl. J. Cunliffe.
1/1535 Cpl. E. C. Darling.
1/1615 Pte. W. Deakin.
1/1422 Pte. J. Dolan.
1/2077 Pte. J. Daffy.
1/2162 L/Cpl. W. P. Eyas.
1/2210 Pte. J. J. Flanning.
1/736 Pte. J. W. Fielding.
1/2084 Pte. S. Friend.
1/2268 Pte. W. Griffiths.
1/1852 Pte. H. Grindley.
20 2 15. 1/1811 Pte A. Whittle.
1/1443 Pte. W. J. Windle.
1/949 Pte. J. Worsley.
22 2 15. 1302 L/Cpl. G. Blackman (d.w.)
2012 Pte. W. Cartwright (d.w.)
5838 Pte. J. Mitson (d.w.)
513 L/Cpl. A. Pimlott (d.w.)

Date List Published.

2/8200 Pte. J. Hamer.
2/6490 Cpl. J. McGovern.
2/6856 Pte. J. Marshall.
2/1420 Pte. J. Taylor.
2/7923 Pte. P. Taylor.
2/2325 Pte. D. Connor (d.w.)
2/3067 Pte. T. A. Harrison (d.w.)
2/1890 Pte. G. Ogden (d.w.)
18 2 15. 1/1681 Pte. T. Magee (d.w.)
6470 Pte. G. Robinson (d.w.)
19 2 15. 1741 L/Cpl. H. Parsonage (d.w.)
20 2 15. 4150 Actg-Sgt. W. Williams.
20 2 15. 1/819 Pte. S. Fitton (d.w.)
1/2226 L/Cpl. J. Gloagg (d.w.)
1/1897 Pte. F. G. Jones (d.w.)
1/935 Pte. G. E. Mall (d.w.)
1/1609 Pte. J. Murphy (d.w.)
1/7926 Pte. G. Nugent (d.w.)
1/2147 Pte. W. Taylor (d.w.)
1/7463 L/Cpl. W. D. Adams.
2063 Cpl. R. Kennedy.
8 3 15. 2077 Pte. H. Edwards.
9488 L/Cpl. W. Ferris.
9 3 15. 3118 Pte. H. Hill.
6178 Pte. S. Rimmer.
9 3 15. 2390 Pte. E. Wall.
22 3 15. 2421 Pte. W. Dunn.
23 3 15. 1/3488 Pte. A. Gresty.
28 3 15. 2/2503 Pte. J. Cavanah.
2/8050 Actg-Sergt. W. Robinson.
2/6845 Actng-Cpl. T. Shaw.
30 3 15. 2724 Pte. A. Martin.
5 4 15. 9674 Pte. A. B. Dixon.
7607 Pte. L. Pickford.
6 4 15. 1691 Pte. J. Armstrong.
2281 Pte. J. Riley.
9 4 15. 2329 Pte. C. Farrel (d.w.)
12 4 15. 1924 Pte. H. Price (d.w.)
1334 Pte. A. Holden.
1807 Pte. A. Robinson.
1837 Pte. W. Sheil (d.w.)
14 4 15. 763 Pte. H. Wrigley.
15 4 15. 1761 Pte. G. H. Avis (d.w.)
2812 Cpl. J. Laffin (d.w.)
3087 Pte. J. Talbot (d.w.)
8185 Pte. A. Cunningham.
17 4 15. 2743 Actg-Sergt. R. Collings.
2413 Pte. R. Taylor.
2805 Pte. J. Clarkson (d.w.)
1962 Pte. F. Sheppard (d.w.)
2063 Pte. R. Williamson (d.w.)

Date List Published.

5726 L/Cpl. O. Robinson (d.w.)
2229 L/Cpl. P. Rowden (d.w.)
2023 L/Cpl. S. Shrimpton (d.w.)
8039 L/Cpl. W. Spencer (d.w.)
1827 L/Cpl. J. Thornton (d.w.)
1269 Cpl. A. Unsworth (d.w.)
5533 Pte. A. J. Ward (d.w.)
2364 Pte. F. Marler.
1/9706 Pte. D. Grimshaw.
26 2 15. 2/8862 Pte. H. Bates.
2/8778 Pte. J. Brown.
2/5466 L/Cpl. W. Mattock.
2/8093 Pte. D. Murphy.
1 3 15. 2/ 461 Pte. C. W. Gamble (d.w.)
2/2625 Pte. D. Turton.
1/776 Pte. W. Hinchcliffe.
3 3 15. 2825 Pte. S. Cook.
2/8909 Pte. J. McCabe (d.w.)
2/1531 Cpl. F. E. Poole (d.)
6 3 15. 6707 Pte. A. Ord. (d.)
2/2567 Pte. T. Phillips.
2/2651 Pte. J. Southern.
2/8196 Pte. C. Molloy (d.w.)
1/9241 Bandr. C. Buxton (d.w.)
1/2844 Pte. T. Durkin (d.w.)
30 4 15. 2/2061 Pte. E. Griffiths (d.w.)
3 5 15. 1/927 Pte. F. Irvine.
1/816 Pte. J. Walsh (d.w.)
5 5 15. 1/3593 Pte. F. C. Hibbs.
1/1757 Pte. J. E. Hughes.
1/2492 Pte. R. Humphries.
1/7888 Bandsn. R. Couchman (d.)
6 5 15. 2/2051 Pte. C. Ashley.
2/9104 Pte. J. Goulden.
2/1932 Pte. J. McDonald.
2/771 Pte. W. O'Brien
2/887 Pte. W. Russell.
10 5 15. 2/8996 Pte. A. Whittaker.
11 5 15. 2/205 Pte. H. Eyres.
14 5 15. 1/1392 Pte. 5. Wood.
15 5 15. 2/5800 Pte. W. Sallows.
17 5 15. 2/6368 Pte. D. Crawford.
2/5977 Pte. J. Hailstone.
2/2998 Pte. W. Martin.
2/2424 Pte. T. Ryan.
2/2268 Pte. W. Southworth.
2/2071 Pte. J. Wemyess.
2/2421 Pte. W. Whitehead.
2/2467 Pte. W. Grant.
19 5 15. 2/2362 Pte. W. Burton.
2/185 Pte. W. Fitzpatrick.

Date List Published.

19 4 15. 1606 Pte. H.D ean.
1153 L/Cpl. W. Jones.
5701 Pte. McBride.
1209 Pte. G. Coldough (d.w.)
1097 Pte. T. Maddox (d.w.)
19 4 15. 1524 Pte. W. Barlow (d.w.)
6868 L/Cpl. E. Jones (d.)
20 4 15. 2035 Pte. J. W. Garnham.
1638 Pte. O. Morley (d.w.)
22 4 15. 2187 Pte. C. Barker (d.w.)
23 4 15. 16490 Pte. W Bell.
1729 Pte. J. Daniels.
1410 Pte. A. Jackson.
2575 Pte. J. Strong.
2983 Pte. T. Wheatcroft (d.w.)
25 4 15. 1/2411 Pte. J. Mills (d.w.)
28 4 15. 2/1758 Pte. J. Carpenter.
2/9571 Pte. Crowther.
2/2869 Pte. E. Curley.
2/6830 Pte. J. Kendall.
1/1265 Pte. W. Gilson.
1/2539 Pte. T. Hancock.
1/2293 Pte. W. Jackson.
1/909 Pte. D. Johnson.
1/1674 Pte. A. Kierney.
1/1645 Pte. T. Mason.
1/1411 Sergt. R. J. Mercer.
1/2816 Pte. T. Pass.
1/2407 Pte. W. Roberts.
1/1765 Pte. T. Southall.
1/2886 Pte. D. Sullivan.
1/2106 Pte. F. Taylor.
1/1372 Pte. A. F. Wearer.
1/2246 Pte. R. Wilcox.
2 6 15. 2/2683 Pte. G. Cooper.
5 6 15. 1/6610 Pte. J. Collins (d.w.)
1/1780 Pte. G. Walsh (d.w.)
1/2555 Pte. L. Waterhouse (d.w.)
9 6 15. 2/805 Pte. A. Adland.
2/2498 Pte. J. Chappell.
2/2963 Pte. E. Fully.
2/9171 L/Cpl. M. McDonough.
2/6973 Pte. J. Naylor.
2/3026 Pte. G. Sharkey.
2/1250 Pte. S. Allen (d.w.)
11 6 15. 2/2341 Pte. J. Hennegan.
2/8681 Pte. J. Logan.
2/1996 Pte. T. Royle.
14 6 15. 2/2710 Pte. J. Oldham (d.w.)
2/1436 Pte. A. Wood.
16 6 15. 1/2485 Pte. J. Nicholas (d.w.)

Date List Published.		
	2/9484	Pte. J. Gavin.
	2/6473	Sergt. J. Hamblett.
	2/5538	Actg-Sergt. H. Tunnicliffe
	2/2563	Pte. T. Royston (d.w.)
25 5 15.	1/2697	Pte. P. Quinn.
27 5 15.	2/7933	Pte. A. Cunningham (d.w.)
	2/682	Pte. H. Rosenthal.
28 5 15.	2/173	Pte. W. Barker.
	2/3558	Pte. J. Kelley.
	2/2147	Pte. M. Ryan.
	2/1494	Pte. F. Matthews (d.w.)
	2/2893	Pte. J. Rushton (d.w.)
29 5 15.	1/2656	Pte. P. Booth.
	1/2128	Pte. W. Boyle.
	1/1529	Pte. H. Clifton.
	1/868	Pte. P. Connor.
29 5 15.	1/868	Pte. P. Connor.
	1/1328	Pte. J. Curry.
	1/2130	Pte. S. Dutton.
	1/8910	Pte. G. Egerton.
26 6 15.	2/7784	Pte. W. Crofton.
29 6 15.	1/8890	L/Cpl. A. Martin.
	2/4	Pte. A. D. Bakerville (d.w.)
	2/2242	Pte. J. Nederman (d.w.)
30 6 15.	2/8799	L/Cpl. J. Aspinall (d.w.)
7 7 15.	2/2760	Pte. W. Hampson.
5 7 15.	1/937	Sergt. A. Riley (d.w.)
	1/9522	Cpl. F. Underwood (d.w.)
	2/104	Pte. A. Fletcher (d.w.)
	3/3121	Pte. A. Hood (d.w.)
	2890	Pte. J. Hurd (d.)
	1/2011	L/Cpl H. Goulden (d.w.)
6 7 15.	1/2543	L/Cpl. E. Callaghan (d.w.)
7 7 15.	1/1211	Sergt. T. McNally (d.w.)
8 7 15.	2/2236	Pte. A. Boothman.
	2/2234	Pte. B. Lewis.
	2/6855	L/Cpl. M. McKenna (d.w.)
9 7 15.	2/6303	Pte. W. Jones.
	2/5268	Sergt. C. E. Kirby.
14 7 15.	1/2657	Pte. G. H. Booth.
	2/4708	Pte. E. Heppinstall.
	2/3037	Pte. J. H. Vernon.
	2/5339	Pte. T. Williamson.
	2/2593	Pte. J. Young.
15 7 15.	1/906	Pte. M. Flanagan (d.)
16 7 15.	2/3136	Pte. W. Marshall.
	2/2977	Pte. S. Walker.
23 7 15.	1/2861	Pte. T. McGann.
	1/2826	Pte. A. Baggoley.
24 7 15.	1/2122	Pte. R. Adland.
	2/9914	Pte. T. W. Gilday.

Date List Published.		
	1/15999	Pte. E. Morrisey (d.w.)
	1/2831	Pte. W. Maugan (d.)
17 6 15.	2/1581	Pte. M. Connor.
	2/8154	Pte. E. Evans.
	2/2379	Pte. W. Gregory.
	2/3335	Pte. J. Hart.
	2/2194	Pte. J. Heywood.
	2/811	Cpl. G. Hillman.
	2/5482	Cpl. J. Mooney.
	2/2157	Pte. E. Rogers.
	2/7709	L/Cpl. J. Walron (d.w.)
	2/1560	Sergt. J. Wharton (d.w.)
18 6 15.	2/2000	Pte. W. Baxter.
	2/1185	Pte. T. Cummings.
	2/9411	Pte. A. Tudor.
	2/8913	Cpl. J. Wolstenholme.
21 0 15.	2/3503	Pte. F. Brown (d.w.)
24 6 15.	2/8798	Pte. J. Croft.
25 6 15.	1/54	Pte. T. Melia.
	1/1168	L/Cpl. J. Rose.
4 9 15.	1/16378	Pte. E. Bradburn.
	2/2179	Pte. T. Higgins.
	1/2486	Pte. J. O'Neill.
7 9 15.	2/2785	Pte. M. Muldoon (d.w.)
18 9 15.	1/2061	Pte. W. Stanley.
22 9 15.	1/3012	Pte. T. Williams.
24 9 15.	2/6108	Pte. F. E. Fielding.
25 9 15.	1/881	Pte. D. Jones.
	1/1813	Pte. E. R. Stout.
	2/300	Pte. W. Halpin.
	2/2403	Pte. J. McCann.
2 10 15.	1/9166	Pte. H. Sterrett.
4 10 15.	1/1652	L/Cpl. W. Deane.
	1/1828	Pte. H. Edler.
	1/1508	Pte. W. McCarthy.
	1/856	Pte. J. Williams.
	1/1595	L/Cpl. L. Shepherd.
11 10 15.	1/2245	Pte. W. Collins.
12 10 15.	4/1442	Pte. T. Atkinson.
	3/1530	Pte. F. Connor.
14 10 15.	2/2800	Pte. D. Williams.
22 10 15.	1/1221	L/Cpl. —. Bamford.
25 10 15.	1/9414	Pte. H. Hibbert.
29 10 15.	1/4765	Pte. E. Doyle.
2 11 15.	2/2323	Pte. W. A. White (d.)
	4/2635	Pte. A. Longworth.
3 11 15.	2/6289	Pte. G. Alexander (d.)
10 11 15.	1/23774	Pte. A. T. Goodwin (d.w.)
12 11 15.	1/2052	Pte. A. Bailey (m.k.)
	1/5230	L/Cpl. A. Williams (d.)
15 11 15.	2/2582	Pte. C. Genner.

Date List Published.	
	2/2266 Pte. W. Walker.
26 7 15.	1/1295 Sergt. W. Marshall.
29 7 15.	1/2732 Pte. H. Holland.
	2/2179 Sergt. D. Driscoll.
	2/1449 Cpl. J. Farrington.
	2/16854 Pte. J. R. Rose.
2 8 15.	1/1950 Pte. A. Scott.
4 8 15.	2/5192 Pte. W. Brereton.
	2/2285 L/Cpl. G. Robinson (d.w.)
5 8 15.	1/2768 Pte. H. Howarth.
14 8 15.	2/2070 Pte. H. Bennett.
	2/4586 Pte. H. Ollerenshaw.
17 8 15.	2/2028 Pte. H. Smith.
19 8 15.	2/2688 Pte. T. Dyer (d.w.)
20 8 15.	1/2785 Pte. S. Gorman.
	1/4565 Pte. W. Hampson.
	1/3597 Pte. J. Mannion.
	1/2330 Pte. M. Walsh.
23 8 15.	1/2247 Pte. T. Eccleston.
30 8 15.	1/6653 Pte. W. Nuttall.
5 1 16.	2/284 Pte. P. Gray.
0 1 16.	3/24320 Pte. G. McDonald.
29 1 16.	2/4638 Pte. H. Eccles.
14 2 16.	1/1399 Pte. A. Roberts.
	3/2230 Pte. M. Evans.
23 2 16.	4/5415 Pte. C. Affleck.
	2/2740 Pte. R. Bowker.

Date List Published.	
	2/9413 Pte. A. McCluskey.
18 11 15.	1/5237 Pte. M. Walsh.
	2/779 Actg-Sergt. W. Buckley.
20 11 15.	1/5230 L/Cpl. A. Williams.
	2/9399 Pte. F. Rooney (d.w.)
	2/1817 Pte. J. Holt (d.)
24 11 15.	2/8620 Pte. J. Fannon.
25 11 15.	2/6767 Pte. R. Steward (d.w.)
	2/74 Pte. E. Nuttall.
3 12 15.	2/160 Pte. P. Jones (d.w.)
6 12 15.	1/2787 Pte. H. Reavey.
	3/2866 Pte. J. Grimes (d.)
7 12 15.	2/3203 Pte. J. Splains.
13 12 15.	2/8830 Pte. G. Marshall.
17 12 15.	1/2357 L/Cpl. A. F. Freeth (d.w.)
21 12 15.	2/8010 Pte. A. Webster (d.)
24 12 15.	2/2660 Dr. E. A. George (m.k.)
27 12 15.	2/9622 Pte. J. Keelty.
3 1 16.	2/7958 L/Cpl. McEwen (d.)
	2/8580 Pte. J. Gilpin.
	2/2732 Pte. G. Preece (d.)
3 2 16.	3/9513 L/Cpl. A. Adshead (d.)
8 3 16.	2/2504 Pte. R. Owen.
	3/2175 Pte. J. Kelly.
13 3 16.	2/9320 Pte. J. Gorman.
21 3 16.	4/1771 Pte. H. Gibbin (d.w.)

N.C.O.'S AND MEN OF THE 1ST, 2ND, 3RD, AND 4TH BATTALIONS KILLED, DIED OF WOUNDS, OR DIED *BEFORE* 1st *APRIL*, 1915, NOT INCLUDED IN *WAR OFFICE LISTS*.

2/775 Pte. A. Ashton.
2/2309 Pte. Barlow.
2/9283 Pte. G. Bowers.
1/2593 Pte. W. Bradley.
1/700 Pte. W. Bryant.
1/6053 Pte. W. Buckley.
2/8999 Pte. P. Burke.
1/1826 Pte. T. Claney.
2/2486 Pte. J. Cronshaw.
2/9075 Pte. C. Donaldson.
1/2210 Pte. J. J. Fanning.
1/9959 Pte. W. A. Fitzpatrick.
2/7288 Pte. W. Ford.
9914 Pte. T. V. Gilday.
1/1987 Pte. W. G. Gregory.
9961 Pte. H. H. Hacking.
2/8931 Pte. J. Hogan.
1/5085 Sergt. M. Jordan.
1/7632 Pte. F. Joy.
2/2574 Pte. A. Kaines.
1/794 Pte. G. Legg.
2/9004 L/Cpl. J. Lord.
2/7961 Pte. J. Lowe.
6548 Pte. T. Madden.
2/9539 Pte. R. Murphy.
1/8515 Sergt. J. Novell.
1/7262 Cpl. E. J. Percival.
2/9023 Pte. J. Plant.
1/1647 Pte. S. Simms.
2/9181 Pte. W. Smith.
1/5523 Co.-Sergt.-Mjr. R. Stanley.
1/1289 Pte. E. Thompson.
1/253 Sergt. J. Turner.
2/9040 Pte. A. Waite.
1/1475 Pte. W. White.

N.C.O.'S AND MEN KILLED OR DIED FROM WOUNDS RECEIVED IN ACTION.

11th (Service) Battalion

Date List Published.

3196 Pte. R. Atherton.
3603 Pte. P. T. Harvey.
2968 Pte. J. Marsden.
15724 Pte. E. Weeks.
3126 Pte. D. Green.
13326 Pte. S. Bentley.
9647 Pte. A. Biddlescombe.
23427 Pte. A. Broomhead.
3476 L/Sergt. J. A. Buckley.
3694 L/Cpl.H. Capes.
3323 Pte. A. E. Connell.
2397 Co.-Sergt.-Mjr. A. Dale.
9586 Pte. H. Dye.
13371 Pte. R. Davidson.
2399 Co.-Sgt.-Mjr. J. A. Duncan.
3726 L/Cpl. J. H. Espin.
3615 Pte. H. Eyre.
3818 Cpl. J. Williamson.
18 9 15. 24731 Pte. J Brooks.
13315 Pte. J. Ellis.
22 9 15. 3157 Pte. J. Andrew.
13565 Pte. A. Cain.
13942 Pte. J. W. Johnson.
2956 Pte. H. Clark.
9588 Pte. R. Clarkson.
3859 Pte. T. Dickenson.
3135 Pte. R. Duff.
3433 Pte. F. Hibbert.
2931 Pte. T. G. Hyland.
13473 Pte. H. Kelly.
3449 Pte. F. Lee.
24 9 15. 5513 Pte. W. Chevery.
27 9 15. 13443 Pte. P. Place.
3022 Pte. J. E. Wild.
13080 Pte. J. H. Adams.
3216 Pte. W. J. Blowe.
13630 Pte. G. Gilbert.
3248 Pte. S. Green.
5562 Pte. T. Gudgeon.
3248 Pte. A. Moston.
2790 Sergt. G. Roberts.
4745 Pte. H. Saxon.
3572 Pte. A. Wildfall.
12952 Pte. J. Collins.
27 9 15. 2979 Pte. J. W. Briers (a.k.)
2932 Pte. W. Hibbert (a.k.)

Date List Published.

3782 Pte. F. Fletcher.
3064 Actg Co.-Q.M.S. O. J. Ford.
3702 Pte. E. Gill.
2644 Pte. P. Green.
3722 Pte. C. Higginson.
13236 Pte. C. Hindley.
3445 Pte. M. Killoran.
13441 L/Cpl. J. H. Markey.
3319 Pte. E. Marsh.
2593 Cpl. W. Middleton.
3695 L/Cpl. C. Mooney.
2395 Co.-Q M.-Sergt. J. Norris.
3743 Pte. J. J. Reeves.
5237 Sergt.-Mjr. P. Steeden.
13691 Pte. S. Sumner.
3581 Pte. T. Taylor.
2632 Sergt. E. D. Wharedale.
14 10 15. 9656 Pte. G. Harrison.
24791 Pte. H. Taylor.
15 10 15. 3969 Pte. F. McGlynn (d.w.)
19 10 15. 3596 Pte. R. McGrear (d.w.)
22 10 15. 15765 Pte. D. Clegg
1747 Pte. H. Batera (d.w.)
23756 Pte. G. Spittle
27 10 15. 6008 Pte. T. Monaghan (d.)
1 11 15. 9650 Pte. C. W. Acton.
2 11 15. 15527 Pte. F. Seeran (d.w.)
4 11 15. 24062 Pte. J. Murphy (d.)
3349 Pte. L. Grimshaw (m.d.)
5095 Pte. J. McLaughlin (m.d.)
5 11 15. 4447 Pte. W. J. Gallagher.
15537 Pte. F. Ferrano (d.w.)
8 11 15. 9695 Pte. J. T. Boulton.
8 11 15. 3574 Pte. J. Gregory.
8530 Pte. J. Scott.
9 11 15. 16042 Actng-Cpl. J. Griffiths.
12 11 15. 5333 Pte. T. Dewhurst (d.w.)
16 11 15. 13539 Cpl. J. O'Connor
17 11 15. 3553 Pte. R. Wood.
11 10 15. 3470 L/Cpl. T. Breen.
20 11 15. 1793 Pte. F. O'Gara (d.w.)
22 11 15. 3/2574 Pte. W. H. Johns (d.w.)
155538 Pte. C. Mainwaring (d.w.)
15919 Pte. F. Smethurst (d.w.)
23 11 15. 14/24083 Pte. W. Oakes (d.)
26 11 15. 24729 Pte. E. Turton (d.w.)

Date List
Published.
28 9 15. 2353 Pte. W. Beech.
29 9 15. 13635 Pte. G. Ackerley.
2594 Sergt. S. Carroll.
1215 Actng Co.1Sgt.-Mjr. Lane.
3102 Pte. D. McCormick.
15523 Pte. 9 Montgomery.
1 10 15. 3891 Pte. R. Reddington.
5 10 15. 3425 Pte. A. Rawlings.
7 10 15. 3538 Pte. J. Goodwin.
11 10 15. 3518 Pte. J. T. Elwell.
13 10 15. 3864 Pte. R. Clegg.
23431 Pte. J. H. Ellis.
3505 Pte. A. McEwen.
3208 Pte. A. Wilson.

Date List
Published.
29 11 15. 13286 Pte. J. Milligan (d.)
9 12 15. 4/2629 Pte. F. W. Young (d.w.)
10 12 15. 413539 Cpl. J. O'Connor.
17 12 15. 2692 Pte. C. Knight (d.w.)
3/23639 Pte. W. G. Wells (d.)
23 12 15. 128 Pte. J. Dunne.
21 12 15. 15610 Pte. H. Coady (d.)
4/5407 Pte. G. Crawford (d.)
3 1 16. 3/2540 Pte. J. Higgins (m.k.)
5478 Pte. G. Lewis (m.k.)
7 1 16. 3/2257 L/Cpl. R. Griffiths (d.)
17 1 16. 18098 Pte. J. Fowler.
24 1 16. 15567 Pte. R. Burtoft (m.k.)
3 9 15. 13475 Pte. E. T. Lloyd.

12th (Service) Battalion

Date List
Published.
21 9 15. 4277 Pte. T. Doran.
27 9 15. 4801 Pte. J. H. Oldham.
5312 Pte. L. Waterhouse.
4 10 15. 4908 Pte. T. Stock.
6 10 15. 24840 Pte. L. B. Wittch.
6038 Pte. P. Price.
24 12 15. 4953 Pte. T. Barton.
13181 Pte. J. Cookson.
4686 Pte. T. Daffy.
3976 Pte. J. Gillbody
4856 Pte. W. Holt.
24878 L/Cpl. W. Toole.
23485 Pte. R. Vanson.
14/13714 Pte. T. W. Wheaton.
5234 Pte. A. Brownhill.
29 12 15. 4966 L/Sergt. H. Greenfield.
9 9 15. 4311 Pte. T. Cooney (d.w.)
16991 Pte. F. Robinson (d.w.)
1 3 16. 3/24632 Pte. W. Bainford.
7 3 16 14/13564 Pte. B. H. Ray.
4018 Pte. H. T. Stott.
14/16464 Pte. W. Culshaw (d.w.)
12/4271 Pte. E. Waring (d.w.)
3/27999 Pte. A. Ward (d.w.)
9 3 16. 13939 Cpl. F. Bamber.
13223 Pte. W. Cullen.
9645 Pte. J. Danion.
1364 Pte. J. Ellis.
3932 Cpl. G. Heath.

Date List
Published.
9 10 15. 5293 Pte. W. V. Turner.
18 10 15. 5371 Pte. D. Aston.
23 11 15. 13580 Pte. J. Blease (d.w.)
24 11 15. 13559 Pte. W. Pugh.
14 12 15. 4128 Pte. W. H. Hamilton.
23326 Pte. A. Isherwood.
4946 Pte. J. McBride.
5325 Pte. J. Timms.
14 1 16. 14/16351 Pte. J. Duckworth.
4247 Pte. J. W. Barker.
3910 Pte. P. Byrne.
5213 Pte. R. Martin.
3796 Pte. E. Shannon.
4328 Pte. J. Tynan.
4278 Pte. W. Yates (a.k.)
25 8 15. 3925 Pte. J. T. Wilksen.
1529 Cpl. D. Howard.
3965 L/Cpl. T. O'Dea.
13591 Pte. J. O'Hara.
29940 Pte. H. Rathmill.
13646 Pte. T. H. Reece.
4691 Pte. J. Ritchie.
13032 L/Sgt. W. Sharrocks.
13370 Pte. W. Simpson.
4/13708 Pte. A. E. Cording (d.w.)
7999 Pte. A. Greenhalgh (d.w.)
18 3 16. 5497 Pte. A. Kite.
4598 Pte. A. Mason.
5210 Pte. A. Cox (d.w.)

13th (Service) Battalion

17 1 16. 14/16191 Pte. J. Berry (d.)

16th (Service) Battalion (1st City)

Date List Published.	
12 2 16.	6266 L/Cpl. C. H. Kelly.
	6929 Pte. F. Slater (a.k.)
3 3 16.	6582 Pte. C. Bentley.
	7370 L/Cpl. W. E. Eckersley.
	7359 Pte. J. H. Gleave.
	6642 Sgt. F. A. Luckman (d.w.)
7 3 16.	6921 Pte. G. Pollitt (d.w.)
21 2 16.	7391 Pte. H. Hughes (d.w.)
	7011 Pte. F. Jelly (d.w.)
	6266 L/Cpl. C. H. Kelly.
	7618 Pte. T. Rae (d.w.)
16 3 16.	7097 Pte. A. Doleman.
20 3 16.	6219 Cpl. W .J. Brown (a.k.)
	6977 Pte. J. Cowell (a.k.)
	6553 L/Cpl. E. Thomas (a.k.)
7 2 16.	17/9110 Pte. W. Ashworth.
2 3 16.	6582 Pte. C. Bentley.
	7370 L/Cpl. W. E. Eckersley.
	7359 Pte. J. H. Glease.
	6643 Sgt. F. A. Luckman (d.w.)

17th (Service) Battalion (2nd City)

Date List Published.	
31 12 15.	8638 Pte. J. P. Holt.
14 2 16.	8050 Pte. J. C. Atkinson.
	8432 Pte. G. H. Bagshaw.
	8445 Pte. R. Bradshaw (d.w.)
17 2 16.	17/8228 Pte. J. McKenna (d.w.)
31 12 15.	8638 Pte. J. P. Holt.
14 2 16.	8445 Pte. R. Bradshaw (d.w.)
17 2 16.	8228 Pte. J. McKenna (d.w.)
21 2 16.	8538 Pte. H. Eckersall (d.w.)
29 2 16.	17/8609 Pte. H. Hollingsworth (d.w.)
6 3 16.	17/9496 Pte. T. Ogden.
16 3 16.	17/2512 Pte. J. Davidson.
	17/8142 Pte. J. Fitzpatrick.
	17/8553 Pte. R. Frost.
	8355 L/Cpl. D. Wolstencraft (d.w.)
25 2 16.	8301 Pte. A. Smith.
29 2 16.	8609 Pte. H. Hollingsworth (d.w.)
6 3 16.	9496 Pte. T. Ogden (d.w.)

18th (Service) Battalion (3rd City)

Date List Published.	
3 2 16.	11005 Pte. B. Browne.
	10486 Pte. R. Davies.
	10105 Pte. A. Davis.
	10985 Pte. H. Grange.
	10273 L/Cpl. D. Logan.
	10195 Pte. S. H. Parry.
	20722 L/Cpl. E. S. Sherridan.
	10895 Pte. R. Thorpe.
	10517 Cpl. J. Webster.
	10232 L/Cpl. W. Wickman.
7 3 16.	9953 Pte. D. Wilkinson.
8 3 16.	10538 Pte. D. George.
3 2 16.	11005 Pte. B. Browne.
	10486 Pte. R. Davies.
	10547 Pte. J. Harrington.
8 2 16.	11128 Pte. T. A. Hatfield (d.w.)
9 2 16.	9872 Cpl. O. Hutton.
16 2 16.	10747 Pte. T. Wood (d.w.)
17 2 16.	10431 Pte. H. Morris.
19 2 16.	10559 Pte. E. L. Moss (d.w.)
	10547 Pte. J. Harrington.
1 3 16.	10070 Pte. S. Aldred.
16 3 16.	11081 Pte. H. W. Bridge.
	10240 Pte. E. Cooper.
	10153 Pte. T. Knight.
	10974 L/Cpl. A. O. Scott (d.w.)
17 2 6.	10431 Pte. H. Morris.
22 2 16.	11240 Pte. F. Matthews (d.w.)
23 2 16.	10164 Pte. H. Loughler.
	9932 Pte. J. E. Sumner.
	1001 L/Cpl. R. H. Williams.
18 3 16.	10975 Pte. R. Kay (d.w.)
28 2 16.	11023 Pte. D. Hanvey (d.w.)
1 3 16.	10070 Pte. S. Aldred.
	10125 Pte. A. Davies.
	10985 Pte. H. Grange.
	10273 L/Cpl. D. Logan.
	10195 Pte. S. H. Parry.
	20722 L/Cpl. E. S. Sheridan.
	10895 Pte. R. Thorpe.

Date List Published.
22 2 16. 11240 Pte. F. Matthews.
23 2 16. 10164 Pte. H. Loughler.
9934 Pte. J. E. Sumner.
10001 Pte. L. Williams.

Date List Published.
10517 Cpl. J. Webster.
10232 L/Cpl. W. Wickman.
8 3 16. 10538 Pte. D. George.

19th (Service) Battalion (4th City)

Date List Published.
9 2 16. 12599 Pte. M. White.
14 2 16. 21/12473 Pte. W. E. Thirlwell (d.w)
12103 Sgt. J. Heywood (d.w.)
12524 Pte. A. Robinson (d.w.)
11735 Pte. W. Baillee (d.w.)
29 2 16. 12114 Pte. P. F. Hover.
12248/ Pte. J. Wolley.
8 2 16. 11735 Pte. W. Baillie (d.w.)
9 2 16. 12500 Pte. M. White.
14 2 16. 21/12473 Pte. W. E. Thirlwell.
12103 Sgt. J. Heywood.
12525 Sergt. A. Robinson.
16 2 16. 11715 Sgt. H. Woodfin (a.k.)
19 2 16. 11753 Sgt. A. Brandreth (d.w.)
21 2 16. 11790 Sgt. H. Dickenson (d.w.)
12410 Sgt. S. Massey (d.w.)

Date List Published.
11897 Pte. S. Newman (d.w.)
1 3 16. 12043 L/Cpl. S. Coudliffe.
12834 Pte. T. Wilson.
11 3 16. 12033 Sgt. S. Carter.
16 3 16. 12421 Pte. A. G. Penn.
20 3 16. 12363 Pte. H. Grundy.
12934 Sgt. T. Wilkinson (d.w.)
25 2 16. 12044 Sgt. F. R. Cooke.
12056 Cpl. G. A. Crowe.
12113 Pte. G. W. Kope.
28 2 16. 12659 Pte. H. Hodkinson (d.w.)
22 2 16. 12114 Pte. P. F. Hover.
12248 Pte. J. Woolley.
11897 Pte. S. Newman (d.w.)
1 3 16. 12043 L/Cpl. Condliffe.
12834 Pte. T. Wilson.

20th (Service) Battalion (5th City)

Date List Published.
29 1 16. 17863 Pte. T. W. Curtis.
17706 Pte. A. Marrow.
17 3 16. 18356 Pte. H. Woods.
21 2 16. 17039 L/Cpl. J. Carruthers.

Date List Published.
23 2 16. 26107 Pte. P. Kelly.
17340 Sgt. S. Dunn (d.)
29 1 16. 17865 Pte. T. W. Curvis.

21st (Service) Battalion (6th City)

Date List Published.
7 3 16. 19898 Pte. M. G. Ramsden (a.k.)

Date List Published.
18 3 16. 21/19165 Pte. J. Johnson (d.w.)

22nd (Service) Battalion (7th City)

Date List Published.
8 12 15. 21499 Pte. W. Woollams (d.)
16 3 16. 27/25696 Pte. J. Chesney (d.w.)
8 12 15. 21499 Pte. W. Woollams (d.)
28 2 16. 20770 Pte. J. E. Ball (d.w.)

Date List Published.
29 2 16. 21400 Pte. R. Beswick (d.w.)
18 3 16. 25673 Pte. J. Burke.
1 3 16. 20541 Sgt. S. Anderson (d.w.)
21400 Pte. R. Beswick (d.w.)

23rd (Service) Battalion (8th City)

Date List Published.

16 3 16. 22179 Pte. M. Cunningham (d.w.)

24th (Service) Battalion (Oldham)

Date List Published.

9 3 16. 15153 Pte. F Whitebread.
21 3 16 24/15431 Pte. R. Green.
24/14898 Pte W. H. Kenyon.
24/14238 Pte. A. Park.
28 2 16. 28097 Pte. G. Brierley.
14616 Pte. J. H. Brownhill.
26008 Pte. H. Connolly.
14472 Co.-Sgt.-Mjr. E. Coop.
15186 Pte. H. Dakin.
15318 Pte. W. Fothergill.

Date List Published.

14098 Sgt.-Mjr. A. Gartside.
14518 Pte. H. Hardman.
28133 Pte. A. Higgins.
14519 Pte. E. James.
14823 Pte. J. Ogden.
14585 Pte. G. O'Neil.
14593 Pte. W. Schofield.
14344 Pte. W. Smith.
14650 Pte. F. Thomson.
14597 L/Cpl. L. Thorpe.

Prisoners of War.

1st and 2nd Battalions.

Addis, T., Pte., 9824.
Appleton, G., Cpl., 1972.
Ashcroft, T., Pte., 2051.
Bailey, J., Cpl., 1812.
Brown, J., Pte., 9915.
Brown, W., Pte., 29.
Brown, J., Pte., 138.
Brown, M., L/Cpl., 2291.
Booth, F., Pte., 7955.
Beresford, J., Cpl., 539.
Berry, F., Pte., 1338.
Budd, —, Pte., 9526 (died).
Bass, J., Pte., 45.
Blill, D., Pte.
Brown, J., Pte., 9915.
Clarke, J., Pte., 9085.
Carroll, P., Pte., 8954.
Cosgrove, H., Pte., 1549.
Cronshaw, A., Pte., 7974.
Cooper, W., Cpl., 8514.
Crook, J., Pte., 8045.
Cushworth, C., Pte., 8662.
Clay, J., Pte., 9135.
Campbell, J., Pte., 2542.
Campbell, W., Pte., 9930.
Cummins, T., Pte., 9732.
Cahill, M., L/ Sergt., 429.
Collins, J., Pte., 2500.
Clarke, A., Pte.
Downey, W., Pte., 9074.
Dickeson, J., Pte., 7910.
Devonshire, J., Sergt., 8581.
Daly, P., Pte., 2091.
Daley, P., Pte., 2091.
Darville, P. Pte.
Eyres, J., Drm., 1530.
Elson, H., Pte., 3.
Edwards, W., Pte., 9585.
England, W., Pte., 7938.
Fletcher, G., Pte., 8599.
Farrand, A., Pte., 9605.
Foster, J., Pte., 173.
Fox, G., Pte., 9024.
Fenton, J., Pte., 2464.
Furber, T., Pte., 9749.
Fudge, J., Pte., 9983.
Fielding, H., Pte., 8103.
Freeth, A. J., Cpl., 1074.
Freeman, G. H., Cpl., 5840 (died).
Foster, H., Pte., 51.
Gregory, J., L/Cpl., 4498.
Gorton, E., Pte., 7598.
Gill, T., Pte., 2529.
Gettings, J., Pte., 8589.
Hilton, T., Pte., 9861.
Haigh, R., Pte., 107.
Hill, M., Pte., 2611.
Hodges, W., Pte., 1991.
Hilton, W., Pte., 2598.
Henderson, J., Pte., 335.
Hill, C., Pte., 2529.
Howard, C., Pte., 9756.
Hadfield, W., L/Cpl., 1928.
Harland, H., Pte., 9694.
Hamer, W., Pte., 8142.
Heaton, W., Pte., 2629.

Harrison, R., Pte., 8741.
Hilditch, J., Pte., 8708.
Hutchinson, A. E., Pte., 5475.
Henderson, J., Pte., 836.
Hollis, J., Pte., 133 (died).
Hughes, W., Pte.
Iveson, W., Pte., 9677.
Jones, F., Pte., 1653.
Jacobs, A., Pte., 2618.
Jones, G., Pte., 2421.
Kenny, C., Pte., 1218.
Kelly, W., Pte., 2596.
Kendrick, R., Pte., 8549.
King, T., Pte., 878.
Keefe, T., Pte., 1527.
Leek, J., Pte., 9955.
Leaberry, S., Cpl., 1802.
Lowe, H., Pte., 8071.
Lewis, H., Pte., 2672.
Langley, G., Pte., 2637.
Lumby, J., Cpl., 273
Leaver, T., L/Cpl., 9311.
Linney, W., L/Cpl., 1949.
Lamb, R., L/Sergt., 256.
Leigh, W., L/Cpl., 2495.
Morley, J., Pte., 8601.
Moulding, H., Pte., 2578.
Mullholland, T., Pte. 2521.
Munroe, T., Pte., 7990.
Murphy, W., Pte., 8687.
Maloney, M., Pte., 8634.
Morrow, J., Pte., 9552.
Mullen, P., Pte., 2769.
Moore, T., Pte., 7752.
Mannion, J., Pte., 8648.
McBride, D., Pte., 2014.
Mackin, T., Pte., 9410.
Mullen, S., Pte., 9133.
McPherson, W., L/Cpl., 9758.
Murphy, J., Pte., 9692
Metcalfe, R., Pte., 7989.
Mangin, A., Pte., 2528.
Molloy, T., L/Cpl., 9923.
Moore, W., Cpl..
Morrison, —, Pte.
Murphy, J., Pte., 9692.
O'Donnell, J., L/Cpl., 9210.
O'Brien, P., Drm., 641.
O'Donnell, J., Pte., 8616.
Phillips, C., Pte., 9910.
Pinchin, F., Sergt., 6800.
Pocock, E., Pte., 8826.
Porter, C., Pte., 9402.
Peach, A., Pte., 2235.
Phillips, C., Pte., 9910.
Pimlett, A., L/Cpl., 114.
Poynter, W., Pte., 1356.
Riddell, A., L/Cpl., 2.
Roberts, A., L/Cpl., 38.
Rothwell, J., Pte., 4426.
Ryan, R., Pte., 290.
Rose, C., Pte., 2633.
Rothwell, J., Pte., 9671.
Reddy, J., Pte., 9854.
Ryan, S., Pte., 2772.
Ryder, J., Cpl., 177.
Riddell, H., L/Cpl., 21.
Roberts, J., Pte., 2224.
Roche, J., Pte., 9718 (?).
Rourke, J., L/Cpl., 2324.
Roy, J., Pte.
Ryan, S., Pte., 2772.
Schofield, J., Pte., 9117.
Shaw, R., L/Cpl., 8603.
Smith, J., Pte., 2429.
Shelsher, W., Drm., 2383.
Shuley, J., Pte., 8701.
Smith, J., Pte., 8892.
Sladen, N., Pte., 2336.
Smith, C., Pte., 9155.
Smith, J., Pte., 313.
Simmons, W., Pte., 155.
Smith, J., 9019.
Thompson, A., Pte., 9881.
Tomlins, C., Pte., 384.
Taylor, A., L/Cpl., 6118.
Townsend, A., Pte., 6574.
Tobin, G., Pte., 9764.
Taylor, W., Pte., 8987.
Taylor, W. J., L/Cpl., 70.
Taylor, T., Pte., 8502.
Thompson, W., Pte., 9077.
Thornley, W., Pte.
Trott, T., L/Cpl., 1414.
Walmsley, E., L/Cpl., 8013.
Wall, S., Pte., 2615.
Westby, T., Pte., 8702.
Williams, E., Pte., 2370.
Woodall, J., Pte., 9451.
Webb, J., Pte., 53.
Walker, J., Pte., 9968.
Ward, F., Pte., 182.
Walker, —, Pte., 921.
Walencting, E., Pte.
White, J., Sergt., 1152.
Yates, E., Pte., 8786.

Lieut-Colonels commanding Regular, Militia and Special Reserve Battalions of the Manchester Regiment, on January 1st each year since 1876.

	63rd Foot (Regular)	96th Foot (Regular)			6th Royal Lancashire Militia	
1876	V. H. Bowles	G. F. C. Bray			T. E. Wilbraham	
1877	R H. Browne	do.			do.	
1878	R. J. Hughes	do.			do.	
1879	do.	J. Briggs			do.	
1880	W. F. F. Gordon	do.			J. H. Chambers	
	MANCHESTER REGIMENT					
	1st Battalion (Regular)	2nd Battalion (Regular)			3rd Battalion (Militia)	4th Battalion (Militia)
1881	W.L. Auchinleck	J. Briggs			J. H. Chambers	
1882	do.	do.			do.	
1883	do.	W. O. Barnard			do.	
1884	do.	do.			do.	
1885	do.	do.			do.	
1886	A. G. H. Church	do.			do.	J. C. Wray
1887	do.	A. D. Saportas			do.	do.
1888	do.	do.			do.	do.
1889	C. J. Ryan	do.			H. G. Matthews	T. P. Powell
1890	do.	do.			do.	do.
1891	H. C. Manyat	R W. Studdy			do.	do.
1892	do.	do.			do.	do.
1893	do.	J. A. Barlow			do.	do.

1894	H. C. Manyat	J. A. Barlow			A. G. P. Foley	T. P. Powell
1895	B. L. Anstruther	do.			do.	do.
1896	do.	do.			do.	C. D. Leyden
1897	do.	C. P. Ridley			J. B. Irving	do.
1898	do.	do.			do.	do.
1999	A. E. R. Curran	do.			do.	do.
1900	do.	do.			W. J. Bosworth	do.
			3rd Battalion (Regular)	4th Battalion (Regular)	5th Battalion (Militia)	6th Battalion (Militia)
1901	do.	C. T. Reay	J. P Gethin	L. L. Steele	W. J. Bosworth	C. D. Leyden
1902	do.	do.	do.	do.	H. Crosbie	do.
1903	A. B. Maxwell	do.	do.	do.	do.	do.
1904	do.	do.	do.	do.	do.	do.
1905	do.	J. E. Watson	J. H. A. Anderson	C. C. Melville	do.	H. A. Johnson
1906	do.	do.	do.	do.	do.	do.
1907	R. D. Vizard	do.	do.	Disbanded	do.	do.
			Disbanded			
					3rd Battalion (Special Reserve)	4th Battalion (Special Reserve)
1908	do.	do.			H. Crosbie	H. A. Johnson
1909	do.	C. C. Melvill			do.	do.
1910	do.	H. C. E. Westropp			do.	do.
1911	A. H. Baldwin	do.			do.	do.
1912	do.	do.			do.	do.
1913	do.	H. L. James			H. K. Oram	do.
1914	do.	do.			do.	J. H. M. Jebb
1915	E. P. Strictland	do.			do.	do.
1916	R. N. Hardcastle	N Luxmoore			do.	do.

THE MANCHESTER REGIMENT

Depot		Lt.-Col. H. L. James, C.B.	In command.
1st Battn.	Regular Line	Major R. N. Hardcastle, D.S.O.	do.
2nd do.	do.	Lt.-Col. (temp.) N. Luxmore.	do.
3rd do.	Special Reserve	Lt.-Col. H. K. Oram.	do.
4th do.	Extra Reserve	Lt.-Col. J. H. M. Jebb, D.S.O.	do.
1/5th do.	Territorial	Lt.-Col. (temp.) H. C. Darlington.	do.
2/5th do.	do.	Lt.-Col. (temp.) G. D. Timmis.	do.
3/5th do.	do.	Major (temp.) W. Hughes-Ridge.	do.
1/6th do.	do.	Lt.-Col. C. R. Pilkington, C.M.G.	do.
2/6th do.	do.	Lt.-Col. (temp.) T. H. Davies-Colley.	do.
3/6th do.	do.	Major H. D. Lowe.	do.
1/7th do.	do	Lt.-Col. H. Canning.	do.
2/7th do.	do.	Lt.-Col. (Hon. Col.) J. H. Pollitt, V.D.	do.
3/7th do.	do.	Major (Hon. Lt.-Col.) H. Hawkins, V.D.	do.
1/8th do.	do.	Lt.-Col. F. I. Bentley, T.D.	do.
2/8th do.	do.	Lt.-Col. (temp.) J. C. H. Crossland.	do.
3/8th do.	do.	Major (temp.) H. D. Halstead.	do.
1/9th do.	do.	Lt.-Col. H. D. Wade.	do.

2/9th Battn.	Territorial	....	Lt.-Col. (temp.) C. C. Heywood.	In command.
3/9th do.	do.	....	Major E. Garside.	do.
1/10th do.	do.	....	Lt.-Col. J. B. Rye, V.D.	do.
2/10th do.	do.	....	Lt.-Cl. (tem.) (Hon. Cl.) W. Patterson, V.D.	do.
3/10th do.	do.	....	Major G. W. Hardman.	do.
11th do.	Service	....	Lt.-Col. (temp.) B. A. Wright, D.S.O.	do.
12th do.	do.	....	Lt.-Cl. (tem.) E. G. Harrison, C.B., D.S.O.	do.
13th do.	do.	....	Lt.-Col. H. J. Jones, D.S.O.	do.
14th do.	Second Reserve	....	Lt.-Col. (temp.) T. M. Greer.	do.
16th do.	Service	....	Lt.-Col. (temp.) C. L. R. Petrie, D.S.O.	do.
17th do.	do.	....	Lt.-Col. (temp.) H. A. Johnson.	do.
18th do.	do.	....	Lt.-Col. (temp.) W. A. Fraser.	do.
19th do.	do.	....	Lt.-Col. (temp.) Sir H. B. Hill, Bt.	do.
20th do.	do.	....	Lt.-Col. (temp.) S. Mitchell.	do.
21st do.	do.	....	Bt.-Col. W. W. Norman.	do.
22nd do.	do.	....	Lt.-Col. (temp.) P. Whetham.	do.
23rd do.	do.	....	Lt.-Col. (temp.) R. P. Smith.	do.
24th do.	do.	....	Lt.-Col. (temp.) J. B. Batten.	do.
25th do.	Local Reserve	....	Lt.-Col. (temp.) F. R. McConnel.	do.
26th do.	do.	....	Bt.-Col. R. B. Hawes, C.B.	do.
27th do.	do.	....	Lt.-Col. (temp.) H. Ledward.	do.
1st Garrison Battalion		....	Lt.-Col. (temp) H. W. K. Bretherton.	do.
1st Cadet Battalion		....	Capt. (Cadet Major) G. F. Falkner.	do.

WARRANT OFFICERS
(Class I.)

SERGEANT-MAJORS—

Depot. J. W. Atkinson (temp.) 3 Oct. 14.
1st Bn. W. Finney. 11 Feb. 11.
2nd Bn. J. Parker. 2 Aug. 11.
Do. E. Wade (temp.) 11 Mar. 15.
Do. G. Hastewell. 14 Oct. 15.
3rd Bn. D. A. Carter. 25 Aug. 14.
4th Bn. R. Williams. 2 Mar. 13.
11th Bn. — Macdonald.
12th Bn. — Casey.
13th Bn. E. Pomfret (temp.) 7 Dec. 14.
14th Bn. G. T. Prosser. 13 Oct. 14.
16th Bn. R. Cheetham (temp.) 12 Sept. 14.
17th Bn. A. Harrey (temp.) 19 Sept. 14.
Do. H. Coates (temp.) 17 Feb. 15.
18th Bn. T. C. Pearce (temp.) 22 Sept. 14.
Do. B. Hall (temp.) 7 Dec. 14.
Do. W. Reynolds (temp.) 15 Mar. 15.
Do. J. Murnagham (temp.) Nov. 15.
19th Bn. J. O'Malley (temp.) 17 Sept. 14.
Do. H. Waddington (temp.) 26 June 15.
20th Bn. W. H. Hague (temp.) 19 Nov. 14.
Do. J. Kennelly (temp.)
21st Bn. T. Richards (temp.)
Do. T. Wade (temp.)
22nd Bn. J. Hughes (temp.) 3 May 15.
Do. S. Bennett (temp.) Nov. 15.
23rd Bn. J. E. Dunn (temp.) 19 Dec. 14.
24th Bn. A. Gartside (temp.) 1 Feb. 15 (Killed in action 6 Mar. 16).
25th Bn. J. Cush (temp.) 12 Aug. 15.
26th Bn. W. H. Hague. 7 June 15.
27th Bn. W. Mullins (temp.)

BANDMASTERS—

1st Bn. H. Jones. 18 July 02.
2nd Bn. L. L. Hoyle. 1 Apr. 09.

The Regular and Special Reserve Officers who are serving or have served in the Manchester Regiment during the present War, including Officers attached from other Regiments.

Part I.

The Officers of the 1st and 2nd Regular, 3rd and 4th Reserve, 11th, 12th, 13th and 15th Service, 14th Second Reserve, 1st Garrison Battalions, and the Depot.

ADAMS, 2nd Lieut. F. H., 1 Bn. First Appt. 20 Aug. 15.

ADAMS, 2nd Lieut. (temp.) J., 12 (S.) Bn. First Appt. 14 Dec 14. **War Services**—The War of 1914-16. To France to 12 (S.) Bn. 16 Dec. 15.

ADAMSON, 2nd Lieut. W., 4 (Extra Res.) Bn. Spec. Res. of Off. (on prob.) 18 April 15.

ADDISON, 2nd Lieut. (temp.) M. C. B., attd.2/10 Bn. from 14 (Res.) Bn.

AGNEW, Lieut.-Col. Q. G. K., M.V.O., D.S.O. (Gent. at Arms), Major ret. pay, Res. of Off. Comdg. 3 (Res.) Bn. R. Scotch Fus. First Appt. 28 April 86, Lieut.-Col. 8 Oct. 10. **War Services**—Burmese Exp. 1885-6. **(Despatches)**—Op. on N.-W. Frontier of India 1897. S. African War 1899-1902—Relief of Ladysmith, Pieters Hill—**(Despatches, D.S.O.).**

AIKEN, Major J. B., 3 (Res.) Bn. Spec. Res. of Off., Capt. 18 Mar. 96, Major 8 Aug. 12. **War Services**—S. African War 1899-1901—Oper. in Or. Riv. Col.

ALBRECHT, Lieut. V. A., attd. R.F.C. First Appt. (from S.R.) 8 June 12, Lieut. 28 Feb. 14, to R.F.C. 6 Jan. 16. **War Services**—The War of 1914-16—France, sailed with B.E.F. with 2 Bn—Mons, Bavay, Le Cateau (Severely wounded 26 Aug. 14). Rejoined 2 Bn. 4 Jan. 15—Ypres (wounded 19 May 15)—**Awd. Military Cross 1 Jan. 16—Despatches.**

ALDERSON, 2nd Lieut. (temp.) P., attd. 14 (Res.) Bn. from 13 (S.) Bn. First Appt. 29 Dec. 14. **War Services**—The War of 1914-16—France, with 13 (S.) Bn 6 Sept. 15 (Invld. to England 26 Oct. 15.)

ALLCOTT, 2nd Lieut. (temp.) A., attd. 14 (Res.) Bn. from 12 (S.) Bn. 9 Dec. 14. **War Services**—The War of 1914-16—France, with 12 (S.) Bn. 15 July 15. (Invld. to England 1 Dec. 15.)

ALLEN, Lieut. (temp.) A. L., 11 (S.) Bn. Lieut. (temp.) 28 Dec. 14. **War Services**—The War of 1914-16—Gallipoli, 7 Aug. 15—Suvla Bay (Wounded 7-11 Aug. 15). Rejoined Bn.—Suvla Bay, Imbros, 19 Dec. 15—Alexandria, 20 Jan. 16.

ALLURED, 2nd Lieut. (temp.) W., 13 (S.) Bn. First Appt. 16 Jan. 15. **War Services**—The War of 1914-16, to Med. Exp. Force 21 Nov. 15.

ANDERSON, Major C. A. First Appt. from Vols. to Reg. Army 5 May 1900, Major 1 Sept. 15, Adjut. 4 Bn. 7 Dec. 11 to 4 Feb. 16. **War Services**—S. African War 1899-02, Supply Officer, Olivier's Noek. The War of 1914-16.

ANDERSON, 2nd Lieut. C. B. W., 4 (Extra Res.) Bn. (Spec. Res. of Off.) First Appt. 16 May 15.

ANDERSON, Lieut.-Col. F. W. A., 1 Bn. attd. to 6 Bn. R. Lanc. R. First Appt. (Manch. R.) Oct. 1891, Major 1906, transfd. to R. Lanc. R. 1908, Lieut.-Col. Sept. 1914. **War Services**—The War of 1914-16—Mediterranean. **Died Jan. 1916.**

ANDERSON, Bt.-Col. J. H. A., Brig. Comdr. (graded as A.A.G.) 29 Jan. 15. First Appt. 11 May 78, Bt.-Col. 17 Feb. 07. **War Services**—Miranzai Expd. 1891. S. African War 1899-1900—Oper. in Or. Riv. Col. and Cape Col.

ANLEY, Lieut.-Col. (temp.) B. D. L. G., D.S.O., Staff. First Appt. 10 Oct. 94, Major 20 July 12, Lieut.-Col. (temp.) 14 Jan. 16, Genl. Staff Off. 12 Mar. 09 to 8 Jan. 15, Dep. A. Q.M.G. 8 Jan. 15 to 8 June 15, Genl. Staff Off. (1st Grade) Ripon Training Centre 5 Sept. 15. **War Services**—S. African War 1899-1900—**Despatches twice, D.S.O.** The War of 1914-16—France, with B.E.F. as A.P.M. 5th Division, materially assisted reorganisation of retreat after Lecateau at Estrees, Comd. 1 Bn. Jan. to Mar. 15 (Invld. to England)—**Despatches 5 April 15.**

ANTHONY, Capt. G. H., 3 (Res.) Bn., Spec. Res. of Off., Capt. 12 Mar. 07. **War Services**—The War of 1914-16—France, with 2 Bn. 11 Mar. 15—Messines, Kemmel, Ypres (wounded 7 April 15).

ARCHER, 2nd Lieut. (temp.) T. S., 14 (Res.) Bn. First Appt. 13 May 15.

ARMSTRONG, 2nd Lieut. (temp.) T. W., 13 (S.) Bn. First Appt. 26 Mar. 15. **War Services**—The War of 1914-16, to Med. Expd. Force 15 Nov. 15.

ASHWORTH, 2nd Lieut. (temp.) H., 14 (Res.) Bn. from 12 June 15 to 8 Nov. 15.

ASSIG, 2nd Lieut. H. L., 3 (Res.) Bn., Spec. Res. of Off. First Appt. 16 Dec. 14.

ATHERLEY, Capt. J. E. M., 4 (Extra Res.) Bn., Spec. Res. of Off. First Appt. 20 Mar. 12, Lieut. 1 Oct. 14, Capt. 26 June 15. **War Services**—The War of 1914-16—France, attd. 1 Bn. 3 May 15 (Invld to England 14 Oct. 15).

ATKIN, Capt. B. G., Attd. West African Regt. 30 July 13. First Appt. 28 July 09, Lieut. 5 Mar. 13, Capt. 10 June 15. **War Services**—S. African War 1901-2. The War of 1914-16—Cameroons (**Awd. Military Cross 3 June 15**).

ATKINS, 2nd Lieut. W., 3 (Res.) Bn., Spec. Res. of Off. 29 May 15.

AUSTIN, 2nd Lieut. (temp.) J., 15 (S.) Bn. 3 Mar. 15. **War Services**—The War of 1914-16—Med. Expd. Force 12 Jan. 16.

BAILEY, Capt. G. (ret. pay) (Res. of Off.), Capt. of Invalids' R. Hospital, Chelsea. First Appt. 26 June 01, Capt. (local) 14 Sept. 11.

BAILEY, 2nd Lieut. G. N. R., R. Warr. R. First Appt. 26 July 15. **War Services**—The War of 1914-16—France, attd. 2 Bn. Manch. R. Jan. 15—Messines. Kemmel, Ypres, Maricourt (to Mach. Gun Corps Dec. 15).

BALDWIN, Brig.-General (temp.) A. H., Comd. 38th Inf. Bgd. from 5 Sept. 14 to 10 Aug. 15. First Appt. (from Mila) 14 May 84, Brig.-Gen. (temp.) 24 Aug. 14. **War Services**—Miranzai Expd. 1891, S. African War 1902, the War of 1914-16, Med. Expd. Force—Gallipoli. **Killed in Action 10 Aug. 15.**

BALSHAW, 2nd Lieut. W., 2 Bn. (from Spec. Res.) 2 Aug. 13. **War Services**—The War of 1914-16—France, with 2 Bn. 23 Sept. 14—Aisne, Lorgies. **Missing since 20 Oct. 14.**

BANCROFT, 2nd Lieut. (temp.) W., 14 (Res.) Bn. First Appt. 24 Dec. 15.

BARKER, Lieut. A., Gov. Mil. Prison. First Appt. 10 Oct. 14. Lieut. 18 Dec. 14. **War Services**—The War of 1914-16——France, on Gen. H.Q. Staff—**Despatches 5 April 15.**

BARKER, 2nd Lieut. (temp.) H. V., 15 (S.) Bn. First Appt. 7 Dec. 14. **War Services**—The War of 1914-16, to Med. Expd. Force 11 Oct. 15.

BARKER, 2nd Lieut. (temp.) J. W., 13 (S.) Bn. First Appt. 25 Feb. 15. **War Services**—The War of 1914-16—France, with 13 (S.) Bn. 6 Sept. 15—Salonica 6 Nov. 15.

BARKER, 2nd Lieut. N. C., 3 (Res.) Bn., Spec. Res. of Off. First Appt. 19 May 15.

BARNARD, Major-General W. O., Colonel Manchester Regt., born 10 Aug. 38. First Appt. to 96 Foot 15 April 56, Lieut.-Col. comdg. 2 Bn. Manch. R. 8 Feb. 82, Major-Gen. 10 June 96, Ret. 16 Aug. 99. Apptd. Col. Manch. R. 9 Jan. 04. **War Services**—Egyptian Expd. 1882, Comd. 2 Bn. Manch. R., and comd. troops in charge of Res-el-Tin after the bombardment of Alexandria.

BARR, 2nd Lieut. (temp.) W. J., 15 (S.) Bn. First Appt. 7 Dec. 14. **War Services**—The War of 1914-16, to Med. Expd. Force 23 Aug. 15

BARRY, Lieut. J. H., R.A.M.C. **War Services**—The War of 1914-16—France, joined 2 Bn. 4 Mar. 15—Messines, Kemmel, Ypres, Maricourt—**Despatches 1 Jan. 16.**

BARWELL, 2nd Lieut. (temp.) G. M., 14 (Res.) Bn. from 10 Mar. 15 to 25 July 15. (Rel. commd. on acc. of ill-health.)

BATE, Lieut. (temp.) H., 13 (S.) Bn. First Appt. 22 Sept. 14, Lieut. (temp.) 12 Dec. 14. **War Services**—The War of 1914-16, to France, attd. 12 (S.) Bn. 16 Dec. 15.

BATES, Major (temp.) H. C., 11 (S.) Bn. First Appt. (from Mila) 21 April 1900, Major (temp.) 19 Mar. 15. **War Ser-**

vices—The War of 1914-16, Med. Expd. Force—Gallipoli, 7 Aug. 15. **Killed in action, landing Suvla Bay, 7-11 Aug. 15.**

BATTY, 2nd Lieut. (temp.) W. R., 13 (S.) Bn. 18 Dec. 14. **War Services**—The War of 1914-16—France, with 13 (S.) Bn. 6 Sept. 15—Salonika 6 Nov. 15.

BAXTER, Lieut. (temp.) P. R. E. (Lieut. Res. of Off. Manch. R.), Empld. Ind. Working Bn. A.S.C. First Appt. 17 Jan. 02. Lieut. (temp.) 8 Aug. 14. **War Services**—S. African War 1902—Oper. in Transvaal and Cape Col. while attd, to A.S.C. The War of 1914-16—France, with 1 Bn. To Mesopotamia 9 Dec. 15 (Missing from 11 Mar. 16).

BEAL, 2nd Lieut. (temp.) F. A., 12 (S.) Bn. York. and Lanc. R. from 12 (S.) Bn. First Appt. 22 Dec. 14, to Y. and L. R. 2 Sept. 15.

BEDFORD, 2nd Lieut. (temp.) C. C., 1 Bn. First Appt. 24 July 15. **War Services**—The War of 1914-16—France, with 1 Bn. To Mesopotamia 9 Dec. 15 (Killed in action 13 Mar. 16).

BEELEY, Capt. (temp.) F. M., 13 (S.) Bn. First Appt. 22 Sept. 14, Lieut. (temp.) 12 Dec. 14, Capt. (temp.) 25 Mar. 15. **War Services**—The War of 1914-16—France, with 13 (S.) Bn. 6 Sept. 15—Salonika 6 Nov. 15.

BEER, 2nd Lieut. (temp.) H. H., 14 (Res.) Bn. First Appt. 12 Oct. 15. **War Services**—The War of 1914-16, to Medit. Expd. Force 16 Feb. 16.

BELL, 2nd Lieut. (temp.) E. V., 11 (S.) Bn. First Appt. 24 Oct. 14. **War Services**—The War of 1914-16, Medit. Expd. Force—Gallipoli, 7 Aug. 15. **Killed in Action, landing Suvla Bay 7-11 Aug. 15.**

BENSON, 2nd Lieut. (temp.) G. F., 15 (S.) Bn. First Appt. 20 Feb. 15, transfd. to R.E. 16 Oct. 15.

BENSON, Major (temp.) T. C., 1 Gar. Bn. (Capt. ret. pay late R. Irish Fus.). First Appt. 29 July 82, Capt. 30 Dec. 91, Ret. 20 Dec. 02, Major (temp.) 23 Sept. 14, to Manch. R. 8 Sept. 15. **War Services**—Burmese Exped. 1885-9—**Despatches,** S. African War 1901.

BENTLEY, 2nd Lieut. C. L., 2 Bn. First Appt. 8 Aug. 14. **War Services**—The War of 1914-16—France, with 2 Bn. **Killed in Action 28-29 Oct. 14.**

BENTON, Capt. (temp.) W. M., attd. Ripon Training Staff from 12 (S.) Bn., Lieut. (temp.) 8 Mar. 15, Capt. (temp.) 28 April 15. **War Services**—The War of 1914-16—France, 15 July 15 (wounded, to England Oct. 15).

BETTINGTON, 2nd Lieut. J. B., attd. 1 Bn. from 3 (Res.) Bn. Shrops. L.I. from 15 Aug. 14 to 14 Feb. 15, to Reg. Army as 2nd Lieut. (Shrops. L.I.) 15 Feb. 15, Lieut. 21 Mar. 15, empld. with 3 Bn. Nigeria Regt. 30 June 15. **War Services**—The War of 1914-16—France, attd. 1 Bn.—Neuve Chapelle (wounded, to England).

BETTS, Capt. (temp.) J. H., 12 (S.) Bn. First Appt. 12 Sept. 14, Lieut. (temp.) 8 Dec. 14, Capt. (temp.) 27 April 15. **War**

Services—The War of 1914-16—France, with 12 (S.) Bn. 15 July 15.

BERTRAM, Major W. (Lieut.-Col. and Hon. Col. ret. Vols.), Res. of Off. First Appt. 14 Sept. 78, Emp. 11 (S.) Bn. 1 Sept. 14. **War Services**—Egyptian Exped. 1882, S. African War 1899-1900. **Died at Grantham 18 Feb. 15.**

BILLINGE, Lieut. F., Attd. R.F.C. from 3 (Res.) Bn., Spec. Res. of Off. First Appt. 15 Aug. 14, Lieut. 2 Feb. 15. **War Services**—The War of 1914-16—France, Attd. to 2 Bn. 11 Mar. 15—Neuve Chapelle, Ypres (wounded April 15).

BLANCH, Major L. K., 4 (Extra Res.) Bn., Spec. Res. of Off., Lieut. 6 Jan. 1900, Major 30 May 14.

BLANE, Capt. E. R., Spec. Res. of Off. First Appt. 1 July 11, Lieut. 29 Sept. 14, Capt. 9 Feb. 15, working on Munitions. **War Services**—The War of 1914-16—France, attd. to 2 Bn. 15 Oct. 14—Wuluerghem (invld. to England Dec. 14). Rejoined 2 Bn.—Ypres 5 May 15 (invld. to England 19 May 15).

BLEAKLEY, 2nd Lieut. (temp.) A. D., 14 (Res.) Bn. First Appt. 1 Nov. 14. **War Services**—The War of 1914-16, to Medit. Exped. Force 29 Sept. 15, attd. 11 (S.) Bn.—Gallipoli (Suvla Bay), Imbros 19 Dec. 15, Alexandria 20 Jan. 16.

BOLTON, Capt. C. A., General Staff Off. (2nd Grade) 10 Jan. 16. First Appt. 29 Jan. 02, Capt. 1 Dec. 14, Staff College. **War Services**—The War of 1914-16—Medit. Exped. Force Staff. **Despatches 20 May 15**—France.

BOLTON, Capt. (temp.) M. B., 11 (S.) Bn. from 22 Aug. 14 to 17 June 15. First Appt. 22 Aug. 14, Capt. (temp.) 3 June 15, to 5 (Terr.) Bn. East Lancs. R. 17 June 15.

BOSTOCK, Capt. L. C., 4 (Extra Res.) Bn., Spec. Res. of Off. First Appt. 19 Sept. 08, Lieut. 25 May 12, Capt. 10 June 15, attd. 1 Bn. Nigeria Regt. 27 Aug. 13.

BOSWELL, 2nd Lieut. (temp.) J., 14 (Res.) Bn. First Appt. 22 July 15.

BOURNE, 2nd Lieut. H. E. First Appt. 4 Nov. 15 from N. Lanc. R.

BOURNE, 2nd Lieut. L. P. S., 3 (Res.) Bn., Spec. Res. of Off. 16 May 15. **War Services**—The War of 1914-16, to Medit. Exped. Force.

BOUSKILL, 2nd Lieut. (temp.) E., Attd. 2/10 Bn. from 14 (Res.) Bn. First Appt. 6 May 15.

BOYLE, 2nd Lieut. G. A., Attd. 20 (S.) Bn. Durham L.I. from 2 Bn. First Appt. (Spec. Res. of Off.) 13 Mar. 08, to Reg. Army 22 June 15. **War Services**—The War of 1914-16—France, with 2 Bn. Manch. R. 9 Feb. 15—Messines, Kemmel (wounded, to England 31 Mar. 15). Rejoined 2 Bn. 17 June 15—Ypres, Maricourt (invld. to England 16 Aug. 15).

BOX, Lieut. (temp.) R., 14 (Res.) Bn., Lieut. (temp.) 5 Jan. 15. **War Services**—The War of 1914-16, to France 17 Nov. 15, attd. 12 (S.) Bn.

BRADBEER, 2nd Lieut. A. H., 3 (Res.) Bn., Spec. Res. of Off. (on prob.). First Appt. 28 Dec. 15.

BRADBURY, 2nd Lieut. (temp.) A., 13 (S.) Bn. First Appt. 5 Feb. 15, Mach. Gun Officer. **War Services**—The War of 1914-16—France, with 13 (S.) Bn. 6 Sept. 15—Salonika 6 Nov. 15.

BRETHERTON, Lieut.-Col. (temp.) H. W. K., Comdg. 1 (Gar.) Bn. (Col. ret. Terr. Force), Lieut.-Col. (temp.) 24 Dec. 15.

BRIGGS, 2nd Lieut. (temp.) F. H., 14 (Res.) Bn. First Appt. 29 Nov. 15.

BRIGHT, 2nd Lieut. H. N. First Appt. 4 Jan. 16, from Yorkshire Regt.

BRISTER, 2nd Lieut. (temp.) J. F., 14 (Res.) Bn. from 11 (S.) Bn. First Appt. 16 Nov. 14.

BROADHEAD, 2nd Lieut. (temp.) R. W., 14 (Res.) Bn. First Appt. 23 Feb. 15.

BRAYSHAW, 2nd Lieut. H. H., 4 (Extra Res.) Bn., Spec. Res. of Off. 23 May 15.

BROCKLEHURST, 2nd Lieut. (temp.) T. S., 14 (Res.) Bn. First Appt. 9 Nov. 14. **War Services**—The War of 1914-16, to Medit. Exped. Force 23 Sept. 15, attd. 11 (S.) Bn.—Gallipoli (Suvla Bay). **Killed in Action Nov. 15.**

BRODRIBB, Lieut. W. C., 2 Bn., Lieut. 6 Feb. 09. **War Services**—The War of 1914-16—France, sailed with B.E.F. with 2 Bn.—Mons, Bavay, Le Cateau, severely wounded and missing. **Presumed to have been killed in action 26 Aug. 14.**

BRODRICK, Lieut. (temp.) E., 13 (S.) Bn. First Appt. 27 Nov. 14. Lieut. (temp.) 24 Mar. 15. **War Services**—The War of 1914-16—France, with 13 (S.) Bn—Salonika 6 Nov. 15.

BRODRICK, Lieut.-Col. (temp.) L. St. J., Comdg. 1 Scottish Horse from 14 (Res.) Bn., Hon. Capt. in Army 30 July 02, Capt. (temp.) 13 (S.) Bn. 28 Oct. 14, to Res. Bn. 17 May 15, Lieut.-Col. and to commd. Bn. **War Services**—S. African War 1902, served with Imp. Yeo.

BROOKHOUSE, 2nd Lieut. (temp.) H., 14 (Res.) Bn. First Appt. 13 Feb. 15.

BROUGHTON, 2nd Lieut. (temp.) J. W., 2 (Gar.) Bn. Northumberland Fus. from 14 (Res.) Bn. First Appt. 12 June 15.

BROWELL, Capt. (temp.) H. F., 12 (S.) Bn., Capt. (temp.) 9 Sept. 14. **War Services**—The War of 1914-16—France, with 12 (S.) Bn. 15 July 15.

BROWN, 2nd Lieut. A. W., attd. R.F.C. from 3 (Res.) Bn. 31 Aug. 15, Spec. Res. of Off. First Appt. 3 Feb. 15. **War Services**—The War of 1914-16—France, with 2 Bn.—Ypres, Maricourt, also with R.F.C. in France. Missing and Pris. of War 11 Nov. 15.

BROWN, 2nd Lieut. (temp.) E. C. H., 13 (S.) Bn. First Appt. 26 Jan. 15. **War Services**—The War of 1914-16—France, with 13 (S.) Bn. 6 Sept. 15—Salonika 6 Nov. 15.

BROWN, 2nd Lieut. (temp.) G. M., 15 (S.) Bn. First Appt. 2 Mar. 15. **War Services**—The War of 1914-16—Medit. Exped. Force 12 Jan. 16.

BROWN, 2nd Lieut. (temp.) J. B., 14 (Res.) Bn. First Appt. 11 Sept. 15.

BROWN, 2nd Lieut. (temp.) S. J., 14 (Res.) Bn. First Appt. 29 June 15.

BROWNE, Capt. R. G., 1 Bn. First Appt. (from Mila) 19 Oct. 01, Capt. 1 Dec. 14. **War Services**—S. African War 1901. The War of 1914-16, with 1 Bn.—Gwenchy, Neuve Chapelle (wounded, to England 12 Mar. 15).

BROWNE, Capt. T. W., R.A.M.C., Capt. 30 Jan. 10. **War Services**—The War of 1914-16—France, sailed with B.E.F. with 2 Bn.—Mons, Bavay, Aisne, Richebourg, Lorgies, La Quinque Rue, Wulverghem, Messines (invld. to England 19 Jan. 15.

BRYAN, Capt. (Bt.-Major) H. C. M. G., Colonial Secretary Gold Coast. (Res. of Off.) First Appt. 18 June 92, Capt. 26 July 99. **War Services**—West Africa 1897-8, Lagos, **Despatches,** W. Africa (N. Nigeria) 1900 (slightly wounded) **Despatches,** 1900 Ashanti **Despatches,** 1901 Gambia **Despatches.**

BUCHAN, Capt. E. N., D.S.O., Brigade Major 1 Sept. 15. First Appt. (from Mila) 4 May 01, Capt. 1 Dec. 12. **War Services**—S. African War 1899-1902. **Despatches, D.S.O.** The War of 1914-16—France, with 1 Bn.—Gwenchy, Neuve Chappelle. **Killed in Action 25-26 Sept. 15.**

BUCKLEY, 2nd Lieut. (temp.) A., 14 (Res.) Bn. First Appt. 28 Jan. 15. **War Services**—The War of 1914-16, to Medit. Exped. Force 15 Nov. 15.

BUCKLEY, 2nd Lieut. (temp.) H., 12 (S.) Bn. 14 Nov. 14. **War Services**—The War of 1914-16—France, with 12 (S.) Bn. 15 July 15.

BULLOUGH, 2nd Lieut. (temp.) E., 14 (Res.) Bn. First Appt. 27 Feb. 15.

BURDON, 2nd Lieut. (temp. Lieut.) J., 1 Bn. First Appt. 13 Jan. 15, Lieut. (temp) 1 Sept. 15. **War Services**—The War of 1914-16—France, with 1 Bn. To Mesopotamia 9 Dec. 16 (Missing from 13 Mar. 16).

BURNLEY, 2nd Lieut. (temp.) B., 14 (Res.) Bn. First Appt. 29 June 15.

BURROWS, Lieut. R. F. G., 2nd Bn. First Appt. 25 Feb. 14, Lieut. 25 Nov. 14. **War Services**—The War of 1914-16—France, sailed with B.E.F. with 2 Bn.—Mons, Bavay, Le Cateau (Wounded and Prisoner of War 26 Aug. 14.

BUTCHER, 2nd Lieut. R. W., 4 (Extra Res.) Bn., Spec. Res. of Off. First Appt. 22 May 15.

BUTLER, 2nd Lieut. (temp.) H. M., 12 (S.) Bn. 19 Nov. 14. **War Services**—The War of 1914-16—France, with 12 (S.) Bn. 15 July 15.

BUTLER, 2nd Lieut. W. E., 2 Bn., Res. of Off. 14 June 13. **War Services**—The War of 1914-16—France, sailed with B.E.F. with 2nd Bn.—Mons, Bavay, Le Cateau (Wounded and Prisoner of War 26 Aug. 14).

BUTTERWORTH, 2nd Lieut. B., 3 (Res.) Bn., Spec. Res. of

Off. (on prob.) 20 Feb. 15. **War Services**—The War of 1914-16—France, Attd. 1 Bn., to Mesopotamia 9 Dec. 15 (Wounded 4 Mar. 16).

CADDELL, Capt. W. W. de V., Res. of Off., Empld. 3 (Res.) Bn. (Late Capt. 4 Vol. Bn.). First Appt. (Vols.) 4 Mar. 1890, Capt. 18 Oct. 02. **War Services**—Matabele Campaign 1896, Bechuanaland 1896, S. African War (Rhodesia F. Force), Natal 1906.

CALLAN-MACARDLE, 2nd Lieut. (temp.) K., 14 (Res.) Bn. First Appt. 6 April 15. **War Services**—The War of 1914-16, to France. Attd. 12 (S.) Bn. 8 Feb. 16.

CALLIS, Lieut. (temp.) J. A. F., 13 (S.) Bn. First Appt. 22 Sept. 14, Lieut. (temp.) 12 Dec. 14. **War Services**—The War of 1914-16—France, with 13 (S.) Bn. 6 Sept. 15—Salonika 6 Nov. 15.

CAMPBELL, Lieut. (temp.) C., 11 (S.) Bn. First Appt. 22 Sept. 14, Lieut. (temp.) 31 Dec. 14. **War Services**—The War of 1914-16, to France 17 Nov. 15, attd. 12 (S.) Bn. (Wounded 22 Dec. 15).

CAMPBELL, Capt. (temp.) G. L. (Capt. T.F., Res. of Off.). First Appt. from Vols. 16 April 03, Capt. 29 Aug. 07, Empld. Rec. Duties 9 Aug. 14 to 14 Oct. 14, Capt. (temp. Reg. Army) and Adjutant Depot Manch. R. 15 Oct. 14 to 19 Aug. 15. Capt. (temp.) R.F.A. (Reg. Army) 7 July 15, to 181 Bgde. R.F.A. 19 Aug. 15.

CAMPBELL, Lieut. (temp.) H., 11 (S.) Bn., Lieut. (temp.) 31 Dec. 14. **War Services**—The War of 1914-16—Medit. Exped. Force, Gallipoli 7 Aug. 15, Landing Suvla Bay. **(Killed in Action 22 Aug. 15).**

CAMPBELL, Lieut. R. J. P., 3 (Res.) Bn., Spec. Res. of Off. First Appt. 15 Aug. 14, Lieut. 2 Feb. 15. **War Services**—The War of 1914-16—France, attd 1 Bn.

CAREY, Lieut. (temp.) H., 14 (Res.) Bn. First Appt. as Lieut. (temp.) 13 Feb. 15. **War Services**—The War of 1914-16, to Medit. Exped. Force 13 May 15 (Wounded).

CARR, Lieut. (temp.) S. T., 14 (Res.) Bn. First Appt. 23 Oct. 14, Lieut. (temp.) 5 Jan. 15. **War Services**—The War of 1914-16—Gallipoli, attd. 11 (S.) Bn.—Suvla Bay, Imbros 19 Dec. 15, Alexandria 20 Jan. 16.

Carter, 2nd Lieut. (temp.) A. C., 14 (Res.) Bn. First Appt. 16 Nov. 15. **War Services**—The War of 1914-16—France, attd. 12 (S.) Bn. 8 Feb. 16.

CAULFIELD, Lieut. J. C., 2 Bn. from A. S.C. 20 Oct. 14. First Appt. 9 Sept. 11. **War Services**—The War of 1914-16—France, with 2 Bn. **Killed in Action 18 Nov. 14.**

CAWLEY, 2nd Lieut. (temp.) J., 14 (Res.) Bn. First Appt. **War Services**—The War of 1914-16—Medit. Exped. Force 12 Jan. 16.

CHAPMAN, 2nd Lieut. (temp.) F. A., 14 (Res.) Bn. First Appt. 29 June 15. **War Services**—The War of 1914-16, to Medit. Exped. Force 16 Feb. 16.

CHARLTON, Capt. J. E., 4 (Extra Res.) Bn., Spec. Res. of

Off. First Appt. 1 July 02, Capt. 5 May 06. **War Services**—S. African War 1901, served with N. Zealand Mounted Infantry.

CHEETHAM, Bt. Lieut.-Col. C. J., ret. R.M.A. First Appt. 5 Nov. 69, Bt. Lieut.-Col. 21 May 95, ret. full pay 30 May 95, Apptd. Chief Rec. Off. 63rd R.D. Rec. Area 23 Mar. 15. **War Services**—Ashanti War 1873-4. Egyptian Exped. 1882—Bombardment of Forts of Alexandria.

CHITTENDEN, 2nd Lieut. A. G. B., 2 Bn. First Appt. 24 Jan. 14. **War Services**—The War of 1914-16, sailed with B.E.F. with 2 Bn.—Mons, Bavay, Le Cateau, Marne. **Died of wounds received in action 9 Sept. 14.**

CHUTE, Capt. R. A. B., Res. of Off., 1 Bn. First Appt. (from Mila) 9 April 92, Capt. 26 May 1900, Emp. A.S.C. 6 Aug. 14. **War Services**—S. African War, 1899-1900—Relief of Ladysmith, Colenso, Spion Kop. Tugela Heights, Pieter's Hill, Laings Nek, **Despatches.** The War of 1914-16—France, with 1 Bn., afterwards empld. at Base.

CLARE, Lieut. (temp.) S., Adjut. 1 (Gar.) Bn. First Appt. as Temp. Qr.-Mr. and Hon. Lieut. 30 Sept. 15, Lieut. (temp.) and Adjut. 12 Dec. 15.

CLARK, Major (temp.) W. C., attd. 32 Bn. Royal Fus. from 14 (Res.) Bn. First Appt (1 Bn. Manch. R.) 23 April 02, Lieut. (temp.) 30 Oct. 14, Major (temp.) 23 Dec. 14. **War Services**—S. African War 1901.

CLARKE, 2nd Lieut. (temp.) H., 14 (Res.) Bn. First Appt. 2 April 15.

CLARKE, 2nd Lieut. (temp.) J., 14 (Res.) Bn. First Appt. 29 June 15.

CLARKE, 2nd Lieut. (temp.) J. H., 14 (Res.) Bn. First Appt. 5 Feb. 15. **War Services**—The War of 1914-16, to Medit. Exp. Force 15 Nov. 15.

CLARKE, 2nd Lieut. (temp.) L., 14 (Res.) Bn. First Appt. 11 Mar. 15.

CLAYTON, 2nd Lieut. (temp.) H. V., 14 (Res.) Bn. First Appt. 7 Dec. 14. **War Services**—The War of 1914-16, to Medit. Exped. Force 23 Sept. 15, attd. 76 Bn.—Gallipoli (Invld. to England).

CLIMO, Major V. C., Ret. Pay. Res. of Officers. First Appt. 22 Aug. 88, Major 27 June 1900, General Staff Officer (2nd Grade) 27 Aug. 14. **War Services**—Ashanti Exped. 1895-6—S. African War 1901—Spec. Serv. Officer. The War of 1914-16 France, on Staff of 35th Division.

CLOSE-BROOKS, Capt. A. B., 3 (Res.) Bn., Spec. Res. of Off. First Appt. 10 Oct. 14, Capt. 1 June 15. **War Services**—The War of 1914-16—France, attd. 2 Bn. 1 Mar. 15—Messines. Kemmel, Ypres (Invld. to England 23 July 15). **Awarded Military Cross 24 July 15. Despatches.**

CLOUGH, 2nd Lieut. (temp.) H. C., 14 (Res.) Bn. First Appt. July 15.

COE, 2nd Lieut. E. R. C., attd. R.E. from 3 (Res.) Bn. 20 May 15, Empld. on Sig. Serv. 30 Sept. 15.

COLLEY, 2nd Lieut. (temp.) W. D., Machine Gun Corps from 14 (Res.) Bn. 17 Mar. 15.

COLLIER, 2nd Lieut. H. C. de Z., 3 (Res.) Bn., Spec. Res. of Off (on prob.) 24 July 15.

CONNELL, Lieut. (temp.) S. D., 1 Bn. First Appt. 24 Jan. 14, Lieut. (temp.) 31 Aug. 14. **War Services**—The War of 1914—France, **Despatches, 17 Feb. 15. Killed in Action 21 Dec. 14.**

CONNERY, Hon. Lieut. and Quar.-Master W. L., 3 (Res.) Bn. First Appt. 27 Mar. 09. **War Services**—S. African War 1899-1902—Elandslaagte, Defence of Ladysmith, **Despatches (twice).** The War of 1914-16—France, sailed with B.E.F. with 2 Bn.—Mons, Bavay, Le Cateau, Marne, Aisne, Richebourg, Messines, Ypres (Invld. to England April 15). **Despatches, 17 Feb. 15.**

COOMBES, 2nd Lieut. (temp. Lieut.) A. E., Empld. with West African F.F. (Gambia Comp.). First Appt. 23 May 15, Lieut. (temp.) 7 July 15. **War Services**—The War of 1914-16—Cameroons (Wounded).

COOPER, 2nd Lieut. (temp.) A., 14 (Res.) Bn. First Appt. 16 Nov. 15. **War Services**—The War of 1914-16, to France 8 Feb. 16, attd. 12 (S.) Bn.

COOPER, 2nd Lieut. E., 3 (Res.) Bn., Spec. Res. of Off. 29 May 15.

COOPER, 2nd Lieut. (temp.) J., 14 (Res.) Bn. First Appt. 25 Mar. 15. **War Services**—The War of 1914-16, to Medit. Exp. Force 23 Sept. 15—Gallipoli (Suvla Bay), Imbros, 19 Dec. 15, Alexandria 20 Jan. 16.

COOPER, 2nd Lieut. R. P., 3 (Res.) Bn., Spec. Res. of Off. First Appt. 16 May 15.

CORLEY, 2nd Lieut. (temp.) H. H., 15 (S.) Bn. First Appt. 6 Dec. 14. **War Services**—The War of 1914-16—Gallipoli, attd. 11 (S.) Bn., Suvla Bay 23 Aug. 15, Imbros 19 Dec. 15, Alex-Andria 20 Jan. 16.

COSGROVE, Lieut. E. T., 3 (Res.) Bn., Spec. Res. of Off. First Appt. 15 Aug. 14, Lieut. 2 Feb. 15. **War Services**—The War of 1914-16—France, attd. 2 Bn. 25 Feb. 15—Messines (Invld. to England 12 Mar. 15).

COULTER, 2nd Lieut. (temp.) A. K., 12 (S.) Bn. First Appt. 22 Dec. 14. **War Services**—The War of 1914-16—France, with 12 (S.) Bn. 15 July 15.

COURT, 2nd Lieut. (temp.) R. H., 14 (Res.) Bn. First Appt. 16 Aug. 15.

COWLEY, 2nd Lieut. (temp.) J., 14 (Res.) Bn. First Appt. 12 May 15.

COX, 2nd Lieut. (temp.) J. P., 12 (S.) Bn. First Appt. 28 Nov. 15.

CRAWFORD, Lieut.-Col. (temp.) J. C., Comdg. Convalescent Camp, Egypt. First Appt. (from Mila) 9 May 88, Adjut. (Mila) 98 to 03, Major 18 April 03, Commanded Depot Manc. R. 1907 to 1910, Rec. Staff Off. Birmingham 1910 to 1914, Commanded 16 (S.) Bn. Manch. R. 1 Sept 14 to 10 Mar 15, Lieut.-Col. 10 Mar. 15, Commd. 1 Bn. 10 Mar. 15 to Oct. 15.

War Services—S. African War 1901-2, **Despatches.** The War of 1914-16—France, in command of 1 Bn.

CRAWHALL, Lieut. N. G., 1 Bn. First Appt. 25 Feb. 14, Lieut. 1 Dec. 14. **War Services**—The War of 1914-16—France, attd. to E. Lancs. R. (Wounded April 15).

CRAWSHAW, 2nd Lieut. (temp.) J. E., 14 (Res.) Bn. First Appt. 23 Feb. 15. **War Services**—The War of 1914-16, to Medit. Exped. Force 2 Feb. 16.

CREAGH, Capt. L., 1 Bn. First Appt. (from Mila) 4 Jan. 99, Capt. 27 Nov. 01. **War Services**—S. African War 1899—Lombard's Kop, Defence of Ladysmith. The War of 1914-16—France, with Indian Cont. 26 Sept. 14—Givenchy. **Killed in Action 20-21 Dec. 14.**

CREALOCK, Capt. (temp.) J. M. S. (Lieut. Res. of Off. 1 May 97), Capt. 4 Bn. (Spec. Res. of Off.) Notts. and Derby R., to Manch. R. (temp. Capt.) 11 Sept. 14, with 12 (S.) Bn. Rel. Commn. on acc. of ill-health 23 Aug. 15. **War Services**—S. African War 1899-1900.

CRICHTON, 2nd Lieut. (temp.) H. C., 14 (Res.) Bn. First Appt. 24 July 15.

CUNNINGHAM, 2nd Lieut. C. M. S., 3 (Res.) Bn. (Spec. Res. of Off.) 11 May 15. **War Services**—The War of 1914-16—Gallipoli, attd. 11 (S.) Bn., Suvla Bay, Imbros 19 Dec. 15—Alexandria 20 Jan. 16.

CURTIS, 2nd Lieut. W., 1 Bn. First Appt. 29 Dec. 14. **War Services**—The War of 1914-16—France, with 1 Bn.—Neuve Chapelle. **Killed in Action 13 or 14 Mar. 15.**

CURWEN, 2nd Lieut. (temp.) G. E., 13 (S.) Bn. First Appt. 10 Feb. 15, Transport Off. **War Services**—The War of 1914-16—France, with 13 (S.) Bn. 6 Sept. 15—Salonika 6 Nov. 15.

DAVIDSON, Lieut. M. R....First Appt. 15 Aug. 14, Lieut. 1 Dec. 14. **War Services**—The War of 1914-16—France, with 1 Bn.—Neuve Chapelle (Wounded 12 Mar. 15).

DAVIDSON, Lieut. R. I. M., 1 Bn. First Appt. 18 Sept. 09, Lieut. 30 July 13. **War Services**—The War of 1914-16—France, with Indian Cont. 26 Sept. 14. **Died of wounds received in action 24 Nov. 14.**

DAVIES, Lieut. (temp.) G. A., 14 (Res.) Bn. First Appt. Lieut. (temp.) 7 Jan. 15. **War Services**—The War of 1914-16, to Medit. Exped. Force 26 Nov. 15—Egypt (Comd. Comp. Coy. of Highlanders).

DAVIES, 2nd Lieut. R. C., 1 Bn. First Appt. 3 (Res.) Bn. 30 Dec. 14, to Reg. Army 15 Aug. 15. **War Services**—The War of 1914-16—France, with 1 Bn. (Wounded 13 June 15). Rejoined 1 Bn.—France. To Mesopotamia 9 Dec. 15. **Killed in Action 11 Mar. 16.**

DEAN, 2nd Lieut. (temp.) W. P., Attd. 2/10 Bn. from 14 (Res.) Bn. First Appt. 12 May 15.

DEARDEN, Capt. J. A., Adjut. 9 (T.) Bn. Manch. R. 12 Mar. 12. First Appt. (from Mila.) 28 Jan. 03, Capt. 1 Dec. 14. **War Services**—S. African War 1902. The War of 1914-16,

Medit. Exped. Force—Gallipoli, with 9 Bn. 9 May 15 (Invld. to England).

DE JONGH, 2nd Lieut. V. H. P., 4 (Extra Res.) Bn., Spec. Res. of Off. First Appt. 31 Mar. 15.

DEMPSTER, Major (temp.) J. F., 13 (S.) Bn. Ches. R., Res. of Off. (late Capt. 5 Bn.) (Hon. Capt. in Army), Capt. 8 May 1900, Major (temp.) 11 Sept. 14, Staff Capt. 20 Mar. 15. **War Services**—S. African War 1901—Oper. in Or. Riv. Col.

DE PUTRON, Capt. H., Staff. First Appt. (from Mila.) 28 Aug. 01, Empd. with African Frontier Force 12 Oct. 07 to 17 Mar. 12, Capt. 30 Oct. 14, Gen. Staff Off. (3rd Class) War Office—on Staff Dir. of Home Defence 5 June 15. **War Services**—S. African War 1900. West Africa 1900—Oper. in Ashanti. The War of 1914-16—France, with 2 Bn. 6 Sept 14—Tournan, Marne, Aisne, Richebourg (Invld. to England Oct. 14).

DERBY, Rt. Hon. E. G. V., Earl of, K.G., G.C.V.O., C.B. (Temp. Lieut.-Col. Comdg. 1 Dock Bn. Liverpool R.), Hon. Col. 4 (Extra Res.) Bn. Manch. R. 24 Dec. 02.

DIGBY, Hon. Major H. M. (Res. of Off.), Capt. 11 May 02, Rec. Offr. 63rd R.D. Rec. Area from 11 Oct. 14 to 31 May 15. **War Services**—S. African War 1900-02.

DIXON, Capt. G., 3 (Res.) Bn., Spec. Res. of Off. First Appt. 7 Aug. 12, Capt. 2 Feb. 15. **War Services**—The War of 1914-16—France, with 2 Bn. 23 Sept. 14—Aisne, La Basse (Wounded and Prisoner of War 20 Oct. 14). **Despatches 17 Feb. 15.**

DONALDSON, 2nd Lieut. (temp.) A., 14 (Res.) Bn. First Appt. 29 Dec. 14. **War Services**—The War of 1914-16, to Medit. Exped. Force 21 Sept. 15—Gallipoli (Suvla Bay), Imbros 19 Dec. 15—Alexandria 20 Jan. 16.

DONALDSON, 2nd Lieut. (temp.) R. C., 2/5 Bn. from 13 (S.) Bn. First Appt. 29 April 15.

DORLING, Major (temp.) F. H., Staff of Dir. Home Defence. First Appt. 8 Sept. 97, Capt. 5 Jan. 01, Major (temp.) 10 Mar. 15, General Staff Off. (3rd Grade) 13 Mar. 15, Empld. with S. African Constabulary 30 Mar. 01 to 30 June 04, O.C. Coy. Gent. Cadets, R. Mil. Coll. 17 Sept. 06 to 16 Sept. 10. **War Services**—S. African War 1900-2 (on Staff). The War of 1914-16—France, sailed with B.E.F. as Staff Capt. 14 Inf. Bgde.—Mons, Bavay, Le Cateau, Marne, Aisne, Richebourg, Lorgies (Invld. to England).

DOUGHTY, 2nd Lieut. (temp.) G. H., 14 Res.) Bn. First Appt. 29 June 15.

DRUITT, 2nd Lieut. (temp.) T. R., 15 (S.) Bn. First Appt. 26 Feb. 15. **War Services**—The War of 1914-16—Medit. Exped. Force 12 Jan. 16.

DRUMMOND, Major K. M., Res. of Off., 2nd in Commd. 13 (S.) Bn. First Appt. 22 Oct. 81, Major 8 July 99, to Manch. Regt. 8 Oct. 14. **War Services**—The War of 1914-16—France, with 13 (S.) Bn. 6 Sept. 15—Salonika 6 Nov. 15.

DUFFY, 2nd Lieut. (temp.) K., 14 (Res.) Bn. from 24 Nov. 14 to 8 Nov. 15.

DUKE, 2nd Lieut. (temp.) F. R., 14 (Res.) Bn. First Appt. 3 Nov. 15.

DUNCAN, 2nd Lieut. A., 4 (Extra Res.) Bn., Spec. Res. of Off. (on prob.) 21 Oct. 15.

DUNLOP, Capt. F. C. S., 1 Bn. First Appt. 1 Dec. 97, Adjut. Indian Vols. 1906 to 1911, Capt. 12 Mar. 01. **War Services**—S. African War 1899-1901—Defence of Ladysmith. The War of 1914-16—France, with Indian Cont. 26 Sept. 14. **Killed in Action 8 Nov. 14.**

DUNLOP, 2nd Lieut. (temp.) M. J., 14 (Res.) Bn. First Appt. 14 June 15. **War Services**—The War of 1914-16, to Medit. Exped. Force 16 Feb. 16.

DU VAL, 2nd Lieut. (temp.) B., 12 (S.) Bn. First Appt. 18 Feb. 15, Lieut. (temp.) 26 April 15. **War Services**—The War of 1914-16—France 15 July 15.

DYSON, 2nd Lieut. (temp.) S. W., 14 (Res.) Bn. First Appt. 18 Dec. 14. **War Services**—The War of 1914-16, to Medit. Exped. Force 22 Sept. 15—Gallipoli (Suvla Bay), Imbros, 19 Dec. 15—Alexandria 20 Jan. 16.

DUGUID, 2nd Lieut. (temp.) C. F., 14 (Res.) Bn. from 13 (S.) Bn. First Appt. 23 Feb. 15.

EARLE, 2nd Lieut. (temp.) P. A., Attd. 14 (Res.) Bn. from 12 (S.) Bn. First Appt. 30 Nov. 14.

ECKHARD, Lieut. (temp.) O. P., 12 (S.) Bn. First Appt. 14 Sept. 14, Lieut. (temp.) 27 April 15. **War Services**—The War of 1914-16—France, with 12 (S.) Bn. 15 July 15.

EDDOWES, Major W. B., Attd. 13 (S.) Bn. North'd. Fus. 28 Aug. 15, Commd. 10 Bn. Yorks. Regt. First Appt. 24 June 99, Capt. 5 Feb. 03, Major 1 Sept. 15, Empd. with Indian Cont. to 28 Aug. 15. **War Services**—S. African War 1889-1902—Lombard's Kop, Defence of Ladysmith (Wounded).

EDMINSON, 2nd Lieut. (temp.) L. O., 12 (S.) Bn. First Appt. 3 Mar. 15. **War Services**—The War of 1914-16, to France to 12 (S.) Bn. 15 Oct. 15.

EDWARDS, Lieut. (temp.) S. B., 13 (S.) Bn., Lieut. (temp.) 28 Jan. 15. **War Services**—The War of 1914-16—France, with 13 (S.) Bn. 6 Sept. 15—Salonika 6 Nov. 15.

ELLAM, Capt. (temp.) J. E., 12 (S.) Bn., Lieut. (temp.) 15 Oct. 14, Capt. (temp.) 29 April 15. **War Services**—The War of 1914-16—France, with 12 (S.) Bn. 15 July 15 (Invld. to England). Rejoined 12 (S.) Bn. 4 Feb. 16.

ELLERSHAW, Capt. H., Adjut. 11 (S.) Bn. First Appt. (from Mila.) 19 Oct. 01, Asst. Supt. Gymnasium 24 April 07 to 23 April 11, Capt. 1 Dec. 14. **War Services**—S. African War 1899-02. The War of 1914-16—Gallipoli, 7 Aug. 15, Suvla Bay Landing (Wounded, to England 7-11 Aug. 15). **Despatches 11 Dec. 15.**

EMBERTON, 2nd Lieut. (temp.) J. W., 1 (Gar.) Bn. First Appt. 8 July 15 (Ches. R.), to Manch. R. 28 Nov. 15.

EMMOTT, 2nd Lieut. H., 3 (Res.) Bn., Spec. Res. of Off. 23

Jan. 15. **War Services**—The War of 1914-16—France, attd. to 1 Bn. (Returned to England).

ERSKINE, Capt. B. L., 4 (Extra Res.) Bn., Spec. Res. of Off., Lieut. 1 Feb. 12, Capt. 1 Sept. 14.

ERSKINE, Lieut.-Col. (temp.) J. D. B., Res. of Off., Comdg. 8 (S.) Bn. Shrops. L.I. First Appt. 6 June 96, Capt. 9 June 1900, Major (temp.) and 2nd in Commd. 13 (S.) Bn. Manch. R. 5 Oct. 14 to 8 Mar. 15, Lieut.-Col. (temp.) 8 Mar. 15. **War Services**—S. African War 1900-02.

ESSENHIGH, 2nd Lieut. (temp.) R. C., Attd. 2 Bn. from 14 (Res.) Bn. First Appt. 10 Mar. 15. **War Services**—The War of 1914-16—France, with 2 Bn. 12 Oct. 15—Maricourt.

EVANS, 2nd Lieut. I. B., 1 Bn. First Appt. 14 July 15. **War Services**—The War of 1914-16—France, with 1 Bn.

EVANS, 2nd Lieut. R. F. O., 3 (Res.) Bn., Spec. Res. of Off. (on prob.). First Appt. 30 Nov. 15.

EVANS, Major W. K., D.S.O., Staff. First Appt. (from Mila.) 21 April 1900, Capt. 18 Dec. 07, Major 1 Sept. 15, Genl. Staff Off. 2 Aug. 15, Comdg. 2 Bn. 29 Sept. 14 to 26 Nov. 14, and then Adjut. up to 13 July 15. **War Services**—S. African War 1900-2. The War of 1914-16—France, with 2 Bn. 16 Sept. 15—Richebourg, Lorgies, La Quinque Rue, to Hd. Qr. 3rd Army 13 July 15. **To be Comp. Dist. Service Order 18 Feb. 15. Despatches 17 Feb. 15.**

EVILL, 2nd Lieut. G., 4 (Extra Res.) Bn., Spec. Res. of Off. 15 Aug. 14. **War Services**—The War of 1914-16—France, attd. to 2 Bn. 5 May 15—Ypres, Maricourt.

EWEN, Capt. (temp.) G. T., Brigade Mach. Gun Off., 3 (Res.) Bn., Spec. Res. of Off. First Appt. 28 Oct. 14, Lieut. (temp.) 2 Feb. 15, Capt. (temp.) 17 June 15. **War Services**—The War of 1914-16—France, attd. to 2 Bn., afterwards to 1 Bn. To Mesopotamia 9 Dec. 15 (Missing from 11 Mar. 16). **Awd. Military Cross 1 Jan. 16.**

FALCONER, 2nd Lieut. H., 3 (Res.) Bn., Spec. Res. of Off. (on prob.). First Appt. 4 Nov. 15.

FARRAR, 2nd Lieut. H. R., 3 (Res.) Bn. Leic. R. 15 Aug. 14. **War Services**—The War of 1914-16—France, attd. 2 Bn. Manch. R. Nov. 15. **Killed in Action 24 Dec. 14.**

FARRELLY, Capt. (temp.) F. J., 14 (Res.) Bn. from 19 Jan. 15 to 2 June 15.

FARROW, 2nd Lieut. (temp.) E. P., 14 (Res.) Bn. First Appt. 13 Nov. 14.

FAUX, 2nd Lieut. S. E., 3 (Res.) Bn., Spec. Res. of Off. (on prob.). First Appt. 28 Dec. 15.

FERGUSON, Capt. (temp.) J. M., Attd. 14 (Res.) Bn. from 11 (S.) Bn., Lieut. (temp.) 16 Sept. 14, Capt. (temp.) 16 April 15. **War Services**—The War of 1914-16—Medit. Exped. Force, Gallipoli, 7 Aug. 15, Suvla Bay Landing (Invld. to England).

FENNYHOUGH, 2nd Lieut. S., 4 (Extra Res.) Bn., Spec. Res. of Off. First Appt. 22 May 15.

FINCH, Major W. R. E. H., 3 (Res.) Bn., Spec. Res. of Off. (Hon. Capt. in Army 6 July 1901), Capt. 22 Oct. 14, Major

2 Feb. 15. **War Services**—The War of 1914-16—France, attd. to 1 Bn., since been empld. at Base.

FINDLATER, 2nd Lieut. L., 3 (Res.) Bn., Spec. Res. of Off. 6 Feb. 15. **War Services**—The War of 1914-16—France, attd. to 1 Bn. (Wounded, to England 29 Sept. 15). **Despatches 15 Oct. 15, Awd. Military Cross 29 Oct. 15.**

FISHER, Capt. H., D.S.O., 1 Bn. First Appt. (from Mila.) 4 May 98, Capt. 14 July 01. **War Services**—S. African War 1899-1902—Elandslaagte, Lombard's Kop, Def. of Ladysmith (severely wounded), **Despatches (four times), D.S.O.** The War of 1914—France (Givenchy). **Killed in Action 16 Dec 14.**

FLANAGAN, 2nd Lieut., Attd. Indian Vols. First Appt. 8 Nov. 15.

FOORD, Major A. G., Empld. on Inst. Duties. First Appt. 5 Jan. 01, Capt. 1 Dec. 12, Major 5 Jan. 16. **War Services**—The War of 1914-16—France, sailed with B.E.F. with 2 Bn. —Mons, Bavay, Le Cateau, Marne (Severely Wounded 9 Sept. 14).

FORMAN, 2nd Lieut. (temp.) E. B., 14 (Res.) Bn. First Appt. 11 Feb. 15.

FORTH, Major, N. B. de L. First Appt. 19 May 1900, Capt. 20 July 12, Major 1 Sept. 15, Empld. Egyptian Army. **War Services**—S. African War 1900-1, Soudan 1908 (Slightly Wounded), Soudan 1910. The War of 1914-15—Egypt. **Awd. Military Cross 10 Mar. 15.**

FOWKE, Capt. M. C. First Appt. (from Mila.) 5 Jan. 01, Empd. with King's Afr. Rifles 26 Nov. 08 to 23 Nov. 13, Capt. 1 Dec. 12. **War Services**—S. African War 1901-2. East African (Somaliland) 1908-10. The War of 1914-16—France, sailed with B.E.F. with 2 Bn.—Mons, Bavay, Le Cateau. Reptd. Severely Wounded and Missing. **Afterwards declared "Killed in Action 26 Aug. 14."**

FOX, 2nd Lieut. (temp.) G. A., 14 (Res.) Bn. First Appt. 29 June 15.

FRANKLIN, 2nd Lieut. H. First Appt. 10 July 15. **War Services**—The War of 1914-16—France, with 1 Bn. as Act. Sgt.-Maj. **Prom. 2nd Lieut. for Services in the Field, 10 July 15.**

FRAZER, 2nd Lieut. (temp.) M. Mc. L., 14 (Res.) Bn. First Appt. 10 April 15.

FRAZIER, Hon. Lieut. C. H., Quartermaster 11 (S.) Bn. 25 Aug. 14. **War Services**—The War of 1914-16, Medit. Exped. Force—Gallipoli 7 Aug. 15—Suvla Bay Landing, Imbros 19 Dec. 15—Alexandria 20 Jan. 16.

FREEMAN, Capt. W. R., Attd. to R. Flying Corps. First Appt. 22 Feb. 08, Lieut. 27 Mar. 12, Flying Officer 28 April 14, Flight Commdr. 17 Mar. 15, Capt. 10 June 15. **War Services**—The War of 1914-16—France. **Awd. Military Cross 27 Mar. 15, Despatches 5 April 15.**

FRITH, Lieut. (temp.) W. H., 1 (Gar.) Bn. First Appt. 10 Dec. 14, Lieut. (temp.) 2 June 15, to Res. Bn. 7 Sept. 15, to Gar. Bn. 30 Oct. 15.

FRYER, 2nd Lieut. P., 3 (Res.) Bn., Spec. Res. of Off. First

Appt. 17 April 15. **War Services**—The War of 1914-16—France, attd. 1 Bn.

GADSBY, 2nd Lieut. C., 4 (Extra Res.) Bn., Spec. Res. of Off. First Appt. 7 May 15.

GANDY, 2nd Lieut. (temp.) L., 14 (Res.) Bn. First Appt. 11 Mar. 15.

GARDINER, 2nd Lieut. P. W., 4 (Extra Res.) Bn., Spec. Res. of Off. (on prob.). First Appt. 25 Sept. 15.

GARRETT, Hon. Major G., Res. of Off. First Appt. 28 April 1900, Hon. Capt. 28 April 10, Hon. Major 27 July 15, Apptd. Quartermaster Depot Manch. Regt. 5 Aug. 14. **War Services**—S. African War 1899 to 1902. **Despatches.**

GATENBY, Lieut. (temp.) J., 14 (Res.) Bn. First Appt. Lieut. (temp.) 5 Jan. 15. **War Services**—The War of 1914-16, to Medit. Exped. Force 2 Feb. 16.

GAUNTLETT, 2nd Lieut. (temp.) J., 14 (Res.) Bn. First Appt. 31 May 15.

GAUKROGER, 2nd Lieut. (temp.) H., 1 Bn. First Appt. 7 Nov. 15. **War Services**—The War of 1914-16. To Mesopotamia (Wounded 10 Mar. 16).

GELLIBRAND, Capt. J., Res. of Off. First Appt. 21 Oct. 93, Capt. 26 May 1900, Empld. special work not under War Office. **War Services**—S. African War 1899-1900—Relief of Ladysmith, Tugela Heights, and Pieter's Hill.

GERARD, 2nd Lieut. T. O., 4 (Extra Res.) Bn., Spec. Res. of Off. First Appt. 10 Mar. 15.

GIBSON, 2nd Lieut. C. H., 1 Bn. First Appt. 15 Sept. 15. **War Services**—The War of 1914-16—France, with 1 Bn.

GICK, 2nd Lieut. (temp.) T. M., 14 (Res.) Bn. First Appt. 18 Dec. 14. **War Services**—The War of 1914-16, to Medit. Expd. Force 11 Jan. 16, Attd. 1/8 (T.) Bn.

GILL, 2nd Lieut. C. T., 4 (Extra Res.) Bn., Spec. Res. of Off. First Appt. 28 April 15.

GILLIAT, 2nd Lieut. (temp.) F., 14 (Res.) Bn. First Appt. 12 June 15.

GLEN, 2nd Lieut. D. A., Attd. to R. Flying Corps. First Appt. 12 May 15. Flying Officer 24 July 15. **War Services**—The War of 1914-16—France (Missing since 30 Dec. 15).

GLOVER, Lieut. G. M., 2 Bn. First Appt. 15 Sept. 14, Lieut. 1 Dec. 14. **War Services**—The War of 1914-16—France, with 2 Bn. 6 Oct. 15—Maricourt.

GOLDSMICHT, Lieut. (temp.) J. P., 13 (S.) Bn. First Appt. 24 Nov. 14, Lieut. 12 Dec. 14. **War Services**—The War of 1914-16, Medit. Exped. Force, with 13 (S.) Bn. 14 Jan. 16—Salonika.

GOODWIN, Lieut. (temp.) E. L., Attd. 14 (Res.) Bn. from 13 (S.) Bn. First Appt. 16 Nov. 14, Lieut. (temp.) 1 Feb. 15. **War Services**—The War of 1914-16—France, with 13 (S.) Bn. 6 Sept. 15 (Injured by fall in trench. To England 19 Sept. 15).

GOODWIN, Major W. M., 1 Bn. Devon R., Attd. 2 Bn. Manch. R. as 2nd in Commd., Major 16 July 14. **War Services**—The

War of 1914-16—France, Attd. to 2 Bn. Manch. R. 26 Aug. 15—Maricourt (Invld. to England 2 Sept. 15).

GOUGH, 2nd Lieut. (temp.) J. S., 14 (Res.) Bn. First Appt. 28 Nov. 14.

GRAHAM, 2nd Lieut. E. C., 3(Res.) Bn., Spec. Res. of Off. First Appt. 26 May 15.

GRAHAM, 2nd Lieut. L. M., 3 (Res.) Bn., Spec. Res. of Off. (on prob.). First Appt. 25 Sept. 15.

GRANGE, 2nd Lieut. (temp.) F., Attd. 2/10 Bn. from 14 (Res.) Bn. First Appt. 6 May 15.

GRAY, 2nd Lieut. (temp.) E. C., 14 (Res.) Bn. First Appt. 13 Nov. 14. **War Services**—The War of 1914-16, to Medit. Exp. Force 21 Sept. 15, Attd. 11 (S.) Bn.—Gallipoli (Suvla Bay), Imbros 19 Dec. 15—Alexandria 20 Jan. 16.

GRAY, 2nd Lieut. F., 3 (Res.) Bn., Spec. Res. of Off. First Appt. 8 May 15.

GREEN, 2nd Lieut. C. C., 3 (Res.) Bn., Spec. Res. of Off. First Appt. 26 May 15.

GREEN, Capt. (temp.) H. R. C., 2 Bn. First Appt. (Spec. Res. of Off.) 4 Jan. 13, to Reg. Army 14 Aug. 14, Lieut. 1 Dec. 14, Capt. (temp.) 1 Aug. 15. **War Services**—The War of 1914-16—France, with 2 Bn. 3 Dec. 14—Wulverghem, Messines (Invld. to England 11 Feb. 15). Rejoined 2 Bn. April 15—Ypres, Maricourt.

GREENGRASS, 2nd Lieut. (temp.) R. P. W., 14 (Res.) Bn. First Appt. 16 Nov. 15.

GREENWOOD, 2nd Lieut. (temp.) T. S., 14 (Res.) Bn. First Appt. 16 Aug. 15. **War Services**—The War of 1914-16, to France 17 Nov. 15, Attd. to 12 (S.) Bn. (Wounded 22 Dec. 15).

GREER, Capt. (temp.) J. J. MacC., Adjut. 14 (Res.) Bn. 8 June 15 Capt. (temp.) 15 Mar. 15.

GREER, Lieut.-Col. (temp.) T. M., Spec. Res. of Off., Capt. 15 Jan. 02, Major 1 April 11, Lieut.-Col. (temp.) and to Commd. 14 (S.) Bn. Manch. R. 12 Nov. 14. **War Services**—S. African War 1900-2, Empld. with Imp. Yeo.

GRIFFIN, 2nd Lieut. (temp.) H. R. First Appt. 28 Nov. 15.

GRIFFIN, 2nd Lieut. (temp.) G. B. First Appt. 28 Nov. 15.

GRINDEL, Lieut. J. H., 2 Bn. First Appt. 20 Dec. 14, Lieut. 27 April 15. **War Services**—The War of 1914-16—France, with 2 Bn.—Ypres (Wounded, to England 15 May 15). Rejoined 2 Bn.—Maricourt.

GRUNDY, 2nd Lieut. F., 4 (Extra Res.) Bn., Spec. Res. of Off. First Appt. 8 April 15, Empld. Sig. Off. Humber Garrison.

GUDGEON, 2nd Lieut. S., 3 (Res.) Bn., Spec. Res. of Off. First Appt. 15 Aug. 14. **War Services**—The War of 1914-16—France, with 2 Bn. 25 Feb. 15—Messines, Kemmel, Ypres (Wounded 1 April and 19 April 15). **Killed in Action 14 May 15.**

GUINNESS, Lieut. A. R., Attd. H.Q. Staff Northern Commd. from 4 (Extra Res.) Bn., Spec. Res. of Off. First Appt. 15 Aug. 14, Lieut. 4 May 15. **War Services**—The War of 1914-

16—France, with 2 Bn. 10 May 15—Ypres (Wounded, to England 10 June 15).

GUINNESS, Capt. W. E., Musketry Officer Humber Defences, 4 (Extra Res.) Bn., Spec. Res. of Off. First Appt. 8 Feb. 02, Empld. with W. African Frontier Force 21 Sept. 07 to 30 Oct. 10, Capt. (Spec. Res. of Off.) 3 May 13, Capt. (Reg. Army) 1 Sept. 14. **War Services**—S. African War 1901 (Empld. with Imp. Yeo.). The War of 1914-16—France, with 1 Bn. Feb. 15—Ypres (Wounded, to England 26 Apl. 15).

GUNNING, Lieut.-Col. O. G., C.M.G., 35 Sikhs, Attd. 3 (Res.) Bn. Manch. R. 28 Aug. 14 to Jan. 15. First Appt. 22 Aug. 88 (1 Bn. Manch. R.), to Ind. S.C. 19 Feb. 92. **War Services**—Maranza (2nd) Exped. 1891. Exped. to Dongola 1896. N.-W. Front. India 1897-8—Malakand. Oper. in Bajaur and Mamund Country—Otman Khel (Severely Wounded). **Despatches (twice).** The War of 1914-16—France, with Ind. Cont. from Jan. 15.

GWYTHER, Capt. H. J., 3 (Res.) Bn., Spec. Res. of Off. First Appt. 15 Aug. 14, Lieut. 2 Feb. 15, Capt. 1 June 15. **War Services**—The War of 1914-16—France, Attd. to 2 Bn. 25 Feb. 15—Messines, Kemmel, Ypres (Wounded, to England 25 April 15). Rejoined 2 Bn.—Maricourt. **Despatches 15 Oct. 15. Awd. Military Cross 1 Jan. 16.**

GWYTHER, Capt. J. R., Spec. Res. of Off. First Appt. 4 Jan. 13, Capt. 2 Feb. 15, Capt. (temp. in Reg. Army) 18 June 15. **War Services**—The War of 1914-16—France, with 1 Bn., afterwards attd. to Tunnelling Coy. R.E. **Despatches 15 Oct. 15.**

HADFIELD, Lieut. (temp.) J. R., 13 (S.) Bn. First Appt. 22 Sept. 14, Lieut. (temp.) 31 July 15. **War Services**—The War of 1914-16—France 6 Sept. 15—Salonika 6 Nov. 15 (Empld. as Bn. Sig. Off.).

HAIGH-WOOD, 2nd Lieut. M .H., 2 Bn. First Appt. 12 May 15. **War Services**—The War of 1914-16—France, with 2 Bn. 8 Aug. 15—Marlancourt, Maricourt.

HALL, 2nd Lieut. (temp.) J. N., 15 (S.) Bn. First Appt. 7 Dec. 14. **War Services**—The War of 1914-16—Gallipoli, Attd. 11 (S.) Bn.—Suvla Bay 23 Aug. 15—Imbros 19 Dec. 15—Alexandria 20 Jan. 16.

HALLER, Capt. (temp.) J. H. L., E. Surrey R. **War Services**—The War of 1914-16—France, Attd. to 2 Bn. Manch. R. Nov. 14 to 5 Jan. 15—Messines. **Since Killed in Action.**

HAMILTON, Gen. Sir I. S. M., G.C.B., D.S.O., Col. Gordon Highlanders q.s., Hon. Col. 3 (Res.) Bn. Manch. R. 9 Aug. 08.

HAMPSON, 2nd Lieut. H. B., 3 (Res.) Bn., Spec. Res. of Off. First Appt. 19 May 15.

HAND, 2nd Lieut. (temp.) L. O., 14 (Res.) Bn. First Appt. 11 Mar. 15. **War Services**—The War of 1914-16. to Medit. Exp. Force 15 Nov. 15.

HANKINSON, 2nd Lieut. (temp.) R. H., 14 (Res.) Bn. First

Appt. 22 Dec. 14. **War Services**—The War of 1914-16, to Medit. Exped. Force 2 Feb. 16.

HANNAFORD, 2nd Lieut. (temp.) R. S., 14 (Res.) Bn. First Appt. 5 Jan. 15. **War Services**—The War of 1914-16, to Medit. Exped. Force 21 Sept. 15, Attd. to 11 (S.) Bn.—Gallipoli (Suvla Bay), Imbros 19 Dec. 15—Alexandria 20 Jan. 16.

HARDCASTLE, Major R. N., D.S.O., Comdg. 1 Bn. First Appt. (from Mila.) 1 Dec. 97, Capt. 9 Jan. 01, Major 27 April 15. **War Services**—S. African War 1899-1902—Elandslaagte, Lombard's Kop, Defence of Ladysmith. **Despatches, D.S.O.** The War of 1914-16—France, with 2 Bn. 16 Sept. 14—Aisne, Richebourg, Lorgies (Wounded, to England 29 Oct. 14). Returned to France to 1 Bn. as 2nd in Commd. June 15, sailed to Mesopotamia 9 Nov. 15.

HARDINGHAM, Capt. A. G. M., Instructional Duties. First Appt. (from Mila.) 29 Jan. 02, Empld. with W. African Fr. Force 3 July 09 to 26 May 14, Capt. 1 Dec. 14, Genl. Staff Off. (2nd Grade) 17 Nov. 15. **War Services**—The War of 1914-16—France, sailed with B.E.F. with 2 Bn.—Mons, Bavay, Le Cateau, Marne, Aisne, Richebourg (Invld. to England Oct. 14).

HARDMAN, 2nd Lieut. (temp.) W. G., Attd. to 14 (Res.) Bn. from 13 (S.) Bn. First Appt. 26 Mar. 15.

HARPER, Capt. J. S., Bgde. Mach. Gun Off. First Appt. 16 Aug. 05, Capt. 27 April 15. **War Services**—The War of 1914-16—France, sailed with B.E.F. with 2 Bn.—Mons, Bavay, Le Cateau, Marne, Aisne, Richebourg, Lorgies (Wounded, to England 26 Oct. 14). Rejoined 2 Bn.—Ypres 27 June 15 (Invld. to England 1 Aug. 15). **Despatches 19 Oct. 14, Awd. Military Cross 1 Jan. 15.** To 93 Bgde. as Mach. Gun Off.

HARRIS, 2nd Lieut. (temp.) P., 14 (Res.) Bn. First Appt. 2 April 15. **War Services**—The War of 1914-16—Medit. Exped. Force 12 Jan. 16.

HARRISON, Lieut. A. A., 4 (Extra Res.) Bn., Spec. Res. of Off. First Appt. 15 Aug. 14, Lieut. 4 May 15.

HARRISON, Lieut.-Col. (temp.) E. G., C.G., D.S.O. (Bt.-Major ret. pay), Comdg. 12 (S.) Bn. 9 Jan. 15. First Appt. 23 May 85, Bt.-Major 25 Jan. 99, Lieut.-Col. (temp.) 8 Jan. 15. **War Services**—East Africa 1895-6, Oper. against Mazroi Rebels—Uganda 1897-8, Commd. in capture of Kabagambi. **Despatches, Bt. of Major, D.S.O.** The War of 1914-16—France, with 12 (S.) Bn. 15 July 15 (Wounded, to England). Rejoined 12 (S.) Bn. **Despatches 15 Oct. 15.**

HARRISON, Capt. H. G., 2nd in Commd. 19 Bn. Lanc. Fus. First Appt. (from Mila.) 4 June 1900, Capt. 18 Dec. 14. **War Services**—S. African War 1902. The War of 1914-16—France, with 2 Bn. 20 Aug. 15—Suzanne, Maricourt, Attd. to Lanc. Fus. Jan. 16.

HARTLEY, Lieut. (temp.) E. H., 11 (S.) Bn. First Appt. Lieut. (temp.) 17 Dec. 14. **War Services**—The War of 1914-16—Gallipoli 7 Aug. 15 (Suvla Bay) (Wounded, to England 7-11

Aug. 15). Rejoined 21 Nov. 15—Imbros 19 Dec. 15—Alexandria 20 Jan. 16.

HASLAM, 2nd Lieut. (temp.) H., 14 (Res.) Bn. First Appt. 29 June 15.

HASTINGS, Major (temp. Lieut.-Col.) W. C. N., D.S.O., Comdg. Sierra Leone Bn. West Afr. Fr. Force 17 April 15. First Appt. (from Mila.) 24 June 99, Capt. 25 Dec. 01, Major 1 Sept. 15, Lieut.-Col. (temp.) 17 April 15, Empld. with W. Afr. Fr. Force 28 Mar. 03 to 3 Aug. 09. **War Services**—Oper. in Sierra Leone 1898-9 (Slightly Wounded). S. African War 1900-2, **Despatches, D.S.O.** West African (N. Nigeria) 1906. The War of 1914-16—France, with Indian Cont.—Givenchy. To Cameroons Mar. 15.

HAUGHTON, 2nd Lieut. (temp.) J. P., 14 (Res.) Bn. First Appt. 10 Feb. 15. **War Services**—The War of 1914-16, to Medit. Exped. Force 21 Sept. 15—Gallipoli (Suvla Bay), Imbros 19 Dec. 15—Alexandria 20 Jan. 16.

HAWKINS, 2nd Lieut. (temp.) V. H., 14 (Res.) Bn. from 11 (S.) Bn. First Appt. 16 Nov. 14.

HAWORTH, 2nd Lieut. C. W. B., 3 (Res.) Bn., Spec. Res. of Off. (on prob.). First Appt. 16 July 15.

HAYNES, 2nd Lieut. (temp.) T. C. W., 14 (Res.) Bn. First Appt. 12 May 15.

HAYWARD, 2nd Lieut. (temp.) A. B., Mach. Gun Corps from 14 (Res.) Bn. First Appt. 2 2June 15.

HEALEY, 2nd Lieut. P., 3 (Res.) Bn., Spec. Res. of Off. First Appt. 20 Feb. 15. **War Services**—The War of 1914-16—France, Attd. to 1 Bn. L.N. Lanc. R. **Killed in Action Oct. 16.**

HEALY, 2nd Lieut. (temp.) E., 13 (S.) Bn. First Appt. 4 Jan. 15. **War Services**—The War of 1914-16, to Medit. Exped. Force 26 Nov. 15.

HEELIS, Major J. R., Staff of Ripon Training Centre. First Appt. 4 May 01, Empld. with W. Afr. Fr. Force 21 Sept. 07 to 31 May 09, Capt. 1 Dec. 12, Brig. Major 22 Oct. 15, Major 8 Jan. 16. **War Services**—The War of 1914-16—France, with Indian Cont. with 1 Bn. as Adjut.—Givenchy, Ypres (Wounded, to England 26 April 15). **Despatches 5 April 15, Awd. Military Cross 3 June 15.**

HENDERSON, 2nd Lieut. E. E. J., Attd. to 3 (Res.) Bn. First Appt. 22 Dec. 15.

HENDERSON, Lieut. (temp. Capt.) G. S., 1 Bn. First Appt. 24 Jan. 14, Lieut. 9 Nov. 14, Capt. (temp.) 26 April 15. **War Services**—The War of 1914-16—France, with Indian Cont. with 1 Bn. 26 Sept. 14—Picantui, Festubert, Givenchy, Neuve Chapelle, Ypres. **Awd. Military Cross 3 July 15.**

HENDERSON, 2nd Lieut. H. W., 3 (Res.) Bn., Spec. Res. of Off. (on prob.). First Appt. 21 July 15.

HENDERSON, Lieut.-Col. R. A. (Ret. pay), Comdg. Depot Bed. Regt. First Appt. 13 Aug. 79, Lieut.-Col. 1 April 04, to Depot Bed. R. 22 Aug. 14. **War Services**—Egyptian Exped. 1882. Burmese Exped. 1885-7.

HENDRIE, 2nd Lieut. H., 4 (Extra Res.) Bn., Spec. Res. of Off. First Appt. 5 May 15.

HEYS, 2nd Lieut. (temp.) G. H., 14 (Res.) Bn. First Appt. 23 Aug. 15. **War Services**—The War of 1914-16, to Med. Exped. Force 2 Feb. 16.

HEWITT, 2nd Lieut. R. C., 3 (Res.) Bn., Spec. Res. of Off. (on prob.). First Appt. 4 Oct. 15.

HEYWOOD, 2nd Lieut. (temp.) B., 14 (Res.) Bn. First Appt. 21 Oct. 15.

HEYWOOD, Col. B. C. P., T.D. (T.F. Res. of Off.), Col. 1 Apl. 08, Commd. 19 (S.) Bn. (4th City) Manch. R. from formation to date of death 29 Oct. 14. **War Services**—S. African War 1900-1.

HEYWOOD, Capt. F. J., Attd. Depot from 4 (Extra Res.) Bn., Spec. Res. of Off. First Appt. 8 June 89, Capt. 1 April 15.

HEYWOOD, 2nd Lieut. H., 1 Bn. First Appt. 16 Aug. 15. **War Services**—The War of 1914-16—France, with 1 Bn. **Killed in Action 25 Sept. 15.**

HIGGINBOTTOM, 2nd Lieut. G. L., 4 (Extra Res.) Bn., Spec. Res. of Off. (on prob.). First Appt. 8 April 15.

HIGGINBOTTOM, 2nd Lieut. (temp.) R. P., 15 (S.) Bn. First Appt. 7 Dec. 14. **War Services**—The War of 1914-16—Gallipoli (Suvla Bay) 11 Oct. 15—Imbros 19 Dec. 15—Alexandria 20 Jan. 16.

HILL, 2nd Lieut. G. A., 4 (Extra Res.) Bn., Spec. Res. of Off. First Appt. 13 May 15. **War Services**—The War of 1914-16. Medit. Exped. Force 12 Jan. 15—Salonika (Empld. as Intell. Officer).

HILLS, 2nd Lieut. C. H., 3 (Res.) Bn., Spec. Res. of Off. (on prob.). First Appt. 4 Oct. 15.

HILTON, 2nd Lieut. (temp.) F., 14 (Res.) Bn. First Appt. 16 Aug. 15.

HITCHINS, Lieut.-Col. H. W. E., Commanded 1 Bn. from 10 Mar. 15 to 26 April 15. First Appt. 25 Aug. 86, Adjut. Vols. 1 Nov. 97 to 30 April 03, Lieut.-Col. 10 Mar. 15. **War Services**—The War of 1914-16—France, with 1 Bn.—Picantin, Givenchy (Wounded, to England 21 Dec. 14). Rejoined 1 Bn.—Ypres (2nd Battle). **Killed in Action 26 April 15. Despatches 5 April 15 and 15 Oct. 15.**

HOFFERT, Lieut. (temp.) W. H., 11 (S.) Bn. First Appt. 26 Aug. 14, Lieut. (temp.) 16 April 15. **War Services**—The War of 1914-16—Gallipoli 7 Aug. 15 (Suvla Bay) (Wounded, to England 7-11 Aug. 15).

HOLBERTON, Major P. V., Staff. First Appt. 8 Jan. 01, Capt. 1 Dec. 12, Arjut. 6 Bn. Manch. R. 4 Nov. 11 to Dec. 15, Major 8 Jan. 16. **War Services**—The War of 1914-16—Gallipoli 7 May 15. **Despatches 22 Sept. and 11 Dec. 15, Brev. of Major for Service in Field 8 Nov. 15.** Egypt (Staff of Army Corps).

HOLDEN, 2nd Lieut. (temp.) H. D., 15 (S.) Bn. First Appt. 1 Mar. 15.

HOLLINGWORTH, Lieut. F. V., 4 (Extra Res.) Bn., Spec. Res. of Off. First Appt. 15 Aug. 14, Lieut. 4 May 15.

HOLME, Major J. H. (Ret. Mila), Adjut. Depot. First Appt. 19 June 82, Capt. 29 Oct. 84, Capt. (temp. Reg. Army) 5 Oct. 14, Major (temp.) 25 Sept. 15.

HOLMES, Lieut. E. B., 1 Bn. First Appt. 17 Sept. 14, Lieut. 11 Dec. 14. **War Services**—The War of 1914-16—France, with 1 Bn.

HOLNESS, 2nd Lieut. H. H. J., Attd. to 4 (Extra Res.) Bn. from 1 Bn. First Appt. 10 Jan. 15. **War Services**—The War of 1914-16—France, with Grenadier Guards as Coy. Q.M.S. **Prom. 2nd Lieut. for Service in the Field.** Joined 1 Bn. Jan. 15—Neuve Chapelle (Wounded, to England 13 Mar. 15).

HOPKINS, Capt. R. B., Res. of Off. First Appt. 11 Feb. 99, Capt. 10 Oct. 1900, Specially empld. 1 Feb. 06 to 31 Mar. 12. **War Services**—S. African War 1900-1. **Despatches, Prom. Captain.**

HORN, 2nd Lieut. F. C., 4 (Extra Res.) Bn., Spec. Res. of Off. First Appt. 23 Dec. 14.

HORN, 2nd Lieut. W. B. F., 4 (Extra Res.) Bn.. Spec. Res. of Off. First Appt. 21 Oct. 14.

HORRIDGE, 2nd Lieut. R., 2 Bn. from 4 (Extra Res.) Bn., Spec. Res. of Off. First Appt. 18 Oct. 11. **War Services**—The War of 1914-16—France, with 2 Bn. 15 Oct. 14—Richebourg, Lorgies. **Killed in Action 17 Nov. 14.**

HOWARD, 2nd Lieut. B. H. E., 4 (Extra Res.) Bn., Spec. Res. of Off. (on prob.). First Appt. 2 Oct. 15.

HOWARD, 2nd Lieut. (temp.) C. M., Mach. Gun Corps from 14 (Res.) Bn. First Appt. 18 Dec. 14.

HOWARD, 2nd Lieut. W. E., 4 (Extra Res.) Bn., Spec. Res. of Off. (on prob.). First Appt. 24 July 15.

HUGHES, 2nd Lieut. E. D. G., 4 (Extra Res.) Bn., Spec. Res. of Off. First Appt. 14 May 15.

HUMPHRYS, Capt. N. W., Adjut. 4 (Extra Res.) Bn. Attd. from 2 Bn. First Appt. Lieut. 18 Dec. 07, Capt. 11 Dec. 14, Adjutant 4 Bn. 4 Feb. 16. **War Services**—The War of 1914-16—France, sailed with B.E.F. (2 Bn. Transport Off.)—Mons, Bavay, Le Cateau, Marne, Aisne, Richebourg, Messines, Kemmel, Ypres, Maricourt (Invld. to England Oct. 15). **Despatches 5 April 15.**

HUMPHRIS, Capt. (temp.) J. P., 14 (Res.) Bn., Capt. (temp.) 18 Sept. 14, Attd. to Northern Command Training Staff as a Grenade Officer.

HUTCHINSON, 2nd Lieut. (temp.) L., 14 (Res.) Bn. First Appt. 6 April 15.

INNES, 2nd Lieut. (temp.) R. S., 11 (S.) Bn. First Appt. 27 Nov. 14 from Public Schools Bn. **War Services**—The War of 1914-16—Gallipoli 7 Aug. 15 (Suvla Bay). **Killed in Action 7 Aug. 15.**

IRWIN, Capt. C. D., Attd. 4 (Extra Res.) Bn. from 2 Bn. First Appt. 22 May 01, Capt. 11 Dec. 12, Brigade Major 11

Oct. 15 to 10 Jan. 16. **War Services**—The War of 1914-16—France, with 2 Bn. Oct. 14—La Quinque Rue, Wulverghem, Messines, Kemmel (Invld. to England 6 April 15). **Despatches 5 April 15, Awd. Military Cross 3 June 15.**

JACKSON, Capt. D. W. G., 3 (Res.) Bn., Spec. Res. of Off., Capt. 6 Feb. 15.

JACKSON, Capt. W. E., 3 (Res.)Bn., Spec. Res. of Off. First Appt. 15 Aug. 14, Lieut. 2 Feb. 15, Capt. (temp.) Reg. Army from 27 May 15 to 27 Sept. 15 while attd. 1 Bn., Capt. (S.R.) 1 June 15. **War Services**—The War of 1914-16—France, attd. 1 Bn. (Invld. to England Sept. 15).

JAMES, Lieut. H. H., Attd. 11 (S.) Bn. from 1 Bn. First Appt. 23 Dec. 14, Lieut. 15 May 15. **War Services**—The War of 1914-16—France, with 1 Bn.—Neuve Chapelle (Wounded, to England 11 Mar. 15) To Gallipoli, Attd. 11 (S.) Bn.—Suvla Bay, Imbros 19 Dec. 15—Alexandria 20 Jan. 16.

JAMES, Lieut.-Col. H. L., C.B., Comdg. 2 Bn., Attd. Depot Manch. R. to Commd. (temp.). First Appt. (from Mila.) 6 May 85, Lieut.-Col. 24 Feb. 08. **War Services**—S. African War 1900-1, **Despatches.** The War of 1914-16—France, sailed with B.E.F. in Commd. 2 Bn.—Mons, Bavay, Le Cateau, Marne, Aisne, nr. Le Basse (Invld. to England). **To be Comp. Order of Bath for Service in the Field 17 Feb. 15, Despatches 19 Oct. 14.**

JANION, Lieut. (temp.) F. J., Attd. 14 (Res.) Bn. from 11 (S.) Bn. First Appt. 1 July 15, Lieut. (temp.) 17 Nov. 15, Empld. as Divisional Grenade Officer, Brocton Camp.

JARVIS, 2nd Lieut. (temp.) T. S. W., 14 (Res.) Bn. from 13 (S.) Bn. First Appt. 18 Dec. 14. **War Services**—The War of 1914-16, to Medit. Exped. Force 23 Sept. 15. Attd. 1/6 Bn.—Gallipoli, Egypt.

JEBB, Lieut.-Col. J .H. M., D.S.O., Res. of Off., Comdg. 4 (Extra Res.) Bn. First Appt. 28 Sept 95, Major 8 May 12, Lieut.-Col. (S.R.) 19 May 13. **War Services**—S. African War 1900-2, **Despatches (twice), D.S.O.** The War of 1914-16—France.

JENNISON, 2nd Lieut. (temp.) A. D., 14 (Res.) Bn. First Appt. 29 June 15. **War Services**—The War of 1914-16, to Medit. Exped. Force 15 Nov. 15.

JENNISON, 2nd Lieut. (temp.) R., 12 (S.) Bn. First Appt. 24 Dec. 14. **War Services**—The War of 1914-16—France 15 July 15 (to England), to Medit. Exped. Force 11 Jan. 16.

JESSOP, Capt. (temp.) G. L., Comdg. "C" (Wigan Pals) Coy. 14 (Res.) Bn. First Appt. as temp. Capt. 21 Dec. 14.

JESSOP, 2nd Lieut. (temp.) T. D., 14 (Res.) Bn. First Appt. 2 Mar. 15. **War Services**—The War of 1914-16—France, Attd. 12 (S.) Bn. (Wounded, to England 6 Nov. 15).

JOHNSON, 2nd Lieut. (temp.) D. F. G., 15 (S.) Bn. First Appt. 26 Feb. 15. **War Services**—The War of 1914-16—France Attd. 2 Bn. 5 Dec. 15.

JOHNSON, Lieut.-Col. (temp.) H. A., Col. ret. Spec. Res.), Major 17 Oct. '94, Commd. 6 and 4 (Mila.) Bns. Manch. R.

1905 to 1913, Lieut.-Col. (temp. Reg. Army) and to Commd Service Bn. 1 Sept. 14. **War Services**—The War of 1914-16—France, with 17 (S.) Bn. 7 Nov. 15.

JOHNSON, Capt. L. C., 4 (Extra Res.) Bn., Spec. Res. of Off. First Appt. 4 Sept. 14, Capt. 26 June 15. **War Services**—The War of 1914-16—France, Attd. 2 Bn. 3 May 15—Ypres, Maricourt.

JONES, 2nd Lieut. A. J. W., 3 (Res.) Bn., Spec. Res. of Off. First Appt. 9 May 15.

JONES, Lieut.-Col. H. J., D.S.O. (Ind. Army), Comdg. 13 (S.) Bn. First Appt. 23 Aug. 84, Lieut.-Col. 25 Aug. 08, to Manch. R. 19 Sept. 14. **War Services**—Soudan Exped. 1884-85—Nile. Hazara Exped. 1888. Burma 1891-2. Oper. in Chitral 1895 (Wounded), **Despatches, D.S.O.** The War of 1914-16—France, in Commd. 13 (S.) Bn. 6 Sept. 15—Salonika 6 Nov. 15.

JONES, Capt. (temp.) H. R., 13 (S.) Bn. First Appt. Lieut. (temp.) 12 Dec. 14, Capt. (temp.) 25 Mar. 15. **War Services**—The War of 1914-16—France, with 13 (S.) Bn. 6 Sept. 15—Salonika 6 Nov. 15 (Invld. to England 24 Nov. 15).

JONES, 2nd Lieut. (temp.) J. A., 14 (Res.) Bn. First Appt. 10 April 15.

JONES, 2nd Lieut. (temp.) J. N., 14 (Res.) Bn. (on prob.). First Appt. 20 Jan. 16.

JONES, Hon. Lieut. (temp.) J. R., Quartermaster 14 (Res.) Bn. 22 Oct. 14.

JONES, 2nd Lieut. R., 3 (Res.) Bn., Spec. Res. of Off. (on prob.). First Appt. 30 Dec. 15.

JONES, 2nd Lieut. (temp.) T. A. E. E., 11 (S.) Bn. First Appt. 1 Sept. 14. **War Services**—The War of 1914-16, Medit. Expd. Force—Gallipoli 7 Aug. 15 (Suvla Bay Landing). **Killed in Action 7-11 Aug. 15.**

JOWETT, 2nd Lieut. J. S., 4 (Extra Res.) Bn., Spec. Res. of Off. First Appt. 15 Aug. 14. **War Services**—The War of 1914-16, to Medit. Exped. Force, Attd. Munster Fus. 11 Oct. 15

JUKES, Lieut. (temp.) M. E. E., 14 (Res.) Bn., Lieut. 14 Jan. 15. Accidentally Killed at Lichfield 4 Sept. 15

KAVANAH, 2nd Lieut. (temp.) E., 14 (Res.) Bn. First Appt. 5 Jan. 15. **War Services**—The War of 1914-16, to France 8 Feb. 16, Attd. 12 (S.) Bn.

KEMP, 2nd Lieut. (temp.) C. M., 14 (Res.) Bn. First Appt. 23 Aug. 15.

KENT, Capt. (temp.) R. E. D., 12 (S.) Bn., Capt. (temp.) 13 Oct. 14. **War Services**—The War of 1914-16—France 15 July 15.

KERANS, Capt. A. L., 3 (Res.) Bn., Spec. Res. of Off., from N. Lanc. R. First Appt. (Reg. Army) 5 May 1900, Capt. 22 April 05.

KERRY, 2nd Lieut. A. J. St. L. First Appt. 4 Dec. 15.

KING, 2nd Lieut. (temp.) A. B., Attd. 14 (Res.) Bn. from 12 (S.) Bn. First Appt. 9 Jan. 15.

KINGSLEY, 2nd Lieut. (temp.) E., 12 (S.) Bn. First Appt. 13 Nov. 14. **War Services**—The War of 1914-16—France, with 12 (S.) Bn. 15 July 15 (Wounded, to England). Rejoined 12 (S.) Bn. 8 Feb. 16.

KNOX, Major H., Staff Capt. First Appt. (from Mila.) 18 April 1900, Capt. 1 April 09, Staff Capt. 11 Aug. 15, Major 1 Sept. 15. **War Services**—S. African War 1900-2, Empld. with Mtd. Inf. The War of 1914-16—France, sailed with B.E.F. with 2 Bn.—Mons, Bavay, Le Cateau (Wounded, to England 26 Aug. 14), **Despatches 19 Oct. 14.**

KOHNSTAMM, 2nd Lieut. N. M. J., 3 (Res.) Bn., Spec. Res. of Off. First Appt. 9 May 15. **War Services**—The War of 1914-16—Gallipoli, Attd. 11 (S.) Bn., Suvla Bay, Imbros 19 Dec. 15—Alexandria 20 Jan. 16.

KROLIK, 2nd Lieut. P. D., 4 (Extra Res.) Bn., Spec. Res. of Off. (on prob.). First Appt. 18 April 15.

LAKE-GREER, Major E., 3 (Res.) Bn. Bord. R., Spec. Res. of Off., Major 2 Feb. 15, Appt. R.T.O. 11 Dec. 14. **War Services**—The War of 1914-16—France, Attd. to 2 Bn. (Returned to England).

LANE, 2nd Lieut. E. A. M., 3 (Res.) Bn., Spec. Res. of Off. First Appt. 27 Oct. 14, Lieut. 2 Feb. 15, to Reg. Army as 2nd Lieut. 4 Oct. 15. **War Services**—The War of 1914-16—France, with 1 Bn. To Mesopotamia 9 Dec. 15 (Missing from 11 Mar. 16).

LASHMAR, 2nd Lieut. (temp.) S., 1 (Gar.) Bn. First Appt. 6 July 15, to Manch. R. 16 Sept. 15.

LASKEY, Capt. F. S., 4 (Extra Res.) Bn., Spec. Res. of Off., Lieut. 1 Oct. 12, Capt. 1 Sept. 14.

LATIMER, 2nd Lieut. (temp.) F., Attd. 14 (Res.) Bn. from 12 (S). Bn. First Appt. 4 Dec. 14.

LAUGHLAND, 2nd Lieut. (temp.) W., 14 (Res.) Bn. First Appt. 23 Aug. 15.

LAVINGTON, Lieut. (temp.) H. J., Attd. 14 (Res.) Bn. from 13 (S.) Bn. First Appt. Lieut. (temp.) 12 Dec. 14.

LAWRENCE, 2nd Lieut. J. D. First Appt. 20 Oct. 15, Attd. Mach. Gun Corps.

LEACH, Lieut. J., V.C., Instructional Duties (Signal). First Appt. 1 Oct. 14, Lieut. 11 Dec. 14. **War Services**—The War of 1914-16—France, with Northampt. R. as Cpl. **Prom. 2nd Lieut. for Service in the Field.** With 2 Bn. Manch. R. Oct. 14—La Quinque Rue, Wulverghem (Invld. to England Nov. 14). **Awd. Victoria Cross 17 Feb. 15, Despatches 22 Dec. 14 and 17 Feb. 15.** Rejoined 2 Bn. 14 April 15—Ypres (Invld. to England 16 April 15).

LECKLER, 2nd Lieut. (temp.) A. N., 15 (S.) Bn. First Appt. 3 Mar. 15. **War Services**—The War of 1914-16—Medit. Expd. Force 16 Feb. 16.

LEES, 2nd Lieut. (temp.) K., 11 (S.) Bn. First Appt. 6 Jan. 15. **War Services**—The War of 1914-16, Medit. Exped. Force—Gallipoli 7 Aug. 15, Landing Suvla Bay (Wounded, to England 7-11 Aug. 15).

LEVICK, 2nd Lieut. H. G., 4 (Extra Res.) Bn., Spec. Res. of Off. First Appt. 15 Aug. 14. **War Services**—The War of 1914-16—France, Attd. 2 Bn. 5 Dec. 14—Messines (Wounded, to England 17 Jan. 15).

LEWIN, 2nd Lieut. (temp.) I., Attd. 2/10 Bn. 14 (Res.) Bn. First Appt. 12 May 15.

LEWIN, 2nd Lieut. (temp.) T. M., 14 (Res.) Bn. First Appt. 11 Sept. 15.

LEWIS, 2nd Lieut. (temp.) M. G., 14 (Res.) Bn. First Appt. 5 April 15. **War Services**—The War of 1914-16, to Medit. Exped. Force 21 Sept. 15—Gallipoli, Attd. 11 (S.) Bn. (Suvla Bay), Imbros 19 Dec. 15—Alexandria 20 Jan. 15.

LEWTAS, 2nd Lieut. O., 3 (Res.) Bn., Spec. Res. of Off. First Appt. 6 Jan. 15. **War Services**—The War of 1914-16—France, Attd. 2 Bn. 25 May 15—Ypres, Maricourt (Wounded, to England 25 Nov. 15).

LIDIARD, 2nd Lieut. A. S., 3 (Res.) Bn., Spec. Res. of Off. (on prob.). First Appt. 31 July 15.

LIDIARD, 2nd Lieut. B. S., 3 (Res.)Bn., Spec. Res. of Off. First Appt. 26 May 15.

LION, Lieut. L. H., 4 (Extra Res.) Bn., Spec. Res. of Off. First Appt. 15 Aug. 14, Lieut. 4 May 15. **War Services**—The War of 1914-16—France, Attd. 2 Bn. 29 Nov. 15—Messines (Wounded, to England 2 Feb. 15). Rejoined 2 Bn. 1 Dec. 15—Maricourt (Wounded, to England 2 Feb. 16).

LITHIBY, Lieut. (temp.) J. S., 11 (S.) Bn. First Appt. Lieut. (temp.) 31 Dec. 14. **War Services**—The War of 1914-16, Med. Exped. Force—Gallipoli 7 Aug. 15, Suvla Bay (Wounded, to England 7-11 Aug. 15), **Despatches 11 Dec. 15.**

LOCKHART, 2nd Lieut. (temp.) A. R., 15 (S.) Bn. First Appt. 2 Mar. 15. **War Services**—The War of 1914-16, to Medit. Exped. Force 12 Jan. 16.

LOMAS, 2nd Lieut. (temp.) G. G., 14 (Res.) Bn. First Appt. 23 Feb. 15.

LOWE, 2nd Lieut. (temp.) W. H., Attd. 14 (Res.) Bn. from 12 (S.) Bn. First Appt. 16 Jan. 15. **War Services**—The War of 1914-16, to Medit. Exped. Force 4 Nov. 15, Attd. 11 (S.) Bn.—Gallipoli (Suvla Bay), Imbros 19 Dec. 15—Alexandria 20 Jan. 16.

LUFFMAN, 2nd Lieut. C. F., Attd. 3 (Res.) Bn. First Appt. 24 Nov. 15.

LUMBY, 2nd Lieut. C. D. R., 4 (Extra Res.) Bn., Spec. Res. of Off. (on prob.) First Appt. 2 Sept. 15.

LUNN, 2nd Lieut. (temp.) P., 12 (S.) Bn. First Appt. 4 Jan. 15. **War Services**—The War of 1914-16—France, with 12 Bn. 15 July 15 (Wounded, to England 3 Sept. 15). Rejoined 12 (S.) Bn. 8 Feb. 16.

LUXMORE, Lieut.-Col. (temp.) N., Comdg. 2 Bn. (Major Devon R.). First Appt. 12 Dec. 94, Major 14 Feb. 15, to Manch. R. 11 Sept. 15, Lieut.-Col. (temp.) 13 Nov. 15. **War Services**—S. African War 1899-1902 (Dangerously wounded)—Relief of Ladysmith, Colenso, Spion Kop, Vaal Kranz, Tugela

Heights, Pieter's Hill, **Despatches.** The War of 1914-16—France, Attd. 2 Bn. 11 Sept. 15—Maricourt.

LYE, 2nd Lieut. G., 4 (Extra Res.) Bn., Spec. Res. of Off. First Appt. 8 June 15.

LYNCH, Lieut. (temp. Capt.) R. F., 1 Bn. First Appt. 18 Sept. 09, Lieut. 1 Dec. 13, Capt. (temp.) 1 Sept. 15. **War Services**—The War of 1914-16—France, with Indian Cont. 26 Sept. 14—Picantin, Givenchy (Wounded, to England 19 Dec. 14). Rejoined 1 Bn.—France, sailed from Marseilles 9 Dec. 15. To Mesopotamia. **Killed in Action 11 Mar. 16.**

LYONS, 2nd Lieut. (temp.) A., Attd. 14 (Res.) Bn. from 12 (S.) Bn. First Appt. 24 Nov. 14. **War Services**—The War of 1914-16. to Medit. Exped. Force 4 Nov. 15, Attd. 11 (S.) Bn.—Gallipoli (Suvla Bay), Imbros 19 Dec. 15—Alexandria 20 Jan. 16.

LYONS, 2nd Lieut. (temp.) J. J., 14 (Res.) Bn. First Appt. 24 Jan. 15.

MacBEAN, Capt. W. W., Attd. 3 (Res.) Bn. from Cam. High., Spec. Res. of Off., Capt. 4 Sept. 14.

McCONNAN, 2nd Lieut. (temp.) J., 14 (Res.) Bn. First Appt. 10 Mar. 15. **War Services**—The War of 1914-16, to Medit. Exped. Force 21 Sept. 15, Attd. 11 (S.) Bn.—Gallipoli (Suvla Bay), Imbros 19 Dec. 15—Alexandria 20 Jan. 16.

McCONNELL, 2nd Lieut. P. McK., 3 (Res.) Bn. Scot. Rifles, Spec. Res. of Off. First Appt. 24 Mar. 15. **War Services**—The War of 1914-16. Medit. Exped. Force, Attd. 11 (S.) Bn.—Gallipoli (Suvla Bay), Imbros 19 Dec. 15—Alexandria 20 Jan. 16.

McELROY, 2nd Lieut. (temp.) J. O., 14 (Res.) Bn. First Appt. 20 July 15.

McFARLANE, Major (temp.) E. J., 12 (S.) Bn. First Appt. Capt. (temp.) 19 Sept. 14, Major (temp.) 12 May 15. **War Services**—The War of 1914-16—France, with 12 (S.) Bn. 15 July 15.

MacGOWAN, 2nd Lieut. W. S., 4 (Extra Res.) Bn., Spec. Res. of Off. 12 June 15.

MacKAY, 2nd Lieut. C. L., 5 (Res.) Bn. Worcest. R., Spec. Res. of Off. **War Services**—The War of 1914-16—France, Attd. 2 Bn. Manch. R. 20 Jan. 15—Messines, Kemmel, Ypres (Wounded 28 May 15). **Died of wounds at Boulogne 7 June 15.**

McKEAN, Capt. (temp.) H., 12 (S.) Bn. First Appt. Capt. (temp.) 18 Dec. 14. **War Services**—The War of 1914-16—France, with 12 (S.) Bn. 15 July 15.

McKELVEY, Hon. Lieut. (temp.) J. W., 1 (Gar.) Bn. First Appt. 12 Dec. 15.

McKIEVER, 2nd Lieut. V. C., 3 (Res.) Bn., Spec. Res. of Off. First Appt. 15 Aug. 14. **War Services**—The War of 1914-16—France, Attd. 2 Bn. 24 Mar. 15—Messines, Ypres. **Died of wounds received in action 18 May 15.**

MACLEAN, Capt. L. F. C., 4 (Extra Res.) Bn., Spec. Res. of

Off. First Appt. 13 Dec. 05, Lieut. 30 June 09, Capt. 8 April 10.

McLELLAN, 2nd Lieut. H. N., 3 (Res.) Bn., Spec. Res. of Off., transferred from 13 (S.) Bn. Manch. R. First Appt. 11 Mar. 15, to 3 Bn. 3 April 15. **War Services**—The War of 1914-16—France, Attd. 2 Bn. 31 Aug. 15—Sailly Lorette, Maricourt.

MACLURCAN, Hon. Col. J. L. R., late R. Mar. First Appt. 19 Sept. 77, Major 25 Jan. 95, Retired on Half-Pay 27 May 01, Hon. Col. 02, Apptd. Rec. Off. 63rd R.D. Rec. Area 14 July 15. **War Services**—Soudan Exped. 1884-5—Defence of Suakin and Oper. in vicinity; actions at Hasheen and Tofrek, attack on convoy 24 Mar. (Wounded). China 1900.

McMULLAN, Capt. (temp.) A., Second in Commd. 14 (Res.) Bn. First Appt. Capt. (temp.) 26 Nov. 14.

MAIR, Capt. B. V., Assist. Mil. Landing Off. First Appt. 22 April 03, Capt. 11 Dec. 14, A.M.L.O. 16 July 15. **War Services**—The War of 1914-16—France, with Indian Cont. (1 Bn. Manch. R.) 26 Sept. 14—Picantin, Givenchy, Neuve Chapelle (Wounded, to England 11 Mar. 15). **Awd. Military Cross 27 Mar. 15, Despatches 5 April 15.**

MAITLAND-ADDISON, 2nd Lieut. (temp.) C. B., 14 (Res.) Bn. First Appt. 6 May 15.

MAITLAND-ADDISON, 2nd Lieut. (temp.) R. C. A., 14 (Res.) Bn. First Appt. 5 Mar. 15.

MAKIN, Lieut. (temp.) J. H. W., 14 (Res.) Bn. from 10 Mar. 15 to 13 Aug. 15 (late Lieut. R. Innis. Fus.).

MALCOMSON, 2nd Lieut. (temp.) T., 14 (Res.) Bn. First Appt. 20 July 15.

MALLAM, 2nd Lieut. (temp.) G. L., 14 (Res.) Bn. from 13 (S.) Bn. First Appt. 30 Nov. 14.

MANSERGH, Lieut. W. G., 2 Bn. First Appt. (from Mila.) 14 Sept. 01, Empld. with W. African Frontier Force 3 Oct. 03 to 25 Feb. 08 and 3 April 09 to 14 Mar. 14. **War Services**—S. African War 1900-2. The War of 1914-16—France, sailed with B.E.F. with 2 Bn.—Mons, Bavay, Le Cateau. **Killed in Action 26 Aug. 14.**

MANTEGANI, 2nd Lieut. (temp.) C., 14 (Res.) Bn. First Appt. 13 Mar. 15.

MARDEN, Major A. W., D.S.O., Ret. Pay (Res. of Off.), D.A.D. Railway Transport. First Appt. 11 Feb. 88, Major 1 June 02, Railway Trans. Off. 5 Aug. 14, D.A.Q.M.G. 18 June 15. **War Services**—S. African War 1899-1902—Elandslaagte, Def. of Ladysmith, **Despatches (five times), D.S.O.**

MARLEY, 2nd Lieut. V. D. K., 4 (Extra Res.) Bn., Spec. Res. of Off. First Appt. 15 Aug. 14. **War Services**—France, Attd. 1 Bn. 9 May 15. To Mesopotamia 9 Nov. 15. (Wounded 5 Mar. 16).

MARRIOTT, 2nd Lieut. S. A., 3 (Res.) Bn., Spec. Res. of Off. First Appt. 29 May 15.

MARSDEN, 2nd Lieut. (temp.) C. W., 12 (S.) Bn. First Appt.

18 Dec. 14. **War Services**—The War of 1914-16—France, with 12 (S.) Bn. 15 July 15.

MARSHALL, 2nd Lieut. (temp.) J. T., 1 (Gar.) Bn. E. Yorks. R. from 14 (Res.) Bn. First Appt. 25 Jan. 15.

MARSLAND, Lieut. (temp.) S. H., 11 (S.) Bn. First Appt. 7 Sept. 14, Lieut. (temp.) 3 June 15. **War Services**—The War of 1914-16, Medit. Exped. Force—Gallipoli (Suvla Bay) 7 Aug. 15. **Killed in Action 7-11 Aug. 15.**

MARTEN, 2nd Lieut. H. H., 2 Bn. from 6 Bn. K. R. Rif. C. 14 Feb. 15. **War Services**—The War of 1914-16—France, with 2 Bn. 3 Dec. 14—Messines, Kemmel, Ypres, Maricourt. **Killed in Action 13 Aug. 15. Despatches.**

MARTIN-ROWE, Lieut. C., R.A.M.C. **War Services**—The War of 1914-16—France, Attd. 2 Bn. as M.O. 19 Jan. 15—Messines (Wounded, to England 4 Mar. 15).

MASSE, Lieut. C. H., A.S.C. from 1 Bn. First Appt. 10 Dec. 13, Lieut. 30 Oct. 14, Transfd. A.S.C. as 2nd Liuet. 15 May 15. **War Services**—The War of 1914-16—France, with Ind. Cont. (1 Bn. Manch. R.) 26 Sept. 14 (Wounded).

MATHER, 2nd Lieut. (temp.) A. R., 1 (Gar.) Bn. E. York. R. from 14 (Res.) Bn. First Appt. 31 May 15

MATHER, 2nd Lieut. (temp.) J., 1 (Gar.) Bn. Notts. and Derby R. from 14 (Res.) Bn. First Appt. 11 Mar. 15.

MATTHEWS, 2nd Lieut. (temp.) W. C., 1 Bn. First Appt. 7 Nov. 15.

MATTHEWS, Capt. and Hon. Major W. J. R., late 6 (Mila.) Bn. Manch. R. (Hon. Capt. in Army) (Res. of Off.), Capt. 5 Jan. 98, Staff Capt. 10 Oct. 14. **War Services**—S. African War 1902—Oper. in Cape Colony.

MAULE, 2nd Lieut. (temp.) R., 15 (S.) Bn. First Appt. 7 Dec. 14. **War Services**—The War of 1914-16, to Medit. Exped. Force 11 Oct. 15.

MAXWELL, Bt. Col. A. B., Commanded 11 (S.) Bn. Lanc. Fus. First Appt. 1 May 78, Brev. Col. 30 Aug. 04. **War Services**—Egyptian Exped. 1882. S. African War 1900-2, **Despatches, Brev. of Lieut.-Col.**

MEADE, 2nd Lieut. (temp.) J. M., 15 (S.) Bn. First Appt. 28 Nov. 14. **War Services**—The War of 1914-16, Medit. Exped. Force, Attd. 11 (S.) Bn. 23 Aug. 15—Gallipoli (Suvla Bay), Imbros 19 Dec. 15—Alexandria 20 Jan. 16.

MEDWORTH, Lieut. (temp.) F. O., 13 (S.) Bn. First Appt. 24 Nov. 14, Lieut. (temp.) 31 July 15. **War Services**—The War of 1914-16—France, with 13 (S.) Bn. 6 Sept. 15—Salonika 6 Nov. 15.

MELVILLE, Bt. Col. C. C., Commanded Depot 6 Aug. to 7 Sept. 14. First Appt. 13 Aug. 79, Bt. Col. 24 Feb. 04. **War Services**—Egyptian Exped. 1882. S. African War 1899-1900—Elandslaagte. **Despatches.**

MEUGENS, Capt. (temp.) G. E., 11 (S.) Bn. First Appt. Lieut. (temp.) 31 Dec. 14, Capt. (temp.) 17 May 15. **War Services**—The War of 1914-16, Medit. Exped. Force, with 11 (S.) Bn. 7 Aug. 15—Gallipoli (Suvla Bay), (Wounded 7-11

Aug. 15). Rejoined Bn.—Suvla Bay, Imbros 19 Dec. 15—Alexandria—20 Jan. 16.

MIDELTON, 2nd Lieut. (temp.) E. W., 14 (Res.) Bn. First Appt. 22 July 15. **War Services**—The War of 1914-16, to Medit. Exped. Force 15 Nov. 15.

MILLER, Capt. R. T., 3 (Res.) Bn., Spec. Res. of Off., Capt. 2 Feb. 15. **War Services**—The War of 1914-16—France, sailed with B.E.F. with 2 Bn.—Mons, Bavay, Le Cateau. (Wounded and Prisoner of War 26 Aug. 14. **Despatches 17 Feb. 15.**

MILLIS, 2nd Lieut. C. H. G. First Appt. 4 Jan. 16 from Notts. and Derby R.

MINCHER, Capt. (temp.) P. W., 1 (Gar.) Bn. Lincoln R. from 14 (Res.) Bn., Lieut. (temp.) 23 Oct. 14, Capt. 25 Jan. 15.

MOODY, 2nd Lieut. (temp.) H. J. G., 14 (Res.) Bn. First Appt. 7 Aug. 15.

MOORE, 2nd Lieut. (temp.) A. A., 14 (Res.) Bn. First Appt. 28 Dec. 14.

MOORE, Capt. A. G., Attd. R. Flying Corps from 4 (Extra Res.) Bn., Spec. Res. of Off., Capt. 22 April 05. **War Services**—S. African War 1901-2. The War of 1914-16.

MOORE, Lieut. A. W. W., Attd. 3 (Res.) Bn. from 2 Bn. First Appt. 8 Aug. 14, Lieut. 1 Dec. 14 **War Services**—The War of 1914-16—France, with 2 Bn. 16 Sept. 14—Aisne (Wounded 19 Sept. 14)—France, with 1 Bn. Jan. 15 (Invld. to England).

MOORE, 2nd Lieut. F. S., 4 (Extra Res.) Bn., Spec. Res. of Off. (on prob.). First Appt. 24 July 15.

MOORE, 2nd Lieut. (temp.) W. H. E., 15 (S.) Bn. First Appt. 2 Mar. 15. **War Services**—The War of 1914-16, to Medit. Exped. Force 12 Jan. 16.

MOORHEAD, 2nd Lieut. C. D., Attd. 3 (Res.) Bn. First Appt. 11 Aug. 15. **War Services**—The War of 1914-16, to Medit. Exped. Force Jan. 16.

MOORHOUSE, Lieut. (temp.) A. J., 12 (S.) Bn. First Appt. Lieut. (temp.) 9 Feb. 15. **War Services**—The War of 1914-16—France, with 12 (S.) Bn. 15 July 15.

MORLEY, Capt. C., 2 Bn. First Appt. 17 Feb. 1900, Empld. with W. Afr. Frontier Force 30 Nov. 01 to 1 June 06 and 29 Dec. 06 to 16 Mar. 10, Capt. 9 Aug. 08. **War Services**—The War of 1914-16—France, sailed with B.E.F. with 2 Bn.—Mons, Bavay, Le Cateau (Wounded and Prisoner 26 Aug. 14.

MORRIS, 2nd Lieut. C., 1 Bn. First Appt. 16 Aug. 15. **War Services**—The War of 1914-16—France, with 1 Bn. To Mesopotamia 9 Dec. 15 (Missing from 11 Mar. 16).

MORRIS, Lieut. H. M., Attd. 19 Bn. Lanc. Fus. from 4 (Extra Res.) Bn., Spec. Res. of Off. First Appt. 15 Aug. 14, Lieut. 26 June 15. **War Services**—The War of 1914-16—France, Attd. 2 Bn. 5 May 15—Ypres, Maricourt. To 19 Bn. Lanc. Fus. Jan. 16.

MOSES, 2nd Lieut. (temp.) B., Attd. 14 (Res.) Bn. from 12 (S.)

Bn. First Appt. 15 Jan. 15. **War Services**—The War of 1914-16, to Medit. Exped. Force 11 Jan. 16.

MOTLER, 2nd Lieut. J. F., 4 (Extra Res.) Bn., Spec. Res. of Off. First Appt. 23 May 15.

MOULTON, 2nd Lieut. (temp.) W. R. O., Attd. 14 (Res.) Bn. from 12 (S.) Bn. First Appt. 2 Dec. 14.

MURPHY, Capt. J. L., 3 (Res.) Bn., Spec. Res. of Off. First Appt. 17 Jan. 1900, Capt. 8 Feb. 05. **War Services**—S. African War 1900-2 The War of 1914-16—France, Attd. to 1 Bn.

MURPHY, 2nd Lieut. (temp. Capt.) P. First Appt. 27 June 15, Capt. (temp.) 8 Aug. 15. **War Services**—The War of 1914-16—France, as Sergt.-Major. **Prom. 2nd Lieut. for Service in the Field.** Medit. Exped. Force, Attd. 1/8 Bn. Manch. R.

MUSSON, Capt. E. L. First Appt. 28 Jan. 05, Attd. 4 (Uganda) Bn. Afr. Rifles 27 Feb. 13, Capt. 18 Dec. 14. **War Services**—The War of 1914-16—German East Africa, **Awd. Military Cross 18 Feb. 15.**

NASH, Major (temp. Lieut.-Col.) W. P. (Ret. Pay), Comdg. 31 (Res.) Bn. Royal Fus. First Appt. 11 Feb. 75, Major 19 Aug. 91, Ret. 11 June 95, to 12 (S.) Bn. as 2nd in Commd. 7 Oct. 14, Temp. Lieut.-Col. while commdg. Bn. 20 Oct. to 19 Nov. 15. **War Services**—Egyptian Exped. 1882. The War of 1914-16—France, with 12 (S.) Bn. 7 Aug. 15 (Invld. to England).

NEILD, 2nd Lieut. (temp.) W., Attd. Depot from 14 (Res.) Bn. First Appt. 11 Mar. 15 (Lost right arm as result of bombing accident while training at Lichfield 1 Nov. 15).

NEPEAN, Capt. (temp.) E. A. R. (2nd Lieut. Res. of Off.), Empld. with A.S.C. First Appt. 30 Aug. 14, Lieut. (temp.) 1 Dec. 14.

NEWBIGGING, Bt. Lieut.-Col. W. P. E., D.S.O., Comdg. Sig. Serv. 3rd Army. First Appt. (from Mila.) 22 Mar. 92, Major 22 Mar. 11, Chief Inst. Sch. of Signalling 3 July 12 to 4 Aug. 14, Attd. to R.E. for Army Sig. Service. **War Services**—S. African War 1899-1902—Elandslaagte (severely wounded), Empld. with Mounted Inf., Relief of Ladysmith, Tugela Heights, **Despatches (twice), D.S.O.** The War of 1914-16—France—**Despatches 19 Oct. 14 and 15 Oct. 15, Brev. Lieut.-Col. 18 Feb. 15.**

NEWMAN, 2nd Lieut. (temp.) G. T., 13 (S.) Bn. First Appt. 4 Jan. 15. **War Services**—The War of 1914-16—France, with 13 (S.) Bn. 6 Sept. 15—Salonika 6 Nov. 15.

NEWMAN, 2nd Lieut. (temp.) J. P., 14 (Res.) Bn. First Appt. 1 Oct. 15.

NEWSON-SMITH, Major (temp.) H. H., 13 (S.) Bn. (late 6 Mila. Bn. Manch. R.), Capt. 14 Mar. 1900, Capt. (temp. Reg. Army) 30 Sept. 14, Major (temp.) 2 June 15. **War Services**—The War of 1914-16—France, with 13 (S.) Bn. 5 Sept. 15—Salonika 5 Nov. 15.

NICHOLAS, 2nd Lieut. E. A., 3 (Res.) Bn., Spec. Res. of Off. First Appt. 9 Dec. 14. **War Services**—The War of 1914-16—

France, Attd. to 1 Bn. To Mesopotamia 9 Dec. 15 (Wounded 10 Mar. 16).

NICHOLL, Capt. (temp.) F., Comdg. "B" Coy. 14 (Res.) Bn. First Appt. as Lieut. (temp.) 15 Feb. 15, Capt. (temp.) 27 Nov. 15.

NIGHTINGALE, 2nd Lieut. (temp.) G. O., 14 (Res.) Bn. First Appt. 13 Nov. 14. **War Services**—The War of 1914-16, to Medit. Exped. Force 21 Sept. 15, Attd. 11 (S.) Bn.—Gallipoli (Suvla Bay), Imbros 19 Dec. 15—Alexandria 20 Jan. 16.

NISBET, Capt. F. S., 2 Bn. First Appt. 7 May 98, Capt. 14 July 01, Adjut. 2 Bn. 1 Dec. 12. **War Services**—S. African War 1900-2. The War of 1914-16—France, sailed with B.E.F. with 2 Bn.—Mons, Bavay, Le Cateau, **Despatches 19 Oct. 14. Killed in Action 26 Aug. 14.**

NORBURY, 2nd Lieut. (temp.) A. L., 11 (S.) Bn. First Appt. 22 Aug. 14. **War Services**—The War of 1914-16, Medit. Expd. Force—Gallipoli 7 Aug. 15—Suvla Bay, Imbros 19 Dec. 15 —Alexandria 20 Jan. 16.

NORMAN, Lieut. S. S., 1 Bn. First Appt. 18 Sept. 09, Lieut. 27 Aug. 13. **War Services**—The War of 1914-16—France, with Indian Cont. 26 Sept. 14—Picautin, Givenchy. **Killed in Action 20-21 Dec. 14.**

O'BRIEN, Hon. Lieut. and Qr.-Mr. P., 1 Bn. 4 Sept. 09. **War Services**—The War of 1914-16—France, with Indian Cont. 26 Sept. 14—Picautin, Givenchy, Neuve Chapelle, Ypres (2nd Battle).

ODLVM, 2nd Lieut. (temp.) D. G. J., 14 (Res.) Bn. First Appt. 3 Dec. 14.

O'CONNOR, 2nd Lieut. E. R., 1 Bn. First Appt. 10 Jan. 15. **War Services**—The War of 1914-16—France, as Co. S. Major Grenadier Guards. **Promd. 2nd Lieut. for Services in the Field 10 Jan. 15.** Attd. 3 (Res.) Bn. 10 Jan. 15, to Medit. Exped. Force, Attd. 11 (S.) Bn.—Gallipoli (Suvla Bay), Imbros 19 Dec. 15—Alexandria 20 Jan. 16.

O'GRADY, 2nd Lieut. (temp.) W. M., 14 (Res.) Bn. First Appt. 9 Nov. 14. **War Services**—The War of 1914-16, to Medit. Exped. Force 2 Feb. 16.

O'LEARY, 2nd Lieut. H. H., 4 (Extra Res.) Bn., Spec. Res. of Off. First Appt. 15 Aug. 14. **War Services**—The War of 1914-16—France, Attd. 2 Bn 17 May 15—Ypres (Wounded, to England 11 June 15). To Medit. Exped. Force 11 Oct. 15 Attd. 11 (S.) Bn.—Gallipoli (Suvla Bay), Imbros 19 Dec. 15—Alexandria 20 Jan. 16.

OLIVER, 2nd Lieut. (temp.) G. H. L., 14 (Res.) Bn. First Appt. 5 Jan. 15. **War Services**—The War of 1914-16, to Medit. Exped. Force 2 Feb. 16.

OLIVER, Capt. (temp.) J.F. (Lieut. Res. of Off.). First Appt. (from ranks of Roberts' Horse) 19 May 1900. Lieut. 13 July 01. Capt. (temp) 2 Oct. 14. **War Services**—S. African War 1899-01—Relief of Kimberley, Paardeberg, Lainge Nek. The War of 1914-16, Medit. Exped. Force 7 Aug. 15—Gallipoli

(Landing Suvla Bay), (Wounded, to England 7-11 Aug. 15). **Despatches 11 Dec. 15.**

O'MEARA, Capt. A. E., 1 Bn. First Appt. (from Mila.) 19 Oct. 01. Capt. 1 Dec. 14, Empld. with W. Afr. Fr. Force 14 Sept. 10 to Nov. 15. **War Services**—S. African War 1900-2. The War of 1914-16—Cameroons. To England Nov. 15. To 1 Bn. Feb. 16.

ORAM, Lieut.-Col. H. K., Comdg. 3 (Res.) Bn., Spec. Res. of Off., Major 27 Dec. 01, Lieut.-Col. and to Commd. Res. Bn. 8 Aug. 12. **War Services**—S. African War 1901-2, Act. Prov. Mar. and Oper. in Orange Riv. Col, **Despatches.** The War of 1914-16—France (Tour.).

ORRELL, 2nd Lieut. (temp.) J. R., 14 (Res.) Bn. First Appt. 2 Dec. 14. **War Services**—The War of 1914-16, to Medit. Exped. Force 21 Sept. 15, Attd. 11 (S.) Bn.—Gallipoli (Suvla Bay), Imbros 19 Dec. 15—Alexandria 20 Jan. 16.

OSBORN, 2nd Lieut. (temp.) C. C. F., Attd. 14 (Res.) Bn. from 11 (S.) Bn. First Appt. 24 Nov. 14.

OST, 2nd Lieut. R. E., 3 (Res.) Bn., Spec. Res. of Off. (on prob.). First Appt. 9 May 15.

OWEN, Lieut. A. P., 3 (Res.) Bn., Spec. Res. of Off. First Appt. 15 Aug. 14, Lieut. 2 Feb. 15. **War Services**—The War of 1914-16—France, Attd. to 2 Bn. 15 Mar. 15—Neuve Chapelle, Messines, Ypres (Wounded, to England 19 April 15), to 1 Bn. Jan. 16. To Mesopotamia (Missing from 11 Mar. 16).

PAGE, 2nd Lieut. (temp.) S. J., 14 (Res.) Bn. First Appt. 24 July 15.

PAINTER, Lieut. (temp.) H. S., 11 (S.) Bn. First Appt. 3 Sept. 14, Lieut. (temp.) 17 May 15. **War Services**—The War of 1914-16, Medit. Exped. Force with 11 (S.) Bn.—Gallipoli (Landing Suvla Bay) 7 Aug. 15 (Wounded, to England 7-11 Aug. 15).

PALMER, 2nd Lieut. (temp.) R. G.

PAPE, 2nd Lieut. (temp.) W. G., Attd. 14 (Res.) Bn. from 12 (S.) Bn. First Appt. 27 Nov. 14. **War Services**—The War of 1914-16—France, with 12 (S.) Bn. 12 July 15 (Invld. to England 29 Sept. 15).

PARKER, 2nd Lieut. A., 3 (Res.) Bn., Spec. Res. of Off. First Appt. 29 May 15.

PARKER, Capt. E. D. (Maj. Ret. Mila., Capt. Res. of Off.) First Appt. (Manch. R.) 7 Jan. 67, Capt. 5 Jan. 98, Retired 2 April 98, to 5 (Militia) Bn. Royal Fus. 2 April 98, Assist. Private Sec. to Parl. Under-Secretary of State for War (Earl of Hardwicke), to Spec. Res. Manch. R. as Capt. 26 Nov. 14. **War Services**—S. African War 1901-2—Oper. in Or. Riv. Col., **Despatches.** The War of 1914-16—France, Attd. 2 Bn. 13 Jan. 15—Messines. **Killed in Action 20 Mar. 15.**

PARKER, Lieut. Royal Army Medical Corps, Attd. 11 (S.) Bn. Manch. R. **War Services**—The War of 1914-16, Medit. Expd. Force—Gallipoli (Landing at Suvla Bay) 7 Aug. 15. **Killed in Action 7-11 Aug. 15.**

PARKS, 2nd Lieut (temp.) G. E. H., Sig. Offr. 14 (Res.) Bn. First Appt. 24 July 15.

PARKES, 2nd Lieut. D. V., 3 (Res.) Bn., Spec. Res. of Off. First Appt. 5 Nov. 15.

PARLANE-GOLDSCHMIDT, Capt. (temp.) P., 13 (S.) Bn. First Appt. 24 Nov. 14, Capt. (temp.) 8 Mar. 15. **War Services**—The War of 1914-16—France, with 13 (S.) Bn. 6 Sept. 15—Salonika 6 Nov. 15.

PARMINTER, Lieut. (temp. Capt.) R. H. R., 1 Bn. First Appt. 5 Feb. 13, Lieut. 15 Sept. 14, Capt. (temp.) 1 Aug. 15. **War Services**—The War of 1914-16—France, with Ind. Cont. 26 Sept. 14—Picantin, Givenchy, Neuve Chapelle, **Awd. Military Cross 27 Mar. 15, Despatches 5 April 15.** To England. Rejoined 1 Bn.—France.

PARROT, Lieut. (temp.) W. E., Attd. Mach. Gun Corps from 12 (S.) Bn. First Appt. 22 Sept. 14. Lieut. (temp.) 9 Feb. 15, to Mach. Gun Corps 22 Nov. 15. **War Services**—The War of 1914-16—France, with 12 (S.) Bn. 15 July 15 (Wounded, to England 9 Aug. 15).

PARRY, Lieut. A. E. First Appt. 17 Oct. 14, Lieut. 22 Dec. 14. **War Services**—The War of 1914-16—France (Wounded).

PARTINGTON, 2nd Lieut. (temp.) J. S., 14 (Res.) Bn. First Appt. 6 Dec. 15.

PATERSON, Lieut. M. C., 4 (Extra Res.) Bn., Spec. Res. of Off. First Appt. 15 Aug. 14, Lieut. 4 May 15.

PATON, Major D. R., Res. of Off., Dist. Rec. Off. No. 6 Dist. First Appt. (from Mila.) 9 Sept. 93, Major 20 Jan. 12, Empld. Dist. Rec. Off. No. 3 Dist. Feb. to July 15, Commd. Depot 20 July to Aug. 15 with temp. rank of Lieut.-Col. **War Services**—S. African War 1899-1902—Elandslaagte (Severely wounded).

PAULSON, Capt. P. Z., Army Sig. Services. First Appt. (from Mila.) 12 Nov. 02, Empld. with W. Afr. Fr. Force 12 Nov. 02 to 30 Oct. 05, Adjut. Vols. and Terr. 20 Aug. 07 to 25 Aug. 12, Capt. 9 Nov. 14, Secd. for emp. with A. Sig. Serv. 2 Nov. 15. **War Services**—S. African War 1899-1900. West African (S. Nigeria) 9101-2—Aro Exped. W. African (N. Nigeria) 1903-4—Oper. against Okpotos, and 1904 against Kilba tribe. The War of 1914-16—France, with 1 Bn.—Givenchy (Wounded 27 Oct. 14). Rejoined 1 Bn.—Ypres (Wounded, to England 26 April 15).

PEAK, 2nd Lieut. (temp.) N., 15 (S.) Bn. First Appt. 26 Feb 15.

PECK, 2nd Lieut. (temp.) E. K. B., 4 (Extra Res.) Bn., Spec. Res. of Off. from 15 (S.) Bn. First Appt. 26 Feb. 15. **War Services**—The War of 1914-16—France, Attd. 2 Bn. 5 Dec. 15—Maricourt.

PEEL, Lieut. (temp.) R. (late Capt. Manch. R., Militia), 1 (Gar.) Bn. Cheshire R., Lieut. (temp.) 22 Dec. 15.

PEIRCE, Capt. W. G. K., 3 (Res.) Bn., Spec. Res. of Off. First Appt. 20 May 99, Capt. 25 Dec. 01, Capt. Spec. Res. of Off. 11 May 12. **War Services**—S. African War 1899-1901. The

War of 1914-16—France, Attd. to 2 Bn. 16 Sept. 14—Aisne, Lorgies. **Killed in Action 26-27 Oct. 14.**

PEMBROKE, 2nd Lieut. S. K., 3 (Res.) Bn., Spec. Res. of Off. First Appt. 28 Nov. 14, Lieut. 2 Feb. 15, to Reg. Army as 2nd Lieut. 4 Oct. 15. **War Services**—The War of 1914-16—France, Attd. 1 Bn.

PETRIE, 2nd Lieut. (temp.) C. H. B., 1 (Gar.) Bn. East Yorks. R. from 14 (Res.) Bn. First Appt. 28 May 15.

PETRIE, Major (temp. Lieut.-Col.) C. L. R., D.S.O. (Maj. ret. pay), Res. of Off., Comdg. 16 (S.) Bn. First Appt. 5 Feb. 87, Major 21 Dec. 01, Sec. in Commd. Depot 6 Aug. 14 to 27 Jan. 15, Brigade Major 111 Inf. Bgde. 28 Jan. 15 to 21 June 15, Lieut.-Col. (temp.) 21 June 15. **War Services**—Uganda 1901. **Despatches (twice) D.S.O.** (Wounded). East Africa 1902-3—Oper. in Somaliland (on Staff), **Despatches.** The War of 1914-16—France, in commd. 16 (S.) Bn. (1st City).

PHILLIPS, Capt. F. G. P., 3 (Res.) Bn. Shrop. L.I., Spec. Res. of Off., Capt. 11 April 1900. **War Services**—S. African War 1901, Staff Off. to Dist. Commandant. The War of 1914-16—France, Attd. to 1 Bn. Manch. Regt.

PHILLIPS, 2nd Lieut. (temp.) P. T., 14 (Res.) Bn. First Appt. 23 Dec. 14. **War Services**—The War of 1914-16, to Medit. Exped. Force 10 Aug. 15, Attd. 6 Bn. East Lancs. Regt.

PICKSTONE, 2nd Lieut. (temp.) D., 14 (Res.) Bn. First Appt. 31 July 15.

PLATT, 2nd Lieut. (temp.) S. F., 14 (Res.) Bn. First Appt. 12 June 15, Empld. on Recruiting Duties, Leicester.

PLENTY, 2nd Lieut. E. P., Attd. R.F. Corps. First Appt. 17 April 15, Flying Offr. 30 Aug. 15.

POMFRET, Capt. H. T., Attd. 3 (Res.) Bn., Res. of Off. First Appt. 29 July 02, Lieut. 18 Nov. 14 (Hon. Capt. in Army, late Mila. Lieut.). **War Services**—S. African War 1899-1900 (Severely wounded). The War of 1914-16—France, with 2 Bn. 7 Jan. 15—Messines, Kemmel, Ypres (Invld. to England 16 May 15), **Despatches 5 April 15.**

POOLE, Hon. Lieut. (temp.) W., Quartermaster 13 (S.) Bn., Attd. 14 (Res.) Bn. First Appt. 3 Dec. 14. **War Services**—The War of 1914-16—France, with 13 (S.) Bn. 6 Sept. 15 (Invld. to England Oct. 15).

PORTER, 2nd Lieut. A. E., 3 (Res.) Bn., Spec. Res. of Off. (on prob.). First Appt. 16 Aug. 15.

POWELL, Lieut. (temp.) P. J., 14 (Res.) Bn. First Appt. as Lieut. (temp.) 15 Mar. 15. **War Services**—The War of 1914-16. to Medit. Exped. Force 21 Aug. 15—Gallipoli (Suvla Bay), Attd. 11 (S.) Bn. (Invld. to England).

PRICE, 2nd Lieut. H. W., 4 (Extra Res.) Bn., Spec. Res. of Off. First Appt. 15 Aug. 14. **War Services**—The War of 1914-16—France, Attd. to 2 Bn. 10 May 15—Ypres (Wounded, to England 2 June 15). Rejoined 2 Bn.—Maricourt.

PRICE, Hon. Major and Qr.-Mr. H. W., 4 (Extra Res.) Bn., Spec. Res. of Off. First Appt. 23 Feb. 01, Hon. Capt. 23

Feb. 11. **War Services**—N.-W. Frontier of India 1897-8—Mohmand.

PRICE, 2nd Lieut. (temp.) J. E., 14 (Res.) Bn. First Appt. 25 Nov. 15.

PRIOLEAU, Major L. H., Res. of Off. First Appt. 22 Oct. 81, Major 7th April 1900, Empld. Rec. Duties 26 Sept. 14. **War Services**—Egyptian Exped. 1882.

PRIESTLEY, 2nd Lieut. (temp.) H. S., 15 (S.) Bn. First Appt. 7 Dec. 14. **War Services**—The War of 1914-16, to Medit. Exped. Force 23 Aug. 15—Gallipoli, Attd. 11 (S.) Bn., Suvla Bay (Wounded, to England Oct. 15).

PURCELL, Major (temp.) H. Y. (late Mila. Manch. R.), 13 (S.) Bn. from 15 Jan. 15 to 2 June 15. First Appt. 5 Feb. 02. **War Services**—S. African War 1902—Oper. in Cape Colony.

PURCELL, 2nd Lieut. M. T., 4 (Extra Res.) Bn., Spec. Res. of Off. (on prob.). First Appt. 6 May 15.

PYMAN, Capt. J., from 3 Bn. Border Regt., Capt. 18 May 06. **War Services**—The War of 1914—France, Attd. 2 Bn. **Killed in Action 18 Nov. 14.**

RAPHAEL, 2nd Lieut. R. A., 4 Bn. R. Wan. Regt. First Appt. 13 Feb. 15. **War Services**—The War of 1914-16—France, Attd. to 2 Bn. Manch. R. Dec. 14—Ypres (Wounded, to England 28 April 15).

RAYNER, 2nd Lieut. O. C., 3 (Res.) Bn., Spec. Res. of Off. First Appt. 17 Feb. 15. **War Services**—The War of 1914-16—France, Attd. 2 Bn. 9 June 15—Ypres, Maricourt.

READE, Lieut. J. H. L., 2 Bn. First Appt. (from Mila.) 29 Jan. 02, Lieut. 3 Oct. 03. **War Services**—S. African War 1901-2. The War of 1914-16—France, sailed with the B.E.F. with 2 Bn.—Mons, Bavay, Le Cateau, Marne, Lorgies, **Despatches 19 Oct. 15. Killed in Action 28-29 Oct. 14.**

REIDY, Lieut. (temp.) E. Mc., 11 (S.) Bn. First Appt. 16 Nov. 14, Lieut. (temp.) 17 May 15. **War Services**—The War of 1914-16, Medit. Exped. Force—Gallipoli 7 Aug. 15, Landing Suvla Bay (Wounded 7-11 Aug. 15). Rejoined 11 (S.) Bn.—Suvla Bay. Imbros 19 Dec. 15—Alexandria 20 Jan. 16.

REYNOLDS, 2nd Lieut. H. J. S., 4 (Extra Res.) Bn., pSec. Res. of Off. (on prob.). First Appt. 26 June 15.

RHEAD, 2nd Lieut. (temp.) A. W., 14 (Res.) Bn. First Appt. 30 July 15.

RHIND, 2nd Lieut. (temp.) H. P., 14 (Res.) Bn. First Appt. 18 Dec. 14., transf. to 5 (Terr.) Bn. Border R. 21 Aug. 15.

RHODES, 2nd Lieut. (temp.) E., 13 (S.) Bn. First Appt. 3 Jan. 15. **War Services**—The War of 1914-16, to Medit. Exped. Force 11 Jan. 16, Attd. 8 (T.) Bn. Manch. R.—Egypt.

RICHARDSON, Lieut. J. C., Empld. with W. African R. First Appt. 20 Nov. 14, Lieut. 27 April 15. **War Services**—S. African War (Ranks. Manch. R.), **Despatches, D.C.M.** The War of 1914-16—France, as Col.-Sergt. Manch. R., to West Afrn. R. (attd.) from Manch. R. 20 Nov. 14—German West Africa.

RICHARDSON, 2nd Lieut. R. F., 3 (Res.) Bn., Spec. Res. of Off. (on prob.). First Appt. 7 Dec. 15.

RIDLEY, Hon. Brig. Gen., C. P., C.B., Temp.Brig.-General 30 Sept. 14. First Appt. 9 Aug. 73, Hon. Brig.-Genl. 24 Aug. 12. **War Services**—Egyptian Exped. 1882, Miranzai Exped. 1891. S. African War 1899-1900, on Staff, **Despatches, C.B.**

RIGBY, 2nd Lieut. (temp.) L., 14 (Res.) Bn. First Appt. 10 April 15.

RIORDAN, 2nd Lieut. E. E., 3 (Res.) Bn., Spec. Res. of Off. First Appt. 22 June 15.

RIPPINGALL, Lieut. N. F. R., Spec. Res. of Off. (late Lieut. Norfolk R. F. Res. A.), Lieut. 9 June 02, Depot Manch. R. 15 Oct. 14 until Rel. Commn. on acc. of ill-health 17 Sept. 15.

RITT, Hon. Lieut. (temp.) G., Quartermaster 12 (S.) Bn. 10 Dec. 14. **War Services**—The War of 1914-16—France, with 12 (S.) Bn. 15 July 15.

ROACH, 2nd Lieut. R. E., 3 (Res.) Bn., Spec. Res. of Off. (on prob.). First Appt. 26 June 15.

ROBERTS, 2nd Lieut. G. B., Unattached List for Indian Army 15 Aug. 14. **War Services**—The War of 1914-16—France, Attd. 1 Bn. Manch. R. **Died of Wounds received in action 11 May 15.**

ROBERTSON, 2nd Lieut. (temp.) A., 4 (Extra Res.) Bn., Spec. Res. of Off. First Appt. 15 (S.) Bn. 3 Mar. 15. **War Services**—The War of 1914-15, to France 5 Dec. 15, Attd. 2 Bn. —Maricourt (Wounded, to England 3 Mar. 16).

ROBERTSON, 2nd Lieut. C. W., 3 (Res.) Bn., Spec. Res. of Off. (on prob.). First Appt. 16 Nov. 15.

ROBINSON, 2nd Lieut. (temp.) A. H., 1 Bn. First Appt. 20 Mar. 15. **War Services**—The War of 1914-16—France, with 1 Bn. (Wounded and Missing 18 June 15)

ROBINSON, Lieut. (temp.) F. W., 14 (Res.) Bn. First Appt. 11 Jan. 15, Lieut. (temp.) 4 Nov. 15.

ROBINSON, Lieut. K., M.B., R.A.M. Corps. War Services—The War of 1914-16—France, Attd. 12 (S.) Bn. 15 July 15. **Killed in Action 27 Sept. 15.**

ROMAN, 2nd Lieut. (temp.) E. O., 14 (Res.) Bn. First Appt. 30 July 15.

ROOKE, 2nd Lieut. (temp.) W. H. C., 2/10 Bn. Manch. R. from 14 (Res.) Bn. First Appt. 5 May 15, to 2/10 Bn. 12 Dec. 15.

ROSE, Capt. A. B., Instructional Duties, Cambridge. First Appt. 27 July 01, Empld. Somaliland Mila. 5 June 07 to 31 Mar. 08, King's Afr. Rifles 1 April 08 to 13 June 10, Local Force British Guiana 27 Mar. 12 to 6 Nov. 14, Capt. 25 Aug. 14. **War Services**—S. African War, 1901, Empld. with New Zealand Contgt. East Africa (Somaliland) 1908-10 (Severely wounded). The War of 1914-16—France, with Ind. Contgt. with 1 Bn. 26 Sept. 14—Givenchy (Wounded, to England 21 Dec. 14).

ROSS, 2nd Lieut. (temp.) E. A., 13 (S.) Bn. First Appt. 14 Jan. 15. **War Services**—The War of 1914-16, to Medit. Expd. Force 11 Jan. 16, Attd. 8 (T.) Bn. Manch. R.—Egypt.

ROUTLEY, Lieut. (temp.) W. F., Comdg. "A" Coy. 14 (Res.) Bn. from 11 (S.) Bn. First Appt. Lieut. (temp.) 7 Dec. 14.

ROYLE, Capt. (temp.) R. H., 11 (S.) Bn. First Appt. 26 Aug. 14, Capt. (temp.) 6 Sept. 15. **War Services**—The War of 1914-16, Medit. Exped. Force—Gallipoli, with 11 (S.) Bn. 7 Aug. 15, Landing Suvla Bay **(Invld. to Cairo).**

RUDDICK, 2nd Lieut. (temp.) S., 2/5 Bn. Manch. R. from 13 (S.) Bn. First Appt. 9 April 15.

RUDDY, Lieut. T., 1 Bn. First Appt. 21 Dec. 14, Lieut. 10 June 15. **War Services**—The War of 1914-16—France, sailed with B.E.F. with 2 Bn. in ranks—Mons, Bavay, Le Cateau, Marne, Aisne, Richebourg. **Prom. 2nd Lieut. for Services in the Field, 21 Dec. 14. Despatches 17 Feb. 15.** To England, Attd. 4 (Extra Res.) Bn., to France with 1 Bn.

RYALL, 2nd Lieut. (temp.) G., 15 (S.) Bn. First Appt. 3 Mar. 1915.

RYMER, Capt. (temp.) J. H., 11 (S.) Bn. from 14 (Res.) Bn. First Appt. as Lieut. (temp.) 21 Dec. 14, Capt. (temp.) 15 Mar. 15, to 11 (S.) Bn. 27 May 15. **War Services**—S. African War 1899-1901. The War of 1914-16, Medit. Exped. Force—Gallipoli, with 11 (S.) Bn. 7 Aug. 15, Landing Suvla Bay. **Killed in Action 7-11 Aug. 15.**

RYND, Capt. G. C., Res. of Off. First Appt. 3 May 90, Capt. 24 Jan. 98. **War Services**—S. African War 1900-2.

SALISBURY, 2nd Lieut. C. D., 4 (Extra Res.) Bn., Spec. Res. of Off. (on prob.). First Appt. 18 April 15.

ST. JOHN, Lieut. (temp.) H. G., Machine Gun Corps from 14 (Res.) Bn. First Appt. 9 Nov. 14, Lieut. (temp.) 7 Jan. 15.

SALMON, 2nd Lieut. (temp.) W., 12 (S.) Bn. from 24 Nov. 14 to 22 Jan. 15, to Army Cyclist Corps.

SAPORTAS, 2nd Lieut. (temp. Lieut.) H. A. First Appt. 2 May 14, Lieut. (temp.) 11 Sept. 14. **War Services**—The War of 1914-16—France, with Indian Contgt. with 1 Bn. 26 Sept. 14—Picantiu, Givenchy (Wounded, to England). Joined 2 Bn. 24 May 15—Ypres. **Killed in Action 16 July 15.**

SAVAGE, 2nd Lieut. (temp. Capt.) G. R., 3 (Res.) Bn. Essex R., Spec. Res. of Off. First Appt. 2 May 15, Capt. (temp.) 23 Oct. 15. **War Services**—The War of 1914-16, Medit. Exped. Force—Gallipoli, Attd. 11 (S.) Bn. Manch. R. (Suvla Bay), Imbros 19 Dec. 15—Alexandria 20 Jan. 16.

SAYERS, Major R. C., 3 (Res.) Bn. E. Surrey R., Spec. Res. of Off., Major 2 Sept. 14, Apptd. Governor Detention Barr. 5 Sept. 15. **War Services**—The War of 1914-16—France, Attd. to 2 Bn. Manch. R. 3 Dec. 14—Messines (Invld. to England 23 Jan. 15).

SAXON, 2nd Lieut. (temp.) F. C., 14 (Res.) Bn. First Appt. 14 June 15. **War Services**—To Medit. Exped. Force 17 Nov. 15.

SCHOLES, 2nd Lieut. (temp.) W. N., 13 (S.) Bn. First Appt. 18 Dec. 14, Mach. Gun Officer. **War Services**—The War of 1914-16—France, with 13 (S.) Bn. 6 Sept. 15—Salonika 6 Nov. 15.

SCULLY, Capt. A. J. First Appt. 22 Feb. 08, Empld. with

African R. 5 Mar. 13 to 24 Sept. 14, Attd. 2 Bn. Manch. R. 4 Aug. 14 to 24 Sept. 14, Capt. 10 June 15. **War Services—The War of 1914-16**—France, sailed with B.E.F. with 2 Bn. Mons, Bavay, Le Cateau, Marne, Aisne, Richebourg, Lorgies, La Quinque Rue, Wulverghem (Invld. to England 20 Nov. 14). Rejoined 2 Bn.—Neuve Chapelle 11 Mar. 15—Kemmel, Ypres, Maricourt. **Despatches 17 Feb. 15, Awd. Military Cross 18 Feb. 15.**

SERGEANT, Capt. F. W. B., Attd. 3 (Res.) Bn., Spec. Res. of Off. First Appt. 10 Feb. 12, Capt. 9 Feb. 15. **War Services**—The War of 1914-16—France, with 2 Bn. 17 Feb. 15—Messines (Invld. to England 27 April 15).

SHACKLADY, 2nd Lieut. E. A., 3 (Res.) Bn., Spec. Res. of Off. First Appt. 14 April 15. **War Services**—The War of 1914-16—France, Attd. 2 Bn. 31 Oct. 15—Maricourt (Invld. to England).

SHARPINGTON, 2nd Lieut. (temp.) F. W., 14 (Res.) Bn. First Appt. 24 July 15.

SHARROCKS, 2nd Lieut. (temp.) T. F., Machine Gun Corps from 14 (Res.) Bn. First Appt. 16 Jan. 15.

SHAW, 2nd Lieut. (temp.) A. G., 13 (S.) Bn. First Appt. 3 Jan. 15. **War Services**—The War of 1914-16—France, with 13 (S.) Bn. 6 Sept. 15—Salonika 6 Nov. 15.

SHEPPARD, 2nd Lieut. C. J. L. First Appt. 12 May 15. **War Services**—The War of 1914-16—France, with 2 Bn. (Invld. to England).

SHIELDS, 2nd Lieut. (temp.) W., 15 (S.) Bn. First Appt. 2 Mar. 15. **War Services**—To Medit. Exped. Force 12 Jan. 16.

SHIPSTER, Lieut. (temp. Capt.) W. N., Attd. 3 Bn. from 1 Bn. First Appt. 18 Sept. 09, Lieut. 3 May 13, Capt. (temp.) 1 Sept. 15. **War Services**—The War of 1914-16—France, with Indian Contig. 26 Sept. 14—Bethune (Wounded, to England 26 Nov. 14). **Despatches 15 Oct. 15, Awd. Military Cross 1 Jan. 16.**

SILLERY, Major J. J. D., 11 (S.) Bn. (Ret. Ind. Army). First Appt. 5 Feb. 87, Major (Manch. R.) 13 Sept. 14. **War Services**—The War of 1914-16, Medit. Exped. Force—Gallipoli, with 11 (S.) Bn. 7 Aug. 15 (Landing Suvla Bay). **Killed in Action 7-11 Aug. 15. Despatches 11 Dec. 15.**

SIMPSON, 2nd Lieut. (temp.) G. G., 1 (Gar.) Bn. First Appt 8 July 15 (Ches. R.), to Manch. R. 28 Nov. 15.

SINCLAIR, 2nd Lieut. (temp.) G. W., 14 (Res.) Bn. First Appt 9 April 15.

SINCLAIR, 2nd Lieut. (temp.) R. F., Attd. R. Flying Corps from 14 (Res.) Bn. First Appt. 9 Nov. 14. War Services—The War of 1914-16, to Medit. Exped. Force 21 Sept. 15—Gallipoli (Suvla Bay), Attd. 11 (S.) Bn. (Wounded, to England 1 Oct. 15).

SKINNER, 2nd Lieut. (temp.) E. D., 15 (S.) Bn. First Appt. 1 Mar. 15. **War Services**—The War of 1914-16, to Medit. Exped. Force 12 Jan. 16.

SLADE, Capt. (temp.) C. J., 13 (S.) Bn. from 27 Sept. 14 to

26 Oct. 15. **War Services**—The War of 1914-16—France, with 13 (S.) Bn. 5 Sept. 15—Salonika 6 Nov. 15.

SLOMAN, Lieut. A. J., 4 (Extra Res.) Bn., Spec. Res. of Off. First Appt. 15 Aug. 14, Lieut. 4 May 15. **War Services**—The War of 1914-16—France, Attd. 2 Bn. 10 May 15—Ypres, Maricourt (Wounded, to England 4 Oct. 15).

SMALL, Lieut. (temp.) B. G., Army Cyclist Corps from 11 (S.) Bn. First Appt. 1 Sept. 14, Lieut. (temp.) 3 Feb. 15, to A.C.C. 10 June 15.

SMITH, Lieut. A. G., 3 (Res.) Bn., Spec. Res. of Off. First Appt. 31 Oct. 14, Lieut. 2 Feb. 15. **War Services**—The War of 1914-16—France, Attd. 1 Bn. To Mesopotamia Nov. 15 (Wounded 11 Mar. 16).

SMITH, Lieut. (temp.) A. W., 13 (S.) Bn. First Appt. 16 Nov. 14, Lieut. (temp.) 1 Feb. 15. **War Services**—The War of 1914-16, Medit. Exped. Force—Salonika, with 13 (S.) Bn. 14 Jan. 16.

SMITH, 2nd Lieut. (temp. Lieut.) J. H. M., 2 Bn. First Appt. 27 Sept. 13, Lieut. (temp.) 31 Aug. 14. **War Services**—The War of 1914-16—France, sailed with B.E.F. with 2 Bn.—Mons, Bavay, Le Cateau, Marne. **Died of wounds received in action 9 Sept. 14.**

SMITH, 2nd Lieut. (temp. Lieut.) R. W. First Appt. 2 April 15, Lieut. (temp.) 21 June 15.

SMITH, 2nd Lieut. (temp. Capt.) W. W. (2nd Lieut. Shrop. L.I.). First Appt. 20 Dec. 14, Capt. (temp.) 1 Sept. 15. **War Services**—The War of 1914-16—France, Attd. 2 Bn. Manch. R. Mar. 15—Messines, Kemmel, Ypres, Maricourt.

SMITH-CARRINGTON, 2nd Lieut. (temp.) H. F., 14 (Res.) Bn. First Appt. 23 Feb. 15. **War Services**—The War of 1914-16, to Medit. Exped. Force 23 Sept. 15—Gallipoli, Attd. 11 (S.) Bn.—Imbros 19 Dec. 15—Alexandria 20 Jan. 16.

SMITHERS, 2nd Lieut. (temp.) E. H. K., Attd. 14 (Res.) Bn. from 11 (S.) Bn. First Appt. 9 Sept. 14. **War Services**—The War of 1914-16, Medit. Exped. Force—Gallipoli 7 Aug. 15 (Landing Suvla Bay), (Wounded 7 Aug. 15, to England).

SMYLIE, Capt. (temp.) J. S., 13 (S.) Bn. First Appt. 22 Sept. 14, Capt. (temp.) 1 Feb. 15. **War Services**—The War of 1914-16—France, with 13 (S.) Bn. 6 Sept. 15—Salonika 6 Nov. 15.

SMYTH, Lieut. (temp.) G. W., 1 (Gar.) Bn. Notts and Derby R. from 14 (Res.) Bn. First Appt. as Lieut. 26 Jan. 16.

SNOW, Major A. D., Attd. 1 (Gar.) Bn. Linc. R. from 4 (Extra Res.) Bn., Capt. and Hon. Major late Genl. Res. of Off. West of Scotland R.G.A. First Appt. 18 Oct. 06, Major 6 Oct. 14. **War Services**—S. African War 1902.

SODEN, Major (temp.) C. W., 1 (Gar.) Bn. (Capt. and Hon. Major ret. R. Irish R.), to Manch. R. 6 Jan. 16. **War Services**—Oper. in S. Africa 1897—Served with B.S.A. Police.

SORRELL, 2nd Lieut. S., 3 (Res.) Bn., Spec. Res. of Off. First Appt. 3 April 15. **War Services**—The War of 1914-16—France, Attd. 2 Bn. 8 Oct. 15—Maricourt.

SOTHAM, Capt. E. G., Adjutant 16 (S.) Bn. Manch. R. First Appt. 18 Nov. 03, Empld. with King's African Rifles 28 Oct. 09 to 28 Nov. 12, Adjut. 16 (S.) Bn. 25 Sept. 14, Capt. 11 Dec. 14. **War Services**—The War of 1914-16—France, with 16 (S.) Bn. Nov. 15.

SOUTHON, Lieut. (temp.) H. F., 14 (Res.) Bn. First Appt. as Lieut. (temp.) 4 Jan. 15. **War Services**—The War of 1914-16, to Medit. Exped. Force 13 May 15—Gallipoli, Attd. 6 (T.) Bn. Manch R. (Wounded).

SPROAT, 2nd Lieut. (temp.) G. M., Attd. 14 (Res.) Bn. from 11 (S.) Bn. First Appt. 1 Sept. 14. **War Services**—The War of 1914-16, Medit. Exped. Force—Gallipoli, with 11 (S.) Bn. (Landing Suvla Bay) 7 Aug. 15 (Invld. to England).

SPROAT, 2nd Lieut. J. McC., 17 (S.) Bn. Liverpool R. First Appt. 1 Sept. 14 (also gazetted 11 (S.) Bn. Manch. R. 29 Sept. 14).

SPURLING, 2nd Lieut. (temp.) J. A., 14 (Res.) Bn. First Appt. 7 Aug. 15.

STAFFORD-BADGER, 2nd Lieut. (temp.) V. C., 11 (S.) Bn. First Appt. 24 Nov. 14. **War Services**—The War of 1914-16, Medit. Exped. Force—Gallipoli, with 11 (S.) Bn. 7 Aug. 15 (Landing Suvla Bay), (Invld. to England).

STAITE, 2nd Lieut. (temp.) A. C., Attd. 14 (Res.) Bn. from 12 (S.) Bn. First Appt. 5 Feb. 15. **War Services**—The War of 1914-16, to Medit. Exped. Force 25 Oct. 15.

STANLEY, 2nd Lieut. A. C. U., 3 Bn. R. Innis. Fus. from 4 (Extra Res.) Bn. First Appt. 28 Sept. 14, to R. Innis Fus. 13 Feb. 15.

STAPLEDON, Major C. C., 2 Bn. First Appt. 11 Aug. 1900, Capt. 20 July 12, Major 1 Sept. 15, Adjut. 3 (Res.) Bn. 6 June 14 to Oct. 15. **War Services**—S. African War 1901-2, —Served with Mtd. Inf. The War of 1914-16—France, with 2 Ban.—Maricourt.

STARKEY, 2nd Lieut. (temp.) T., 14 (Res.) Bn. First Appt. 29 Nov. 15.

STEANE, 2nd Lieut. (temp.) C. S., Attd. 14 (Res.) Bn. from 12 (S.) Bn. First Appt. 15 Feb. 15. **War Services**—The War of 1914-16, to Medit. Exped. Force 25 Oct. 15.

STEVENS, Capt. (temp.) J. M., 1 (Gar.) Bn. E. Yorks. R. from 11 (S.) Bn. First Appt. as Capt. 7 Jan. 15, to 11 (S.) Bn. 29 May 15. **War Services**—The War of 1914-16, Medit. Exp. Force—Gallipoli, 7 Aug. 15 (Landing Suvla Bay), (Invld. to England).

STOKOE, 2nd Lieut. (temp.) J. C., 14 (Res.) Bn. First Appt. 25 Nov. 14. **War Services**—The War of 1914-16, to Medit. Exped. Force 23 Sept. 15—Gallipoli, Attd. 6 (S.) Bn. N. Lan. R.—Suvla Bay. **Killed in Action 11 Dec. 15.**

STOTT, Lieut. (temp.) F. C., 12 (S.) Bn. First Appt. 12 Sept. 14. Lieut. (temp.) 9 Feb. 15. **War Services**—The War of 1914-16—France, with 12 (S.) Bn. 15 July 15.

STRICKLAND, Brig. Genl. (temp.) E. P., C.M.G., D.S.O. First Appt. (from Mila.) 10 Nov. 88, Empld. with Egyptian Army

1 April 96 to 31 Mar. 03, Empld. with W. Afr. Rrontier Force 3 Feb. 06 to 2 Aug. 13, Lieut.-Col. 1 June 14, Brig.-Genl. (temp.) 4 Jan. 15. **War Services**—Burmese Exped. 1887-9, Expd. to Dongola 1896, **Despatches.** Nile Expdns 1897, **Despatches (twice).** 1898 Atbara and Khartoum, **Despatches (twice), Brev. of Major.** 1899, White Nile, **D.S.O.** The War of 1914-16—France, Assumed Commd. 1 Bn. Manc. R. (Indian Contg.) at Marseilles 26 Sept. 14—Picantin, Givenchy—**Brev. of Col. 18 Feb. 15, Despatches 17 Feb. 15.**

STURT, 2nd Lieut. (temp.) S., 14 (Res.) Bn. First Appt. 22 July 15. **War Services**—The War of 1914-16, to Medit. Exped. Force 15 Nov. 15.

SUTTON, Lieut. (temp.) H., 14 (Res.) Bn. First Appt. as Lieut. (temp.) 27 Mar. 15. **War Services**—The War of 1914-16, to Medit. Exped. Force 21 Sept. 15—Gallipoli, Attd. 11 (S.) Bn. (Suvla Bay), Imbros 19 Dec. 15—Alexandria 20 Jan. 16.

SWAN, 2nd Lieut. G. G., 4 (Extra Res.) Bn., Spec. Res. of Off. First Appt. 6 May 15.

SWANN, 2nd Lieut. (temp.) C. F., 14 (Res.) Bn. First Appt. 29 June 15.

SWEET, 2nd Lieut. F. G., 3 (Res.) Bn. Essex R., Spec. Res. of Off. First Appt. 10 April 15. **War Services**—The War of 1914-16, Medit. Exped. Force, Attd. 11 (S.) Bn.—Alexandria 20 Jan. 16.

SWIFT, 2nd Lieut. (temp.) J., 12 (S.) Bn. First Appt. 22 Sept. 14. **War Services**—The War of 1914-16—France, with 12 (S.) Bn. 15 July 15.

SWIFT, 2nd Lieut. (temp.) W. F., Attd. 14 (Res.) Bn. from 12 (S.) Bn. First Appt. 23 Feb. 15.

SYKES, 2nd Lieut. F. C., Attd. 3 (Res.) Bn. First Appt. 20 Oct. 15.

TANNER, 2nd Lieut. E., 3 (Res.) Bn., Spec. Res. of Off. First Appt. 14 May 15.

TATTERSHALL, 2nd Lieut. (temp.) H. N., 14 (Res.) Bn. First Appt. 28 May 15. **War Services**—The War of 1914-16, to Medit. Exped. Force 23 Sept. 15—Gallipoli, Attd. 11 (S.) Bn. (Suvla Bay), Imbros 19 Dec. 15—Alexandria 20 Jan. 16.

TAYLOR, 2nd Lieut. (temp.) G. E., 14 (Res.) Bn. First Appt. 23 Aug. 15.

TAYLOR, 2nd Lieut. (temp.) H., 14 (Res.) Bn. First Appt. 3 April 15.

TEMPEST, 2nd Lieut. (temp.) B., 13 (S.) Bn. First Appt. 28 Jan. 15. **War Services**—The War of 1914-16—France, with 13 (S.) Bn. 6 Sept. 15—Salonika 6 Nov. 15.

THEOBALD, Major H. C. W., D.S.O., Rec. Duties, London. First Appt. (from Mila.) 4 May 98, Capt. 13 July 01, Major 1 Sept. 15. **War Services**—S. African War 1899-1902—Def. of Ladysmith (Dangerously wounded), **Despatches, Prom. Capt., D.S.O.** The War of 1914-16—France, sailed with B.E.F. with 2 Bn.—Mons, Bavay, Le Cateau (Severely wounded 26 Aug. 14).

THIERRY, 2nd Lieut. (temp.) L. H., 15 (S.) Bn. First Appt. 1 Mar. 15. **War Services**—The War of 1914-16, to Medit. Exped. Force 12 Jan. 16.

THOMAS, Capt. A. F., Army Signal Service 14 June 15. First Appt. 23 April 02, Empld. with W. Afr. Frontier Force 13 April 07 to 25 May 11, Capt. 1 Dec. 14. **War Services**—S. African War 1901-2. The War of 1914-16—France, sailed with B.E.F. with 2 Bn.—Mons, Bavay, Le Cateau (Severely wounded 26 Aug. 14, to England).

THOMAS, 2nd Lieut. G. R., 4 (Extra Res.) Bn., Spec. Res. of Off. First Appt. 15 Aug. 14. **War Services**—The War of 1914-16—France, Attd. 2 Bn. 23 May 15—Ypres, Maricourt.

THOMAS, 2nd Lieut. J. H., 3 (Res.) Bn., Spec. Res. of Off. First Appt. 24 July 15. **War Services**—The War of 1914-16—France, Attd. 2 Bn.—Maricourt.

THOMPSON, Capt. (temp.) E. R., 12 (S.) Bn. First Appt. as Lieut. (temp.) 15 Sept. 14, Capt. (temp.) 26 April 15. **War Services**—The War of 1914-16—France, with 12 (S.) Bn. 15 July 15.

THOMPSON, Capt. (temp.) J., 13 (S.) Bn. First Appt. 14 Nov. 14, Capt. (temp.) 1 Feb. 15. **War Services**—The War of 1914-16—France, with 13 (S.) Bn. 5 Sept. 15—Salonika 5 Nov. 15.

THORMAN, 2nd Lieut. (temp.) R. C., 14 (Res.) Bn. First Appt. 1 Oct. 15.

THORNE, Capt. (temp.) F. O., Adjut. 13 (S.) Bn. First Appt. as Lieut. (temp.) 28 Jan. 15, Capt. (temp.) 2 June 15, Adjut. 1 Feb. 15. **War Services**—The War of 1914-16—France, with 13 (S.) Bn. 6 Sept. 15—Salonika 6 Nov. 15.

THORNLEY, 2nd Lieut. (temp.) H., 14 (Res.) Bn. First Appt. 23 Aug. 15.

THORNTON, 2nd Lieut. A. M., 3 (Res.) Bn., Spec. Res. of Off. First Appt. 14 May 15. **War Services**—The War of 1914-16—France, Attd. 1 Bn.

THORNYCROFT, Major C. M., Adjutant 3 (Res.) Bn., Spec. Res. of Off. (Capt. ret. pay). First Appt. 12 Aug. 99, Capt. 5 Feb. 03, Major (Spec. Res.) 2 Feb. 15, Adjut 3 (Res.) Bn. 30 Oct. 15. **War Services**—S. African War 1900-2—On Staff, **Despatches.** The War of 1914-16—France, Attd. 2 Bn. 4 Jan. 15—Messines, Kemmel, Ypres, Maricourt (Invld. to England 30 Aug. 15). **Despatches 15 Oct. 15, to be Comp. Dist. Service Order 1 Jan. 16.**

THOROLD, Bt.-Col. H. D. (Lieut.-Col. Res. of Off.). First Appt. 14 Jan. 80, Bt.-Col. 30 Nov. 07, Commd. Depot Manch. R. 10 Feb. 15 to 18 June 15, Apptd. O.C. No. 6 District 18 June 15. **War Services**—Oper. in S. Africa 1896, **Despatches.** S. African War 1900-2—Relief of Kimberley, Paardeberg, Poplar Grove, Dreifontein.

TILL, 2nd Lieut. (temp.) G. F., 14 (Res.) Bn. First Appt. 22 April 15.

TILLARD, Capt. A. G., 3 (Res.) Bn., Spec. Res. of Off. First Appt. 20 Feb. 95, Capt. 4 Jan. 13. **War Services**—S. African

War 1899-1902—Lombard's Kap, Def. of Ladysmith. The War of 1914-16—France, Attd. 2 Bn. 16 Sept. 14—Aisne, Lorgies. **Killed in Action 20 Oct. 14.**

TILLARD, Capt. A. K. D. First Appt. 8 May 01, Capt. 11 Dec. 12. **War Services**—S. African War 1901-2. The War of 1914-16—France, with 1 Bn.—Neuve Chapelle, Ypres (Wounded, to England 26 April 15). Returned to France Attd. 1 Bn. Ches. R. **Despatches 5 April 15.**

TIMMS, 2nd Lieut. (temp.) C. A. S., 14 (Res.) Bn. First Appt. 7 May 15. **War Services**—The War of 1914-16, to France 8 Feb. 16.

TITJEN, Lieut. (temp.) C. F. H., Attd. 3 (Res.) Bn. from 11 (S.) Bn. First Appt. as Lieut. 6 Jan. 15, Attd. 3 (Res.) Bn. 15 Feb. 16. **War Services**—The War of 1914-16, to Medit. Exped. Force 23 Sept. 15—Gallipoli, with 11 (S.) Bn. (Suvla Bay). (Invld. to England).

TOMBE, Capt. (temp.) H. E. (Ret. Suffolk R.). First Appt. (from Mila.) 11 Oct. 79, Capt. 26 April 86, Ret. 1894. Apptd. Rec. Off. 63rd R.D. Rec. Area 8 Oct. 14. **War Services**—Egyptian Exped. 1882. S. African War 1899-02.

TOMBLIN, 2nd Lieut. H. R., 3 (Res.) Bn. Spec. Res. of Off. First Appt. 13 Mar. 15. **War Services**—The War of 1914-16—France, Attd. 2 Bn.—Maricourt.

TORRANCE, 2nd Lieut. (temp. Lieut.) K. S., 2 Bn. First Appt. 22 Jan. 15, Lieut. (temp.) 5 May 15. **War Services**—The War of 1914-16—France, with 2 Bn. 5 May 15—Ypres, Maricourt.

TOWER, Lieut. (temp.) F., 12 (S.) Bn. First Appt. 22 Sept. 14, Lieut. (temp.) 28 April 15. **War Services**—The War of 1914-16—France, with 12 (S.) Bn. 15 July 15.

TOWERS, 2nd Lieut. W. G., 4 (Extra Res.) Bn., Spec. Res. of Off. (on prob.). First Appt. 21 Oct. 15.

TRENCH, Lieut. S. J. le P., 12 (S.) Bn. from Staff. Yeo. 15 July 15, Lieut. 21 Aug. 12. **War Services**—The War of 1914-16—France, with 12 (S.) Bn. 15 July 15.

TRISTRAM, 2nd Lieut. A. M., Attd. Mach. Gun Corps from 4 (Extra Res.) Bn., Spec. Res. of Off. from 15 (S.) Bn. 11 Dec. 14.

TRUEMAN, Capt. C. Fitz G. H., 2 Bn. First Appt. 8 Sept. 97, Assist. Inst. of Gymnasia, Aldershot Commd. 1 Sept. 09 to 22 April 12, Capt. 5 Jan. 01. **War Services**—S. African War 1900-1. The War of 1914-16—France, sailed with B.E.F. with 2 Bn.—Mons, Bavay, Le Cateau. **Killed in Action 26 Aug. 15.**

TUCHMANN, Lieut. (temp.) M. J., Attd. 14 (Res.) Bn. from 12 (S.) Bn. First Appt. as Lieut. (temp.) 5 Sept. 14. **War Services**—The War of 1914-16—France, with 12 (S.) Bn. 15 July 15 (Invld. to England).

TUCKER, Lieut.-Col. (temp.) A. C. (Capt. Res. of Off.), 2nd in Commd. 14 (Res.) Bn. from 17 Nov. 14 to 2 Oct. 15, Lieut.-Col. and to Commd. 1 (Gar.) Bn. York R. 2 Oct. 15. **War**

Services—S. African War 1899-1900, Act. Adj. and Qr.-Mr. Imp. Irregular Corps Depot—Martizburg.

TUCKER, Lieut. D. H. M., 4 (Extra Res.) Bn., Spec. Res. of Off. First Appt. 15 Aug. 14, Lieut. 26 June 15. **War Services**—The War of 1914-16, to Medit. Exped. Force 23 Aug. 15—Gallipoli, Attd. 11 (S.) Bn. (Suvla Bay), (Invld. to England).

TUCKER, 2nd Lieut. G. M., 4 (Extra Res.) Bn., Spec. Res. of Off. First Appt. 2 Dec. 14.

URQUHART, 2nd Lieut. (temp.) 14 (Res.) Bn. First Appt. 25 Sept. 15. **War Services**—The War of 1914-16, to France 29 Nov. 15, Attd. 12 (S.) Bn.

VAIL, 2nd Lieut. J .A., 4 (Extra Res.) Bn., Spec. Res. of Off. First Appt. 28 April 15.

VANDERSPAR, Lieut. E. R., 2 Bn. First Appt. 5 Oct. 10, Lieut. 20 Feb. 14. **War Services**—The War of 1914-16—France, sailed with the B.E.F. with 2 Bn.—Mons, Bavay, Le Cateau, Marne, Aisne, Richebourg (Wounded, to England 13 Sept. 14). Rejoined 2 Bn., France 4 June 15—Ypres. **Died of wounds received in action 24 June 15.**

VASEY, Capt. P. W., 3 (Res.) Bn. Dorset R., Spec. Res. of Off., Lieut. (Unattd. List T.F.) 26 Oct. 13, Capt. (Spec. Res.) 2 Feb. 15. **War Services**—The War of 1914-16—France, Attd. to 1 Bn. Manch. R. (Ret. to England).

VAUDREY, Capt. C. H. .S., Res. of Off., 3 (Res.) Bn. (Hon. Lieut. in Army), late Capt. 4 (Extra Res.) Bn. First Appt. as Lieut. 24 July 1900, Assist. Dist. Commd., Sierra Leone, 17 April 09 to 1914. **War Services**—S. African War 1902—Oper. in Or. Riv. Col. The War of 1914-16—France, Attd. 1 Bn. (Ret. to England).

VAUGHAN, Major E., Instruc. Duties, Ripon. First Appt. (from Mila.) 10 Sept. 90, Empld. Transvaal Vols. 7 July 02 to 30 Sept. 08, Empld. West Afr. Regt. 11 Dec. 12, Major 17 Feb. 04, Lieut.-Col. (temp.) 30 Sept. 14 to 5 Jan. 16. **War Services**—S. African War 1899-02, **Despatches (twice), Brev. of Maj.** The War of 1914-16—Cameroons (Ret. to England).

VICKERS, Hon. Capt. G. E., Quartermaster 2 Bn. First Appt. as Hon. Lieut. 5 Feb. 02, Hon. Capt. 5 Feb. 12, Qr.-Mr. 3 (Res.) Bn. from 5 Feb. 02 to 17 July 15. **War Services**—S. African War 1900-2. The War of 1914-16—France, with 2 Bn. 17 July 15—Ypres, Maricourt.

VIZARD, Bt.-Col. R. D., Res. of Off., Appt. 23 April 81, Brev.-Col. 30 Aug. 06, Apptd. Inspec. of Infantry with rank of Brig.-Genl. (temp.) 28 Oct. 14. **War Services**—Egyptian Expedition 1882. S. African War 1899-1902—Defence of Ladysmith. **Despatches, Brev. of Lieut.-Col.**

WALKER, 2nd Lieut. A. D., 4 (Extra Res.) Bn.. Spec. Res. of Off. First Appt. 6 May 15.

WALKER, Lieut. (temp.) C. D., 13 (S.) Bn. First Appt. 24 Nov. 14, Lieut. (temp.) 24 Mar. 15. **War Services**—The War of 1914-16—France, with 13 (S.) Bn. 6 Sept. 15—Salonika 6 Nov. 15.

WALKER, Major E. J. H., Attd. 3 (Res. Bn. from 1 Bn. First Appt. 29 Nov. 90, Empld. Gold Coast Const. and W. Afr. Frontier Force 6 Mar. 97 to 14 Sept. 02, Major 4 Mar. 05, Attd. 3 Bn. 22 Aug. 14. **War Services**—The War of 1914-16 —France, with Indian Contg. with 1 Bn. 26 Sept. 14 (Invld. to England 4 Jan. 15).

WALKER, 2nd Lieut. R. F., 2 Bn. First Appt. 12 Aug. 14. **War Services**—The War of 1914-16—France, with 2 Bn. 10 Sept. 14—Marne, Aisne, Lorgies. **Died of wounds received in action 21 Oct. 14.**

WALKER, 2nd Lieut. (temp.) W., 14 (Res.) Bn. First Appt. 13 May 15.

WALKLEY, Hon. Capt. D., Qr.-Mr. ret. pay (Qr.-Mr. and Hon. Capt. T.F. Res. of Off.). First Appt. 1 Mar. 1900, Hon. Capt. 1 Mar. 10, Chief Rec. Off. Manch. Rec. Area 11 Aug. 14. **War Services**—Soudan Exped. 1884-5—Nile.

WAINE, Capt. (temp.) W. H., 14 (Res.) Bn. First Appt. as Capt. (temp.) 8 Feb. 15. **War Services**—The War of 1914-16, to Medit. Exped. Force 13 May 15—Gallipoli, Attd. 6 (Terr.) Bn. Manch. R. **Killed in Action 7 Aug. 15.**

WALSH, 2nd Lieut. (temp.) A. St. G., 15 (S.) Bn. First Appt. 26 Feb. 15.

WARBURTON, 2nd Lieut. W. E., 3 (Res.) Bn., Spec. Res. of Off. (on prob.). First Appt. 4 Oct. 15.

WARE, 2nd Lieut. (temp.) E. M., 13 (S.) Bn. First Appt. 25 Feb. 15. **War Services**—The War of 1914-16—France, with 13 (S.) Bn. 6 Sept. 15—Salonika 6 Nov. 15.

WASHINGTON, 2nd Lieut. J. N. First Appt. 12 May 15., Attd. R. Flying Corps, Flying Officer 21 Aug. 15. **War Services**—The War of 1914-16—France (Missing from 25 Sept. 15).

WATSON, 2nd Lieut. B. S., 3 (Res.) Bn., Spec. Res. of Off. First Appt. 9 Jan. 15. **War Services**—The War of 1914-16—France, Attd. to 1 Bn.

WATSON, Capt. H. T., 3 (Res.) Bn. Liverpool R., Spec. Res. of Off., Capt. 1 Sept. 14. **War Services**—The War of 1914-16—France, Attd. 2 Bn. **Died of wounds received in action 6 Mar. 15.**

WATSON, 2nd Lieut. (temp.) J. A., Attd. 2/10 Bn. from 14 (Res.) Bn. First Appt. 3 May 15.

WATSON, Col. (temp. Brig.-Genl.) J. E., C.B. First Appt. 11 May 78, Col. 27 Nov. 07, Commd. No. 5 Dist. N. Comd. 24 June 11 to 1 April 15, Brig.-Genl. (temp.) 1 April 15. **War Services**—Egyptian Exped. 1882. Maranzai Exped. 1891. S. African War 1899-1902—Elandslaagte, Def. of Ladysmith, **Despatches (four times), Brev. of Lieut.-Col.**

WEBSTER, 2nd Lieut. H. A., 4 (Res.) Bn., Spec. Res. of Off. (on prob.). First Appt. 18 April 15.

WELLWOOD, 2nd Lieut. (temp.) D. N., 2/5 Bn. from 13 (S.) Bn. First Appt. 9 April 15.

WENDER, 2nd Lieut. (temp.) L., 1 (Gar.) Bn. First Appt. 8 July 15 (Ches. R.), to Manch. R. 28 Nov. 15.

WESTON, Major (temp. Lieut.-Col.) R. S., C.M.G., Comdg. 12 (Res.) Bn. East Lanc. R. First Appt. 22 Aug. 88, Major 23 Sept. 03, Lieut.-Col. (temp.) 8 Feb. 15. **War Services**—N.-W. Frontier of India 1897-8—Malakland. The War of 1914-16—France, sailed with B.E.F. with 2 Bn.—Mons, Bavay, Le Cateau, Marne, Aisne, Richebourg (Wounded, to England 13 Sept. 14). Rejoined 2 Bn. 8 Nov. 14—Wulverghem. Commd. 2 Bn. 8 Jan. 15 to 13 Nov. 15—Messines, Kemmel, Ypres, Maricourt, Suzance (Wounded slightly 30 Oct. 15, to England 5 Nov. 15). **Despatches 5 April 15, to be Comp. Order St. Michael and St. George for services in the field 3 June 15.**

WESTROPP, Brig.-Genl. (temp.) H. C. E., Staff. First Appt. (from Militia) as Lieut. 12 May 83, Adjut. Reg. Bn. 18 April 92 to 17 April 96, Adjut. (Mila. Bn.) 13 July 92 to 12 Jan. 02, Lieut.-Col. 6 Oct. 07, Commd. 12 (S.) Bn. Manch. R. from Sept. 14 to 30 Dec. 14, Brig.-Genl. (temp.) 30 Dec. 14, Commd. 111th afterwards 90th Bdge. (Manch. City Bns.) 37th Division from 30 Dec. 14 to Nov. 15. **War Services**—S. African War 1901-2, served as Adjut. 5 Bn. Lanc. Fus.—Oper. in Or. Riv. Col. **Despatches.**

WHITE, 2nd Lieut. H. E., 3 (Res.) Bn., Spec. Res. of Off. First Appt. 9 May 15. **War Services**—The War of 1914-16—France, Attd. to 1 Bn.

WHITE, Capt. (temp.) J.H. M., 12 (S.) Bn. First Appt. as Lieut. (temp.) 9 Feb 15, Capt. (temp.) 9 July 15. **War Services**—The War of 1914-16—France, with 12 (S.) Bn. 15 July 15 (Wounded, to England 26 Feb. 16).

WHITE, 2nd Lieut. W., 4 (Extra Res.) Bn., Spec. Res. of Off. First Appt. 22 May 15.

WHITE-COOPER, 2nd Lieut. (temp.) R. C., 14 (Res.) Bn. First Appt. 22 July 15.

WHITEHEAD, 2nd Lieut. E. P. First Appt. 26 Jan. 16.

WHITEHEAD, 2nd Lieut. (temp.) G., 1 (Gar.) Bn. E. Yorks. R. from 12 (S.) Bn. First Appt. 22 Dec. 14. **War Services**—The War of 1914-16—France, with 12 (S.) Bn. 15 July 15 (to England).

WHITFIELD, 2nd Lieut. L. O. G., 3 (Res.) Bn., Spec. Res. of Off. (on prob.). First Appt. 28 Dec. 15.

WHITMORE, 2nd Lieut. H. F., 3 (Res.) Bn., Spec. Res. of Off. (on prob.). First Appt. 7 Aug. 15.

WHYTE, 2nd Lieut. C .C., 3 (Res.) Bn., Spec. Res. of Off. (on prob.). First Appt. 25 Sept. 15.

WICKHAM, 2nd Lieut. (temp.) H. St. B., 14 (Res.) Bn. First Appt. 28 April 15. **War Services**—The War of 1914-16, to Medit. Exped. Force 23 Sept. 15 Attd. 11 (S.) Bn.—Gallipoli (Suvla Bay), Imbros 19 Dec. 15—Alexandria 20 Jan. 16.

WICKHAM, 2nd Lieut. W. T. D., Attd. 3 (Res.) Bn. First Appt. 16 June 15.

WICKHAM, Lieut. (local Capt.) T. S., D.S.O., 1 Bn. First

Appt. 14 Sept. 01, Empld. with R. W. Afr. Frontier Force 24 June 04 to 13 Feb. 09 and 8 Mar. 11. **War Services**—Oper. in S. Africa 1896. S. African War 1899-1902—Relief of Ladysmith, **Despatches (four times) D.S.O.** W. African (N. Nigeria) 1906. The War of 1914—Camercons. **Killed in Action 25 Aug. 14.**

WILKINS, 2nd Lieut. A. R., 3 (Res.) Bn., Spec. Res. of Off. First Appt. 17 Feb. 15. **War Services**—The War of 1914-16—France, Attd. 1 Bn. To Mesopotamia Nov. 15. **Killed in Action 11 Dec. 16.**

WILKINS, 2nd Lieut. H. T., 3 (Res.) Bn., Spec. Res. of Off. First Appt. 26 Aug. 15.

WILKINSON, 2nd Lieut. (temp.) R. W., 1 (Gar.) Bn. Notts and Derby R. from 14 (Res.) Bn. First Appt. 2 Dec. 14.

WILLIAMS, 2nd Lieut. (temp.) H. P., 14 (Res.) Bn. (on prob.). First Appt. 18 Jan. 16.

WILLIAMS-GREEN, 2nd Lieut....First Appt. 4 Dec. 15.

WILLIAMSON, Lieut. (temp.) A. H., Attd. 14 (Res.) Bn. from 12 (S.) Bn. First Appt. 17 Oct. 14, Lieut. (temp.) 29 April 15.

WILLIAMSON, Capt. G. W., Attd. R. Flying Corps from 3 (Res.) Bn., Spec. Res. of Off. First Appt. 20 Sept. 11, Capt. 2 Feb. 15. **War Services**—The War of 1914-16—France, Attd. 2 Bn. 15 Oct. 14—Lorgies, La Quinque Rue (Wounded, to England 10 Dec. 14). Rejoined 2 Bn. 8 May 15—Ypres (Invld. to England 21 May 15). **Despatches 17 Feb. 15, Awd. Military Cross 18 Feb. 15.**

WILLIAMSON, 2nd Lieut. H. A., 2 Bn. First Appt. (Spec. Res. of Off.) 3 Mar. 15, to Reg. Army 4 Oct. 15. **War Services**—The War of 1914-16—France, Attd. 2 Bn. (Wounded, to England 27 Nov. 15).

WILLIAMSON, Capt. W. H., Res. of Off., Capt. 28 July 95. **War Services**—S. African War 1901-2.

WILLIAMSON-JONES, 2nd Lieut. (temp.) C. E., 1 Bn. First Appt. 20 Mar. 15. **War Services**—The War of 1914-16—France, with 1 Bn.

WILLIS, 2nd Lieut. (temp.) M. F., Attd. R.E. (Wireless) from 14 (Res.) Bn. First Appt. 17 Oct. 14. **War Services**—To Medit. Exped. Force 9 July 15.

WILLOUGHBY, 2nd Lieut. H. L., 3 (Res.) Bn., Spec. Res. of Off. First Appt. 18 May 15. **War Services**—The War of 1914-16, to Medit. Exped. Force Jan. 16.

WILMOT, Capt. (temp.) G. A., 4 (Extra Res.) Bn., Spec. Res. of Off., R. Wan. R., Lieut. 1 Nov. 14, Capt. (temp.) 1 Jan. 15. **War Services**—The War of 1914-16—France, Attd. 2 Bn. Manch. R. 6 Dec. 14—Wulverghem (Invld. to England 30 Jan. 15).

WILSON, Lieut. A. K., 1 Bn. from Spec. Res. of Off. First Appt. 3 July 12, Lieut. 29 Sept. 14. **War Services**—The War of 1914-16—France, Attd. 1 Bn.—Neuve Chapelle. **Killed in Action 20 Mar. 15.**

WILSON, 2nd Lieut. (temp.) B., 12 (S.) Bn. First Appt. 28 Jan. 15. **War Services**—The War of 1914-16, to Medit. Exp. Force 5 Nov. 15.

WINKWORTH, 2nd Lieut. (temp.) L. S., 2/5 Bn. from 13 (S.) Bn. First Appt. 7 April 15.

WOMERSLEY, 2nd Lieut. D. N., 4 (Extra Res.) Bn., Spec. Res. of Off. First Appt. 14 May 15.

WOMERSLEY, 2nd Lieut. (temp.) F. G., 12 (S.) Bn. First Appt. 26 Jan. 15. **War Services**—The War of 1914-16, to Medit. Exped. Force 4 Nov. 15, Attd. 8 (Terr.) Bn.

WOOD, 2nd Lieut. (temp.) A. S., 14 (Res.) Bn. First Appt. 22 July 15.

WOOD, Capt. (temp.) M., 14 (Res.) Bn. First Appt. 9 Nov. 14, Lieut. (temp.) 10 Jan. 15, Capt. (temp.) 7 Oct. 15. **War Services**—The War of 1914-16, to Medit. Exped. Force 21 Sept. 15, Attd. 11 (S.) Bn.—Gallipoli (Suvla Bay), Imbros 19 Dec. 15—Alexandria 20 Jan. 16.

WOODBRIDGE, 2nd Lieut. F. H., 3 (Res.) Bn., Spec. Res. of Off. (on prob.). First Appt. 22 June 15.

WOODHOUSE, 2nd Lieut. (temp.) M. L., 14 (Res.) Bn. First Appt. 13 Mar. 15.

WOODHOUSE, Major (temp.) W. S., Draft Conducting Officer, Temp. Major 12 (S.) Bn. from 26 Sept. 14 to 8 May 15.

WORRALL, 2nd Lieut. (temp.) E. A., 14 (Res.) Bn. First Appt. 2 April 15.

WRIGGLESWORT, 2nd Lieut. A. G., 3 (Res.) Bn., Spec. Res. of Off. (on prob.). First Appt. 30 Dec. 15.

WRIGHT, Lieut.-Col. (temp.) B. A., D.S.O., Comdg. 11 (S.) Bn. Manch. R. First Appt. 28 Sept. 95, Empld. with W. Afr. Frontier Force 6 May 99 to 26 June 01, Major (Manch. R.) 24 Feb. 12, Lieut.-Col. (temp.) 19 Aug. 14. **War Services**—Oper. on N.-W. Frontier of India 1897-8. West Africa 1900—Relief of Kumassi, **Despatches, D.S.O.** The War of 1914-16, Medit. Exped. Force—Gallipoli, in Commd. 11 (S.) Bn. 7 Aug. 15 (Landing Suvla Bay), (Wounded, to England 9 Aug. 15). Rejoined 11 (S.) Bn. 19 Oct. 15—Suvla Bay, Imbros 19 Dec. 15—Alexandria 20 Jan. 16. **Despatches 11 Dec. 15.**

WRIGHT, 2nd Lieut. (temp.) F. H., 15 (S.) Bn. First Appt. 2 Mar. 15.

WRIGHT, Capt. H. T. R. S. First Appt. 2 May 03, Empld. with Egyptian Army 24 June 14, Capt. 11 Dec. 14. **War Services**—The War of 1914-15—Egypt.

WYATT, 2nd Lieut. (temp.) H. E., 14 (Res.) Bn. First Appt. 22 July 15.

WYMER, Capt. G. P., 2 Bn. First Appt. 5 May 1900, Capt. 1 April 09. **War Services**—S. African War 1899-1902, **Despatches, Medal for Dist. Conduct in the Field.** The War of 1914-16—France, sailed with B.E.F. with 2 Bn.—Mons, Bavay, Le Cateau (Wounded and Prisoner of War 26 Aug. 14.

YANDELL, 2nd Lieut. (temp.) B., 14 (Res.) Bn. First Appt. 16 Jan. 15. **War Services**—The War of 1914-16, to Medit. Exped. Force 21 Sept. 15—Gallipoli (Wounded).

YATES, 2nd Lieut. (temp.) W. G., Attd. 3 (Res.) Bn. First Appt. 20 Oct. 15.

Part II.

The Officers of the 16th, 17th, 18th, 19th, 20th, 22nd, 23rd and 24th Service and the 25th, 26th and 27th Local Reserve Battalions. Raised by the Lord Mayor of Manchester and the Mayor of Oldham.

ADAMS, 2nd Lieut. D. J. C., (Res.) Bn. 9 Dce. 15.

ADAMS, Capt. (temp.) H. T., 26 (Res.) Bn. First Appt. Mar. 00, Capt. (temp.) 18 Bn. Middx. R. 27 Sept. 14, to Manch. R. 20 Apr. 15, to Res. Bn. 7 Nov. 15.

AGNEW, Capt. (temp.) C. G., 26 (Res.) Bn. Capt. (temp.) Sept. 14, to Res. Bn.

AGNEW, 2nd Lieut. (temp.) E. K., 20 (S.) Bn. 17 Dec. 14. **War Services**—The War of 1914-1916—France, with 20 (S.) Bn. 9 Nov. 15.

AITKEN, Major (temp.) J. K., 25 (Res.) Bn. Capt. (temp.) 8 Nov. 14, Major (temp.) 1 Jan. 15, to Res. Bn. 7 Sept. 15.

ALDERTON, 2nd Lieut. (temp.) C. F., 25 (Res.) Bn. 6 Sept. 15.

ALLEN, 2nd Lieut. (temp.) F. B., 23 (S.) Bn. 14 Apr. 15. **War Services**—The War of 1914-16—France, with 23 (S.) Bn. Jan. 16.

ALLEN, 2nd Lieut. (temp.) K. H., 26 (Res.) Bn. First Appt. 6 Aug. 15, to Res. Bn. 7 Nov. 15.

ALLEN, Major (temp.) R. J., 26 (Res.) Bn. First Appt. (Vols.) Mar. 00, Major Reg. Army (temp.) 22 Sept. 14, to Res. Bn. 18 Aug. 15.

ALLEN, 2nd Lieut. (temp.) S. R., 16 (S.) Bn. 20 Mar. 15. **War Services**—The War of 1914-16—France, with 16 (S.) Bn. Nov. 15.

ALLFREY, Major C. M., 2nd in Commd. 22 (S.) Bn., Major 3 Bn. (Spec. Res. of Off.) R. W. Kent R. 26 Sept. 14, to Manch. R. Nov. 15. **War Services**—S. African War 1902. The War of 1914-16—France, with 22 (S.) Bn. Nov. 15.

ANDREW, Lieut. (temp.) H., 24 (S.) Bn. First Appt. 22 Dec. 14. Lieut (temp.) 2 June 15 **War Services**—The War of 1914-16—France, with 24 (S.) Bn. Nov. 15.

ARNOLD, Bt.-Col. A. J., D.S.O., Commandg. 20 (S.) Bn. from 8 Nov. 14 to 20 July 15. First Appt. 23 Aug. 93, Brev.-Col. 8 July 05. **War Services**—W. Africa 1895-6, Oper. on the Niger 1897—**Despatches, Prom. Capt., D.S.O.** W. Africa 1897-8—**Despatches, Prom. Major, Brev. of Lt.-Col.**

ASHTON, 2nd Lieut. (temp.) J., 27 (Res.) Bn. First Appt. 22 Feb. 15, to Res. Bn. 19 Oct. 15.

ASHWORTH, Capt. (temp.) J. H., 27 (Res.) Bn. Lieut. (temp.) 3 Dec. 14, Capt. (temp.) 18 Mar. 15, to Res. Bn. 8 Nov. 15.

ATKINSON, 2nd Lieut. (temp.) A. W., 26 (Res.) Bn. First Appt. 1 Mar. 15, to Res. Bn. 7 Nov. 15.

BAGSHAW, Lieut. (temp.) H. S., 20 (S.) Bn. 3 Mar. 15, Lieut. (temp.) 5 Mar. 15. **War Services**—The War of 1914-1916—France, with 20 (S.) Bn. 9 Nov. 15.

BAGSHAW, Capt. (temp.) W. B., 20 (S.) Bn. First Appt. 3 Mar. 15, Lieut. (temp.) 5 June 15, Capt. (temp.) 20 Oct. 15. **War Services**—The War of 1914-1916—France, with 20 (S.) Bn. 9 Nov. 15.

BALL, Hon. Lieut. (temp.) J. T., Quartermaster 16 (S) Bn. 11 Mar. 15. **War Services**—The War of 1914-16—France, with 16 (S.) Bn. Nov. 15.

BALLAN, 2nd Lieut. (temp.) L., 27 (Res.) Bn. First Appt. 18 Oct. 15, to Res. Bn. 19 Oct. 15.

BANNANTYNE, Major (temp.) J. F. (Capt. 11th Hussars), 2nd in Commd. 23 (S.) Bn., Capt. 14 Nov. 14, Major (temp.) and to Manch. R. 9 Nov. 15. **War Services**—The War of 1914-16—France, with 23 (S.) Bn. Jan. 16.

BARBER, 2nd Lieut. (temp.) G. A., 16 (S.) Bn. 30 Apr. 15. **War Services**—The War of 1914-16—France, with 16 (S.) Bn. Nov. 15.

BARKWORTH, Major H. A. S. (Staff College), (Maj. Ret. Pay). 18 (S.) Bn. 23 Oct. 14. First Appt. 30 Nov. 76, Major 7 July 97, Ret. 15 Mar. 02 (Resigned Com. on account of ill-health). To be Staff Capt. 19 Jany. 16.

BARDSLEY, 2nd Lieut. (temp.) H. C., 26 (Res.) Bn. First Appt. 23 June 15, to Res. Bn. 7 Sept. 15.

BARNARD, 2nd Lieut. (temp.) L. H., 27 (Res.) Bn. First Appt. 3 Apr. 15, to a Res. Bn. 20 Nov. 15. **War Services**—The War of 1914-16—France, attchd. 23 (S.) Bn. 26 Jany. 16.

BARTON, 2nd Lieut. (temp.) J. E. B., 26 (Res.) Bn. First Appt. 10 Nov. 15.

BATE, Capt. (temp.) F. J. First Appt. 31 Mar. 15, Capt. (temp.) 20 Apr. 15. To Genl. List for Emp. as Bgde. Machine-Gun Officer, 25 Aug. 15.

BATEMAN, Lieut. (temp.) R. W., 24 (S.) Bn. First Appt. 10 Dec. 14, Lieut. (temp.) 2 Aug. 15. **War Services**—The War of 1914-16—France, with 24 (S.) Bn. Nov. 15.

BATTEN, Lieut.-Col. (temp.) J. B., Comdg. 24 (S.) Bn. (Capt. R. Fus. Special Reserve of Off.) First Appt. 4 May 01. Lieut.-Col. (temp.) and to Manch. R. 13 Oct. 15. **War Services**—The War of 1914-16—France, with 24 (S.) Bn. Nov. 15.

BAYLISS, 2nd Lieut. (temp.) B. B., 27 (Res.) Bn. First Appt. 11 Dec. 15.

BEARD, 2nd Lieut. (temp.) O. G., 27 (Res.) Bn. First Appt. 27 Mar. 15 (11 Bn. W. Riding R.) To Manch. R. 5 Apr. 15.

BEAUMONT, Lieut. (temp.) J. S., 18 (S.) Bn. First Appt. 24 Dec. 14, Lieut. (temp.) 12 May 15. **War Services**—The War of 1914-16—France, with 18 (S.) Bn. Nov. 15.

BEHRENS, Lieut. (temp.) F. E., 16 (S.) Bn. First Appt. 8

Oct. 14, Lieut. (temp.) 8 Dec. 14. **War Services**—The War of 1914-16—France, with 16 (S.) Bn. Nov. 15 (wounded 9 Dec. 15).

BENOIST, 2nd Lieut. (temp.) L. M., 23 (S.) Bn. 27 Aug. 15. **War Services**—The War of 1914-16—France, with 23 (S.) Bn. Nov. 15.

BENTLEY, 2nd Lieut. (temp.) H., 21 (S.) Bn. 3 Apr. 15. **War Services**—The War of 1914-16—France, with 21 (S.) Bn. 7 Nov. 15.

BERRY, Capt. (temp.) D., 18 (S.) Bn. First Appt. 22 Sept 14, Capt. (temp.) 30 Dec. 14. **War Services**—The War of 1914-16 —France, with 18 (S.) Bn. Nov. 15.

BEST, Capt. (temp.) A., 24 (S.) Bn. First Appt. Capt. (temp.) 1 Dec. 14. **War Services**—The War of 1914-16 —France, with 24 (S.) Bn. Nov. 15.

BETTELEY, Capt. (temp.) C. E. R., 27 (Res.) Bn. First Appt. 1 April 15, Capt. (temp.) 20 April 15, to Res. Bn. 25 Sept. 15.

BINNING, 2nd Lieut. (temp.) K. R., R.F.C. from 20 (S.) Bn. First Appt. 19 Dec. 14. To R.F.C. 18 Nov. 15.

BIRLEY, Capt. (temp.) H. K., 19 (S.) Bn., Capt. (temp.) 21 Sept 14. **War Services**—The War of 1914-16—France, with 19 (S.) Bn. 7 Nov. 15.

BLACKFORD, Hon. Lieut. (temp.) C. W., Quartermaster 25 (Res.) Bn. 12 Aug. 15.

BLAND, Capt. (temp.) A. E., 22 (S.) Bn. First Appt. as Lieut. (temp.) 1 Feb. 15, Capt. (temp.) 26 Apr. 15. **War Services**—The War of 1914-16—France, with 22 (S.) Bn. Nov. 15.

BLENKIRON, 2nd Lieut. (temp.) D., 18 (S.) Bn. 25 Jan. 15. **War Services**—The War of 1914-16—France, with 18 (S.) Bn. Nov. 15. Missing from 30 Jany. 16. Prisoner of War.

BLENCH, 2nd Lieut. (temp.) A. C., 20 (S.) Bn. First Appt. 3 Apr. 15. **War Services**—The War of 1914-16—France, with 20 (S.) Bn. 9 Nov. 15.

BLES, 2nd Lieut. (temp.) G. M., 25 (Res.) Bn. First Appt. 16 Mar. 15, to Res. Bn. 7 Sept. 15.

BLYTHE, 2nd Lieut. (temp.) N. H., 25 (Res.)Bn. First Appt. 3 Aug. 15, to Res. Bn.

BLYTHE, Lieut. (temp.) P. A., 18 (S.) Bn. First Appt. 21 Sept. 14, Lieut. (temp.) 2 Feb. 15. **War Services**—The War of 1914-16—France, with 18 (S.) Bn. Nov. 15.

BOLTON, 2nd Lieut. (temp.) T. T., 25 (Res.) Bn. First Appt. 21 July 15, to Res. Bn. 7 Sept 15.

BOWER, Lieut. (temp.) H. G. S., 18 (S.) Bn. First Appt. as Lieut. (temp.) 9 Feb. 15. **War Services**—The War of 1914-16—France, with 18 (S.) Bn. Nov. 15.

BOWLES, 2nd Lieut. (temp.) K. A., Attd. Machine Gun Corps from 25 (Res.) Bn. First Appt. 26 Feb. 15, to Res. Bn. 7 Sept. 15.

BOWLY, Lieut. (temp.) R. W., 22 (S.) Bn. First Appt. 1 Apr. 15, Lieut. (temp.) 1 Aug. 15. **War Services**—The War of 1914-16—France, with 22 (S.) Bn. 7 Nov. 15.

BOXALL, 2nd Lieut. (temp.) F. S., 19 (S.) Bn. 19 Jan. 15. **War**

Services—The War of 1914-16—France, with 19 (S.) Bn. 7 Nov. 15.

BRAINE, 2nd Lieut. (temp.) H. E., 24 (S.) Bn. 18 Oct. 15. **War Services**—The War of 1914-16—France, with 24 (S.) Bn. Nov. 15.

BRETT, 2nd Lieut. (temp.) F. J., 25 (Res.) Bn. First Appt. 30 Aug. 15, to Res. Bn. 7 Oct. 15.

BROOKS, 2nd Lieut. (temp.) F. S., 20 (S.) Bn. 4 Dec. 14. **War Services**—The War of 1914-16—France, with 20 (S.) Bn. 9 Nov. 15.

BROOKS, Capt. (temp.) H. J., Adjt. 21 (S.) Bn. 7 Jan. 15. First Appt. as Lieut. (temp.) 7 Jan. 15, Capt. (temp.) 18 May 15. **War Services**—The War of 1914-16—France, with 21 (S.) Bn. 7 Nov. 15.

BROWN, 2nd Lieut. (temp.) A. H. M., 27 (Res.) Bn. First Appt. 18 Oct. 15, to Res. Bn. 9 Nov. 15.

BROWN, 2nd Lieut. (temp.) M. W., 17 (S.) Bn. 12 May 15. **War Services**—The War of 1914-16—France, with 17 (S.) Bn. Nov. 15.

BROWNE, 2nd Lieut. (temp.) I. W. H., 16 (S.) Bn. 16 Feb. 15. Rel. Commission on account of ill-health 9 Oct. 15.

BRUNTON, 2nd Lieut. (temp.) M., 18 (S.) Bn. 29 Apr. 15. **War Services**—The War of 1914-16—France, with 18 (S.) Bn. Nov. 15.

BRYANT, Capt. (temp.) F., Adjt. 20 (S.) Bn. First Appt. 24 Nov. 14, Adjt. 9 Feb. 15, Capt. (temp) 5 Mar. 15. **War Services**—The War of 1914-16—France, with 20 (S.) Bn. 9 Nov. 15.

BURCHILL, Lieut. (temp.) V., 22 (S.) Bn. First Appt. 1 Feb. 15, Lieut. (temp.) 15 Apr. 15. **War Services**—The War of 1914-16—France, with 22 (S.) Bn. Nov. 15.

CAIN, Hon. Lieut. (temp.) A. A., Quartermaster 20 (S.) Bn. 18 Nov. 14. **War Services**—The War of 1914-16—France, with 20 (S.) Bn. 9 Nov. 15.

CALDWELL, Lieut. (temp.) J. A., 19 (S.) Bn. First Appt. 8 Dec. 14, Lieut. (temp.) 1 Nov. 15. **War Services**—The War of 1914-16—France, with 19 (S.) Bn. 9 Nov. 15.

CALVERT, 2nd Lieut. (temp.) R. M., 25 (Res.) Bn. First Appt. 8 Apr. 15, to Res. Bn. 7 Sept. 15.

CAMERON, Lieut. (temp.) A. G., 17 (S.) Bn. First Appt. 23 Feb. 15, Lieut. (temp.) 8 Dec. 15. **War Services**—The War of 1914-16—France, with 17 (S.) Bn. Nov. 15 (wounded, to England 11 Feb. 16).

CANSINO, 2nd Lieut. (temp.) J., 26 (Res.) Bn. First Appt. 1 Dec. 15.

CAPSTICK, Capt. (temp.) A. E., 23 (S.) Bn. First Appt. 19 Jan. 15, Lieut. (temp.) 20 July 15, Capt. (temp.) 4 Nov. 15. **War Services**—The War of 1914-16—France, with 23 (S.) Bn. Jan. 16.

CARSTAIRS, Lieut. (temp.) N. M., 21 (S.) Bn. First Appt. as Lieut. (temp.) 12 Feb. 15. **War Services**—The War of 1914-16—France, with 21 (S.) Bn. 7 Nov. 15.

CARTMAN, 2nd Lieut. (temp.) T., 27 (Res.) Bn. (on prob.) 15 Jan. 16.

CASSALL, 2nd Lieut. (temp.) C. V., 26 (Res.) Bn. First Appt. 5 Sept. 15, to Res. Bn. 7 Nov. 15.

CASSWELL, Major (temp.) F. (Capt. Ret. pay), 17 (S.) Bn., from 23 Oct. 14 to 10 Sept. 15.

CAULCOTT, 2nd Lieut. (temp.) J. E., 26 (Res.) Bn. First Appt. 3 Apr. 15, to Res. Bn. 7 Sept. 15.

CHADWICK, 2nd Lieut. (temp.) L. A., 19 (S.) Bn. 2 Nov. 14. **War Services**—The War of 1914-16—France, with 19 (S.) Bn. 9 Nov. 15.

CHADWICK, Capt. (temp.) J. H., 24 (S.) Bn. First Appt. 3 Apr. 15, Capt. (temp.) 1 June 15. **War Services**—The War of 1914-16—France, with 24 (S.) Bn. Nov. 15.

CHAPMAN, Capt. (temp.) J., 21 (S.) Bn., Lieut. 12 Feb. 15, Capt. (temp.) 3 Apr. 15. **War Services**—The War of 1914-16—France, with 21 (S.) Bn. 9 Nov. 15.

CHAPMAN, 2nd Lieut. (temp.) R. C., 27 (Res.) Bn. 6 July 15, to a Res. Bn. 19 Oct. 15.

CHILTON, 2nd Lieut. (temp.) E. S., 25 (Res.) Bn. First Appt. 23 June 15. to Res. Bn. 7 Sept. 15.

CLARKE, Lieut. (temp.) W. F., 16 (S.) Bn. First Appt. 15 Feb. 15, Lieut. (temp.) 13 May 15. **War Services**—The War of 1914-16—France, with 16 (S.) Bn. Nov. 15.

CLARKE, Capt. (temp.) W. M., 19 (S.) Bn. First Appt. 7 Oct. 14, Lieut. (temp.) 20 Jan. 15, Capt. (temp.) 26 May 15. **War Services**—The War of 1914-16—France, with 19 (S.) Bn. 9 Nov. 15.

CLAYTON, 2nd Lieut. (temp.) E. G., 25 (Res.) Bn. First Appt. 27 Mar. 15, to Res. Bn. 7 Sept. 15.

CLAYTON, 2nd Lieut. (temp.) J. L., 26 (Res.) Bn. First Appt. 3 April 15, to Res. Bn. 7 Sept. 15.

CLEGG, 2nd Lieut. (temp.) T. H., 26 (Res.) Bn. First Appt. 7 April 15, to Res. Bn.

CLESHAM, 2nd Lieut. (temp.) T. H., 25 (Res.) Bn. First Appt. 20 July 15, to Res. Bn. 7 Sept. 15.

CLOUGH, Major (temp.) F. N., 27 (Res.) Bn. First Appt. as Major 7 Sept. 14, to Res. Bn. 7 Sept. 15.

COATMAN, 2nd Lieut. (temp.) G., 26 Res. Bn. First Appt. 3 April 15. to Res. Bn.

COE, Lieut. (temp.) W. O., 27 (Res.) Bn. First Appt. as Lieut. (temp.) 1 Feb. 15, to Res. Bn. 7 Sept. 15.

COMYN, Major (temp.) C. D. E. (Lieut. Res. of Off.), 16 (S.) Bn. from 10 Dec. 14 to 24 Nov. 15. **War Services**—S. African War 1899-1901—Oper. in Transvaal and Or. Riv. Col.

COOKE, 2nd Lieut. (temp.) F. J., 27 (Res.) Bn. First Appt. 18 Oct. 15, to Res. Bn. 19 Oct. 15.

COOKE, 2nd Lieut. (temp.) H. R., 25 (Res.) Bn. 18 June 15, to Res. Bn. 7 Sept. 15.

COOPER, Capt. (temp.) A. W., 23 (S.) Bn. First Appt. as Lieut. 3 Dec. 14, Capt. (temp.) 1 May 15. **War Services**—The War of 1914-16—France, with 23 (S.) Bn. Jan. 16.

COOPER, Lieut. (temp.) W. C., 20 (S.) Bn. First Appt. 7 April 15, Lieut. (temp.) 5 June 15. **War Services**—The War of 1914-16—France, with 20 (S.) Bn. 7 Nov. 15.

COTTON, 2nd Lieut. (temp.) H. S., 22 (S.) Bn. 8 Jan. 15. **War Services**—The War of 1914-16—France, with 22 (S.) Bn. Nov. 15.

COTTON, Lieut. (temp.) C., 22 (S.) Bn. from 15 July 15 to 19 Nov. 15.

COTTRELL, 2nd Lieut. (temp.) J. F., 17 (S.) Bn. 3 July 15. **War Services**—The War of 1914-16—France, with 17 (S.) Bn. Nov. 15.

COWAN, Capt. (temp.) W. J., 22 (S.) Bn. First Appt. 12 Mar. 15, Capt. (temp.) 14 May 15. **War Services**—The War of 1914-16—France, with 22 (S.) Bn. Nov. 15.

CRAIG, 2nd Lieut. (temp.) J., 26 (Res.)Bn. First Appt. 3 April 15, to Res. Bn. 22 Oct. 15.

CRANSHAW, Lieut. (temp.) H. H., 18 (S.) Bn. First Appt. 6 Oct. 14, Lieut. (temp.) 26 Mar. 15. **War Services**—The War of 1914-16—France, with 18 (S.) Bn. Nov. 15.

CRASTON, 2nd Lieut. (temp.) N. H., 19 (S.) Bn. First Appt. 22 Mar. 15. **War Services**—The War of 1914-16—France, with 19 (S.) Bn. 9 Nov. 15.

CREWDSON, Lieut. (temp.) T. W., 20 (S.) Bn. First Appt. as Lieut. (temp.) 5 Mar. 15. **War Services**—The War of 1914-16 —France, with 20 (S.) Bn. 9 Nov. 15.

CRINION, 2nd Lieut. (temp.) F., 24 (S.) Bn. 10 Dec. 14. **War Services**—The War of 1914-16—France, with 24 (S.) Bn. Nov. 15.

CRUICKSHANK, 2nd Lieut. (temp.) G. G. L., 26 (Res.) Bn. First Appoint. 16 Jan. 15, to res. Bn.

CUNLIFFE, Capt. (temp.) H. H., 25 (Res.) Bn. First Appt. from Cadet Bn. Manch. R. 12 Sept. 14, to Res. Bn. 12 Aug. 15.

CUNLIFFE, Lieut. (temp.) J. G., 18 (S.) Bn. First Appt. 22 Sept. 14, Lieut. (temp.) 2 Feb. 15. **War Services**—The War of 1914-16—France, with 18 (S.) Bn. Nov. 15.

CUNLIFFE, Lieut. (temp.) J. L., 21 (S.) Bn. First Appt. as Lieut. (temp.) 12 Feb. 15. **War Services**—The War of 1914-16—France, with 21 (S.) Bn. 9 Nov. 15.

CUNLIFFE, Hon. Lieut. (temp.) L., Quartermaster 23 (S.) Bn. 17 Aug. 15. **War Services**—The War of 1914-16—France, with 23 (S.) Bn. Jan. 16.

CUNLIFFE, Capt. (temp.) W. S., 19 (S.) Bn., Capt. (temp.) 21 Sept. 14. **War Services**—The War of 1914-16—France, with 19 (S.) Bn. 9 Nov. 15.

CUSHION, Lieut. (temp.) W. B., 22 (S.) Bn. 3 Feb. 15. **War Services**—The War of 1914-16—France, with 22 (S.) Bn. Nov. 15.

DAGLEISH, Lieut. (temp.) A. B., 16 (S.) Bn. First Appt. 12 Sept. 14, Lieut. (temp.) 8 Dec. 14. **War Services**—The War of 1914-16—France, with 16 (S.) Bn. Nov. 15.

DAVIDSON, 2nd Lieut. (temp.) R. W., 26 (Res.) Bn. First Appt. 10 Nov. 15.

DAVIDSON, Lieut. (temp.) W. S., 16 (S.) Bn. First Appt. 3 Oct. 14, Lieut. (temp.) 8 Dec. 14. **War Services**—The War of 1914-16—France, with 16 (S.) Bn. Nov. 15.

DAWSON, 2nd Lieut. (temp.) W. H. H., 25 (Res.) Bn. First Appt. 22 Sept. 14, to a Res. Bn.

DAY, 2nd Lieut. (temp.) C. E., 25 (Res.) Bn. First Appt. 6 Apr. 15, to Res. Bn. 7 Sept. 15

DEAN-WILLCOCKS, Capt. (temp.) A. H., 20 (S.) Bn. from 29 Nov. 14 to 15 July 15.

DEMPSEY, Lieut. (temp.) G. B., Adjt. 24 (S.) Bn. First Appt. 8 Jan. 15, Lieut. (temp.) 1 June 15. **War Services**—The War of 1914-16—France, with 24 (S.) Bn. Nov. 15.

DENISON, 2nd Lieut. (temp.) G., 26 (Res.) Bn. First Appt. 3 Apr. 15, to Res. Bn. 7 Sept. 15.

DENTON-THOMPSON, Lieut. (temp.) B. J., 26 (Res.) Bn. First Appt. 4 Nov. 14, Lieut. (temp.) 5 Mar. 15, to Res. Bn.

DIXEY, 2nd Lieut. (temp.) A. G. N., 20 (S.) Bn. 5 Dec. 14. **War Services**—The War of 1914-16—France, with 20 (S.) Bn. 9, Nov. 15.

DIXON, Capt. (temp.) T. H., 23 (S.) Bn. First Appt. 3 Dec. 14, Lieut. (temp.) 1 May 15, Capt. (temp.) 4 Oct. 15. **War Services**—The War of 1914-16—France, with 23 (S.) Bn. Jan. 16.

DOWLING, 2nd Lieut. (temp.) A. V., 27 (Res.) Bn. 3 Apr. 15, to Res. Bn.

DOWLING, 2nd Lieut. (temp.) B. B., 25 (Res.) Bn. First Appt. 11 Jan. 15, to Res. Bn.

DONAND, 2nd Lieut. (temp.) E. L., 23 (S.) Bn. 7 June 15. **War Services**—The War of 1914-16—France, with 23 (S.) Bn. Jan. 16.

DRAKE, 2nd Lieut. (temp.) H., 27 (Res.) Bn. (on prob.) 15 Jan. 16.

DUNKERLEY, 2nd Lieut. (temp.) L. R. B., 24 (S.) Bn. 10 Dec. 14. **War Services**—The War of 1914-16—France, with 24 (S.) Bn. Nov. 15.

DURANDEAU, 2nd Lieut. (temp.) R. F., 27 (Res.) Bn. 31 Mar. 15, to Res. Bn. 9 Nov. 15, to Serv. Bn. 19 Nov. 15.

DYER, 2nd Lieut. (temp.) H. de D., 25 (Res.) Bn. First Appt. 5 Jan. 15, to Res. Bn. 18 Dec. 15.

EARLES, Capt. (temp.) F. J., 27 (Res.) Bn. First Appt. 10 Dec. 14, Capt. (temp.) 6 Feb. 15, to Res. Bn.

EATON, 2nd Lieut. (temp.) J. W., 26 (Res.) Bn. First Appt. 30 Nov. 14, to Res. Bn.

ELLERY, 2nd Lieut. (temp.) A. J., 23 (S.) Bn. 12 Aug. 15. **War Services**—The War of 1914-16—France, with 23 (S.) Bn. Jan. 16.

ELSTOB, Capt. (temp.) W., 16 (S.) Bn. First Appt. 3 Oct. 14, Capt. (temp.) 3 Mar. 15. **War Services**—The War of 1914-16—France, with 16 (S.) Bn. Nov. 15.

ELWELL, 2nd Lieut. (temp.) E. E., 17 (S.) Bn. 1 Mar. 15.

War Services—The War of 1914-16—France, with 17 (S.) Bn. Nov. 15.

ENGLAND, Lieut. (temp.) R. S., 18 (S.) Bn. First Appt. 25 Oct. 14, Lieut. (temp.) 12 May 15. **War Services**—The War of 1914-16—France, with 18 (S.) Bn. Nov. 15.

ESSE, 2nd Lieut. (temp.) F. A., 25 (Res.) Bn. First Appt. 18 Aug. 15, to Res. Bn.

ETCHELLS, Capt. (temp.) T., 27 (Res.) Bn. First Appt. 17 (S.) Bn. Manch. R. 6 Oct. 14, Lieut. (temp.) 18 Oct. 14, Capt. (temp.) 29 April 15, to Res. Bn. 7 Sept. 15, to 26 (Bankers) Bn. R. Fusiliers.

ETHERIDGE, Lieut.-Col. C. de C., D.S.O., Comdg. 22 (S.) Bn. Manch. R. from 21 Nov. 14 to 8 July 15. First Appt. 11 May 78, Res. of Off. from R. War R. 28 Dec. 98. **War Services**—Afghan War 1878-9-80—Kurram Valley. Nile Expedition 1898—Khartoum. S. African War 1900-2, Remount Offr. **Despatches—Promd. Lieut.-Col. D.S.O.**

EVANS, 2nd Lieut. (temp.) W., 27 (Res.) Bn. First Appt. 14 Oct. 15, to Res. Bn. 18 Nov. 15.

FAIRHAM, 2nd Lieut. (temp.) F. B., 27 (Res.) Bn. 26 Dec. 15.

FARNSWORTH, 2nd Lieut. (temp.) W. C., 26 (Res.) Bn. First Appt. 23 Sept. 15, t oRes. Bn. 28 Oct. 15.

FAULKNER, 2nd Lieut. (temp.) H. L., 27 (Res.) Bn. 3 April 15, to Res. Bn.

FEARENSIDE, Capt. (temp.) E., 17 (S.) Bn. First Appt. 19 Sept. 14, Capt. (temp.) 19 Dec. 14. **War Services**—The War of 1914-16—France, with 17 (S.) Bn. Nov. 15.

FITZGERALD, 2nd Lieut. (temp.) L. D., 23 (S.) Bn. 28 Mar. 15. **War Services**—The War of 1914-16—France, with 23 (S.) Bn. Jan. 16.

FITZ-PATRICK, Capt. (temp.) J., 21 (S.) Bn. First Appt. as Capt. (temp.) 12 Feb. 15. **War Services**—The War of 1914-16—France, with 21 (S.) Bn. 9 Nov. 15.

FORD, Capt. (temp.) R. J., 17 (S.) Bn. (Temp. Capt. Unatt. List T.F.). First Appt. 20 Nov. 14, Capt. (temp.) 1 Jan. 15, to Manch. R. 6 Nov. 15. **War Services**—The War of 1914-16—France, with 17 (S.) Bn. Nov. 15

FOSTER, Lieut. (temp.) B. La T., 19 (S.) Bn. First Appt. 16 Oct. 14, Lieut. (temp.) 5 July 15. **War Services**—The War of 1914-16—France, with 19 (S.) Bn. 9 Nov. 15.

FOSTER, Lieut. (temp.) P. La T., 19 (S.) Bn. First Appt. 16 Oct. 14, Lieut. (temp.) 3 July 15, Machine Gun Officer. **War Services**—The War of 1914-16—France, with 19 (S.) Bn. 9 Nov. 15.

FOULDS, 2nd Lieut. (temp) W. A., 27 (Res.) Bn. First Appt. 22 June 15, to Res. Bn. 26 Oct. 15.

FOULKES, Capt. (temp.) J. S., 23 (S.) Bn. First Appt. 1 Feb. 15. Lieut. (temp.) 20 May 15, Capt. (temp.) 3 Oct. 15. **War Services**—The War of 1914-16—France, with 23 (S.) Bn Jan. 16.

FRASER, Capt. (temp.) C. J. R., 25 (Res.) Bn. First Appt. as Capt. (temp.) 24 Sept. 14, to Res. Bn. 5 Oct. 15.

FRASER, Lieut.-Col. (temp.) W. A., Comdg. 18 (S.) Bn. Manch. R. (Hon. Lieut.-Col. 3 Bn. Durh. L.I.), to Mila. from Indian S.C. as Capt. 31 Jan. 00, Lieut.-Col. (temp.) 14 Sept. 14. **War Services**—N.-W. Frontier of India 1897-8—Malakand. Tirah 1897-8, S. African War 1902. The War of 1914-16—France, with 18 (S.) Bn. Nov. 15.

FYFE, Capt. (temp.) C., 23 (S.) Bn. from 3 Dec. 14 to 28 Oct. 15.

GALLOWAY, Capt. (temp.) J., 26 (Res.) Bn. First Appt. as Capt. (temp.) 5 Mar. 15, to Res. Bn.

GARNER, Lieut. (temp) F. St. J. W., 23 (S.) Bn. First Appt. as Lieut. (temp.) 13 Feb. 15. **War Services**—The War of 1914-16—France, with 23 (S.) Bn. Jan. 16.

GEARY, Capt. (temp.) Sir W. N. M., Bart., 25 (Res.) Bn. First Appoint. as Capt. (temp.) 18 Jan. 15, to Res. Bn. 7 Sept. 15.

GEMMELL, Capt. (temp.) J. S., 20 (S.) Bn. First Appt. as Lieut. (temp.) 14 Jan. 15, Capt. (temp.) 1 Oct. 15. **War Services**—The War of 1914-16—France, with 20 (S.) Bn. 9 Nov. 15.

GIBBON, Lieut. (temp.) R., 16 (S.) Bn. First Appt. 14 Mar. 15, Lieut. (temp.) 13 May 15. **War Services**—The War of 1914-16—France, with 16 (S.) Bn. Nov. 15.

GIBBONS, Capt. (temp.) W. P., 23 (S.) Bn. First Appt. 21 Jan. 15, Lieut. (temp.) 1 May 15, Capt. (temp.) 21 Nov. 15. **War Services**—The War of 1914-16—France, with 23 (S.) Bn. Jan. 16.

GIFFARD, 2nd Lieut. (temp.) G. G., 20 (S.) Bn. 7 Apr. 15. **War Services**—The War of 1914-16—France, with 20 (S.) Bn. 9 Nov. 15.

GIFFARD, 2nd Lieut. (temp.) J. S., 20 (S.) Bn. 17 Mar. 15. **War Services**—The War of 1914-16—France, with 20 (S.) Bn. 9 Nov. 15.

GILCHRIST, 2nd Lieut. (temp.) G. K., 27 (Res.) Bn. First Appt. Rec. Staff Manch. Rec. Area, 1 Sept. 14, to Manch. R. 18 Nov. 15.

GILLET, 2nd Lieut. (temp.) J. C., 27 (Res.) Bn. First Appt. 8 Feb. 15, to Res. Bn.

GILMORE, Lieut. (temp.) E. F. G., 21 (S.) Bn. First Appt. as Lieut. (temp.) 12 Feb. 15, Signalling Officer. **War Services**—The War of 1914-16—France, with 21 (S.) Bn. 9 Nov. 15.

GOAD, 2nd Lieut. (temp.) F. L., 23 (S.) Bn. 3 July 15. **War Services**—The War of 1914-16—France, with 23 (S.) Bn. Jan. 16.

GODLEE, Capt. (temp.) P., 18 (S.) Bn. First Appt. 3 Oct. 14, Capt. (temp.) 30 Dec. 14. **War Services**—The War of 1914-16—France, with 18 (S.) Bn. Nov. 15.

GOLDSCHMIDT, Major (temp.) S. G. T. D. (Major and Hon. Lieut.-Col. Ret. T.F.), 20 (S.) Bn. from 19 Nov. 14 to 28 Sept. 15.

GOMERSALL, Lieut. (temp.) W. E., 22 (S.) Bn. First Appt. 22 Dec. 15, Lieut. (temp.) 11 May 15. **War Services**—The War of 1914-16—France, with 22 (S.) Bn. Nov. 15.

GOSLING, Capt. (temp.) F. W., 23 (S.) Bn. First Appt. 21

Jan. 15, Lieut. (temp.) 1 April 15, Capt. (temp.) 20 Nov. 15. **War Services**—The War of 1914-16—France, with 23 (S.) Bn. Jan. 16.

GREEN, 2nd Lieut. (temp.) C. N., 25 (Res.) Bn First Appt. 13 July 15, to Res. Bn. 7 Sept. 15.

GREG, Lieut. (temp.) A. H., R.A.M.C. from 17 (S.) Bn. First Appt. 11 Dec. 14, to R.A.M.C. 4 Jan. 15.

GREG, Capt. (temp.) H. S., 16 (S.) Bn. First Appt. as Capt. (temp.) 31 Aug. 14. **War Services**—The War of 1914-16—France, with 16 (S.) Bn. Nov. 15.

GRIGG, 2nd Lieut. (temp.) M. H., 26 (Res.) Bn. First Appt. 12 Aug. 15, to Res. Bn. 7 Sept. 15.

GRIMSHAW, Major (temp.) C., 23 (S.) Bn. First Appt. as Capt. (temp.) 3 Feb. 15, Major (temp.) 7 Dec. 15. **War Services**—The War of 1914-16—France, with 23 (S.) Bn. Jan. 16.

GRIMWOOD, 2nd Lieut. (temp.) H., 22 (S.) Bn. 1 April 15. **War Services**—The War of 1914-16—France, with 22 (S.) Bn. Nov. 15.

GUILLET, Lieut. (temp.) J. C., 23 (S.) Bn. First Appt. 13 April 15, Lieut. (temp.) 1 May 15. **War Services**—The War of 1914-16—France, with 23 (S.) Bn. Jan. 16.

HALDANE, 2nd Lieut. (temp.) C. K., 26 (Res.) Bn. First Appt. 19 Feb. 15, to Res. Bn. 22 Oct. 15.

HALL, Hon. Lieut. (temp.) T. B., Quartermaster 26 (Res.) Bn. 20 July 15. First Appt. as 2nd Lieut. (temp.) 15 Mar. 15.

HAMER, 2nd Lieut. (temp.) R. B., 23 (S.) Bn. 13 April 15. First Appt. 21 Dec. 14, 22 (S.) Bn. **War Services**—The War of 1914-16—France, with 23 (S.) Bn. Jan. 16.

HARFORD, Capt. (temp.) J. F., 20 (S.) Bn. First Appt. as Lieut. (temp.) 30 Sept. 14, Capt. (temp.) 5 Mar. 15. **War Services**—The War of 1914-16—France, with 20 (S.) Bn. 9 Nov. 15.

HARREY, Capt. (temp.) A., Adjutant 25 (Res.) Bn. First Appt. as Capt. (temp.) 7 Jan. 15, to Res. Bn. 7 Sept. 15, to be Adjutant 13 Oct. 15.

HARRIS, Lieut. (temp.) A., 21 (S.) Bn. First Appt. 23 Dec. 14, Lieut. (temp.) 3 April 15. **War Services**—The War of 1914-16—France, with 21 (S.) Bn. 9 Nov. 15.

HARRIS, 2nd Lieut. (temp.) A. A. F., 18 (S.) Bn. 25 Jan. 15. **War Services**—The War of 1914-16—France, with 18 (S.) Bn. Nov. 15.

HARRIS, 2nd Lieut. (temp.) G. S., 21 (S.) Bn. 16 Jan. 15. **War Services**—The War of 1914-16—France, with 21 (S.) Bn. 9 Nov. 15.

HARRIS, Capt. (temp.) T. A., 20 (S.) Bn. First Appt. as Capt. (temp.) 5 Mar. 15. **War Services**—The War of 1914-16—France, with 20 (S.) Bn. 9 Nov. 15.

HARRIES-JONES, 2nd Lieut. (temp.) L. A., 27 (Res.) Bn. First Appt. 10 Dec. 14, to Res. Bn. 19 Oct. 15.

HARRISON, 2nd Lieut. (temp.) F. A., 22 (S.) Bn. 6 Jan. 15.

War Services—The War of 1914-16—France, with 22 (S.) Bn. Nov. 15.

HARRISON, 2nd Lieut. (temp.) G., 22 (S.) Bn. First Appt. 11 Nov. 15. **War Services**—The War of 1914-16—France, with 22 (S.) Bn. Nov. 15.

HARRISON, Lieut. (temp.) H. B., 18 (S.) Bn. First Appt. 24 Dec. 14, Lieut. (temp.) 12 May 15. **War Services**—The War of 1914-16—France, with 18 (S.) Bn. Nov. 15.

HARRYMAN, 2nd Lieut. (temp.) G. C., 25 (Res.) Bn. 20 Sep. 15.

HARTLEY, Capt. (temp.) R. L., 26 (Res.) Bn., Lieut. 5 Mar. 15, Capt. (temp.) 5 July 15, to Res. Bn. 7 Sept. 15.

HARVEY, 2nd Lieut. (temp.) G. M., 27 (Res.) Bn. First Appt. 30 Sept. 15, to Res. Bn. 15 Nov. 15.

HASLAM, 2nd Lieut. (temp.) H., 27 (Res.) Bn.

HAWES, Bt.-Col. B. R., C.B. (ret. pay), Comdg. 26 (Res.) Bn. 12 Aug. 15. First Appt. 20 Nov. 75, Lieut.-Col. 17 Feb. 00. **War Services**—Burmese Exped. 1885-9—South African War 1901—Spec. Service Officer—**Despatches.**

HAWKINS, Capt. (temp.) J. N., 27 (Res.) Bn. First Appt. as Lieut. (temp.) 30 Nov. 14, Capt. (temp.) 1 April 15, to Res. Bn. 19 Oct. 15.

HAWORTH, Lieut. (temp.) P. G. Du V., 18 (S.) Bn. First Appt. 6 Jan. 15, Lieut. (temp.) 5 June 15. **War Services**—The War of 1914-16—France, with 18 (S.) Bn. Nov. 15.

HEADINGTON, Lieut. (temp.) P. E., 23 (S.) Bn. First Appt. 14 (Res.) Bn. as Lieut. (temp.) 5 July 15, to 23 (S.) Bn. 29 July 15. **War Services**—The War of 1914-16—France, with 23 (S.) Bn. Jan. 16.

HEARD, Lieut. (temp.) J. L., 23 (S.) Bn. First Appt. 27 Mar. 15, Lieut. (temp.) 21 Nov. 15. **War Services**—The War of 1914-16—France, with 23 (S.) Bn. Jan. 16.

HEATH, Capt. (temp.) W. E., Army Cyclist Corps from 23 (S.) Bn. First Appt. as Lieut. (temp.) 3 Dec. 14, Capt. (temp.) 1 May 15, to A.C.C 8 Sept. 15.

HEATHCOTE, Capt. (temp.) G., 25 (Res.) Bn. First Appt. as Capt. (temp.) 30 Oct. 14, to Res. Bn. 7 Sept. 15.

HEATHER, 2nd Lieut. (temp.) C., 26 (Res.) Bn. First Appt. 15 Sept. 15, to Res. Bn.

HENDRIE, 2nd Lieut. (temp.) H. A., 26 (Res.) Bn. First Appt.

HENDRIQUES, 2nd Lieut. (temp.) G. L. Q., 16 (S.) Bn. 10 Oct. 14. **War Services**—The War of 1914-16—France, with 16 (S.) Bn. Nov. 15.

HENSHALL, Capt. (temp.) C., 18 (S.) Bn. First Appt. 28 Sept. 14, Lieut. (temp.) 30 Dec. 14, Capt. (temp.) 12 May 15. **War Services**—The War of 1914-16—France, with 18 (S.) Bn. Nov. 15.

HENSHALL, 2nd Lieut. (temp.) F., 19 (S.) Bn. 9 Nov. 14. **War Services**—The War of 1914-16—France, with 19 (S.) Bn. 9 Nov. 15.

HEYWOOD, Lieut. (temp.) A. T., 19 (S.) Bn. First Appt. 23 Sept. 14, Lieut. (temp.) 6 July 15. **War Services**—The War of 1914-16—France, with 19 (S.) Bn. 9 Nov. 15.

HEYWORTH, Lieut. (temp.) E. L., 17 (S.) Bn. First Appt. 18 Sept. 14, Lieut. 15 Oct. 14. **War Services**—The War of 1914-16—France, with 17 (S.) Bn. Nov. 15.

HIGGINS, Lieut. (temp.) J. B., 19 (S.) Bn. First Appt. 28 Sept. 14, Lieut. (temp.) 20 Jan. 15. **War Services**—The War of 1914-16—France, with 19 (S.) Bn. 9 Nov. 15.

HILL, Lieut.-Col. (temp.) Sir H. B., Bt., Comdg. 19 (S.) Bn. Manch. R. 4 June 15 (Capt. Res. of Off.) (Bt.-Maj. ret. pay). First Appt. 10 Nov. 88, Res. of Off. from R. Irish Fus. 3 June 08, Lieut.-Col. (temp.) 23 Jan. 15. **War Services**—Nile Exped. 1898—Khartoum. **Despatches (twice) Brev. of Major,** Nile Exped. 1899, **Despatches.** The War of 1914-16—France, with 19 (S.) Bn. 9 Nov. 15.

HILLER, Lieut. (temp.) A. H., 17 (S.) Bn. from 26 Nov. 14 to 23 Nov. 15. Rel. Comm. on account of ill-health.

HIRST, 2nd Lieut. (temp.) H. H., Empl. Sig. Serv. from 21 (S.) Bn. First Appt. 1 Mar. 15.

HISLOP, Capt. (temp.) J. A., 19 (S.) Bn. First Appt. 28 Sept. 14, Lieut. (temp.) 30 Jan. 15, Capt. (temp.) 26 May 15. **War Services**—The War of 1914-16—France, with 19 (S.) Bn. 9 Nov. 15.

HOARE, Capt. (temp.) G. E., Adjut. 18 (S.) Bn. First Appt. as Capt. (temp.) and Adjut. 28 Sept. 14. **War Services**—The War of 1914-16—France, with 18 (S.) Bn. Nov. 15.

HOBBS, 2nd Lieut. (temp.) C. E., 25 (Res.) Bn. First Appt. 8 April 15, to Res. Bn. 7 Sept. 15.

HOBKIRK, Capt. (temp.) R., 18 (S.) Bn. First Appt. 3 Oct. 14, Lieut. (temp.) 30 Dec. 14, Capt. (temp.) 18 Oct. 15. **War Services**—The War of 1914-16—France, with 18 (S.) Bn. Nov. 15.

HOBSON, Capt. (temp.) C. J. M., 21 (S.) Bn. First Appt. as Capt. (temp.) 12 Feb. 15. **War Services**—The War of 1914-16—France, with 21 (S.) Bn. Nov. 15.

HODGSON, 2nd Lieut. (temp.) C. B. V., 20 (S.) Bn. 3 Mar. 15. **War Services**—The War of 1914-16—France, with 20 (S.) Bn. Nov. 15 (Wounded, to England 17 Feb. 16).

HODGSON, Major (temp.) T. G., 17 (S.) and 25 (Res.) Bns. from 24 Sept. 14 to 5 Jan. 16. Rel. Commn. on account of ill-health.

HOGG, 2nd Lieut. (temp.) J. H. B., 23 (S.) Bn. 17 June 15. **War Services**—The War of 1914-16—France, with 23 (S.) Bn. Jan. 16.

HOLDEN, Lieut. (temp.) S., 24 (S.) Bn. First Appt. as Lieut. (temp.) 1 Feb. 15. **War Services**—The War of 1914-16—France, with 24 (S.) Bn. Nov. 15.

HOLT, 2nd Lieut. (temp.) A. T. S., 17 (S.) Bn. 28 Sept. 14. **War Services**—The War of 1914-16—France, with 17 (S.) Bn. Nov. 15.

HOOK, 2nd Lieut. (temp.) C. W. K., 16 (S.) Bn. 25 Dec. 14. **War Services**—The War of 1914-16—France, with 16 (S.) Bn. Nov. 15.

HORLEY, 2nd Lieut. (temp.) E. L. R., 27 (Res.) Bn. 22 May 15 to a Res. Bn. 4 Sept. 15.

HOUGHTON, 2nd Lieut. (temp.) F., 27 (Res.) Bn. First Appt. 10 Dec. 14, to Res. Bn. 19 Oct. 15.

HOWE, Capt. (temp.) E. H., (Hon. Maj. Ret. Vols.) (Hon. Lieut. in Army), 19 (S.) Bn., Capt. (Vols.) 5 June 95, Capt. (temp. Reg. Army) 27 Oct. 14. **War Services**—S. African War 1899-1901—Emply. with 4 Bn. Railway Pioneer Regt. The War of 1914-16—France, with 19 (S.) Bn. 9 Nov. 15.

HUGHES, Lieut. (temp.) S. J., 12 Bn. L. North Lancs. from 27 (Res.) Bn. First Appt. as Lieut. (temp.) 17 Mar. 15, to Res. Bn. 7 Sept. 15, to L.N. Lancs. 24 Oct. 15.

HUMPHREYS, Lieut. (temp.) L. B., 17 (S.) Bn. First Appt. 3 Oct. 14, Lieut. (temp.) 1 July 15. **War Services**—The War of 1914-16—France, with 17 (S.) Bn. Nov. 15.

HUTCHINSON, 2nd Lieut. (temp.) J., 27 (Res.) Bn. First Appt. 6 Oct. 15, to Res. Bn. 9 Nov. 15.

IBBOTSON, 2nd Lieut. (temp.) L. H. P., 19 (S.) Bn. 6 Sept. 15. **War Services**—The War of 1914-16—France, with 19 (S.) Bn. 9 Nov. 15.

ILETT, 2nd Lieut. (temp.) J. J., 25 (Res.) Bn. First Appt. 19 July 15, to Res. Bn. 7 Sept. 15.

INCE, Lieut. (temp.) N. S., 19 (S.) Bn. First Appt. 16 Oct. 14, Lieut. (temp.) 4 July 15. **War Services**—The War of 1914-16—France, with 19 (S.) Bn. 9 Nov. 15.

JACKSON, 2nd Lieut. (temp.) S. C., 26 (Res.) Bn. First Appt. 25 Nov. 15.

JAMES, 2nd Lieut. (temp.) F., 26 (Res.)Bn. First Appt. 3 Mar. 15, to Res. Bn.

JAMES, 2nd Lieut. (temp.) H. A., 26 (Res.) Bn. First Appt. 18 Oct. 15.

JENNISON, 2nd Lieut. (temp.) N. L., 26 (Res.) Bn. First Appt. 22 April 15, to Res. Bn.

JENSEN, 2nd Lieut. (temp.) C. T., 25 (Res.) Bn. First Appt. 19 July 15, to Res. Bn. 7 Sept. 15.

JOHNSON, Lieut.-Col. (temp.) H. A., Comdg. 17 (S.) Bn. 1 Sept. 14 (Col. Ret. Spec. Res.), Comdg. 4 Bn. Manch. R. 1905 to 1913. **War Services**—The War of 1914-16—France, with 17 (S.) Bn. Nov. 15.

JOHNSON, Capt. (temp.) W. M., 16 (S.) Bn. First Appt. 8 Oct. 14, Capt. (temp.) 3 Mar. 15. **War Services**—The War of 1914-16—France, with 16 (S.) Bn. Nov. 15.

JOHNSTON, 2nd Lieut. (temp.) R. L., 17 (S.) Bn. 16 April 15. **War Services**—The War of 1914-16—France, with 17 (S.) Bn. Nov. 15 **(Killed in Action 13 Dec. 15).**

JOHNSTON, 2nd Lieut. (temp.) W. T., 25 (Res.) Bn. First Appt. 8 April 15, to Res. Bn. 7 Sept. 15.

JONES, 2nd Lieut. (temp.) O. V., 23 (S.) Bn. 31 May 15. **War Services**—The War of 1914-16—France, with 23 (S.) Bn. Jan. 16.

JOYCE, Capt. (temp.) C., 26 (Res.) Bn. First Appt. as Quartermaster 17 Sept. 14, Capt. (temp.) 20 Jan. 15, to Res. Bn. 7 Sept. 15. **War Services**—S. African War 1900.

JOYCE, 2nd Lieut. (temp.) C. D. (Res.) Bn. (on prob.) 8 Jan. 16.

KEELEY, 2nd Lieut. (temp.) A. W., 27 (Res.) Bn. First Appt. 18 Mar. 15, to Res. Bn. 23 Sept. 15, Asst. Adjutant.

KEEFE, 2nd Lieut. (temp.) R. C. M., 25 (Res.) Bn. First Appt. 17 Aug. 15, to Res. Bn. 10 Sept. 15.

KELLY, Lieut. (temp.) T. J., 18 (S.) Bn. First Appt. 25 Oct. 14, Lieut. (temp.) 26 Mar. 15. **War Services**—The War of 1914-16—France, with 18 (S.) Bn. Nov. 15.

KEMP, 2nd Lieut. (temp.) T., 20 (S.) Bn. 12 April 15. **War Services**—The War of 1914-16—France, with 20 (S.) Bn. 9 Nov. 15.

KEMPSTER, Major (temp.) A. C., 16 (S.) Bn. from 11 (S.) Bn. Essex R., Capt. (temp.) 21 Sept. 14, to Manch. R. 13 Sept. 15. **War Services**—The War of 1914-16—France, with 16 (S.) Bn. Nov. 15.

KENWORTHY, Capt. (temp.) S., 17 (S.) Bn. First Appt. 19 Sept. 14, Capt. (temp.) 19 Dec. 14. **War Services**—The War of 1914-16—France, with 17 (S.) Bn. Nov. 15.

KERR, 2nd Lieut. (temp.) L. A., 25 (Res.) Bn. First Appt. 8 April 15, to Res. Bn. 7 Sept. 15.

KETTLEWELL, Bt.-Col. E. A. (ret. Ind. Army), Comdg. 19 (S.) Bn. Manch. R. from 11 Nov. 14 to 4 June 15, Bt.-Col. 6 June 07. **War Services**—Burmese Exped. 1885-7. N.-W. Frontier of India 1897-8. Tirah 1897-8, **Despatches.** China 1900.

KIRKWOOD, Lieut. (temp.) J. D., 17 (S.) Bn. First Appt. 5 Jan. 15, Lieut. (temp.) 1 July 15. **War Services**—The War of 1914-16—France, with 17 (S.) Bn. Nov. 15.

KNIGHT, 2nd Lieut. (temp.) A. F. D., 25 (Res.) Bn. First Appt. 21 Aug. 15. to Res. Bn. 7 Sept. 15.

KNIGHT, Capt. (temp.) H. J., V.C., 20 (S.) Bn. 5 Mar. 15 to 18 Oct. 15. **War Services**—S. African War 1899-1902. **Awd. V.C.**

KNOWLES, 2nd Lieut. (temp.) J., 25 (Res.) Bn. First Appt. 19 July 15, to Res. Bn. 7 Sept. 15.

KNOWLES, Lieut. (temp.) R. K., 16 (S.) Bn. First Appt. 30 Oct. 14, Lieut. (temp.) 12 May 15. **War Services**—The War of 1914-16—France, with 16 (S.) Bn. Nov. 15.

KNOWLES, Lieut. (temp.) W. P., 18 (S.) Bn. First Appt. 22 Sept. 14, Lieut. (temp.) 2 Feb. 15. **War Services**—The War of 1914-16—France, with 18 (S.) Bn. Nov. 15.

KNUDSON, 2nd Lieut. (temp.) O. J., 22 (S.) Bn. First Appt. 3 Dec. 14, to 22 (S.) Bn. 13 April 15. **War Services**—The War of 1914-16—France, with 22 (S.) Bn. Nov. 15.

LAITHEWAITE, Lieut. (temp.) J., 20 (S.) Bn. First Appt. as Lieut. (temp.) 5 May 15. **War Services**—The War of 1914-16—France, with 20 (S.) Bn. Nov. 15. **Killed in Action 24 Feb. 16.**

LANGDON, Lieut. (temp.) G., 21 (S.) Bn. First Appt. as

Lieut. (temp.) 12 Feb. 15. **War Services**—The War of 1914-16—France, with 21 (S.) Bn. 9 Nov. 15.

LAW, 2nd Lieut. (temp.) E. L., 26 (Res.) Bn. (on prob.). First Appt. 6 Jan. 16.

LAWTON, 2nd Lieut. (temp.) S. J., 24 (S.) Bn. 18 Dec. 14. **War Services**—The War of 1914-16—France, with 24 (S.) Bn. Nov. 15.

LEDWARD, Lieut.-Col. (temp.) H., Comdg. 27 (Res.) Bn. 12 Aug. 15. First Appt. as Major 12 Sept. 14, Lieut.-Col. (temp.) 12 Aug. 15.

LEE, Lieut. (temp.) C. H., 24 (S.) Bn. First Appt. 10 Dec. 14, Lieut. (temp.) 1 May 15. **War Services**—The War of 1914-16—France, with 24 (S.) Bn. Nov. 15.

LEE-EVANS, 2nd Lieut. (temp.) G., 21 (S.) Bn. 7 Jan. 15. **War Services**—The War of 1914-16—France, with 21 (S.) Bn. Nov. 15.

LENDON, 2nd Lieut. (temp.) H. C. G., Comdg. Depot (Heaton Park). First Appt. 17 Feb. 15.

LERESCHE, Lieut. (temp.) G., 19 (S.) Bn. First Appt. 4 Dec. 14, Lieut. (temp.) 20 Jan. 15. **War Services**—The War of 1914-16—France, with 19 (S.) Bn. 9 Nov. 15.

LEVINSTEIN, 2nd Lieut. (temp.) G. E., 26 (Res.) Bn. First Appt. 3 April 15, to Res. Bn. 7 Sept. 15.

LEWIS, Lieut. (temp.) J. F., General List from 26 (Res.) Bn. First Appt. 3 Jan. 15, Lieut. (temp.) 3 April 15, to Res. Bn. as Adjut. 12 Aug. 15, to Gen. List 8 Jan. 16.

LILLIE, Lieut. (temp.) A. P., 21 (S.) Bn. First Appt. 23 Dec. 14. Lieut. (temp.) 3 April 15. **War Services**—The War of 1914-16—France, with 21 (S.) Bn. 9 Nov. 15.

LINNELL, 2nd Lieut. (temp.) A. J., 26 (Res.) Bn. First Appt. 14 Aug. 15, to Res. Bn. 7 Nov. 15.

LLOYD, Capt. (temp.) E., 17 (S.) Bn. First Appt. as Hon. Lieut. and Quartermaster 8 Sept. 14, Capt. (temp.) 17 Dec. 14. **War Services**—S. African War 1900. **Despatches, D.C.M.** The War of 1914-16—France, with 17 (S.) Bn. Nov. 15.

LLOYD, Capt. (temp.) C. M., 22 (S.) Bn. First Appt. as Capt. (temp.) 12 May 15. **War Services**—The War of 1914-16—France, with 22 (S.) Bn. 9 Nov. 15.

LLOYD, Major (temp.) W. E. (Lieut.-Col. ret. T.F.), 19 (S.) Bn. 21 Sept. 14. to Res. Bn. 7 Feb. 16. **War Services**—The War of 1914-16—France, with 19 (S.) Bn. 9 Nov. 15, to England 7 Feb. 16.

LOGAN, Major (temp.) R. J., T.D. (Lieut.-Col. ret. T.F.), 21 (S.) Bn. 6 Jan. 15. **War Services**—The War of 1914-16—France, with 21 (S.) Bn. 9 Nov. 15.

LOMAS, Lieut. (temp.) H., 20 (S.) Bn. First Appt. 3 Mar. 15, Lieut. (temp.) 5 June 15. **War Services**—The War of 1914-16—France, with 20 (S.) Bn. 9 Nov. 15.

LORD, 2nd Lieut. (temp.) H. O., 26 (Res.) Bn. First Appt. 20 Oct. 15, to Res. Bn.

LOUGH, 2nd Lieut. (temp.) J., 26 (Res.) Bn. First Appt. 18 Oct. 15.

LUPTON, Major (temp.) G., 18 (S.) Bn., Capt. (Vol.) 4 Aug. 1900, Capt. (temp.) in Reg. Army 22 Sept. 14, Major (temp.) 12 May 15. War Services—S. African War 1902. The War of 1914-16—France, with 18 (S.) Bn. Nov. 15.

LYNDE, Capt. (temp.) G. S., 18 (S.) Bn. First Appt. 3 Oct. 14, Capt. (temp.) 2 Feb. 15. War Services—The War of 1914-16—France, with 18 (S.) Bn. Nov. 15.

MACDONALD, Capt. (temp.) C. L., Adjut. 17 (S.) Bn. 11 June 15. First Appt. as Capt. (temp.) 15 Dec. 14 (Capt. Unatt. List T.F.). War Services—The War of 1914-16—France, with 17 (S.) Bn. Nov. 15.

MACDONNELL, 2nd Lieut. (temp.) J. H. O'C. de C., 25 (Res.) Bn. First Appt. 11 May 15, to Res. Bn. 7 Sept. 15.

MACDONNELL, 2nd Lieut. (temp.) R. A. M. J., 25 (Res.) Bn. 2 Dec. 15.

MACGOWAN, 2nd Lieut. (temp.) A. G., 24 (S.) Bn. 1 Sept. 15. War Services—The War of 1914-16—France, with 24 (S.) Bn. Nov. 15.

MADDEN, Capt. (temp.) J. G., 17 (S.) Bn. (Unatt. List T.F.), Lieut. Off. Training Corps 18 June 13, Lieut. (temp.) 24 Dec. 14, Capt. (temp.) 11 June 15. War Services—The War of 1914-16—France, with 17 (S.) Bn. Nov. 15.

MAGNAY, Major P. M., 2nd in Comd. 24 (S.) Bn. from 5 (Res.) Bn., Royal Fus. Spec. Res. of Off. Capt. 26 Sept. 14, Major 3 Nov. 15. War Services—The War of 1914-16—France, attd. 1 Bn. Royal Fus. (to England), France with 24 (S.) Bn. Manch. R. Nov. 15.

MAIDEN, Hon. Lieut. (temp.) E. L., Quartermaster 22 (S.) Bn. 3 Feb. 15. War Services—The War of 1914-16—France, with 22 (S.) Bn. 9 Nov. 15.

MALIM, Capt. (temp.) J., 17 (S.) Bn. First Appt. as Capt. (temp.) 16 Dec. 14. War Services—The War of 1914-16—France, with 17 (S.) Bn. Nov. 15.

MANSERGH, Lieut. (temp) R. F., 17 (S.) Bn. First Appt. 21 Dec. 14, Lieut. (temp.) 8 Dec. 15. War Services—The War of 1914-16—France, with 17 (S.) Bn. Nov. 15.

MARILLIER-MILLER, 2nd Lieut. (temp.) R., 25 (Res.) Bn. 4 Aug. 15.

MARSDEN, Capt. (temp.) W. M., 26 (Res.) Bn. First Appt. as Capt. (temp.) 21 Nov. 14, to Res. Bn. 7 Sept. 15.

MARSHALL, Capt. (temp.) D., 24 (S.) Bn. First Appt. as Lieut. (temp.) 8 Dec. 14, Capt. (temp.) 1 April 15. War Services—The War of 1914-16—France, with 24 (S.) Bn. Nov. 15.

MARSHALL, Capt. (temp.) F., 24 (S.) Bn. First Appt. 1 Mar. 15. Capt. (temp.) 2 June 15. War Services—The War of 1914-16—France, with 24 (S.) Bn. Nov. 15.

MATHER, Capt. (temp.) R. C., 19 (S.) Bn. First Appt. 26 Sept. 14, Lieut. (temp.) 20 Jan. 15, Capt. (temp.) 26 May 15. War

Services—The War of 1914-16—France, with 19 (S.) Bn. 9 Nov. 15.

MATHEWS, 2nd Lieut. (temp.) F. C. V., 25 (Res.) Bn. First Appt. 9 Aug. 15, to Res. Bn. 7 Sept. 15.

MAWDESLEY, 2nd Lieut. (temp.) E. W., 19 (S.) Bn. 22 Feb. 15. **War Services**—The War of 1914-16—France, with 19 (S.) Bn. 9 Nov. 15.

MAY, Capt. (temp.) C. C., 22 (S.) Bn. First Appt. as Capt. (temp.) 7 Feb. 15. **War Services**—The War of 1914-16—France. with 22 (S.) Bn. 9 Nov. 15.

McCONNEL, Lieut.-Col. (temp.) F. R., Comdg. 25 (Res.) Bn. (Hon. Col. ret. Vols.), Lieut.-Col. (temp.) 12 Aug. 15.

McKENZIE, 2nd Lieut. (temp.) L. C., 27 (Res.) Bn. First Appt. 18 Oct. 15, to Res. Bn. 19 Oct. 15.

McNULTY, Capt. (temp.) E. J., 26 (Res.) Bn. First Appt. as Capt. (temp.) 5 Mar. 15, to Res. Bn.

MEAD, Lieut. (temp.) P. J., 16 (S.) Bn. First Appt. 25 Dec. 14, Lieut. (temp.) 13 May 15. **War Services**—The War of 1914-16—France, with 16 (S.) Bn. Nov. 15 (Wounded 9 Dec. 15.

MEGSON, Lieut. (temp.) R. H., 16 (S.) Bn. First Appt. 3 Oct. 14, Lieut. (temp.) 13 May 15. **War Services**—The War of 1914-16—France, with 16 (S.) Bn. Nov. 15.

MELLOR, Lieut. (temp.) R., 22 (S.) Bn. First Appt. as Lieut. (temp.) 1 Feb. 15. **War Services**—The War of 1914-16—France, with 22 (S.) Bn. Nov. 15.

MERRIMAN, Major (temp.) F. B., 22 (S.) Bn., Capt. (temp.) 20 (S.) Bn. 18 Nov. 14, Major (temp.) 1 Aug. 16. **War Services**—The War of 1914-16—France, with 22 (S.) Bn. Nov. 15.

MILLAR, Lieut. St. Cy. W., Adjut. 23 (S.) Bn., from Liverpool R. 22 Nov. 15. **War Services**—The War of 1914-16—France, with 23 (S.) Bn. Jan. 16.

MILLER, 2nd Lieut. (temp.) J. H., 21 (S.) Bn. 3 April 15. **War Services**—The War of 1914-16—France, with 21 (S.) Bn. 9 Nov. 15.

MILLER, 2nd Lieut. (temp.) R. M., 25 (Res.) Bn. 10 Sept. 15.

MILNE, Lieut. (temp.) D. F., 20 (S.) Bn. First Appt. as Lieut. (temp.) 5 Mar. 15. **War Services**—The War of 1914-16—France, with 20 (S.) Bn. 9 Nov. 15.

MITCHELL, Lieut.-Col. (temp.) S., Comdg. 20 (S.) Bn. 20 July 15, from 24 (S.) Bn. First Appt. as Major 24 Mar. 15, Lieut.-Col. (temp.) 20 July 15. **War Services**—The War of 1914-16—France, with 20 (S.) Bn. 9 Nov. 15.

MONKMAN, 2nd Lieut. (temp.) C. B., 25 (Res.) Bn. 30 Sept. 15.

MOORE, Major (temp.) H., V.D. (Hon. Col. ret. T.F.), 26 (Res.) Bn., Major (temp.) Reg. Army 6 Jan. 15, to Res. Bn.

MORGAN, 2nd Lieut. (temp.) H. H., 26 (Res.) Bn. First Appt. 6 Oct. 15, to Res. Bn.

MORRIS, Lieut. (temp.) G. P., 16 (S.) Bn. First Appt. 12 Sept. 14, Lieut. (temp.) 8 Dec. 14. **War Services**—The War of 1914-16—France, with 16 (S.) Bn. Nov. 15.

MORTON, 2nd Lieut. (temp.) J. L. M., 23 (S.) Bn. First Appt.

3 April 15, to Res. Bn. 7 Sept. 15. **War Services**—The War of 1914-16—France, attd. 23 (S.) Bn. Feb. 16.

MULHOLLAND, 2nd Lieut. (temp.) W., 26 (Res.) Bn. First Appt. 2 April 15, to Res. Bn.

MURDOCK, Lieut. (temp.) T. J. C., 24 (S.) Bn. First Appt. 10 Dec. 14, Lieut. (temp.) 1 Aug. 15. **War Services**—The War of 1914-16—France, with 24 (S.) Bn. Nov. 15.

MURRAY, Capt. (temp.) D., 22 (S.) Bn. First Appt. 25 Jan. 15, Capt. (temp.) 1 April 15. **War Services**—The War of 1914-16—France, with 22 (S.) Bn. Nov. 15.

MURRAY, Lieut. (temp.) D. S., 22 (S.) Bn. First Appt. 18 Jan. 15, Lieut. (temp.) 28 Feb. 15. **War Services**—The War of 1914-16—France, with 22 (S.) Bn. Nov. 15.

MYERS, Capt. (temp.) J. W., Adjut. 19 (S.) Bn. First Appt. 1 Oct. 14, Lieut. (temp.) 20 Jan. 15, Capt. (temp.) 26 May 15. **War Services**—The War of 1914-16—France, with 19 (S.) Bn. 9 Nov. 15.

MYERS, 2nd Lieut. (temp.) W., 26 (Res.) Bn. First Appt. 28 June 15, to Res. Bn. 7 Sept. 15.

NANSON, 2nd Lieut. (temp.) J., 25 (Res.) Bn. First Appt. 21 April 15, to Res. Bn. 7 Sept. 15.

NASH, 2nd Lieut. (temp.) T. A. H.. 16 (S.) Bn. 13 May 15. **War Services**—The War of 1914-16—France, with 16 (S.) Bn. Nov. 15.

NELSON, 2nd Lieut. (temp.) J. L., 18 (S.) Bn. 18 Jan. 15. **War Services**—The War of 1914-16—France, with 18 (S.) Bn. Nov. 15. **Killed in Action 10 Mar. 16.**

NEY, 2nd Lieut. (temp.) G., 24 (S.) Bn. 3 April 15. **War Services**—The War of 1914-16—France, with 24 (S.) Bn. Nov. 15.

NICHOLLS, Capt. (temp.) F., 20 (S.) Bn. First Appt. 3 Mar. 15, Lieut. (temp.) 5 June 15, Capt. (temp.) 10 Dec. 15. **War Services**—The War of 1914-16—France, with 20 (S.) Bn. 9 Nov. 15.

NORMAN, Major (temp.) J. (Major ret. Mila., Hon. Capt. in Army 2 Nov. 1900), 24 (S.) Bn. 1 Mar. 15 to 13 July 15.

NOBLE, Lieut. (temp.) B., 22 Bn. Lancs. Fus. from 23 (S.) Bn. First Appt. 3 Dec. 14, Lieut. (temp.) 5 July 15.

NORMAN, Bt.-Col. W. W. (ret. Ind. Army), Comdg. 21 (S.) Bn. Manch. R. 24 Nov. 14. First Appt. (from Mila.) 23 Oct. 80, Major 23 Oct. 1900, Bt.-Col. 21 Dec. 08. **War Services**—Tirah 1897-8—On Staff. The War of 1914-16—France, with 21 (S.) Bn. 9 Nov. 15.

O'BRIEN, Major (temp.) W. D., 20 (S.) Bn. (Capt. ret. pay, 3 Bn. Spec. Res. of Off., Conn. Rangers). First Appt. as Major (temp.) and to Manch. R. 6 Nov. 15. **War Services**—S. African War 1901-2. The War of 1914-16—France, with 20 (S.) Bn. 9 Nov. 15.

OLDFIELD, 2nd Lieut. (temp.) A. R., 27 (Res.) Bn. 24 Dec. 15.

OLDHAM, Lieut. (temp.) E., 22 (S.) Bn. First Appt. 8 Dec. 14, Lieut. (temp.) 31 Jan. 15. **War Services**—The War of 1914-16—France, with 22 (S.) Bn. Nov. 15.

OLIVER, Lieut. (temp.) J. M., 16 (S.) Bn. First Appt. 8 Oct.

14, Lieut. (temp.) 8 Dec. 14. **War Services**—The War of 1914-16—France, with 16 (S.) Bn. Nov. 15.

O'MALLEY, Hon. Lieut. (temp.) J., Quartermaster 19 (S.) Bn. 20 Jan. 15. **War Services**—The War of 1914-16—France with 19 (S.) Bn. Nov. 15.

OMMANNEY, Major (temp.) F. F. (Lieut.-Col. T.F. Res.), 21 (S.) Bn. 6 Jan. 15. **War Services**—The War of 1914-16—France, with 21 (S.) Bn. 9 Nov. 15.

ORFORD, 2nd Lieut. (temp.) W. K., 17 (S.) Bn. 11 Jan. 15. **War Services**—The War of 1914-16—France, with 17 (S.) Bn. Nov. 15.

ORR, Lieut. (temp.) W. B., 26 (Res.) Bn. First Appt. to Res. Bn.

OUTRAM, 2nd Lieut. (temp.) E., 26 (Res.) Bn. First Appt. 3 April 15, to Res. Bn. 7 Sept. 15.

OWEN, Capt. (temp.) G. H. R. St. J., 19 (S.) Bn. First Appt. 23 Sept. 14, Lieut. (temp.) 20 Jan. 15, Capt. (temp.) 1 Nov. 15. **War Services**—The War of 1914-16—France, with 19 (S.) Bn. 9 Nov. 15.

OWEN, 2nd Lieut. (temp.) S. J., (Res.) Bn. 15 Jan. 16.

PALMER, Capt. (temp.) F. C., (Maj. ret. T.F.), 25 (Res.) Bn. 22 June 15, Capt. (temp.) in Army 22 June 15, to Res. Bn. 7 Sept. 15.

PALMER, 2nd Lieut. (temp.) W. O., 26 (Res.) Bn. First Appt. 5 July 15, to Res. Bn. 7 Sept. 15.

PARKER, Capt. (temp.) R. F., 21 (S.) Bn. First Appt. as Capt. (temp.) 12 Feb. 15. **War Services**—The War of 1914-16—France, with 21 (S.) Bn. 9 Nov. 15.

PARR, 2nd Lieut. (temp.) E. H. T., 27 (Res.) Bn. First Appt. 6 April 15, from 8 Bn. E. Surrey R. to Res. Bn. 7 Sept. 15.

PATEY, Capt. (temp.) M. H. R., 16 (S.) Bn. First Appt. as Capt. (temp.) 2 Dec. 14. **War Services**—The War of 1914-16—France, with 16 (S.) Bn. Nov. 15.

PAYNE, Capt. (temp.) J. J., 16 (S.) Bn. First Appt. 7 Oct. 14, Capt. (temp.) 8 Dec. 14. **War Services**—The War of 1914-16—France, with 16 (S.) Bn. Nov. 15.

Payne, Major (temp.) W., 2nd in Commd. 27 (Res.) Bn. First Appt. as Hon. Lieut. 17 Sept. 14, Capt. (temp.) 7 Dec. 14, Major (temp.) 15 Nov. 15, to Res. Bn. 12 Aug. 15.

PEASE, 2nd Lieut. (temp.) W. H., 23 (S.) Bn. 3 Dec. 14 to 12 Sept. 15. Rel. Commn. on account of ill-health.

PENN-GASKELL, Capt. (temp.) W., 25 (Res.) Bn. First Appt. as Capt. (temp.) 22 Feb. 15, to Res. Bn.

PEPPER, 2nd Lieut. (temp.) A. A., 12 Bn. S. Lancs. R. from 24 (S.) Bn. First Appt. 1 Mar. 15.

PERCY, 2nd Lieut. (temp.) G. B., 26 (Res.) Bn. First Appt. 3 April 15, to Res. Bn. 7 Sept. 15.

PERCY, 2nd Lieut. (temp.) J. E. G., 16 (S.) Bn. 8 Oct. 14. **War Services**—The War of 1914-16—France, with 16 (S.) Bn. Nov. 15.

PETERS, 2nd Lieut. (temp.) H., 26 (Res.) Bn. First Appt. 11 Oct. 15.

PETRIE, Major (temp. Lieut.-Col.) C. L. R., D.S.O. Major ret. pay. Res. of Off.), Comdg. 16 (S.) Bn. 21 June 15. First Appt. 5 Feb. 87, Major 21 Dec. 01, Empld. with E. African Rifles 27 Dec. 99 to 1903, Sec. in Commd. Depot 6 Aug. 14 to 27 Jan. 15, Brigade Major 111th Bgde. 28 Jan. 15 to 21 June 15, Lieut.-Col. (temp.) 21 June 15. **War Services**—Uganda 1901. **Despatches (twice), D.S.O. (wounded).** East Africa 1902-3—Oper. in Somaliland (on Staff)—**Despatches.** The War of 1914-16—France, with 16 (S.) Bn. Nov. 15.

PHILLIPS, Lieut. (temp.) R. O., 16 (S.) Bn. First Appt. 12 Sept. 14, Lieut. (temp.) 14 May 15. **War Services**—The War of 1914-16—France, with 16 (S.) Bn. Nov. 15.

PICKFORD, 2nd Lieut. (temp.) H. A., 26 (Res.) Bn. First Appt. to Res. Bn.

PICKLES, 2nd Lieut. (temp.) F. A., 27 (Res.) Bn. First Appt. 20 Nov. 15.

PICKLES, 2nd Lieut. (temp.) R., 27 (Res.) Bn. First Appt. 25 Sept. 15, to Res. Bn.

PIERCE, Hon. Lieut. (temp.) T. C., Quartermaster 18 (S.) Bn. 7 Dec. 14. **War Services**—N.-W. Frontier of India 1897-8—Tirah. S. African War. The War of 1914-16—France, with 18 (S.) Bn. Nov. 15.

PLUMMER, Capt. (temp.) N., 21 (S.) Bn. First Appt. as Lieut. (temp.) 20 Dec. 14, Capt. (temp.) 3 April 15. **War Services**—The War of 1914-16—France, with 21 (S.) Bn. 9 Nov. 15.

POTTS, Lieut. (temp.) G. F., 17 (S.) Bn. First Appt. 28 Sept. 14, Lieut. (temp.) 1 July 15. **War Services**—The War of 1914-16—France, with 17 (S.) Bn. Nov. 15.

POWELL, Lieut. (temp.) F. J., Royal F. Corps from 18 (S.) Bn. First Appt. 2 Feb. 15, to R.R.C. 25 May 15.

POWELL, 2nd Lieut. (temp.) H. A., 18 (S.) Bn. 4 Feb. 15. **War Services**—The War of 1914-16—France, with 18 (S.) Bn. Nov. 15.

POWER, 2nd Lieut. (temp.) G. H., 27 (Res.) Bn. First Appt. 13 Oct. 15, to Res. Bn. 19 Oct. 15.

POYNTON, 2nd Lieut. (temp.) C. E., 26 (Res.) Bn. First Appt. 8 Dec. 15.

PRENDERGAST, Capt. (temp.) H., 24 (S.) Bn. First Appt. 1 Mar. 15, Capt. (temp.) 1 Aug. 15. **War Services**—The War of 1914-16—France, with 24 (S.) Bn. Nov. 15.

PRESTWICH, 2nd Lieut. (temp.) E., 25 (Res.) Bn. First Appt. 15 Mar. 15, to Res. Bn. 7 Sept. 15.

PRICE, 2nd Lieut. (temp.) H., 17 (S.) Bn. 4 Aug. 15. **War Services**—The War of 1914-16—France, with 17 (S.) Bn. Nov. 15.

PRITCHARD, 2nd Lieut. (temp.) O. T., 26 (Res.) Bn. First Appt. 16 Aug. 15, to Res. Bn. 7 Nov. 15.

PRINCE, Lieut. (temp.) J. F., 22 (S.) Bn. 1 Feb. 15. **War Services**—The War of 1914-16—France, with 22 (S.) Bn. Nov. 15.

PURVIS, 2nd Lieut. (temp.) W. B., 21 (S.) Bn. 3 April 15.

War Services—The War of 1914-16—France, with 21 (S.) Bn. 9 Nov. 15.

RAM, 2nd Lieut. (temp.) P. J., 26 (Res.) Bn. First Appt. 26 Oct. 15.

RAMSBOTTOM, Capt. (temp.) G. O., 22 (S.) Bn. First Appt as Capt. (temp.) 31 Mar. 15. **War Services**—The War of 1914-16—France, with 22 (S.) Bn. Nov. 15.

RAMSBOTTOM, Lieut. (temp.) J. W., 26 (Res.) Bn. First Appt. as Lieut. (temp.) 5 Mar. 15, to Res. Bn.

RAMSDEN, 2nd Lieut. (temp.) H., 26 (Res.) Bn. First Appt. 18 Oct. 15.

RATHBONE, 2nd Lieut. (temp.) H. J., 27 (Res.) Bn. First Appt. 8 Oct. 15.

READ, 2nd Lieut. (temp.) N., 19 (S.) Bn. 5 Feb. 15.

REID, 2nd Lieut. (temp.) W. M. First Appt. 8 Jan. 15, to Res. Bn. 20 Nov. 15. **War Services**—The War of 1914-16—France, attd. 23 (S.) Bn. 26 Jan. 16.

RENSHAW, Capt. (temp.) L., 18 (S.) Bn. First Appt. 3 Oct. 14, Lieut. (temp.) 30 Dec. 14, Capt. (temp.) 8 Nov. 15. **War Services**—The War of 1914-16—France, with 18 (S.) Bn. Nov. 15.

RHODES, 2nd Lieut. (temp.) E. L., 16 (S.) Bn. 3 Oct. 14. **War Services**—The War of 1914-16—France, with 16 (S.) Bn. Nov. 15.

RICKS, 2nd Lieut. (temp.) L. de B., Mach. Gun Corps from 27 (Res.) Bn. First Appt. 6 Oct. 15, to Mach. Gun Corps 22 Nov. 15.

RIDGWAY, Major J. H., 2nd in Comd. 21 (S.) Bn. (Capt. 1st N. Staffs. R.). First Appt. 21 April 1900, Major 7 Nov. 15. **War Services**—S. African War 1899-01—Oper. in Or. Riv. Col. and Oper. in Trans. The War of 1914-16—France, with 21 (S.) Bn. 9 Nov. 15.

RILEY, 2nd Lieut. (temp.) E. L., 22 (S.) Bn. 21 Feb. 14. **War Services**—The War of 1914-16—France, with 22 (S.) Bn. Nov. 15.

ROBERTS, 2nd Lieut. (temp.) D. H., 25 (Res.). Bn. First Appt. 6 July 15, to Res. Bn. 7 Sept. 15.

ROBERTS, 2nd Lieut. (temp.) J., 24 (S.) Bn. 6 July 15. **War Services**—The War of 1914-16—France, with 24 (S.) Bn. Nov. 15.

ROBERTS, 2nd Lieut. (temp.) L. W., 23 (S.) Bn. 3 Dec. 14 to 3 July 15.

ROBERTS, Capt. (temp.) R. E., 16 (S.) Bn. First Appt. as Capt. (temp.) 21 Oct .14. **War Services**—The War of 1914-16—France, with 16 (S.) Bn. Nov. 15.

ROBERTSON, Lieut. (temp.) B., 24 (S.) Bn. First Appt. 10 Dec. 14, Lieut. (temp.) 1 May 15. **War Services**—The War of 1914-16—France, with 24 (S.) Bn. Nov. 15.

ROSE, Lieut. (temp.) M. H., (Res.) Bn. First Appt. 3 April 15, Lieut. (temp.) 28 Jan. 15, to Res. Bn.

ROSS, 2nd Lieut. (temp.) F. G., 20 (S.) Bn. 17 Mar. 15. **War**

Services—The War of 1914-16—France, with 20 (S.) Bn. 9 Nov. 15.

ROTHBAND, Copt. (temp.) J. E., 23 (S.) Bn. First Appt. as Lieut. (temp.) 19 April 15. Capt. (temp.) 20 Dec. 15. **War Services**—The War of 1914-16—France, with 23 (S.) Bn. Jan. 16

ROWLAND, Lieut. (temp.) F. E., Brigade Machine Gun Officer from 23 (S.) Bn. First Appt. 3 Dec. 14, Lieut. (temp.) 1 June 15. **War Services**—The War of 1914-16—France, Nov. 15

ROYLE, Capt. (temp.) F. W., 19 (S.) Bn. First Appt. 25 Sept. 14, Lieut. (temp.) 30 Jan. 15, Capt. (temp.) 26 May 15. **War Services**—The War of 1914-16—France, with 19 (S.) Bn. 9 Nov. 15

ROYLE, 2nd Lieut. (temp.) H. W., 22 (S.) Bn. 20 May 15. **War Services**—The War of 1914-16—France, with 22 (S.) Bn. Nov. 15.

ROYLE, 2nd Lieut. (temp.) T. R., 27 (Res.) Bn. (on prob.). First Appt. 27 Sept. 15. **War Services**—The War of 1914-16—France, attd. 23 (S.) Bn. 26 Jan. 16.

RUSSELL, 2nd Lieut. (temp.) A. S., 21 (S.) Bn. 8 Jan. 15. **War Services**—The War of 1914-16—France, with 21 (S.) Bn. 9 Nov. 15.

RUSSELL, 2nd Lieut. (temp.) J. P., 28 Sept. 15, 24 (S.) Bn. **War Services**—The War of 1914-16—France, with 24 (S.) Bn. Nov. 15.

RYLANDS, 2nd Lieut. (temp.) F., 25 (Res.) Bn.

SADLER, 2nd Lieut. (temp.) C., 25 (Res.) Bn. First Appt. 2 Aug. 15, to Res. Bn. 7 Sept. 15.

SALMON, 2nd Lieut. (temp.) B. B., 25 (Res.) Bn. First Appt. 3 Aug. 15, to Res. Bn.

SAYCE, Capt. (temp.) G. B., 26 (Res.) Bn. First Appt. as Capt. (temp.) 1 Jan. 15, to Res. Bn. 7 Sept. 15.

SCOTT, Lieut. (temp.) H. E., 21 (S.) Bn. First Appt. as Lieut. (temp.) 12 Feb. 15. **War Services**—The War of 1914-16—France, with 21 (S.) Bn. 9 Nov. 15

SCOTT, Lieut.-Col. (temp.) W. T. W. (Major Res. of Off.), Comdg. 24 (S.) Bn. Manch. R. from 19 Nov. 14 to 13 Oct. 15. First Appt. 6 Feb. 84, Res. of Off. from Bed. R. 21 Sept. 12, Lieut.-Col. (temp.) 19 Nov. 14. Rel. Temp. Command on account of ill-health 13 Oct. 15. **War Services**—Burmese Exped. 1888-9.

SCRUTTON, 2nd Lieut. (temp.) F. S., Army Cyclist Corps from 21 (S.) Bn. First Appt. 6 April 15. to A.C.C. 14 Sept. 15.

SHELMERDINE, 2nd Lieut. (temp.) J. A., 22 (S.) Bn. 23 Dec. 14. **War Services**—The War of 1914-16—France, with 22 (S.) Bn. Nov. 15.

SHEPHERD, Lieut. (temp.) C. H. B., 20 (S.) Bn. First Appt. 7 April 15, Lieut. (temp.) 5 June 15. **War Services**—The War of 1914-16—France, with 20 (S.) Bn. 9 Nov. 15.

SIDEBOTHAM, Lieut. (temp.) J. N. W., 17 (S.) Bn. First

Appt. 18 Sept. 14, Lieut. (temp.) 16 Oct. 14. **War Services**—The War of 1914-16—France, with 17 (S.) Bn. Nov. 15.

SIMPSON, 2nd Lieut. (temp.) A., 27 (Res.) Bn. First Appt. 29 Mar. 15, to Res. Bn. 9 Dec. 15.

SIMPSON, 2nd Lieut. (temp.) E. T., 21 (S.) Bn. 1 Feb. 15. **War Services**—The War of 1914-16—France, with 21 (S.) Bn. 9 Nov. 15.

SIMPSON, Lieut. (temp.) G. E., 23 (S.) Bn. First Appt. 21 Jan. 15, Lieut. (temp.) 1 April 15. **War Services**—The War of 1914-16—France, with 23 (S.) Bn. Jan. 16.

SINGTON, Lieut. (temp.) A. J. C., 25 (Res.) Bn. First Appt. as Lieut. (temp.) 8 Dec. 14, to Res. Bn. 7 Sept. 15.

SLACK, 2nd Lieut. (temp.) E. S., 16 (S.) Bn. 29 Mar. 15. **War Services**—The War of 1914-16—France, with 16 (S.) Bn. Nov. 15.

SMALLEY, Major (temp.) E., 20 (S.) Bn. First Appt. to Bn. as Capt. (temp.) 9 Dec. 14, Major (temp.) 5 Mar. 15. **War Services**—The War of 1914-16—France, with 20 (S.) Bn. 9 Nov. 15.

SMITH, Capt. (temp.) A. J., Adjut. 27 (Res.) Bn. First Appt. as Capt. (temp.) 6 Dec. 14, to Res. Bn. 7 Sept. 15, to be Adjut. 15 Nov. 15.

SMITH, 2nd Lieut. (temp.) C. L., 26 (Res.) Bn. First Appt. 7 April 15, to Res. Bn. 22 Oct. 15.

SMITH, 2nd Lieut. (temp.) H. C., R.F.C. from 21 (S.) Bn. First Appt. 25 Jan. 15, to R.F.C. 23 Nov. 15.

SMITH, 2nd Lieut. (temp.) N. A., 25 (Res.) Bn. First Appt. 26 Aug. 15, to Res. Bn. 7 Sept. 15.

SMITH, Lieut.-Col. (temp.) R. P., Comdg. 23 (S.) Bn. from Devon R. (Capt. Res. of Off.). First Appt. as Lieut.-Col. (temp.) and to Manch. R. 18 Aug. 15. **War Services**—The War of 1914-16—France, with 23 (S.) Bn. Jan. 16.

SMITH, 2nd Lieut. (temp.) W. R., 26 (Res.) Bn. First Appt. 9 Jan. 15, to Res. Bn. 7 Nov. 15.

SMITH, 2nd Lieut. (temp.) W. W., 19 (S.) Bn. 3 June 15. **War Services**—The War of 1914-16—France, with 19 (S.) Bn. 9 Nov. 15.

SOLLY, Lieut. (temp.) A. N., attd. R.F.C. from 26 (Res.) Bn. First Appt. 16 Oct. 14, Lieut. (temp.) 5 July 15, to Res. Bn. 7 Sept. 15, attd. R.F.C.

SOMERVILLE, Lieut. (temp.) H., 23 (S..) Bn. First Appt. 5 April 15, Lieut. (temp.) 23 Nov. 15. **War Services**—The War of 1914-16—France, with 23 (S.) Bn. Jan. 16.

SOTHAM, Capt. E. G., Adjut. 16 (S.) Bn. 25 Sept. 14. First Appt. 18 Nov. 03, Empld. with King's Afr. Rifles 28 Oct. 09 to 28 Nov. 12, Capt. 11 Dec. 14. **War Services**—The War of 1914-16—France, with 16 (S.) Bn. Nov. 15.

SPANKIE, 2nd Lieut. (temp.) D. W., 27 (Res.) Bn. 5 April 15, to Res. Bn. 9 Nov. 15.

SPEAKMAN, 2nd Lieut. (temp.) E. V., 26 (Res.) Bn. First Appt. 28 July 15. to Res. Bn. 7 Sept. 15.

STATHAM, 2nd Lieut. (temp.) A. J., 18 (S.) Bn. 1 April 15.

War Services—The War of 1914-16—France, with 18 (S.) Bn. Nov. 15.

STATHAM, 2nd Lieut. (temp.) H. R., attd. R.E. for Sig. Services from 22 (S.) Bn. First Appt. 10 Dec. 14.

STEPHENS, 2nd Lieut. (temp.) C. R., 17 (S.) Bn. 3 June 15. **War Services**—The War of 1914-16—France, with 17 (S.) Bn. Nov. 15.

STEVENS, 2nd Lieut. (temp.) C. G., 21 Bn. Lancs. Fus. from 22 (S.) Bn. First Appt. 3 Dec. 14, to Lancs. Fus. 5 Oct. 15.

STONEHEWER, 2nd Lieut. (temp.) D. W., 27 (Res.) Bn. First Appt. 10 Dec. 14, to Res. Bn. 19 Oct. 15.

STREET, 2nd Lieut. (temp.) E. A., 27 (Res.) Bn. 5 April 15, to a Res. Bn.

SUTCLIFFE, 2nd Lieut. (temp.) J., 27 (Res.) Bn. First Appt. 21 Jan. 15, to Res. Bn. 20 Nov. 15.

SWAIN, 2nd Lieut. (temp.) T. L., 24 (S.) Bn. 19 July 15. **War Services**—The War of 1914-16—France, with 24 (S.) Bn. Nov. 15.

SWAINE, 2nd Lieut. (temp.) G. R., 19 (S.) Bn. 1 Dec. 14. **War Services**—The War of 1914-16—France, with 19 (S.) Bn. 9 Nov. 15.

SWALLOW, Capt. (temp.) H. B., 26 (Res.) Bn. First Appt. as Capt. (temp.) 3April 15, to Res. Bn. 7 Sept. 15.

SWIFT, 2nd Lieut. (temp.) W. F., 26 (Res.) Bn. First Appt. 23 Feb. 15. to Res. Bn. 7 Nov. 15.

TARDREW, 2nd Lieut. (temp.) H. C., 23 (S.) Bn. **War Services**—The War of 1914-16—France, with 23 (S.) Bn. Jan. 16.

TAVARE, 2nd Lieut. (temp.) B. F. N., 25 (Res.) Bn. First Appt. 25 Mar. 15, to Res. Bn. 7 Sept. 15. Rel. Commission on account of ill-health 24 Feb. 16.

TAYLEUR, Major (temp.) W., Draft Cond. Off. from 22 (S.) Bn. (Capt. T.F. Res.). First Appt. as Major (temp.) 1 Mar. 15, to be D.C. Off. 5 Oct. 15.

TAYLOR, Capt. (temp.) A., 16 (S.) Bn. First Appt. Capt. (temp.) 3 Mar. 14, Staff Capt. 90th Brigade. **War Services**—The War of 1914-16—France, Nov. 15.

TAYLOR, Lieut. (temp.) F. T., 21 (S.) Bn. First Appt. as Lieut. (temp.) 12 Feb. 15. **War Services**—The War of 1914-16—France, with 21 (S.) Bn. 9 Nov. 15.

THORNILEY, Lieut. (temp.) P. A. H., 21 (S.) Bn. First Appt. as Lieut. (temp.) 12 Feb. 15. **War Services**—The War of 1914-16—France, with 21 (S.) Bn. 9 Nov. 15.

THOMPSON, 2nd Lieut. (temp.) C. R., (Res.) Bn. (on prob.) 6 Jan. 16.

THOMPSON, 2nd Lieut. (temp.) J. B., 26 (Res.) Bn. First Appt. 3 April 15, to Res. Bn.

TIDY, 2nd Lieut. (temp.) W. E., 19 (S.) Bn. 13 May 15. **War Services**—The War of 1914-16—France, with 19 (S.) Bn. 9 Nov. 15.

TONGE, 2nd Lieut. (temp.) W. R., 17 (S.) Bn. 24 Nov. 14. **War Services**—The War of 1914-16—France, with 17 (S.) Bn. Nov. 15. **(Killed in Action 12 Jan. 16.)**

TOWERS, Lieut. (temp.) F., 26 (Res.) Bn. First Appt. as Lieut. (temp.) 20 Jan. 15, to Res. Bn. 7 Sept. 15.

TOWNSEND, 2nd Lieut. (temp.) A. E., 18 (S.) Bn. 8 Mar. 15. **War Services**—The War of 1914-16—France, with 18 (S.) Bn. Nov. 15 **(Accidentally Killed Dec. 15).**

TOWNSEND, Capt. (temp.) J. E., Adjut. 22 (S.) Bn. 1 April 15. First Appt. as Lieut. 28 Jan. 15, Capt. (temp.) 10 Feb. 15. **War Services**—The War of 1914-16—France, with 22 (S.) Bn. Nov. 15.

TUCKEY, 2nd Lieut. (temp.) R. E. S., 25 (Res.) Bn. 27 Oct. 15.

TUKE, 2nd Lieut. (temp.) E. M., 25 (Res.) Bn. First Appt. 18 June 15, to Res. Bn. 7 Sept. 15.

TURNER, Lieut. (temp.) H. E., 19 (S.) Bn. First Appt. 26 Sept. 14, Lieut. (temp.) 5 July 15. **War Services**—The War of 1914-16—France, with 19 (S.) Bn. Nov. 15.

TURNER, 2nd Lieut. (temp.) S. G., 25 (Res.) Bn. First Appt. 13 May 15, to Res. Bn. 7 Sept. 15.

TURPIN, 2nd Lieut. (temp.) C. T., 25 (Res.) Bn. First Appt. 4 Aug. 15, to Res. Bn. 7 Sept. 15.

TURRELL, Lieut. (temp.) J. W., 27 (Res.) Bn. First Appt. as Lieut. (temp.) 22 Feb. 15, to Res. Bn. 4 Sept. 15 (Acting Quartermaster).

TWIST, 2nd Lieut. (temp.) F. C. O., 25 (Res.) Bn. First Appt. 19 Aug. 15, to Res. Bn.

VAUDREY, Capt. (temp.) N., 17 (S.) Bn. First Appt. as Lieut. (temp.) 17 Oct. 14, Capt. (temp.) 1 June 15. **War Services**—The War of 1914-16—France, with 17 (S.) Bn. Nov. 15.

VAUGHAN, Lieut.-Col. (temp.) W. C., Comdg. 22 (S.) Bn. Lancs. Fus. from 23 (S.) Bn. Manch. R. (late Maj. Res. of Off.), to Manch. R. 20 May 15, Lieut.-Col. and to Lancs. Fus. 23 Nov. 15.

VINER, Capt. (temp.) E., 24 (S.) Bn. First Appt. Lieut. (temp.) 1 Feb. 15, Capt. (temp.) 2 Aug. 15. **War Services**—The War of 1914-16—France, with 24 (S.) Bn. Nov. 15.

WALKER, Capt. (temp.) F., 16 (S.) Bn. First Appt. (Hon. Lieut. Quartermaster), Capt. (temp.) 1 Dec. 14. **War Services**—S. African War. The War of 1914-16—France, with 16 (S.) Bn. Nov. 15.

WALKER, Lieut. (temp.) H. W., 21 (S.) Bn. First Appt. as Lieut. (temp.) 12 Feb. 15. **War Services**—The War of 1914-16—France, with 21 (S.) Bn. 9 Nov. 15.

WALL, Capt. (temp.) W., 24 (S.) Bn. First Appt. Capt. (temp.) 10 Dec. 14. **War Services**—The War of 1914-16—France, with 24 (S.) Bn. Nov. 15.

WALLWORK, 2nd Lieut. (temp.) W., 25 (Res.) Bn. First Appt. 12 Mar. 15, to Res. Bn.

WALSH, 2nd Lieut. (temp.) A., 12 (S.) Bn. L. North Lancs. R. from 22 (S.) Bn. First Appt. 18 Feb. 15.

WALTON, 2nd Lieut. (temp.) C. H., 26 (Res.) Bn. First Appt. 13 July 15, to Res. Bn. 7 Nov. 15.

WARD, 2nd Lieut. (temp.) G. F., 30th Div. Cyclist Corps

from 17 (S.) Bn. First Appt. 25 Sept. 15.

WARD, 2n dLieut. (temp.) W. F., 5 (T.) Bn. L. North Lancs. R. from 23 (S.) Bn. First Appt. 21 Jan. 15.

WATERHOUSE, Hon. Lieut. (temp.) R., Quartermaster 21 (S.) Bn. 5 Dec. 14. **War Services**—S. African War 1900-2. The War of 1914-16—France, with 21 (S.) Bn. 9 Nov. 15.

WATSON, Lieut. (temp.) F., 23 (S.) Bn. First Appt. 21 Jan. 15, Lieut. (temp.) 4 Nov. 15. **War Services**—The War of 1914-16—France, with 23 (S.) Bn. Jan. 16.

WATSON, Lieut. (temp.) H. G., 18 (S.) Bn. First Appt. 28 Sept. 14, Lieut. (temp.) 2 Feb. 15. **War Services**—The War of 1914-16—France, with 18 (S.) Bn. Nov. 15.

WATSON, 2nd Lieut. (temp.) J., 27 (Res.) Bn. First Appt. 13 Mar. 15, to Res. Bn. 20 Nov. 15.

WATSON, 2nd Lieut. (temp.) L. S., Rel. Commission on acc. of ill-health, 24 Sept. 15

WATSON, 2nd Lieut. (temp.) W., 24 (S.) Bn. 21 Jan. 15. **War Services**—The War of 1914-16—France, with 24 (S.) Bn. Nov. 15.

WATTS, Lieut. (temp.) S., 20 (S.) Bn. First Appt. Lieut. (temp.) 5 Mar. 15. **War Services**—The War of 1914-16—France, with 20 (S.) Bn. 9 Nov. 15.

WEIR, 2nd Lieut. (temp.) W. L., 27 (Res.) Bn. First Appt. 5 April 15, to Res. Bn. 19 Oct. 15.

WEST, 2nd Lieut. (temp.) R. W., 26 (Res.) Bn. First Appt. 18 Oct. 15.

WHEATLEY, 2nd Lieut. (temp.) S. L., 22 (S.) Bn. and 27 (Res.) Bn. from 3 April 15 to 10 Feb. 16. Rel. Commission on account of ill-health.

WHEATLEY-CROWE, Capt. (temp.) H. S., 25 (Res.) Bn. First Appt. as Capt. (temp.) 21 Sept. 14, to Res. Bn. 12 Aug. 15.

WHETHAM, Lieut.-Col. (temp.) P., Comdg. 22 (S.) Bn. First Appt. (R.W. Surrey R.) 1 Dec. 97, Major 21 (S.) Bn. 7 Dec. 15. Lieut.-Col. (temp.) and to Command 22 (S.) Bn. 8 July 15. **War Services**—The War of 1914-16—France, with 22 (S.) Bn. Nov. 15.

WHITE, Lieut. (temp.) J. H. B., 23 (R.) Bn. and 27 (Res.) Bn. from 3 May 15 to 25 Feb. 16.

WHITE, Capt. (temp.) J. V., 20 (S.) Bn. First Appt. as Lieut. (temp.) 1 Jan. 15, Capt. (temp.) 10 Dec. 15. **War Services**—The War of 1914-16—France, with 20 (S.) Bn. 9 Nov. 15.

WHITEHEAD, Major (temp.) J. J., 17 (S.) Bn. First Appt. as Capt. (temp.) 11 Dec. 14, Major (temp.) 2 Jan. 15. **War Services**—The War of 1914-16—France, with 17 (S.) Bn. Nov. 15.

WHITTALL, Lieut. (temp.) F. J. G., 17 (S.) Bn. First Appt. as Lieut. (temp.) 19 Oct. 14. **War Services**—The War of 1914-16—France, with 17 (S.) Bn. Nov. 15.

WICKS, 2nd Lieut. (temp.) F. C., 22 (S.) Bn. 25 Jan. 15. **War Services**—The War of 1914-16—France, with 22 (S.) Bn. Nov. 15.

WIGLEY, Lieut. (temp.) E., 17 (S.) Bn. First Appt. 24 Sept

15, Lieut. (temp.) 1 July 15. **War Services**—The War of 1914-16—France, with 17 (S.) Bn. Nov. 15.

WILKINS, 2nd Lieut. (temp.) H. L., 24 (S.) Bn. 18 Oct. 15. **War Services**—The War of 1914-16—France, with 24 (S.) Bn. Nov. 15.

WILKINS, Lieut. (tmep.) W. J., (Res.) Bn. from T.F. Res. First Appt. as Lieut. 15 Jan. 16.

WILLEY, 2nd Lieut. (temp.) H. L., 25 (Res.) Bn. First Appt. 2 Aug. 15, to Res. Bn. 7 Sept. 15.

WILLIAMS, 2nd Lieut. (temp.) C. M., 25 (Res.) Bn. 25 Sept. 15.

WILLIAMS, Hon .Lieut. (temp.) J. E., Quartermaster 23 (S.) Bn. 12 Dec. 14. To Half-Pay List on account of ill-health 17 Aug. 15.

WILLIAMS, Capt. (temp.) J. V., 17 (S.) Bn. First Appt. 19 Sept. 14, Capt. (temp.) 19 Dec. 14. **War Services**—The War of 1914-16—France, with 17 (S.) Bn. Nov. 15.

WILSON, 2nd Lieut. (temp.) C. F., 26 (Res.) Bn. First Appt. 30 Aug. 15, to Res. Bn.

WILSON, Lieut. (temp.) J., 23 (S.) Bn. First Appt. 5 April 15, Lieut. (temp.) 22 Nov. 15. **War Services**—The War of 1914-16—France, with 23 (S.) Bn. Jan. 16.

WILSON, Lieut. (temp.) L. F., 16 (S.) Bn. First Appt. 3 Oct. 14, Lieut. (temp.) 8 Dec. 14. **War Services**—The War of 1914-16—France, with 16 (S.) Bn. Nov. 15.

WILSON, Capt. (temp.) T. J. W., 21 (S.) Bn. First Appt. as Capt. (temp.) 16 Dec. 14. **War Services**—The War of 1914-16—France, with 21 (S.) Bn. 9 Nov. 15.

WINDER, Hon. Lieut. (temp.) A. M., Quartermaster 24 (S.) Bn. 12 Dec. 14. **War Services**—The War of 1914-16—France, with 24 (S.) Bn. Nov. 15.

WOLFENDEN, Capt. (temp.) F., 27 (Res.) Bn. First Appt. as Lieut. (temp.) 8 Dec. 14, Capt. (temp.) 1 May 15, to Res. Bn. 7 Sept. 15.

WOOD, 2nd Lieut. (temp.) A., 27 (Res.) Bn. First Appt. 15 Sept. 15, to Res. Bn. 9 Nov. 15.

WOOD, Lieut. (temp.) E., 24 (S.) Bn. First Appt. 10 Dec. 14, Lieut. (temp.) 2 June 15. **War Services**—The War of 1914-16—France, with 24 (S.) Bn. Nov. 15.

WOOD, 2nd Lieut. (temp.) J., 23 (S.) Bn. First Appt. 5 April 15, Lieut. (temp.) 20 Nov. 15. **War Services**—The War of 1914-16—France, with 23 (S.) Bn. Jan. 16.

WOOD, 2nd Lieut. (temp.) J. P. H., 22 (S.) Bn. 1 April 15. **War Services**—The War of 1914-16—France, with 22 (S.) Bn. Nov. 15.

WOOLAM, Lieut. (temp.) J. L., 20 (S.) Bn. First Appt. 3 April 15, Lieut. (temp.) 10 Dec. 15. **War Services**—The War of 1914-16—France, with 20 (S.) Bn. 9 Nov. 15.

WOOLAM, Capt. (temp.) S. E., 18 (S.) Bn. First Appt. 3 Oct. 14, Lieut. (temp.) 30 Dec. 14, Capt. (temp.) 12 May 15. **War Services**—The War of 1914-16—France, with 18 (S.) Bn. Nov. 15.

WOOLASTON, 2nd Lieut. (temp.) K. R., (Res.) Bn. 11 Jan. 16.

WORTHINGTON, Capt. (temp.) J. H., 16 (S.) Bn. First Appt. 3 Oct. 14, Capt. (temp.) 8 Dec. 14. **War Services**—The War of 1914-16—France, with 16 (S.) Bn. Nov. 15.

WORTHINGTON, Capt. (temp.) T. R., 22 (S.) Bn. First Appt. 4 Feb. 15, Capt. (temp.) 25 April 15. **War Services**—The War of 1914-16—France, with 22 (S.) Bn. Nov. 15.

WYLDE, Capt. (temp.) C. H., 25 (Res.) Bn. First Appt. as Capt. (temp.) 3 Jan. 15, to Res. Bn. 7 Sept. 15.

YARWOOD, Hon. Lieut. (temp.) T. A., Quartermaster 17 (S.) Bn. 14 Jan. 15. **War Services**—The War of 1914-16—France, with 17 (S.) Bn. Nov. 15 (Wounded, to England 11 Feb. 16).

YEANDLE, 2nd Lieut. (temp.) G. G., 26 (Res.) Bn. First Appt. 3 April 15, to Res. Bn. 7 Sept. 15.

Lightning Source UK Ltd.
Milton Keynes UK
08 May 2010

153911UK00001B/19/P